Doireann, Boook. It's Book Granda!

GARRETT MARTIN RICHARD HEARNS

authorHOUSE·

AuthorHouse™ UK
1663 Liberty Drive
Bloomington, IN 47403 USA
www.authorhouse.co.uk
Phone: UK TFN: 0800 0148641 (Toll Free inside the UK)
*   UK Local: (02) 0369 56322 (+44 20 3695 6322 from outside the UK)*

Published by AuthorHouse 07/20/2022

ISBN: 978-1-7283-7433-8 (sc)
ISBN: 978-1-7283-7435-2 (hc)
ISBN: 978-1-7283-7434-5 (e)

For Rosemary

CONTENTS

FOREWORD

My name is Oisín. I am 15 years of age and studying for my junior cert. My granda is the author of this book. At the age of 64, he was awarded a Bachelor of Arts degree in Applied Social Studies (Professional Social Care) from IT Carlow (Wexford Campus), Ireland.

When my younger sister was 3 months old, my granny and granda cared for her three days a week until she was 3 years of age so that Mam and Dad could go to work.

When my sister reached the age of "the terrible twos", my granda started to take notes of daily happenings, with a view to writing a book, which would be educational and of interest to grandparents. It was to help them understand and deal with the daily tantrums of a 2-year-old, which can create havoc and be upsetting at times.

The following are two separate passages from his book:

> "How are you today, Teddy Pink? Doireann left you at home on Wednesday for a well-earned sleep because you were tired," Granda said.

> Teddy Pink didn't talk, as sometimes she got very shy and will only talk to Doireann. Granda handed Teddy Pink back to Doireann, who had been observing everything. She gave Teddy a big hug and a smile. She then thanked Granny and Granda for taking care of her.

***

They then had your normal brotherly/sisterly spats.

Later on, Oisín sat on the bed with Granda, and they talked about different things. They were soon joined by Doireann, who sat on the other side. Granda put his arms around them both and gave them big cuddles. When they got bored, they left.

"Ah, Oisín, leave that for Doireann," Granny told him, meaning her TV seat. While Doireann sat at the kitchen table, finishing her breakfast, Oisín sat in her TV chair, and she was not having it. She continued to kick up until he moved.

Later, Granda went into the dining room, only to see her and Oisín sitting side by side on "her" TV chair, watching the telly as if nothing ever happened.

I have always admired my granda, in that he can bring humour to a situation before it explodes. He has a great interest in young people and in their progress through life.

His main motivation for writing this book, is to offer something back to the educational field, based on what he studied and learned at college.

Oisín

GLOSSARY

aaaaaaah/oooooooh. sounds made when trying to overcome a resistance
amborghini. Lamborghini car
arthur fishal. artificial
A-tishoo! A-tishoo! sneezing
biro. a pen
bolonase. bolognaise
boooks. books
breaked. broke
brekkie. breakfast
byeee. goodbye, elongated
byeeeeeeee. goodbye, elongated
byeeeeeeeeeeeeeeeeeee. goodbye, elongated
byeee, Grannndaa. goodbye Granda, elongated
cardoring. cardigan
'cause. because
Cheerios. a breakfast cereal
co. co. county council
Déise. early settlers in Waterford
Doireann. girl's name in Irish, pronounced 'Dear-rin'
Easist Rist. Jesus Christ
elicious. delicious
excira. Dublin lingo for excited
FA. Football Association
GAA. The Gaelic Athletic Association
Gangar. Granda
Ganny. Granny
Garda / Gardai. policeman / policemen

Granda. Grandad

Grann-daa, Grannnn-daaaaa. Granda, elongated

Granneee. Granny, elongated

here-eeerrrrre. Here, elongated

horhay. Jorge; Spanish for George

Hokey, Hokey Pokey. communal song

howaya. Dublin lingo for "how are you"

howya. Dublin lingo for "how are you"

I catched it. I caught it

I want to do a wheeee. *Wheeeeeeeeeeeeeeeeeeeeeeeeeeeeeeeeeeeeeeeeeeeeeeeeeeeeeeeee eeeeeeee*

lazies. ladies

lelicious. delicious

lellow. yellow

libria. library

Lionel Missy. This is a play on the name Lionel Messi.

Mammeeeeee. Mammy, elongated

Mammmmmmeeeeeee. Mammy, elongated

Man City. Manchester City

Man Utd. Manchester United

me ears. Dublin slang for my ears

mo. moment

moooosic. music by cows, elongated

moosic. music by cows, elongated

NCT. National (Ireland) Car Test

noooooo. no, elongated

noooooooooooooooooooooooooooo. no, elongated

o'glee. of glee

oooooooh. to squirm

oul. slang for 'old'

picmic. picnic

porditch. porridge

puter. computer

Rishie. Richie

sausies. sausages

shaysins. stations

snotted. deposited snot
Snowy. the polar bear
spag-ball. spaghetti bolognese
Spurs. Tottenham Hotspurs
Sudocrem. antiseptic healing cream
talk-a to. talk to
Teddeeeeeeeeeeee.Teddy, elongated
telafouwn. Posh pronunciation of *telephone*
***The Ragged-Trousered Philanthropists* by Robert Tressell**. A reference
    only to the main characters, "painters and decorators" (in this book)
tweetment. treatment
waggly tail. a wagging tail
wee-wee. go to the toilet
wha'. slang for "what"
wheeeeeeeeeeeeeeeeeeeeeeeeeeeeeeeeeeeeeeeeeeeeeeeeeeeeeeeeee. shouted
    as you drive down a ramp
wheeeeeeeeeeeeeeeeeeeeeeeeeeeeeeeeeeeeeeeeeeeeeeeeeeeeeeeeee. screamed
    as you run down a ramp
ya'll. you all
yeaaaaaaaaaaaaaah. yes, elongated.
you're welcome. you are welcome
yous. you all
yuck. a strong distaste or disgust
yum-yums. tasty food

Baby

I'm baby ya'll waited for … and …

Mammy phoned Mammy to say I's on the way
Be ready an' waiting 'cause today is the day

28 July 2015
Its 9:33 and time for a "scream"

I drove Mammy's capsule during the night
As big bro' lay sleeping, with expectant delight

Daddy delivered Mammy at the hospital on time
Mammy delivered me, Doireann, after nine

As I lay there winded, with the odd burp or two
It'd be twenty-four hours afore more family due

Including cat Kafli and Oisín to see
Was I, all excira and oh full o' glee?

Hello to my world, my family, and friends
My story begins, oh life never ends!

CHAPTER 1

The Terrible Twos

5 August

Uncle Gary and Aunt Suzie were on a quick visit from the United Kingdom. They had dinner in Granny and Granda's house. Mammy, Daddy, Oisín, and Doireann were there also. Later, while playing outside in the back garden, Doireann peered in through the kitchen window, with her nose pressed firmly against the glass pane, causing everyone inside to laugh at Miss Piggy.

14 August

"Be careful or you'll have an accident," Granda warned Doireann as she jumped up and down on Granny and Granda's bed. "Do you know what an accident is?" Granda asked her.

"Me?"

Later, when eating cherries, she called Granda over, and pointing at the fruit she was eating, she said, "The nut."

"Good girl, Doireann, and well done for telling Granda." He removed the nut for her.

Granda is called Gangar. Sometimes of late, she giggles cheekily when using his real name, Gary. Granny is called Ganny. Preparing for a visit to Gorey today, she refused offers of help when clearly struggling to put her

1

shoes and socks on. Now frustrated and eager to hurry her along, Granda pretended to leave the house by saying, "Ah, I'm off so—" He closed the hall door behind him. He had hoped this would spur her on.

When he re-entered the house, Granny informed him that Doireann had said, "Bye!"

Back home after their visit, Granny and Granda were given lots of (pretend) tea to drink from Doireann's toy tea service. Following this, she had to go to the shops (the imaginary one halfway down the garden) for tea, sugar, coffee, and vegetables. Granda gave her a paper shopping bag to take with her. Then, when finished with her shopping, she decided to pour water into an already full bucket of water, laughing loudly as it splashed out. Even with her arms freezing cold, she refused to give up and continued playing with the miniature buckets and watering cans and three little plastic boats, floating in a biscuit tin full of water.

23 August

Granny asked Doireann a question, to which she answered, "I done that." Then she immediately corrected herself, saying, "I did that."

That morning, she got a fright sliding down the big slide in the newly opened kiddie's playground in Camolin's Community Grounds. With Granny and Granda's help, she eventually drummed up the courage to slide down the small slide lots of times. Then she inspected the tiny angel doors attached to the trees, as well as two little spiders crawling up and down one of them.

After lunch she played with the water again outside. "Gangar, can I have the boats?"

Then after filling the containers with water, she said, "Come on, Gangar. Help me move them."

Oisín and Mammy called to collect her soon afterwards.

25 August

Granny and Granda took care of Doireann's older brother, Oisín, today also. They took both of them to Camolin Playground. Everything from Doireann now is about *why*. As soon as you give her an answer, she wants to know why. If you say you don't know, she will ask why.

30 August

Doireann arrived wearing a new shoulder carrier bag she got as a present from Horhay (Jorge), their new Spanish student. It held her lunch, soother, and all the other things she normally brings for the day. She took out her bottle of bubbles to play with but spilled it as soon as she stepped outside. She immediately shook the bottle to check the amount left, splashing Granda at the same time. Then Granny added water, but it didn't work.

31 August

Doireann met a little boy called Guy and a baby called Ba with their Spanish mammy at Camolin Playground today. When leaving with Granny and Granda, she gave all of them big waves.

4 September

When visiting the town of Gorey today, Granny sat in the back of the car with Doireann as normal. When Granny moved Doireann's hair away from her eyes, she complained, saying, "Sore eye." And then she pointed her finger at Granny and said, "Don't do that again."

She repeated this a couple of times until Granny, noticing a little grin on her face, realised she was trick acting.

8 September

Granny took Doireann with her when visiting a former work colleague who had just moved into a new house in Camolin. Doireann had orange juice and played with the toys in the attic room while there. Granda collected them later and drove to Camolin Playground.

13 September

When Daddy dropped Doireann off at Granny and Granda's this morning, she was unusually very quiet. They took her and the two teddies she played with in the house to the seaside holiday town called Courtown, where they observed the boats in the harbour from the small bridge. The teddies are named Teddy White and Teddy Brown. They then got closer to the sea after walking down some steps. Both of the teddies watched as Doireann threw stones down a slipway and into the water.

On the way back home, they sang two songs over and over. They were "The School Around the Corner's Still the Same" and "How Much Is That Doggie in the Window?" with Doireann offering her "woof-woof" renditions each time.

For lunch she didn't want her chopped-up egg, preferring Granny's lovely potatoes instead. Then she ate lots of soft cheese triangles from the circular cheese box before having a good two hours of sleep with Teddy White, Teddy Brown, and a book.

Mammy called to the house with Oisín and Horhay to collect Doireann. The two boys battled over who got to lie on Snowy, with Doireann screaming in attendance. Snowy is a large polar bear that Granda won for Granny in Toronto, Canada, forty years ago where they had both worked for three years. When warned by Mammy that there would be no badminton for the boys this evening, silence rapidly descended.

15 September

Doireann and Mammy waited at the field opposite Granny and Granda's house and waved as soon as they arrived home from their early morning gym and swim. When Mammy left for work, Granda got Doireann to wave to a neighbour who was standing at her gate. When she waved back, Doireann and Granda walked up to her. "Would you like to come in?" the neighbour asked.

Doireann nodded with a yes, only to return almost immediately with a huge smile on her face and a Kimberly biscuit in each hand. She also saw the dog, Barney. She spent about an hour savouring each biscuit and licking her lips until she said, "All gone."

Later that morning, Doireann's grand-aunt Ann paid them a visit from Bray, County Wicklow. She had only seen Doireann when she was a baby. Then looking somewhat startled, she said, "oh my God, it's like looking at her mammy when she was little."

"You look so like your mammy," Ann told her.

And Doireann gave her a lovely big smile back.

18 September

On their way home from the gym, Granny and Granda passed Daddy, who had just arrived at Oisín's school (Camolin National School). They didn't stop to disturb him because all the schoolkids had gone into their classrooms. He arrived with Doireann a little while later. She was full of fun and running all over the place. Then she wanted the dance music on and got Teddy White and Teddy Brown to dance with her. She ate a bowl of Granny's porridge and then wanted more. Later on, Granny and Granda took her on her first visit to the Enniscorthy "Famine Grave". When Mammy called to collect Doireann later, Oisín and Horhay played with her in the back garden for a while before they all left for home.

20 September

Granny and Granda took Doireann to Gorey Library today. They parked in a parents' parking bay in Gorey Shopping Centre's underground car park. Doireann visited the kiddie ride machine, situated just inside the two sets of magic doors, which Doireann opened with her outstretched arms.

"Welcome to Toyland and meet all my friends!" Noddy announced.

Then she walked up the travellator to the ground floor, holding Granda's hand. They ran to get the lift to the first floor. Doireann pressed the *up*-call button and, when inside the lift, pressed *1*.

As they exited the lift on the first floor, she ran to the kiddie racing car, opposite the doctor's surgery. She (pretend)drove the car for a while before jumping down and running towards more magic doors. With outstretched arms, she exited the shopping centre and walked towards the library, just beyond Gorey Courthouse.

In the library, Granny read lots of stories from Doireann's chosen books while Granda read the newspapers. Granny told Granda, "It's time to go because we don't have a spare nappy, and she needs a nappy change."

On the way home, they all sang "How Much Is That Doggie in the Window?" and "The School Around the Corner's Still the Same" with the car windows wide open!

22 September

Doireann wore her new shoes today. The toe and sole parts were coloured pink, with the rest of the shoes covered in silvery glitter. "She picked them herself when in the store and refused to take them off. She even got a free glitter stick to wave," Mammy informed Granny and Granda. They were also told that she'd had two bowls of porridge for her breakfast that morning. When Mammy left for work, Doireann asked, "Granny, can I have porditch?"

"You already had two bowls of porridge," Granny reminded her.

"Not here," she replied.

Later, they drove to Gorey. Granny had to get some items in Tesco's Supermarket, and as she shopped, Granda watched over Doireann as she drove the new kiddie London bus outside the store at the drop-off zone. When Granny arrived back out, Granda went for his car and drove it to the drop-off zone, because of the heavy rain. "Doireann drove me into Gorey Town and back in her new London bus," Granny informed Granda as he got out of the car.

When back home, Doireann put a wicker wastebasket over her head and walked around resembling that Irish Australian bandit "Ned Kelly".

25 September

Granny and Granda took Doireann to Cartons Daybreak outlet in Camolin to get the car washed. Doireann got scared when the big rollers arrived, splashing and rocking the car. "Sorry, pet. I won't do that again. I know you got a fright," said Granda as Doireann buried herself in Granny's tight clutches in the back seat.

They then went to Camolin Playground for about forty minutes of fun, and as soon as they readied to leave for home, Doireann had a major meltdown. She screamed and cried, saying, "No. I don't want to." And her legs kicked out as Granda tried to carry her to the car.

"Oh, I am dreading that," said a young mother of two small children, sitting close by and made reference to "the terrible twos".

Later, after a short nap, she had another meltdown.

Oisín walked to Granny and Granda's house after school, and Doireann answered the knock on the hall door to let him in. Soon after, Mammy and Horhay arrived. They couldn't play in the back garden because of heavy dense smoke. A nearby haybarn had caught fire at the weekend and was still smouldering. Doireann forgot to take her favourite Teddy Pink home with her.

26 September

Granny and Granda left for Wicklow Town for an early morning and pre-arranged car service. Doireann had wanted to bring Teddy Pink to bed the night before, and realising she wasn't there, Mammy quickly said to Doireann, "She [Teddy Pink] is having a sleepover at Granny and Granda's tonight."

Doireann thought this was very funny and went to bed with a big smile on her face.

Mammy telephoned Granny early and arranged to collect Teddy Pink after she dropped Oisín to school. Granny left Teddy hidden up the side of the house in a plastic bag. Doireann was delighted to get Teddy Pink back when she called but was upset because Granny and Granda were not at the house.

27 September

When Doireann arrived today, she made Granny and Granda tea and put coffee in with it also for Granny from her toy tea service. Then she mopped up the floor when one of her (empty) cups fell on the floor.

"Gangar, will you read *Peppa Pig*? Mammy says you like *Peppa Pig*?" Doireann said.

Mammy had seen Granda's post on Facebook about the book, which read, "Me and Doireann love *Peppa Pig*." Granda did this because he disagreed with claims that *Peppa Pig* was rude. Now, all Granda could hear from Doireann was, "Read, Gangar. Read, Gangar."

While helping Doireann remove her lunch from her shoulder bag, Granda found yesterday's daily report from her crèche that read, "26 November 2017. Snack – crackers and milk. Lunch – beef casserole with mash potatoes, fruit, and water (refused lunch). Change – 11, wet."

Granda drove Granny into Gorey Curves for a workout on this wet, windy, and miserable day. He then took Doireann to the library, parking in the Gorey Shopping Centre underground car park. Doireann met a new friend, Austin from Enniscorthy, in the library. Granda read lots of kiddies' books for her also.

Granny telephoned them when she was ready, and they went and collected her before driving to Tesco's. Granda had to get petrol for the car on the way and got wet doing so.

"Ha ha ha, Gangar's funny; the blue cloth on his head," Doireann said.

Granda had put the small blue car cloth on his soaking wet head.

A while later, she had to cancel her plans to drive the London bus parked outside Tesco's due to the hazardous conditions and because it was now flooded out. Doireann wheeled the blue plastic shopping trolley around the shop for Granny instead. Then she helped with scanning the bread, milk, and lettuce at the automatic till. She then picked up the change (coins) and receipt, after Granny's money had "disappeared into the machine".

On the way home, Granda put the car heater on high because Doireann's pink and sparkle soft shoes had got wet. They sang "Knees Up Mother Brown" over and over and louder and louder at Doireann's request in the car. It made the journey home very short indeed.

29 September

Doireann was standing waiting with Daddy as Granny and Granda arrived home from the gym and gave them a big wave with a lovely smile before heading straight for the hall door. She wanted to be chased by Granda and, later, by Granny. She put Teddies White and Brown into the cot for a sleep.

When it was time to go to Gorey, she woke them up and got them ready, so as to accompany her on the journey. Extra vigilance was required for Doireann then because she was inclined to just venture off willy-nilly, especially as soon as she got out of the car in the car park.

When, back home, "Will I switch on the smelly?" Granda asked Doireann.

"The telly," she replied in a serious-sounding voice. She liked to sit on the sofa to watch the telly. Granda took the wooden insect thingy with wings down off the hook in the hall where it was hanging for Doireann to inspect. Granny and Granda got it in a charity shop in Greystones, County Wicklow, last Saturday. It had four dangling legs, two wings, a small leprechaun-type cap on its big head with two antennas, an egg-shaped green body, and huge grinning teeth.

"What should we call him?" Granda asked.

"Mick," she said, as she took him for a walk around the room while holding the string.

At lunchtime, Granda was putting her into the high chair at the table when she proclaimed loudly and excitedly, "I farted. I farted!"

Horhay went back to Spain this week and was upset about leaving. This was strange, as, when he'd arrived four weeks ago, he had been upset then too and had to make telephone calls to his daddy in Spain every day until he settled.

2 October

Granda drove Granny and Doireann to Bolger's Hardware Store in Ferns to get furniture oil. He had just returned from his annual doctor/nurse appointment, regarding what he termed "his annual 10,000 miles service". Doireann played in the small kiddie's toy house on display outside in the front yard. She was having such great fun in "her" house, with pretend front and back gardens, that she refused to leave.

Feeling somewhat uncomfortable, with a poo in her nappy, she then offered to leave.

"Ganny, can you fix Teddy Pink's nose?" she asked, because there were frayed threads hanging from it.

Granny stitched them together again.

"Gangar, take the [your] jacket off. I don't like it," he was ordered.

It was a sleeveless in-house jacket that she obviously took a dislike to. Granda removed the jacket and went for his jumper instead. Looking at Doireann as he put his jumper on, Granda started to jump up and down, saying, "Doireann, look at what the jumper is doing; it's turning Granda into a jumper."

There was no response.

Later, Doireann was pushing a buggy up the hall, and because Granda was in the way, he was sternly told, "Gangar, move."

Granda stayed in the same position but started to sway back and forth, lifting one foot off the floor and then putting it back down in the same spot again and so on.

"What are you doing, Gangar?" she asked angrily.

"You told me to move, and I am moving," Granda informed her. "Will I get out of the way?" he continued.

"Get out of the way," she said bluntly.

The roofers installing Granny and Granda's new roof were making a lot of noise today.

"I don't like that noise," Doireann said angrily.

4 October

Doireann has a new saying. "Oh my god."

Mammy said that yesterday she heard her say, "Jesus Christ."

Doireann put Teddy Pink sitting on a chair at the kitchen table, saying, "That's Gangar's."

"Where's mine?" Granny asked.

She pointed to the chair that Granny sits on. "Howya, Mick," she said, looking up at him, as she darted up the hall.

6 October

Doireann ran out of the kitchen, announcing she was going to hide. While searching for her, Granda called out, "Where are you Doireann?"

"In here!" came the reply.

Granny and Granda took her to Gorey Library and parked the car in the usual car park. They took the lift to the first floor, and Doireann held Granda's hand as she walked on the small wall over from the courthouse. She was able to open all the magic doors with outstretched arms. On their return, they stopped outside Dunnes Stores to let Doireann inspect all the new kiddie ride machines. When Granny went into Dunnes Stores for some items, Granda stayed with Doireann to let her mingle with other kiddies and parents, enjoying Dunnes Stores' birthday celebration. She and Granda added their signed card alongside all the other cards on the wall, wishing Dunnes a happy birthday. They then joined up with Granny in the store to look for a roll of plastic bags.

Looking up at the scary Halloween skeleton Witch hanging from the shop ceiling, Doireann laughed at it, saying, "It has a funny face!"

When they arrived back home, Doireann took a selfie with Granda using his phone.

9 October

Mammy telephoned Granny this morning, to say she would be a little late. Doireann decided to do a poo in her nappy, just as they were hurrying out the door.

"That's all right. I will change her nappy," Granny offered. (Granny always kept some spare nappies.)

When Daddy dropped Doireann over, Granny took her to the small bedroom and laid her down on the floor to change her nappy.

"Easist Rist" (Jesus Christ), said Doireann, angrily.

As the day wore on, Doireann would scream if you didn't do as she wanted. Then she reminded Granda with a scrunched-up look on her face, "It's books, Granda," when, after they arrived at the library, he referred to them as *bukes* or *boooks* just to wind her up.

Because she didn't have a coat with her today, and it was cold, they had to hurry her along when outdoors, much to her annoyance.

"Will I put the jelly on for you?" Granda asked after they arrived back home.

"It's telly, Gangar," she said, emphasising the correct pronunciation Lately, Doireann will answer you with a definite 'I did' or 'I did not', instead of a plain 'yes or no'.

11 October

"Don't talk to Ganny," Doireann said to Mammy as soon as they entered Granny and Granda's house.

"Why?" asked Mammy.

"She's *my* Ganny." Doireann then showed off her lovely dress, doing a whirl around for good measure.

Earlier, Mammy had asked Doireann to jump over a large puddle on the road, but she jumped into it instead. Granny removed her wet socks to dry them out. Later, Doireann called out, "Look, Gangar," after she had put the dried-out socks on her hands as gloves. Earlier, when the back door was opened, Doireann looked out at the rain and stuck her bare hands out to feel it. Then she had to do the same at the hall (front) door.

Granda drove to Gorey Library or *Libria*, as Doireann calls it, again today. Picking up a book, Doireann noticed a page had become detached. She brought it to the librarian, who repaired it for her, with some Sellotape. Doireann played hide-and-seek with another little girl at the library's kiddies' section for a while.

Granda picked up a book to show Doireann. It had pictures of lots of different musical instruments. She identified the piano, and Granda named some others for her. After a quick visit to Dunnes Stores, they returned to the car. During the drive home, they all sang "Oh, Hokey Hokey Pokey" and "The Rain in Spain Falls Mainly on the Plain", secure in the knowledge that no one could hear them!

Doireann had her cheese and grapes for lunch. Then Granny changed her nappy, and she slept for two long hours.

13 October

Granny and Granda took Doireann to Gorey Credit Union today to get statements and to lodge some money. Granda parked his car at a pay-for-parking bay on a side street after having driven around twice before finding one. They then walked the rest of the way.

As they queued inside the credit union, the main door was open. Doireann did not like the noise coming from outside on the street, where workmen were digging up footpaths to lay telecommunications cables. On their way back to the car, Doireann held onto both Granny and Granda's hands, dragging out of them and smiling all the while.

During the drive back to Camolin, Granny got Doireann to sing "Twinkle Twinkle Little Star" and was greatly surprised when Doireann sang the six words that follow the opening— "how I wonder what you are"—all on her own.

Before driving straight to the house, they visited Camolin Playground for a while. Doireann helped to dry the equipment in the playground, due to the rain earlier. They used an old red half towel Granny had brought along. A short while later, Doireann slipped while "walking up" one of the slides and got audibly upset from the fright of it.

They took her home because the whole of County Wexford could hear her.

16 October

Granny and Granda didn't have Doireann today because of the forecasted arrival of Hurricane Ophelia. Mammy kept her home with her bro, who had the day off also because his school was closed.

18 October

Granny and Granda arranged, through Mammy, to pick Doireann up in Tesco's car park, Gorey, on their way home from the gym. They were running late that morning because of the heavy traffic in Arklow Town. Daddy had already left Gorey with Doireann to drop Oisín off at school (in Camolin) first and then drop Doireann over to Granny and Granda. While heading back to Tesco, Doireann kept saying, "Daddy, it's the wrong way," knowing where Granny and Granda's house was.

When they arrived, she got out of Daddy's car, delighted to see them. She was wearing her "new" purple duffle coat with red polka dots that was pink on the inside, with a girl's name, "Kacey", on it!

Granda fixed Doireann into the car seat and closed the car door. Then, after he sat into his seat, Doireann said, "Gangar, the door hit my hand."

"Oh, sorry, pet. I didn't mean that," Granda said.

Doireann didn't want to sleep after her lunch today. Granny lifted her out of the cot and got her to help rake up the leaves in the garden after the storm Ophelia. Then she played (pretend) shopping with empty food boxes that Granny gave her to play with. She then showed Granda her shopping.

Later, just as Doireann entered the sitting room, Granda was yawning. "Are you tired, Gangar?" she asked.

"Yes, pet."

"Then go to sleep Gangar," was her advice as she stood there, eyeing up the glass cabinet, full of medals, cups, ornaments, and an "opportunity", perhaps!

20 October

Granny and Granda were running late again after their workout and collected Doireann in Tesco's car park, Gorey, once again.

She was easily upset today. In the car, because Granny had the soother, she just started crying. She then tripped and fell, going in past their gate and really cried, even though she didn't hurt herself. Granny and Granda gave her plenty of loves and hugs and also tried to get her to laugh. Later that morning, some neighbours spoke briefly to Doireann as she was getting back into the car to go to Gorey. Doireann didn't talk, only waved bye-bye.

Granda parked in Pettitt's Supermarket car park and they all walked to a chemist shop on the Main Street. On their return, Doireann pointed to a lady approaching in a wheelchair. The lady put her hand out, but Doireann wouldn't shake it; Granda did though. Doireann just waved bye-bye.

After they got some things in Pettitt's, they went to Tesco's, where Doireann played with the "London bus" parked outside the store.

As soon as they returned home and entered the dining room, Doireann stood and looked into the long mirror on the wall.

"Mirror, mirror on the wall, who is the prettiest of them all?" Granda said.

"She is." Doireann immediately pointed to Granny.

Granny changed her nappy and put her into the cot for a nap. Doireann wanted two teddies with her and then started talking to them. The same thing occurred the other day, and when Granny gave out to Doireann for not sleeping, she ended up having to take her back out of the cot, because Doireann got so upset.

This time, Granny gave out to both Teddy Pink and Teddy White for keeping Doireann awake. "Doireann needs her sleep, and if you two continue talking, I will have to take both of you out of the cot," Granny firmly warned them.

Doireann and both Teddies slept for two long hours.

Mammy arrived for Doireann. As Granny and Mammy chatted in the kitchen, Doireann ran into the sitting room, where Granda was. "Did you have your yum-yums" (lunch)? Granda asked.

Nodding, she said, "Tattoo" (Thank you).

"Was it nice?"

"Cold, Gangar," she said with a scrunched-up nose and face.

23 October

When Granny and Granda arrived home from Arklow, they sneaked up behind Mammy's car, parked outside their house, but no one was in it.

"Boo," shouted Doireann as they neared the front door, where she and Mammy had been hiding all along.

Doireann had a sore ear and looked pale. Mammy had to give her Calpol (liquid medicine) yesterday, because she had a high temperature. Granda blew up a balloon that he picked up at the Expo50 exhibition, in the RDS, Dublin, at the weekend. When he released it, the balloon flew like a rocket around the room.

Doireann, now laughing, thought this was great fun. A "million" goes later (well sort of), she got bored with it, much to Granda's relief.

Later, there was great excitement when Granny put Doireann into the buggy and went to the new playground in Camolin. Back in the house later, Doireann, who didn't take a nap today, laughed as she played with Mick.

When Mick danced on her bare feet, Doireann ran away laughing. At one stage, she ran up the hall towards the toilet, in her nappy, shouting, "I need to use the toilet!"

She continued to greet Teddy with, "How-e-ye, Teddy," in Granda's finest Dublin accent.

When Mammy called later, she was informed that Doireann, still pale-looking with a high temperature, had complained of a pain in her right ear.

24 October

Mammy telephoned Granny to say she took Doireann to the doctor's and had to wait two hours. Doireann was very good and, after about an hour, said, "Ear not sore now Mammy. Let's go." (Perhaps Doireann thought that, by sitting in the doctor's waiting room, you get better!)

When she did get to see the doctor, she was also very good and didn't mind having her ears checked. She was put on a course of antibiotics for a very nasty ear infection.

25 October

Doireann arrived late with Mammy and Oisín, today. Oisín had no school and wanted to stay with Granny and Granda. Doireann was protective of the six free yellow stress balls Granny brought home from the Expo50 exhibition. They were now hers—end of story! As Oisín played with one stress ball, Doireann stood in front of him, pointing her finger and screaming. We don't know what she was saying but she was angry, and let it be known. It was funny because she behaved just like her Mammy when she was little.

Earlier, Doireann took her medicine out of the fridge and would only put it back when Mammy called to collect her. She was so determined and ran up the hall holding it firmly. Granda followed and told her to go back and put it in the fridge. She went back into the kitchen and put it on the table instead. Granny kept on at her, telling her to put her medicine back into the fridge to keep it cool.

Doireann eventually relented, saying angrily, "Okay, Mother," before putting it back into the fridge.

27 October

Mammy told Granny and Granda, that Doireann was acting up again this morning. At one stage, with arms aloft and protesting, she screamed, "Jesus Christ!"

During their trip to Gorey Library, Doireann gave out to Granda, saying, "Don't talk-a to me like that," over something he had said to her.

In the library, whatever Doireann did, a bookshelf came crashing down with a big loud *bang, crash*. Security arrived to check it out and poor Granny had to explain what happened.

Later, when Granda was talking to a friend in the library, he introduced Doireann, but she was not for talking. Doireann offered Teddy Pink as a go-between instead.

30 October

Mammy arrived at the house with Doireann and Oisín, for Granny's birthday. Granny was talking to Selin about Richard, on the telephone. He was in hospital following his motorbike accident in Cambodia.

"Gangar, we got cake, betray" (birthday) "cake," said Doireann.

"Oh, for me?" joked Granda.

"No, for Ganny," she said angrily.

31 October

Doireann and Mammy visited and stayed a while. When Oisín and Daddy arrived, they had to go. Doireann screamed the house down when Daddy tried to get her to move. Then she wanted to get into the buggy, even though they were only going to the car parked outside. You could see that Doireann was very tired.

CHAPTER 2

No Monkeys in Cork!

6 November

When back home, after her October holiday break, Doireann told Granny and Granda all about County Cork—the hotel room she stayed in and the big telephone she played with. She then talked about the animals in Fota Wildlife Park in County Cork.

"What did you have for your brekkie?" Granny asked.

"Chips."

Granny, now laughing with Granda, said, "You don't have chips for brekkie!"

A while later, when Granda kicked the old shoebox on the floor out of his way, Doireann said, "Oh my god."

He picked it up and handed it to her, saying, "There's a cot for Teddy Pink."

"Can I see scary Oisín on your phone, Ganny?" she asked, referring to her brother's Halloween photo.

She tried to remove the catch chain from her soother, saying, "I don't want that." She had screamed when Daddy tried to stop her from removing it, earlier. This is the new thing now, Doireann not wanting the catch chain on her soother.

"Look, Gangar." She showed him her tub of melon pieces before putting them in the fridge, for later. Doireann wanted to visit the library

18

today, and when it was time to go, she would not put her socks on and threw them at Granda instead. When Granda went out the hall door, Doireann soon changed her mind. Pretending he forgot his bottle of water, Granda came back into the house and observed Doireann, now rushing to get ready.

Then, there was another battle when he helped her with her coat. Lately, she is very independent minded and wants to do things all by herself.

On their way to Gorey Library, Granny had to call into Dunnes Stores, and while in there, Granda used his mobile phone to take a photo of Doireann, standing among some in-store dummies, modelling some fancy clothes. In the library, Doireann lay Teddy Pink down on one of the long yellow seats for a sleep. She put her coat over her, to keep her warm.

On the way home in the car, Doireann coughed and said, "Excuse me."

"Ah sure, you don't have to say that, pet," Granda said.

"Excuses anyway!" she insisted.

She kept wanting to see the photo of scary Oisín (dressed as a Halloween clown), as she called him.

She smiled when Granda sat down beside her to watch the TV, saying, "You are Granda's best girl."

Granny then claimed that she was.

Doireann responded firmly and loudly with, "I am!"

8 November

Granny and Granda collected Doireann at her house in Gorey, because Oisín was off from school with a very bad sore throat. Driving down towards an oncoming truck, Doireann said, "Mind the truck, Gangar."

"Thanks for that, Doireann."

"You're welcome," she said.

Because of a very heavy night frost, Granda showed Doireann the cold, white-green grass in the back garden.

"That's cold, Gangar," she said after putting her hands on the frost.

Doireann wanted to put her toast in the fridge and screamed when Granny said no, while explaining that you cover the toast with a plate first. Doireann nodded in agreement and then wanted the toast to eat!

They went to the Aldi store in Gorey today, so Granny could get some firelighters. After parking the car, Granda got out and sat in Granny's seat beside Doireann for company, as usual.

"That's Ganny's," she reminded Granda in a somewhat serious tone.

To deflect attention away, Granda, referring to her recent October holiday, asked her, "Did you see the monkeys in Cork?"

"No, in the zoo!"

"Ah, here's Granny now," Granda said.

"Get out of Ganny's seat," he was ordered.

Later, in Pettitt's Supermarket, Doireann sat inside the trolley. Granda had to spin the trolley for her lots of times and she loved it. Lying back in the trolley at one stage, Doireann said with a smile, "I'm a baby now."

As they approached the cashier's desk, Doireann gave the cashier a lovely big smile and a wave. When leaving, Doireann was handed a free *Jack and the Beanstalk* book and told by the cashier that she was a lovely girl! As they drove home, Granny read the story to Doireann. When it was finished, Doireann wanted it read again and again.

When they arrived home, Doireann made them tea and coffee from her toy plastic tea service. Lately, she objects to taking naps and only slept for about half an hour today.

At the kitchen table, Granda sat facing her while she ate her potatoes and mincemeat that her Mammy made.

"That's Ganny's chair," Granda was told.

Later, as Daddy took her home, she gave Granda the thumbs up.

10 November

Granny and Granda collected both Doireann and Oisín in Gorey today; mainly to drop Oisín off at school and because Mammy and Daddy had to attend a meeting in Dublin. On their journey to Camolin, the conversation with Oisín was about his new cousin, Rosie, in Cambodia.

"I'm not a baby," interrupted Doireann.

Granda jokingly reminded her that she had said she was a baby while lying back in Pettitt's trolley the other day.

"I am not a baby," she screamed loudly.

"Are you a girl then?" Granda asked.

"No, I'm Doireann."

"Are you a princess then?" continued Granda.

"A princess, no. I'm not."

"Are you the boss, Doireann?" Oisín asked.

"I am the boss, ha ha," she replied.

They arrived at Oisín's school just as his classmates were entering the classroom. As Granda stood waiting by the open car window, until Oisín entered the building, Doireann said to him, "Get in the car, Gary!"

When Granda did get back into the car, Doireann said, "Eddie" (Rosie's brother) "has new sister, for goodness' sake!"

13 November

When in the house, Doireann was running back and forth to the fridge with an orange and her lunch. Granny and Granda decided to copy Doireann by running but with a hop also.

"You can't run. You're too big," she objected.

She then, put Teddy Pink into the shoebox, and Granda had to get a blanket (half a towel) for her. Next, she wanted Granda to put it over Teddy because she couldn't.

"I don't have a willie; I have a vagina, Granny," she said. (Relayed to Mammy later and okayed.)

They went to the libria in Gorey, today. On the way, when she spoke, she referred to Ganny and Gary (Granda)!

Granda parked in the underground car park, and they walked through the shopping centre, admiring all the Christmas decorations on the way. Then, Doireann played on all the kiddie ride machines, along the way. There were cars, a spaceship, a helicopter, and more. Afterward, they walked up the stairs to the first floor and walked on the outside wall, opposite the courthouse. Then Doireann ran to and magically opened the library doors with her arms outstretched, before running to the kiddies' corner to select books for Granny to read to her. Granda sat and read the newspapers, as usual.

On their return to the car, by the same route from which they'd entered the centre, Doireann didn't want to leave to go home.

Once back home, Doireann's yum-yums consisted of cold mashed potatoes and peas. She wouldn't let Granny heat them and ate them with no bother. Mammy was surprised when Granny informed her later.

17 November

They were now in Liverpool for Uncle Gary's fortieth Birthday. The following morning, after their respective arrivals, Uncle Gary collected Mammy, Daddy, Doireann, and Oisín from the Travel Lodge Hotel beside Liverpool's Sefton Park and drove them straight down the road to the Hallmark Hotel, where Granny and Granda were staying.

Spotting only Granny, Doireann asked, with a surprised look, "Where's Gangar?"

Then she immediately saw Granda topping up his car engine with motor oil and ran to give him a big hug.

It was then, off to the Albert Docks to take some photos of the small padlocks with the Grandkids' names that Granny and Granda had fitted some months earlier. They were located beside the many other thousands of padlocks of different shapes and sizes, with different messages—all locked on the large industrial chains close to the river Mersey.

Everyone searched for the grandkids' padlocks, displaying their names—Doireann, Oisín, Richie, and Eddie, as well as the most recent padlock for Rosie, which was fitted by Uncle Gary. Doireann, spotting a little boy looking out a museum window on the top floor, gave him a wave. The little boy and his parents all waved back. Then Doireann gave the little boy the thumbs up.

Later at the evening birthday party, a very tired Doireann had a couple of meltdowns as she sat between Granda and Daddy. She screamed for "Liverpool" and "Everton" that night! Her appetite was all right though, as she ate a big dish of spag-ball (spaghetti bolognese) and lots of green and black olives. She then polished that off with birthday cake, after singing Happy Birthday to Uncle Gary.

At about 9.30 p.m., Granny and Granda left the party with Doireann, who was spending the night with them in their hotel bedroom. Doireann was really happy to see that Teddy Pink was waiting in Granda's car for her. She was even more happy to see Teddy White was waiting up for her, back in the hotel room. Granda went downstairs for a pint, while Granny settled Doireann into her cot with her two pals. All three of them slept like little logs.

18 November

As they all got ready for breakfast the next morning, Granny was looking for Doireann's hairclip. Granda found it under the bed and said he would use it for his hair.

"Gangar, you have no hair on your head," laughed Doireann.

When they arrived in the restaurant, for breakfast, the waitress gave Doireann a bottle of orange juice and she drank the lot as they sat by the large bay window facing Sefton Park. She next had Cheerios, rasher, egg, toast, milk, and then more of Granny's toast with loads of real butter. Just as they were finishing their breakfast, Doireann saw Mammy walking into the main entrance and jumped up in excitement. She was so happy with a big smile on her face. Daddy had taken Oisín for a tour of Liverpool FC's pitch and museum at Anfield.

After breakfast, Mammy and Doireann joined Granny and Granda for a walk in Sefton Park, where Mammy got something to eat in the café there, as she did not have a breakfast in her hotel. Doireann, showing us the large autumn leaves she picked up, marvelled at the many colours. She then marvelled at every excitable passing dog "bringing their owners" for a walk!

She had great fun on the swings and the slides in the playground. She saw the red squirrels going up and down the trees and, when one came really close, just inches away, a dog, who obviously had lost its owner, chased the squirrel away. Mammy demonstrated to Doireann how squirrels eat nuts. A while later, Doireann watched closely as a blackbird foraged in the leafy grass just in front of her. She then ran to look at the ducks and swans in the water close by. She loved the huge park and didn't want to leave.

Later, Oisín told us that, during his tour of Anfield Road, he'd sat in the seat the Liverpool FC manager, Jurgen Klopp, sits in for the home games. This added to his excitement; having met Uncle Gary's then future father-in-law at the birthday party, who was a professional footballer. He played for Chester and Blackpool during his career.

24 November

Mammy phoned Granny to say she would be late, as she was bathing Doireann, who got sick during the night.

"Ganny, I farted," shouted Doireann, into the phone.

"Doireann, I don't want to know if you farted," replied Granny.

Later when they arrived at Granny and Granda's house or, as Doireann would say, "our home", Doireann became animated as she explained to Granny how she got sick. Acting out being asleep, she then mimicked vomiting with her mouth wide open.

Later, as they readied to go to the Bank and Pettitt's in Gorey, they battled with her because she refused to put her new coat on. Next, she did not want the coat closed. In Gorey, she helped with the shopping and with putting the items in the car boot also. Then she carried a bag of mushrooms from the car to the house when they got back home. She told Granny and Granda about getting the train and plane home from Liverpool. She said she waved to all the people from the train. The plane was like a helicopter. (Mammy later said it was a small Aer Lingus regional plane with fan blades on the wings.)

27 November

Mammy arrived a little late this morning, having given Doireann a bath. When they knocked on the hall door, Granda opened it, saying, "Hello, ladies."

"Gangar, Mammy is a lady, and I am a girl," replied the serious-talking Doireann.

"What is Granny then, an oul" (old) "one?" asked Granda.

"No, she is a lady," retorted Doireann.

"What is Granda, an oul lad?" he asked.

"No, a man," he was bluntly told.

She couldn't get her ride-along car out from where it was parked in the dining room and said so in a whingy-moany voice.

"Let me help you," Granda said also in a whingy, moany voice.

"Don't cry, Gangar," he was bluntly told.

Because Doireann had taken a shine to Granny's new yellow phone, Granny gave her the old unworkable red one to play with. At going home time, Granda looked out the sitting room window and waved to Doireann, as she walked to Mammy's car. "Bye, love you," she said, while waving back.

29 November

Today, Doireann did her exercises like Mammy. Later, as Granda put his heavy woollen jumper on, she just seemed to stare (perhaps she thought he would start jumping again!). They then had a little bit of fun marching around the house to some music.

Later, when they went to the local playground and parked in the empty carpark, Granda let Doireann sit on his lap and drive his car, a teeny-weeny bit (at least she thought she was, as Granda loudly revved the car engine in neutral). They played some lively Christmas songs, while singing over and over, "Mammy is a lady, Doireann is a girl, Oisín is a boy, and Daddy is a man."

CHAPTER 3

A White Elephant in Camolin?

1 December

Granny and Granda had a battle with Doireann when trying to put her coat on before they left the house for Gorey. Later, in the library, Doireann watched a lady play some lovely music on a grand piano, and when finished, Doireann wanted to "play" it. Granda explained that the piano was there for musicians to play, and it wasn't a toy. Then Granda let her press one key only on the piano before they both legged it to the children's section so as not to be caught. Earlier, they'd visited the credit union and then the motor factors across the road from it to get special black paint for the scratches on Granda's car bonnet. Doireann got to meet some of Granda's friends and a friend of her Mammy's also while in Gorey that day.

"I played the piano one," Doireann proudly said in the car as they drove home.

Back in the house, Doireann couldn't sleep and was crying. Granny took her out of the cot and gave her, her yum-yums (sausages and toast).

While eating her "sausies" as she called them, she had difficulty trying to settle down on the chair's cushion. "Jesus Christ," she said, in a frustrated voice. Then, as she left her yum-yums on the table, she told Teddy Brown to eat up.

As she played at the back door, Granda hid her sausies and toast.

"Where are they?" she asked, alarmed upon realising the sausies and toast were missing.

"You told Teddy Brown to eat up, so he must have eaten them," said Granda.

She was not having this and went looking. Granda then handed them back to her, as Granny gave out to her for leaving the table in the first place. She now had a face on her, like a bulldog chewing a wasp. But she sat up at the table to eat all her sausies and toast, no bother.

Later, she laughed at Granda's loud sneeze into a tissue. As Granda dozed in the sitting room armchair when he was supposed to be minding Doireann, he was suddenly awakened by a very loud "*Boo*," from Doircann, who broke her heart laughing as poor Granda descended back down into his seat after the fright he got.

They then watched the *Teletubbies* on the TV, which Doireann thought was funny.

When Mammy arrived, Doireann got great laughs performing Granda's loud sneeze for her.

4 December

"How are you today, Doireann?" asked Granda, as he put his arms around her.

A little later, when Granda asked for a hug, Doireann loudly replied, "You already got one."

Then later, looking at their Cambodian holiday photos (July 2016) and spotting Uncle Gary, she said, "I love Gary."

Today, on their journey to Gorey and back, they played Christmas CDs in the car. In Gorey, Granda dropped Granny off at the post office to register and post a letter for him. Granny then walked to Dunnes Stores, where they all met up again. Granda did a photoshoot with Doireann, in and around all the Christmas Trees and toys. She gave a Teddy Bear a big hug, and loved the My Little Pony shoulder bag.

5 December

Granny and Granda collected Doireann at Tiggy's Crèche in Gorey at about 12.30 p.m. as arranged. She was staying overnight with them because Mammy and Daddy were away. Doireann was playing on her own, with only her carer there, when they called, as all the other babies were now sleeping.

"Gangar, where's your car?" she asked, as they exited the crèche, and he pointed to it. Then she asked, referring to the crèche, "What were you doing in there?"

"I came to pick you up today," he said.

Now back home, Doireann was driving her toy car, and when Granda handed her her phone, she said firmly, "No, I'm driving," while gesturing him away with her hand.

Doireann has developed a whiny cry now, and everything is punctuated with it. If she doesn't get what she wants immediately, she'll scream with this whiny voice. If a CD is playing in the car and a song she particularly likes comes on, she will request it over and over, with, "Again Gangar. Again Gangar?"

If Granda is too slow with her request (remember he is driving the car now), she gets impatient, and the whiny screaming starts.

Granny, who always sits in the back seat with her for company, has to calm her down. If it's the wrong song, well, it's time to head for the bunker.

This behaviour also came into play when watching TV programmes. When a programme she liked ended, she would immediately call out, "Play it again, Gangar?"

But Granda had to be firm with her and explain why he could not do it. He also explained that Granny and Granda's TV is not like Mammy and Daddy's TV (with an automatic replay option).

When Granda mimicked Doireann's whiny voice, she bluntly told him, "Don't cry, Gangar."

Another time, she giggled, saying, "Gangar is a baby."

"You're a baby," Granda said.

Well, World War III arrived! "I am a girl," she loudly insisted and continued with, "Mammy and Granny are ladies. Oisín is a boy, and Daddy a man."

For these two days, Granny has had a major battle trying to get her to have a midday nap. Her whiny-screaming cries were so fierce she was determined not to be caught napping—if you'll pardon the pun. Granny and Granda surrendered and agreed to a peace deal. Doireann was going to bed early that night. At 7.30 p.m., she was ready for bed and slept right through, for twelve hours.

6 December

After breakfast, Granda did the forty-minute drive to Wexford Town. He dropped Granny off at the tax office in the town and then drove to Tesco's car park, where he and Doireann awaited Granny's arrival. There were long traffic delays, due to road works, near Oylgate, just outside the town.

Granny soon arrived at the car park, with the news that you have to make an appointment for the tax office now. What Granda had to say to that, out of earshot of Doireann, is not for the reader's ears, but he was not happy, at all at all.

Granny and Granda decided to get her a milkshake because, she was "very good" and they had another long boring drive back home.

Doireann was getting mixed up with the words *seeing* and *hearing*. "I can't hear the milkshake," she kept saying.

"There's some still in it," Granny said as she rattled the carton for her.

The other day, Doireann sat watching TV, eating her breakfast.

"I am worried about Doireann's eyesight because she keeps saying she can't see the telly," Granny told Granda.

Granda soon learned what the problem was. He observed her the next time she sat and watched TV. "I can't see the telly!" she shouted.

Granda increased the volume and asked, "Can you see that now, Doireann?"

"Yeah, can see it now," she said.

That afternoon, when Granda nodded off in the sitting room, he was suddenly awakened by a big loud "*Boo*" from a laughing Doireann.

8 December

When Doireann tripped and fell against the dining room radiator today, she cried and cried. Granny gave her loads of cuddles. She then sat on the sofa with a blanket over her, along with her three teddies. They all watched Granny Murray on the *Me Too* television show.

Later on, when she came around after her fall against the radiator, they went into Pettitt's of Gorey to do some shopping. They had trouble trying to get Doireann to wear her woollen hooded jumper and her coat. It was about 1 degree and bitter cold outside. She took her coat off in the car. At Pettitt's, she could not wait to take her coat and woollen top off in the shop. Later, they went to Gorey Library via Dunnes Stores, where Granny read her her favourite books.

Back home, Doireann had something to eat before Granny changed her nappy. Her midday nap followed, but she would not sleep and kept calling out. She was delighted when taken out of the cot. Granda played with her for a while by chasing her around the outside of the cot before she sat with Granda in the sitting room to watch her programmes on the telly. Whenever Granda dozed off, Doireann would "frighten" him awake with a loud "*Boo*", followed by loud laughter.

She was running all over the place today, full of beans, tickles, and giggles. When she found some pants, Granny had bought and stored away, she insisted on putting a pair on, over her nappy. Then she paraded out to the kitchen to show Granda, with Granny in hot pursuit, saying, "Doireann they are too small for over your nappy, which is now digging into your skin."

Another meltdown moment duly arrived!

Doireann had taken to the song "Jingle Bells" and wanted it played so she could march around the house to the sound of it.

She was delighted as usual when Mammy called to collect her. Mammy told Granny and Granda about Doireann the other day. After telling her to stop doing something, Mammy started to count to three. Doireann then looked at Mammy with a cheeky smirk and, with a swagger, started singing "One, Two, Three Little Monkeys"!

9 December

Doireann and Oisín stayed overnight with Granny and Granda, as Mammy and Daddy were attending the Curves staff Christmas party, which entailed an overnight stay in a Kilkenny hotel. Doireann watched a Barney the Dinosaur DVD. She had shepherd's pie for dinner after the removal of all the peas, which she called beans.

Later, as she marched up and down, she ordered Granny to follow her. Granda told her she was full of beans, which caused her to give him a confused look as she darted past. Granda then ran after her, and she giggled excitedly when he caught her. Just before bedtime, she insisted on going in to the sitting room to see her brother, who was watching the big telly. They all watched some of *Strictly Come Dancing*, hosted by Bruce Forsyth on BBC One. Doireann loved the dancing and even got up and danced with Granny.

At night-night time, she refused to get into her sleeping bag and just stood in the cot. She wanted to play and talk to her teddies. Granny told her it was only fifteen sleeps to Santa Claus. Eventually, she put the soother into her mouth and lay down to let Granny fix her into the sleeping bag and zip it up. It wasn't long before she fell fast asleep, snuggled up in her cosy sleeping bag.

10 December

After breakfast, Mammy and Daddy called to take Doireann and Oisín off for the day to find snow to play in. On their way home from Kilkenny, they could see that snow had fallen in the surrounding countryside.

11 December

Doireann told Granny and Granda they built a tower in the snow with Mammy, Daddy, and Oisín, yesterday and threw snowballs.

Next, she put Teddies White and Brown into her cot for a sleep. "Gangar, put a blanket over them," he was ordered.

Then they sang "Baa Baa Black Sheep" for them.

"Can I look at Barney?" she asked Granny.

As she watched the Barney DVD, Granda inflated a balloon and released it. Doireann laughed as it spun noisily around the dining room. After another hundred goes (well sort of), Granda blew it up for the last time and put a knot in it. Doireann had more great fun and giggles throwing, chasing, and kicking the huge balloon around the room with Granda.

Later, they drove to Dunnes Stores, and she played on the kiddie ride machines before going into the food store to help Granny locate the milk. At the automatic pay machine, Doireann put the money in, removed the change, and gave it to Granny. "Ganny, can I have the change?" she asked, chancing her arm with a smile and a little laugh.

"No," was Granny's response.

Then, they went into the fashions section to admire all the new teddies, the Santas, and loads of different Christmassy items. Granda took photos of her with his mobile phone before returning to his car.

"Gangar, put your two hands on the wheel," he was told.

Granda was changing gear as they drove back home.

Doireann wanted to watch Barney again, and Granda switched off the radio news to facilitate this.

After lunch, Granny put her into the cot for a nap, but she refused to sleep. "Gangar, Gangar, Gangar," she bellowed, until Granda took her out of the cot, with Granny's approval.

They all played in the sitting room with the balloon again. Then, Granny and Granda showed her how static electricity worked. Looking into the mirror, she giggled as her hair stuck to the balloon.

13 December

Doireann looked pale today and was grumpy. When Granda gave her a swing, she was still not happy. Looking at the Christmas cards, she helped herself to one and handed it to Mammy to take home. "That's Granny and Granda's," she was told.

Granny then gave Doireann an unused Christmas card. "There, Mammy, mind that," said a contented Doireann.

Granda helped her take Teddy White, Teddy Brown, and Snowy out of the cot to bring them to the dining room. Then they got two blankets for their sleep. Later, Granda sat down beside the bears and closed his eyes.

"Gangar, Gangar," she moaned and was obviously not happy.

"I'm sleeping," said Granda.

"Move, Gangar," she said, and she meant it.

"Doireann, will you get the post in the hall for me?" asked Granny after the postman dropped some mail in through the letter box.

Granda helped her open the envelope. It was a Christmas card with Santa Claus on it. "It's from Granny's cousin," Granda said.

"She's my cousin," Doireann said to a nodding Granny later.

They went to Pettitt's in Gorey today, and Doireann helped Granda put the empty bottles into the recycling bank containers in the car park area. Earlier, as Granda had driven through Camolin, Granny had remarked that a new and long-time vacant building (now "Stone Solutions") was a "white elephant".

"Where, where, where is it?" said Doireann excitedly, scanning the place for this white elephant, while strapped into her car seat.

Granny and Granda laughed and tried to explain to her what that meant. It's very hard to explain that to a child though.

In Pettitt's, Doireann pulled the red plastic trolley along and put the food items into it for Granny. At the checkout, she put the shopping items on the counter. As the food items were scanned, she put them into the shopping bag, while Granny paid with her debit card.

15 December

When Daddy dropped Doireann out to Granny and Granda's house, she told them she had Cheerios for breakfast. Now sitting and watching her favourite DVD, Barney the dinosaur, she helped herself to strawberries, grapes, and melon slices that she had brought with her. Later, they went to the Bridgewater Shopping Mall in Arklow. Doireann played on the kiddie rides—Disney Princess and three other machines—in the shopping centre's large hallways.

Next, while browsing around the pound shop, she gave the reindeers (or "bears with antlers", as she called them) hugs. She then rode on a pole that had a reindeer's head, jumping and skipping as she went along. When she took a fancy to a Christmas card to bring home, she was told no. There was an immediate major meltdown with lots of screaming and crying. It was time for Granny and Granda to evacuate the building.

Then she fell, hurting her knee as they walked to the car. It was now time for Granny and Granda to evacuate Arklow! Granny went to the Aldi store, before they left, and as they waited in the car park, Doireann told Granda to sit in the back seat with her. "Santa will bring presents and a cake, Ho, ho, ho," she told Granda.

Granny arrived back with a packet of apple biscuits, which Doireann really loved.

"Can I have another one?" she asked after she finished her third one!

"No," was Granny's firm response.

She watched her favourite Barney DVD again as soon as they arrived back home. Later, while at the table for lunch, with Doireann strapped into her high chair, she wanted to watch Barney.

"No, we all sit at the table for lunch," Granny insisted.

At one stage, Granda got up from the table to get something.

"Sit down," she told Granda.

He sat on the floor.

"No, sit down," she persisted.

"I am sitting down."

She pointed to his chair.

Granda got up and sat on the left side of the chair.

"No, sit on the chair," she said, still pointing.

Granda moved to the other side of the chair.

"No." She continued to point.

Granda got up, turned, and sat facing the back of the chair.

"Granda, sit there," she said, while continuing to point at the chair.

Granda then sat properly in the chair, and that satisfied her.

After lunch, Granny put her into the cot and read her a story. When Granny finished reading the story, she left her and Teddy White on their own. She started to cry and did not want to sleep, but it wasn't long before she did fall asleep.

She woke up soon after Mammy and Daddy called. When Daddy tried to put her shoes on, there was a major meltdown. She put the shoes on herself, after what seemed like an eternity. She gave Granny and Granda hugs and left.

18 December

Doireann had a bruise on her forehead today. Her hair was ruffled because Mammy washed it last night. This was the first of a total of four required washes to get rid of nits in her hair.

They drove to Bolger's Hardware Shop in Ferns to get fire briquettes for over the Christmas. In the car, Doireann was drawing circles, and then she did triangles. When she spoke in a moany-whingey voice, Granda responded in kind.

"Don't cry, Granda," he was told.

"I'm copying your crying," said Granda.

Well, the roof nearly came off the car. "*I am not crying*," was the loudest response from her to date.

This caused Granda to laugh uncontrollably at the thoughts of her being able to vent her anger with such gusto.

They got a free Christmas diary in Bolger's, which she claimed. Granny and Granda bought her an ice cream on the way home, because she was very good. "It's [d]elicious," she said.

Back in the house, Granny went to talk to Doireann. At the same time, she was (pretend) speaking to her Mammy over the phone. Holding the phone close to her ear, she put her hand up, waving Granny away, saying, "Not now."

Then Granda inflated another balloon and she had great fun with it.

She was very excited today, because Granny had dressed the Christmas tree and put a lot of decorations around the house. Her favourites were the baubles on the tree, the wooden train, the little snowmen, and the cribs.

The Barney DVD was watched over and over and over today. After lunch, Granny eventually succeeded in getting a very reluctant Doireann to sleep. Mammy had to wake her up when she called, and she was still red-faced and sleepy.

20 December

When Granny and Granda played the Kinks CD, Doireann loved it and ran around the kitchen to the music. Then Granda switched on the TV and selected the channel for the Granny Murray programme, but she didn't want to watch it. They had to put Barney on instead.

Later, they went to the library and parked the car in the outdoor car park, close to Dunnes Stores. Doireann and Granda climbed the long stairs to the first floor and met Granny coming off the lift. In the library, Granny read books that Doireann selected, while Granda read the newspapers.

Before leaving for home, they got some bread, pitta bread and a large bread role for Doireann because she said she was hungry. She ate the dried bread in the car, listening to the Jimmy Cricket Christmas song, "Kids You Better Be Good", over and over and over.

Granny put her down for a nap, without any protests. She was very tired now, having been awake since six o'clock this morning.

After her nap, they danced to some Christmas songs, including "Jingle Bells", and she pulled a Christmas cracker. Doireann, now full of energy, played with Teddy Pink. Later, she played with Teddies White and Brown and then with Snowy. Sitting on Snowy and with Teddy White also on board, she tried to drive, but Snowy wasn't for moving.

She was delighted when Mammy and Daddy arrived, and she showed them the star for her Christmas tree. Doireann had a major meltdown just before they left for home, when the telly was switched off.

22 December

Daddy dropped Doireann over to Granny and Granda's today. Granny then phoned Mammy and arranged to meet her in Tesco's car park in Gorey, to pick up Doireann's soother and Teddy Pink before they continued on with their pre-planned trip to Dublin. Doireann invited Mammy to sit in the back of the car with her.

"Ah, Mammy has to go to work, pet," Granny told her. And luckily, she accepted that.

Granny talked to her on the journey, and Doireann then sang along with the music. She even danced in her seat, arms up in the air, to the beat of the music. At one stage, Granny had to tighten her straps after she managed to free herself.

They were running behind time when they arrived at Dunnes Stores in Cabinteely County, Dublin, and the outdoor car park was full of Christmas shoppers. They waited in a long slow-moving queue to access the indoor car park, only to be told it was also full. They then had to queue to exit. It was absolute mayhem, but Doireann didn't seem to mind. Granny and Granda decided to cancel this part of their planned trip.

They drove to Dean's Grange Cemetery and bought a wreath to put on Granny's parents' grave. Her brother, Tony, usually did that but could not visit this year because his wife, Val, was in hospital. Granda took photos of Doireann standing at both Granny and Granda's parents' graves. She then sat on a bench in the graveyard and ate her fruit. While Granny first and then Granda next used the toilets, Doireann played around the headstones as they watched out for her, with many visitors driving in and out of the graveyard at this time of the year.

Driving to Bray, they encountered more heavy traffic on the roads. Luckily, they found a parking spot in Tesco's car park in Bray.

Granda strapped Doireann into the buggy, and they all walked down to the shops in Bray Town, paying a quick visit to Granda's brother on the way. Granny bought Doireann a gingerbread man biscuit in a cake shop, and on their way back to the car, she ate it slowly. She started with one arm and then the other one, next the head and then the upper body, right down to the trousers belt. Once the belt was eaten, the rest of the gingerbread man slowly disappeared, with Doireann savouring every piece of it.

Next, they drove to Bray Head overlooking the Irish Sea for their picnic. Doireann really enjoyed making her own sarnies (rashers and bread) in the back seat of the car. When they all finished their sarnies and tea, they drove down to the long promenade at Bray seafront. Doireann got really excited and laughed as Granny struggled to put the warm astronaut-type jumpsuit on her. Down at the water's edge, they threw stones into the water. "This is nice," she said, with a big smile on her face.

They avoided the dogs poos on the stones, which was disgusting. She did not like the seaweed on the stones; in fact, it scared her. There soon followed a walk on the promenade on the little walls and up and down all the steps, with Doireann looking up at Granda and singing, "You're the king of the castle; get down you dirty rascal." She loved walking down the little slanted walls on either side of the steps and then back up again. On their return, on the small wall nearest the green area, she sang "Jingle Bells" to her heart's content, oblivious to the passing and smiling onlookers listening in. She was really happy with herself at this stage.

Granda showed her a man inside the boathouse near the amusements end of the prom who was building a lovely new wooden boat. Granda told her that, when it was finished, it would be used on the water for sailing and rowing. At this point, she wanted to be lifted up to look out to sea for other boats (on the horizon).

As they walked past the small restaurant, she wanted nothing to do with the man-sized and stiff dummy Santa at the door with a coffee in his hand. She did not like the look of him and gave him a wide berth. Granny phoned Auntie Ann, but she was out doing her Christmas shopping, and they agreed to meet up soon after Christmas. They then drove for home, stopping at a petrol station just outside Bray in Kilmacanogue, which was busy like everywhere else.

As they queued for petrol, Doireann lifted her head up from her little nap on hearing Granda refer to the long queue. Her only comment was, "Jesus," as if she had had enough of all the queueing and delays today!

Granny wanted her to get a long snooze on the journey home, as she had been up since 6 a.m., but Doireann had other ideas. Granny then led the way and closed her eyes. Doireann wasn't having it, and next thing she goes, "Boo, boo, boo," trying to wake Granny up.

Eventually, she did sleep, collapsing in a heap for the rest of the journey home. She woke up just as they pulled up at her house. There was real excitement when Mammy came and took her out of the car. Doireann burped, farted, and then laughed. Mammy drew attention to this with a big smile. There were big hugs for Granny and Granda as they left for home.

24 December

Granny and Granda, Uncle Gary, Mammy, and Doireann and Oisín all went for their annual Christmas Eve walk. They changed the venue this year from Loch Dan, County Wicklow, to the local Sliabh Bui hill walk, just up from Camolin. Uncle Gary had a very bad sore back, which required a lot of ongoing physio-treatment, and Mammy had had a very late night. They parked up from the steep walk to Askamore and put their respective walking boots on. Doireann was having great fun jumping in and out of the big pools of water, with Oisín kicking his football into the water instead. Next thing, there was a splash, with a big loud cry. Doireann had tripped and fallen into a pool of water. What a start to their trek, and poor Mammy had to clean her up. They decided to leave their grub in the cars for when they returned and headed off to do a full circle of a walk, they'd done many times before but in reverse. They took the buggy for Doireann just in case.

Granda produced an assortment of chocolates from his coat pocket and passed them around. Doireann got the chocolate buttons and loved them. "I want the buggy," said a tired-looking Doireann.

"You're the bug in the buggy, Doireann," Granda told her.

It was hard work, wheeling it over the big stones.

Granda introduced some party whistles. When you blew into them, an attached paper chute extended out with the sound of the whistle. Doireann and Oisín took one each.

Later, into their journey, Granda produced a blue balloon and inflated it. He then released it, much to the enjoyment of Doireann. Granda had to do this a hundred times more (well sort of), until the strong wind blew it towards some thorns with the evitable *bang*. Granda introduced a red balloon and tied a knot in it. Doireann wanted to let it go, and of course, the wind shifted it off its tracks. Granda gingerly approached the red balloon, now lying against some thorns and was about to rescue it when there was another loud *bang*, followed by lots of laughter. Granda made sure to bring home the burst balloons.

Doireann was in and out of the buggy. Gary stopped to stretch his sore back at various intervals, and Oisín kicked his football along the track, as they all walked and talked in the lovely fresh mountain air. They took turns pushing the buggy. Then there was a *baa* sound, and Doireann wanted to see the sheep. Granda pushed her along in the buggy until he could get a good close-up look from a farm gate where they were. She wanted Mammy to be there also.

Eventually, they arrived back at the starting line. Gary sat in a portable sun chair; Oisín and Granny sat against the boot of Granda's car; Doireann sat in the buggy; and Mammy sat on one of their trays, kept in Granda's car boot. Granda served the tea, hot chocolate, and milk. They had their lovely sarnies and crisps. Oisín had hot chocolate, and Doireann had milk. Gary had water. Granny, Mammy, and Granda had tea. Then, they had chocolate sponge cake that Granny made. Finally, they had sweets, a variety of chewy jelly-type sweets, and they were lovely. Granda spilled his crisps when pouring more hot chocolate for Oisín. They played around and took photos after their picnic, until it was time to leave.

Granny and Granda and Gary removed their mucky walking gear and prepared themselves for a visit to Aunt Valerie in Wexford General Hospital. There were lots of hugs and bye-byes as they all parted.

Christmas Day

There was a knock at the hall door, and Granda answered it. "Happy Christmas, Granda," said Oisín. He was wearing his lovely Liverpool football gear.

"What did Santa bring you?" Granda asked.

"A PlayStation 4, a lava lamp, a fiery rebounder, and the Liverpool jersey with No. 11 / M. Salah on the back," he declared gleefully.

"Wow, you must have been a very good boy," Granda said.

Then Doireann arrived in her lovely dress Aunt Suzie and Uncle Gary had bought her earlier in the year. Santa brought her a supermarket trolley with loads of (plastic) food in it, a cooker, and some other things. Daddy scratched a scratch card for Doireann, and she won €2.

Doireann and Oisín had great fun, pulling Christmas crackers, wearing the paper hats, reading the jokes, and playing with the tiny toys within during their Christmas dinner. They had turkey, stuffing, ham, gravy, Brussels sprouts, celery, carrots, croquets, roast potatoes, onion-rings and broccoli. For afters, they had jelly and ice cream.

Doireann and Oisín went with Mammy in search of a big Christmas cracker that Santa usually hid somewhere in Granny and Granda's house. They found it behind the sitting room sofa, along with some balloons and some more smaller crackers. After dinner, they opened the family presents from under the Christmas tree.

CHAPTER 4

You Can Do Your Work, I Go See Granda

8 January

This was Doireann's first day back with Granny and Granda after the Christmas break, and she was wearing a lovely black dress and a white cardigan. Later, Granny said to Granda, "Doireann is not comfortable in her dress, so I am taking it off."

"Work away," said Granda.

"Work away," mimicked Doireann, now in her tights.

"You're a little sausage," said Granny, laughing as she sat her up.

"I am not a little sausage." Then, with some difficulty trying to remove some toys from the box of toys, Doireann uttered, "Jesus Christ Almighty," in annoyance, before asking to look at Barney (the DVD) on the telly.

It was still morning time. "I want my (lunchtime) pepperoni," she demanded as she struggled to get it out of the lunch box taken from the fridge. "It's [not] my coming," she said, before eventually succeeding all by herself.

Granda helped her when naming the furry monkey and the tiny magnet horse stuck to the fridge door. The monkey was called Max the monkey, and the horse, Harry the horse.

After lunch, Granny put her into the cot for a nap. "Granny, Granny," she cried and screamed. "Granda, Graandaaaa," was her next target. And when he too ignored her, she yelled, "I'm telling Mammy. I am telling Mammy."

When Mammy did eventually arrive, Doireann ran to the hall door and gave her a big hug.

9 January

Granda drove to Gorey to help Mammy get her car started.

"Are you going to fix Mammy's car?" Doireann asked.

Granda then offered to drive Oisín to school, as he was going back that way.

"Granda fixed your car," said a smiling Doireann to Mammy.

10 January

When Granny and Granda asked Doireann to put her grub away, Granda danced towards the fridge to open the door for her.

"Ha ha ha, you're like a bunny rabbit." She laughed.

Later, they went to the library, but firstly, Granny had to do some shopping. Granda took Doireann into the library and read about five books that she selected as they sat in the tiny kids' seats, in the children's corner. Granny arrived later and took over from Granda, while he went to read the newspapers.

12 January

On the way home from their early morning gym, Granny and Granda went to collect Doireann, who was waiting in Tesco's car park, Gorey, with Daddy. As soon as she got out of Daddy's car, she had to show off her lovely dress and red cardigan first, before getting her shoulder bag.

"Ooh, aren't you very pretty," said Granny.

As they drove to Camolin, Granda played the Jimmy Cricket CD of Christmas songs, and a delighted Doireann sang some of the words.

"Doireann, after breakfast, we have to do some shopping, and will you help Granny and Granda?" Granda asked.

"Yes."

"Thank you," he said.

"You're welcome."

"Teddy Pink is minding your house," Granny told her, on realising that Teddy wasn't in the car. "Teddies White and Brown are waiting for you at home," continued Granny, who was eager to avoid a meltdown.

In the house, Doireann sat and watched Barney and sang along with all the kids singing the numbers songs with Barney.

"Doireann, will you put your grub into the fridge?" requested Granny.

"I did."

"You didn't," Granny told her.

She then inspected the fridge with an "Ooh", before removing her dinner (pepperoni and a drink) from her bag to put it in the fridge. She had a runny nose and a chesty cough and wanted to sleep instead of shop. Granny put her into the cot and read her a story to try and settle her and then tried to leave the room, but Doireann wasn't having it.

When Granny did eventually come out of the bedroom, Doireann was tagging along behind her.

A while later, they went to Tesco's in Gorey to do their weekly shopping. Granny and Granda could not do their normal weekly shopping the night before because of a very thick fog with zero visibility. Doireann sat in the shopping trolley car and was very well behaved as she drove it around the shop, gathering up the shopping items from Granny.

"Are you sitting side-saddle?" Granda asked as she sat with her legs out the window on one occasion.

On their way home, she sang along with Granny and Granda's songs in the car. "The babies on the bus went suck, suck, suck … The dogs on the bus went woof, woof, woof … The monkeys … and then the lions …"

Their next song was "How Much is That Doggie in the Window".

"A big, huge thank you," Granda said to Doireann and gave her a pat on the head. "That's for helping us with the shopping and helping to bring it into the house," he said as she nodded and smiled approvingly.

While watching the telly, she had her juice drink and then had her pepperoni.

Later, as Granny was changing her nappy, she said, "Oh, Granny, I did [a] fart."

"I know. I can smell it. You did it right into my face," complained Granny.

Then Granny got her to take a nap by staying in the bedroom with her, ignoring her protests and telling her, "Be quiet. Granny wants to sleep also."

After a couple of minutes, Doireann fell fast asleep.

When Mammy called to collect Doireann, she told Granny and Granda about her devilment that morning. "What would you like for breakfast"? Mammy asked her.

She thought for a while and then said, "Kafli" (the cat), with a smirk on her face and then, rubbing her belly, continued with, "yum-yum, Mammy, ha ha ha."

Granny and Granda got loads of hugs before she left for home.

15 January

When Granny and Granda arrived home from the gym, they couldn't see who was in Daddy's car until they got close up to the window. It was Mammy and Doireann playing hide-and-seek in the car. Mammy was at the doctors on Saturday and is on antibiotics for a chest infection, and Doireann had a very heavy cold. Granny made an orange juice drink from fresh oranges but spilt it as she handed it to Doireann. Her pants, nappy, chair, cushion, and floor got it. Granda hated anything sticky, and Granny had to mop it up and change Doireann's clothes.

Later, they went to Gorey Library. They walked through Dunnes Stores and up onto the first floor and out the door towards, and past the courthouse. Doireann walked on the walls while holding Granda's hand. Granda read a couple of books for her in the library, while Granny collected a library book she had ordered online. Granny then took over from Granda, and he went to read the daily newspapers. When Granda went back to Granny, Doireann had blocked off the children's area with the round portable plastic pouffe-type seating of varying sizes and colours. It was like a blockade, and the only thing missing was a flag. She then "made an opening" and said, "Come in here, Granda."

When they left the library, they used the elevator.

There were other mammies and kids on the lift, now all very silent, like Doireann. Granda announced, to much amusement and laughter, "Wouldn't it be great if they were like that all the time?"

Doireann held Granda's hand when walking down the travelator to the basement. At lunchtime, Doireann said, "I'm cold."

"How do you do, Cold?" joked Granda, while shaking her hand.

Looking at him innocently, she replied, "How do you do?"

Later, when she was watching Barney with all the music and dance, Granda started to dance. "Stop dancing, Granda," she said angrily.

Next, when Granny and Granda were talking, "Shush," she said.

Granny took her in for a snooze and read her a story first to settle her in the cot. Granny told her she was having a snooze also, but Doireann kicked up by moaning and moaning and then coughing and coughing; until she got her own way.

17 January

Today, Doireann brought a banana only but nothing for her dinner. Everything now from her is "my"—for example, "My do it."

Granny and Granda took her to the Amber Springs Hotel in Gorey this morning to check out its gym and swim facilities, as they were finding the journey to Arklow too long and costly on petrol. As they proceeded to exit the hotel through the hotel foyer, they could smell the breakfasts, and Doireann said, "My hungry."

When they got outside, they took her over to see the water fountain in the hotel grounds. They had to be very careful not to slip on the icy surfaces. Because it was very cold, they did not stay too long either. They went to Lidl's Store to get a warm fleece top for her. She wheeled the kiddies' shopping trolley around the shop. Then she gave cuddles to all the furry lions and zebras stacked on the various shelves. "I love cuddly toys," she said.

As he drove home, Granda said, "Thanks for helping us today, Doireann."

"You're welcome."

She got cranky and upset at lunchtime and cried when Granda closed the straps on her high chair.

"Where's my banana?" Granda asked her as he stood there with a banana on his head.

She started laughing when she saw the banana on Granda's head. She asked for and was given porridge with blueberries for her lunch. After her afternoon nap, she would not give Granda a hug as she headed for home.

19 January

Doireann had a bad chesty cold with a runny nose. Granny helped her build a garage for a place to put all her little toy cars in. "Granda, look," she said, pointing to her new garage for the cars.

Granny wrapped her up well in her jumpsuit before they headed over to Camolin Playground. It was very cold today. She spent a long time on the toddlers' swing.

"Lean back and look up at the sky," Granny suggested.

As the swing swung back and forth, with Granda pushing her, she had a big grin on her face and loved it. Next, she slid down each of the two slides with Teddy Pink. Then Teddy Pink had a few goes herself, with Doireann close behind, sometimes. She didn't like the spinning seat herself but let Teddy Pink have a go anyway. Then she ran to the see-saw; she put Teddy Pink on one end, and she sat on the other. Next, she climbed up into the tree house with Teddy Pink (Granny close behind). Teddy had a great time up there. Doireann sat her down, made her tea, and gave her some toast and then cake. "This is great fun," she said. When her hands got cold, Granny put spare woollen socks on her hands. She found a tennis ball on the perimeter of the playground and took it home.

As Granny prepared lunch, Doireann was strapped in her high chair. "I want out," she demanded.

"No. Wait for your food," Granny told her.

"You can call me when you are ready," she said.

Granda stood up from his chair as he separated the lettuce from the rest of his salad to place it on the lunch box lid.

"Sit down," Doireann said, who thought he was eating his lunch.

Granda ignored her.

"*Sit down*," she roared.

"Please?" said Granda.

"Please?" she said, rather meekly with her head bent down.

"Thank you," Granda said as he sat down.

22 January

Granny and Granda collected Doireann at her house in Gorey this morning. Daddy had taken Oisín to school. Doireann was in great form, and when asking Mammy for the Cheerio's, she'd been promised, she was animated—twisting her two feet in a dancing motion with arms outstretched like a ballerina as she spoke. She gave Mammy a big hug as she said bye-bye, and her and Teddy Pink headed for Granda's car.

"Are you tired, Granny?" she asked after Granny gave a big loud noisy yawn in the back seat of the car.

"Yes."

"Go asleep," Doireann suggested.

The conversation for the rest of their journey to Camolin was Doireann telling Granny all about their flight to Uncle Gary after Christmas. "On the plane we put suitcases up; sat down; played crocodile; ear phones on, and Mammy had hers; plane down and landed."

"Did the plane bump?" asked Granny.

"Yeah, it bump and we got off."

Granny mentioned Uncle Gary's birthday last November to her.

"Where was that?"

"Liverpool," Granny said.

Then she remembered singing him Happy Birthday at his party.

"Do you remember staying with Granny and Granda in their hotel that night, Doireann?" Granda asked.

She remembered and started talking about having breakfast with us the next morning—the lady who'd given her a bottle of orange juice; how Mammy had called; and how we'd gone for a walk in the park, where we fed the ducks, saw the squirrel, and played in the playground.

They went to the library again today. Granny read books for Doireann, while Granda read the newspapers. Then Granda gave Granny a break and read some more books for Doireann. Earlier, as they walked to the library through Gorey Shopping Centre, Doireann played with all the kiddie ride machines on the ground floor outside Dunnes Stores. She climbed the big stairs with Granda and then played in the kiddie ride machine on the first floor before taking a walk outside on the wall opposite the courthouse.

During the drive home, Doireann got great laughs, mimicking Granny and Granda with, "It's a hard life." She repeated this over and over, laughing all the while, and her laughing made them laugh also.

Granny changed her nappy and then gave her lunch.

When finished, Doireann asked, "Where's Granda?"

"He's in the room, working on his computer," Granny told her.

She headed off to see Granda, and when Granny tried to stop her, she said, "You can do your work. I go see Granda."

Granny laughed at that and thanked her, while continuing to laugh.

"You're welcome," was her reply as she sought out Granda.

"What are you doing?" she asked Granda, while scanning his work station for something to get her hands on.

Having heard her conversation with Granny, Granda asked, "Did you leave Granny to do her work?"

"I did," she proudly said, as Granny laughed out loud again in the background.

Granny took Doireann for a snooze, and when she fell asleep, Granny came out and had her lunch.

An hour later, "Mammeeeeee," bellowed Doireann.

"She is on the way," Granny said as she removed her from the cot.

Standing in the hall now, Doireann asked for Teddy Pink, before realising she was still in the cot. Pointing to Granda, she said, "Get it."

Granny and Granda tried to get her to say the word "please", but she went quiet.

"Say please, and Granda will get Teddy," Granny told her.

She pointed to Granny and said, "You get it."

Granda pointed to Doireann and said, "You get it."

And she laughed, saying, "I won't reach," as she walked into the bedroom.

Granda lifted her up, and she was able to reach into the cot and pick Teddy Pink up, while declaring excitedly, "I got her. I got her."

She then went off home without Teddy Pink, and poor Mammy had to dash back before there was a meltdown.

23 January

Mammy called this evening with Doireann, after dropping Oisín to his football training. Doireann did her "I'm a Little Teapot" song and dance routine, for Granny and Granda, and it was brilliant, and they told her so. Then Mammy showed them Uncle Gary's attempt at it on video. Doireann kept asking to see Gary's attempt at it all the time. That evening, Doireann wore a lovely blue and white jacket with hat and pockets, and it looked lovely on her.

24 January

When Doireann removed her shoes, you could see she was wearing her lovely red tights with her red skirt and navy top. Then, when she started dancing around, she slipped and fell, and the storm clouds opened up! Granda read the story about the three pigs building their houses with straw and then wood and then brick because of the wolf going huff and a puff and so on just to calm her down.

Later, when she was being nosey, Granny spotted her and said, "I can see you."

When she put one hand up, in an attempt to cover her face, Granny said, "I can't see you."

She went to get her grub from the fridge after Granny said it was there. When she opened the fridge door, she became alarmed saying, "It's not in it."

"It is," Granny insisted.

Doireann searched again and with her arms now in the air, she said loudly, *"It is not there."*

Then Granny, spotting the grub on the countertop, realised she forgot to put it in the fridge. "I apologise, Doireann. You were right, and I was wrong," conceded Granny.

They took her to Camolin Playground in the buggy, and before she played with the various equipment, Granny wiped the machines dry, using some old towels she had taken with her. It had rained during the night. Doireann and Teddy Pink got plenty of goes on the see-saw. Then it was Granda's turn after Doireann asked him to get on.

They left after about an hour, and before Granda went indoors, Granny asked him to wipe the buggy wheels clean with baby wipes, because she suspected dog poo got on them. Poor Granda!

Granny fed Doireann, changed her nappy, and read some books to her in the cot. Then, both of them lay down for a snooze. Doireann would not settle as Granny pretended to sleep on the bunk bed beside the cot. Doireann started to read stories (well sort of) to Teddy Pink.

Granny gave up and left her reading to Teddy Pink.

It wasn't long before Doireann sent out an SOS. "Granda, Granda, help."

While they waited for Mammy to call, Doireann watched a *Scooby-Doo* episode on the telly. Then they took some photos of Granny, with her red woollen hat on.

25 January

Granny and Granda met Doireann and Mammy in Tesco's this evening. They had dropped Oisín to his football training. "Granda, I was at the doctor's today, and I have a sore throat," Doireann told him. "I got a present," she said.

Mammy later told Granda that the present was nose drops! Doireann's hair was lovely and full of curls because Mammy had bathed her earlier.

Doireann then reminded Mammy to get her her favourite blueberries in Tesco's.

26 January

Granny and Granda collected Doireann at her house in Gorey after their early morning gym and swim. Daddy was home from Galway late last night and was now on his way to Kilkenny this morning, dropping Oisín off at school on the way. Mammy applied the nose drops to Doireann's nose and handed the bottle to Granny. In the car on their way home, Doireann applied the nose drops (bottle only) to Teddy Pink's nose. She then gave some pretend cake to Teddy and also to Granny. When handing Granda some, she said it was "lelicious".

She wanted Granda to play a Christmas song, but he told her she would have to wait until next Christmas. "Do you like Christmas?" he asked.

"Yeah, Santa gave me chocolate Santa" (in the church Christmas morning) "and a high five," she replied.

"What did he say, Doireann?" he asked.

"He said, 'Ho, ho, ho.'"

Granny made Doireann some porridge, even though she had Mammy's earlier for breakfast. Soon after, while watching an animated cartoon film, she responded with facial expressions, such as eyes widening, laughing, head slightly dropping to one side, and so on.

When Granda told her, she was the prettiest girl in the whole world, she showed him her lovely red dress, red tights, and red hair clip. Granny suggested going to the library today, but Doireann wanted the playground. Granda offered to use the car, but she wanted to go in the buggy. They put her "astronaut" jumpsuit on and took the buggy with them. She refused to get into the buggy. They started walking, and after a while, she wanted to get into the buggy. When they reached the wall bordering Camolin Community Grounds, she wanted to walk on it and held Granda's hand.

Inside the grounds, on the walk down towards the playground, she had great fun chasing Granny and Granda's shadows, until she tripped and fell. World War II arrived! She wanted to go home and would not go into the playground.

When some Mammies arrived with their children, she changed her mind. She went into the playground to stop and stare only with a sulky face. Granny eventually got her to play on the slides, swings, and the see-saw. She even sat in the spinning seat this time and had great fun before they left for home, with her in the buggy.

Granny gave her her lunch, changed her nappy, and put her into the cot for a nap. Granny tried to nap also but gave up after about twenty minutes, because Doireann continued to ignore Granny (pretending to sleep) and instead kept reading a (pretend) story to Teddy Pink.

"Granda, Granda, Granda, Granda," she called out.

Granda went to take her out of the cot.

"Put your sleeves down," she ordered. "I don't like it that way," she continued.

So, before Granda was allowed to lift her majesty out of the cot, he had to roll his sleeves down.

When Granda finished his lunch, he took her to the sitting room. "I am looking for some children's stations," Granda told her as he flicked through the channels.

"Granda, what are shaysins?" she asked.

Granda explained them to her and then gave her his sitting room chair.

Flinging Granda's back support cushion onto the floor, she said, "Granda, I need a blanket."

"Doireann, when did your last servant die?"

"I need a blanket," she demanded.

Soon after this, she played hide-and-seek with Granny before setting up a hurdle, made up of books, in the hall and then jumping over them.

She was delighted when Mammy called to collect her and gave Granny and Granda hugs before she left.

CHAPTER 5

Ha, Ha, Ha

2 February

When Granny and Granda arrived home after their gym and swim, Mammy and Doireann were returning from their little stroll. When Doireann saw them driving in, she waved and kept waving, even after they got out of the car. She was delighted with the "new" Barney DVD that Granny bought in a charity shop, and she watched it over and over. Granda showed her how to fit Granny and Granda's new bird feeder to an outside bedroom window by moistening the suckers first. She then helped with topping it up with birdseed, and Granny took a photo using Granda's mobile phone.

When Granny and Granda finished their breakfast, they took her and Teddy White to Camolin Playground. Granda parked the car in the grounds, and then they all ran to the playground. Doireann chased Granny's shadow and then Granda's, with lots of giggles as she tried to step on them. Granda handed her an old towel to wipe down the playground equipment, but it wasn't needed. She had great fun on the slides, the see-saw, the swings and the spinning seat with Teddy White. Then she climbed up into the tree house, where she made tea for Teddy White.

Next, it was to the see-saw again, and when she and Teddy were finished with it, Doireann told Granny and Granda to get on and move up and down. She kept insisting they continue, and like two idiots, they did. Luckily, there was no one else around to see Granny and Granda see-sawing on this sturdy piece of equipment.

Before leaving the playground, Doireann decided to walk the track around the outside of the perimeter fencing, with Granda in hot pursuit. She made it into a chase and started to run. On the final track, she stopped; turned; and, pointing at Granda, said, "No. Don't come near me."

Granda let her walk on but soon followed.

She ran and jumped into Granny's outstretched arms for safety but screamed when Granda, tickled her and made a scary sound. They all giggled at that, and then Doireann, seeing Teddy White sitting at the picnic bench, decided to lie down beside him on the long seat before they left.

Back in the house, she ate two spreadable cheese triangles, which she loved, and then had her lunch. She actually brought Granny into the bedroom for a snooze. Granny changed her nappy first, before reading her some stories. As Granny pretended to sleep on the bed, Doireann was moving her legs up and down noisily in the cot.

"I cannot sleep with that noise," Granny told her, and she just groaned, with the soother in her mouth.

Eventually, Granny appeared back out in the kitchen, minus Doireann, who was now fast asleep. Mammy called to the house early and decided that, rather than wake Doireann, she would collect Oisín at school first, which was just up the road.

Doireann woke from her deep sleep and wanted to see what Granda was doing in the back garden. He was cutting down some overgrown hedge branches. Just then, Mammy and Oisín arrived.

"I am looking forward to the France v Ireland rugby game tomorrow," Oisín said to Granda, who agreed as he stood there with his trousers tucked into his socks.

"Would you like your leggings tucked into your socks like mine, Doireann?" Granda asked.

She shook her head with a disgruntled look and just said, "No."

Granda then put her small empty raisins box inside the empty bird feeder cardboard box and gave it to her as a rattle.

"We don't need more rubbish at home," Mammy joked with a smile.

As they left, Granda ran after Doireann and handed her the new rattle.

"Will you mind it, Granda?"

Mammy, now laughing loudly, said "One up, ha ha."

Later, Mammy sent Granny and Granda a photo of Doireann, reunited with and holding her favourite Teddy Pink very tightly. Teddy had got lost and was found safe and well.

5 February

It was very frosty and cold (0.5 degrees) this morning. Granny and Granda stood at the gate waving when Mammy drove onto their road. Doireann's face displayed plenty of excitement. It was frosty white everywhere, and the road was slippery. As she got out of the car, Doireann immediately held up Teddy Pink.

"Ah, she is back."

"That's great, Doireann," they said.

Then, pointing to the sky, she said, "Granny, look, the bird is flying."

Granny acknowledged this by nodding her head.

"He is flapping his wings," Doireann said.

When inside the house, she showed off her lovely top that had flowers on it.

Then Mammy showed them her other lovely top under it and then a third top also—because of the cold.

"You look lovely," said Granda, and she gave him a lovely smile.

She then sang the song "Old McDonald Had a Farm", and they all clapped their hands while cheering and saying, "Well done."

"That was lovely Doireann."

"Brilliant."

Teddy White and Teddy Brown were sitting opposite each other as they chatted by the dining room stove, when Doireann interrupted them to show them Teddy Pink. Then she ran to open the hall door for Mammy, who had to go to work. "Bye-bye, Mammy, it's slippy," she warned after giving Mammy a big hug.

She put her lunch into the fridge.

"We are going to the library later today," Granda told her, and she nodded her approval with a happy smile.

Granda switched the telly on to play the Barney DVD for her.

Shortly afterwards, "Where's Granda?" she shouted, realising he was not in the room.

Granda suddenly appeared around the door just to let her see he was still there.

"Would you like me to make a juice drink from the orange Mammy left you?" Granny asked.

"Yes, in a cup; I won't spill it," was her response.

Granny used the beaker this time, to be sure—to be sure!

Later, when driving past the Church of the Immaculate Conception (Roman Catholic) in the village, Doireann said, "Santa gave me a chocolate Santa to eat" (on Christmas morning).

"What did Santa say?" Granda asked.

"*Ho, ho, ho*," was her loud response.

Off they went to Gorey Library and parked in one of the parent-child bays in Gorey Shopping Centre underground car park. During the car journey, they all sang "How Much is That Doggie in the Window?"

Then Doireann wanted to sing "The Wheels on the Bus". She started messing. As soon as she and Granny started to sing the "Doggie" song, Doireann would start singing the other song, giggling all the while.

Granny was not impressed. "That's not fair, Doireann," Granny said. "We will sing one song at a time."

But Doireann insisted on switching songs as Granny sang and got great giggles from this.

The car park rescued Granny and Granda. Doireann magically opened the basement electric doors; removed her coat; and ran to sit in Noddy and Minnie's car, parked in the foyer. Next, she ran to the elevator lift and once inside, asked, "Which one? Which one is it?" holding her index finger to the ready.

"It's that one, the number one," said Granda, pointing.

She pressed the button, and off they rose speedily until the carriage came to a stop and the doors opened. Out she dashed to the fire engine kiddie ride on the first-floor opposite, with Teddy Pink and Granda in hot pursuit.

Next, it was on with her coat again, before exiting the now magically opened doors for a walk on the wall that had a water feature, opposite the courthouse. This brought them to the library doors, and, using her outstretched arms and all the power in her body, she managed to get the outer semi-sphere doors to slide open magically. She repeated this exercise when confronted with a similar set of inner sliding doors.

Once inside, she wondered why all the people were there to the right of the entrance to the library. This space was used for various exhibitions and other activities. Off with her coat and cardigan, and down she ran to the kiddies' area and the books. Granda read the newspapers while Granny read books for Doireann.

Next, Doireann used the round plastic seating to close off her area. Then she got a book and read it (mumbled) to Teddy Pink before they left. Granny needed to get some things in Dunnes Stores, so Granda stayed with Doireann as she played in the helicopter, the Peppa Pig spaceship, and other various kiddie ride machines parked in the hallway. As soon as they reached the entrance to Dunnes Stores, Doireann said hello to the two plastic dogs at the store entrance, with donation coin slots for the Irish Guide Dogs association. She then stood on the plinth with the two dogs, and sang, "How much is that doggie in the window? The one with the waggly tail. Woof, woof."

Granny arrived back out, and they all walked down the travelator towards Granda's car. On the journey home, in the back seat of the car, Doireann played hide-and-seek with Granny by covering her face with the small blue cloth and then removing it with a loud, "*Boo.*"

For lunch, she enjoyed her blueberries before eating the spaghetti bolognese that Mammy had made for her.

7 February

Mammy arrived with Doireann today and told Granny and Granda about an incident yesterday. Mammy mentioned to Doireann that they would be going to see her brother, Oisín, singing in the local church with his school at the grandparents' Mass later.

Then, all excited, she asked, "Will I get a present?"

"Noooooo," said Mammy, whereupon, she got very upset and had a major meltdown (obviously because ho, ho, ho wouldn't be there!).

"Did you see Oisín in the church yesterday, Doireann?" Granda asked.

"I did."

"Who else did you see?" continued Granda.

"Everybody!"

Next thing, she pretended to be asleep on the rocking chair and then shouted, "I'm awake. It's your turn, Granda."

She walked into the kitchen and, on her return about twenty seconds later, Granda jumped up with a loud "*Boo*", causing her to jump with fright and then laugh.

The teddies were next to be rocked asleep before Snowy had a go, with Doireann squeezing onto the rocking chair with him also. Earlier, she had great fun when Snowy, encouraged by Granda, chased her from the bedroom, down the hallway, and into the dining room, where she leapt into Granny's arms, screaming. Granda took photos of her playing with and lying on Snowy.

"Are we going to the library?" she asked Granny and was disappointed when informed that they weren't.

After her lunch, she asked for milk.

"Where does milk come from?" Granda asked her.

"Moo cows."

"What moosic do they listen to?" continued Granda.

"The piano!" she said.

Because it was very cold today, only four degrees, Granny took her out the back for a short while to play chase and, next, to drive her toy car.

Back inside, she complained that her hand was sore, and Granda kissed it better. She started doing drawings on some paper. Granda gave her a copybook, and she did lots of different colours and lines. After that, she sat and watched some of her favourite DVDs.

She was so happy and got really excited when Mammy arrived early. "That's Mammy," she said with a big smile.

Mammy was told they had visited Auntie Val in the nursing home today. Mammy told them that, when the grandparents' Mass ended the other day, Doireann was delighted when shespotted Oisín, and ran up to give him a big hug.

9 February

Doireann would normally have breakfast before arriving out to Granny and Granda's house, as was the case today. They were about to head off into Gorey when she asked for porridge.

"You had your breakfast already," Granny said and offered her some toast instead.

"I want porditch," she demanded.

"I want to see my dinner" (lunch), was her next demand.

"No, Doireann. We are going into Gorey now," Granny said firmly.

Then there was a meltdown, followed with a much firmer demand. "I want my dinner."

"I'm going to Gorey on my own," said Granda.

"I not go with you," Doireann told him.

"That put paid to that false manoeuvre," Granda said to Granny.

Granny gave her some porridge, and when she finished it, Granda said, "Come on. We are going now."

Next thing, she said she wanted her dinner.

"No," Granda said firmly.

Doireann, now looking straight into Granda's face, screamed, "*I want my dinner!*" Another meltdown followed, with screams and tears.

Granny calmed her down eventually and suggested we take Teddy Pink along, and she agreed to this. She was also promised a cream cracker, which she duly demolished, leaving all the necessary evidence on the back seat of the car. Granny and Granda volunteered another peace offering—to play Jimmy Cricket's Christmas songs, as demanded, on the journey to and from Gorey.

They drove to the Talk to Tom charity shop in Gorey to purchase an extremely large teddy bear, the size of the shop window, for €5, which Granny had spotted yesterday. Unfortunately, when they got there, it and a few others had all been sold. Granny returned to the car, parked illegally outside, with a large green Baby Bop of Barney the dinosaur fame that only cost €3.

Doireann's face lit up when Granny handed it to her. The expression of delight on her face was something else, and she could not believe it was all hers. "You buy me present, Granny," she said, with a big smile akin to that of the Cheshire cat.

They drove over to Tesco's for some other items and met Uncle Tony there. Doireann refused to give him a kiss but offered him Teddy Pink to kiss instead.

She was still a bit moany on the way home.

"You are feisty today," Granny told her.

"*I am not feisty!*" she shouted (while not even knowing what feisty meant).

"I was there," she said as they passed the Catholic Church in Camolin.

Back home, and they played Barney and other DVDs for her before she had her spaghetti bolognese and looked for more as soon as she finished her first serving. She then had Granny's lemon drizzle cake and loved it.

After her dinner, Granda read out Doireann's Facebook message they had sent to Aunty Selin and cousin Eddie in Cambodia. He also read Aunt Selin's reply, "I love you Doireann. X."

Doireann switched on the bedroom radio and got into Granny's side of the bed for a sleep. Granny arrived and took her into the cot for a nap and read some stories to her first. She loved stories.

12 February

Doireann arrived wearing another pretty dress, with pockets on the sides today. She spoke to Mammy about Baby Bop all weekend. Noticing her lurking around the bathroom, Granda asked, "What do you want there?"

"I want to wash my hands," she said as she walked into the bathroom.

Granda gave her the towel to dry her hands with.

"I like that towel," she said.

She then ran into her bedroom to get Baby Bop and all the teddies, including Snowy. "Teddy Pink lost," she said.

But Mammy corrected her, saying, "Teddy is minding the house for you."

Later, when Granny and Granda forgot to bring Teddy White to Tesco's, they avoided the tears by telling her that Teddy White, Teddy Brown, and Snowy would play with Baby Bop until they returned home, which wouldn't be too long.

She got into the trolley car and put her seat belt on before driving off, with the help of Granda. Then she wanted to get out and walk. Next, she wanted to sit inside the trolley with the shopping. Because there was very little room in the trolley, she got out and walked with Granny.

Granny and Granda had failed to notice Doireann putting her small glass medicine bottle (with safety cap) into her pocket before they had left the house. Granny tried to take it, in case it fell and smashed, but she wouldn't let her. The first item for the trolley was a cardboard carton of tomato juice. Granny handed it to Doireann, who then flung it into the trolley like a tennis ball.

"Doireann, you are to hand the food to me, and I will do the rest," Granda told her firmly.

Her head went down, but she came around soon after.

Granda went to put all of the shopping into the car, while Granny took her to play with the London bus and then she played with Noddy, both parked outside Tesco, at the drop-off zone. Granda arrived with his car to collect them.

"Doireann drove me to Galway and back," Granny told him.

On the way home, Doireann sang "The Wheels on the Bus". When Granny used the lyrics "all day long" at the end of a verse, Doireann corrected her, saying, "it's 'all along the town', Granny."

Driving past Camolin (Catholic) Church, she pointed and said, "I know that."

"What happens in there?" Granny asked her.

"Get a present!"

Doireann offered to help bring in the shopping, which consisted of only two bags. She carried the small container of milk.

It was very cold but with lovely sunshine, and so, before lunch, Granny decided to take her, with Snowy, Baby Bop and the teddies out to the garden to play for a while.

Later, as she ate her lunch, Granda gave her a piece of his beetroot.

"Granda, can I have more beetroot?" she asked. "Granda, could I have some more beetroot?" she asked again. She loved the beetroot.

After lunch, Granny changed her nappy, put her in the cot for a snooze, and sang her some songs.

"Granny, don't sing loud, because Granda is listening to the radio," she was told. (He was actually listening to the news.)

She didn't sleep and was calling for Granny soon after. Granny took her to the sitting room, but she came to visit Granda as he worked on his computer.

"I go back to Granny now," she said.

"Where are you going?" Granda asked because she headed into the dining room instead.

"I want bread," came the reply.

"Granny will get you some," said Granda.

"She is watching the telly."

On hearing this conversation, Granny got up and got her some bread.

When Mammy called with Oisín, she had to print off something from the computer. While they did this, Doireann put the radio on and got into the main bed on Granny's side. She had Baby Bop beside her.

19 February

Because Mammy was on a training course in Birmingham today, Daddy had Doireann and Oisín with him when opening Gorey Curves at 9 a.m. Granny and Granda collected both of them there on their way home from an early morning gym and before driving to Camolin. Daddy forgot Doireann's soother and Teddy Pink, but luckily, Granny had a spare soother at home. Granda stopped the car outside Oisín's school in Camolin, where both of them got out.

"Gary's outside," Doireann said (referring to Granda), with a slight grin and a giggle, as if trying to tease Granny.

When in the house, she told Granny and Granda she was on holidays in Galway last week. They visited the museum (at the Spanish Arch) and the aquarium (in Salthill).

When she sat at the telly to watch a DVD, she immediately started waving her finger, saying, "I don't like it."

Granny got her to sit at the kitchen table to do some drawings. Granny drew a rectangle, a triangle, a circle, and a box and asked her to name them individually. She was able to name them all on her own.

"I have to go to the doctor now," Granda told Doireann as he headed out the door.

"Okay," she said with a lovely smile as she waved bye-bye.

When Granda returned, she agreed to help him move some twigs in the garden. He had cut them off a hedge the day before. Later, when Granny arrived out to help, Doireann put her hand up, shouting, "Stop. Go away."

Granda handed her a small twig.

"No. It's too heavy," Doireann insisted.

At lunchtime, she closed her eyes a couple of times before glancing sideways, towards Granny and Granda, while laughing. Earlier, she'd danced to the rock music on the radio with Baby Bop and then with Teddy White. Granda was out in the garden again as she and Granny looked out the bedroom window. Doireann was calling Granda. Then she pressed her nose up against the window. When Granda did the same thing at the same time as her, she laughed out loud.

Next, she went outside again to play some football and then played with Granda. It was a mild and sunny day, about ten degrees. She then took Granda to the lovely flowers that Granny had shown her and said she would get some for Mammy.

Eventually, Granny put her in the cot for a nap and read her some stories from her books before she lay down to go asleep.

Ten minutes later, "Granda, Granda, Granda. Granneee, Granneee, Graneee."

Granda went into the bedroom, and Doireann immediately said, "I did a poo."

"I know. I can smell it," said Granda.

The poo disturbed her sleep.

As a rather disgruntled Granny changed her nappy, she declared, "I hate these nappy-type pants, because they are easily soiled on the outside if you are not careful."

Doireann had brought her shoes and her boots with her today. Earlier, she had her boots on the wrong feet.

Granda asked her, with a grin on his face, "Do you want to walk like a penguin, pet?"

"No," was the sharp reply, but she would not let Granda fix them.

A while later, all Granny and Granda could hear was, "I did it; I did it," from an excitable Doireann, who had fixed the boots herself.

CHAPTER 6

Teddy Pink is Having a Rest

21 February

Daddy dropped Doireann off today and said Mammy was flying home from Birmingham this evening. Doireann had porridge for her breakfast and was very tired. "You are a great girl, one of my favourites," Granda said to her and continued with, "You are the prettiest girl in Ireland."

Granny then said, "I am," which prompted Doireann to respond immediately with, "I am, 'cause Granda said."

Off she went to play with her teddies, with a hop, a skip, and a jump. She showed Granny and Granda her sore knees, which she got while playing in the playground yesterday.

"I don't like this T-shirt," she later complained, actually referring to a dress.

She sang along with all the children while clapping her hands as she watched the Barney DVD on the telly and was delighted when Baby Bop appeared on the screen.

Then, as they got ready to go to Gorey Library, she put her shoes and coat on all by herself. Granda put his good coat on—one he got in Chester, United Kingdom, many years ago.

"That's nice," Doireann remarked.

Granda was in charge of the soother, and it wasn't long before Doireann came looking for it. In the car, on the way to Gorey, Granny played with

Doireann, Teddy Pink, and the small blue cloth that Granda kept in the car for when the windscreen fogged up. Teddy Pink and Doireann were each pulling the blue cloth, and Doireann gave lovely belly laughs all the while.

"Thanks for showing me where to drive for the library," Granda said as they arrived into Gorey.

"You're welcome. No problem," came the reply. Granny read books in the children's section, while Granda read the newspapers in the newspaper section, a short distance away.

Catching Granda's eye, Doireann waved, and he waved back, giving her the thumbs up. Then she copied Granda and gave him the thumbs up, with a big smile.

"Granny, can I go to Granda?" she asked, and up she ran after Granny nodded yes.

"What are you doing, Granda?" she asked.

"I'm reading today's news in the newspapers," Granda told her.

"I am going back to Granny now." And off she ran.

They left for home, repeating the same journey back to the car but in reverse. Doireann opened the library's magic doors to walk on the small wall outside toward the magic doors leading into Gorey Shopping Centre's first floor. She played in the kiddie car ride again. Next, she pressed the buttons on the elevator lift, bringing it to the ground floor, where she played with more kiddie ride machines, while Granny went to purchase some things in the shop. Doireann was joined by a little boy as she played inside Peppa Pig's spaceship. She sat quietly looking at the little boy pressing all the buttons as Granda and the little boy's mammy looked on. She was having a great time, and when Granny came out of Dunnes Stores, they walked down the travelator to visit Noddy and Minnie in the basement.

When Granny and Granda said they were going to the car, it was meltdown time again. Granda had to lift her up and carry her to the car, as she protested vigorously with loud screams, cries, and kicks. Granny eventually managed to calm her down. As Granda drove the car for home, he flung the blue cloth randomly over his shoulder. Doireann laughed and threw it back before she and Granny then threw it at each other.

When back in the house, Doireann protested with more kicks and moans as Granny tried to change her nappy. When Granda lifted her into the cot for a nap, she continued her little protests. Granny read some stories before lying her down but she got unsettled and would not sleep. She kept calling out to Granny, and when Granda went into her, holding Baby Bop, she got all excited because she knew she was getting up.

She knocked on the dining room door and Granny asked, "Who is that?"

Doireann jumped from behind the door and said, "*Boo.*" Then she ran and gave Granny a big hug.

"Doireann will probably fall asleep in Daddy's car on the way up to the airport later when collecting Mammy," Granda told Granny.

Granny heated up her lunch (sausages and mashed potatoes). She loved sausages. And when she finished that, she had loads of beans as she sat in her high chair watching a DVD on the telly.

"I'm doing a wee," she said.

"You're all right. You have a nappy on," Granny informed her.

"Do you want to be taken out of your chair?" Granda asked.

Holding the palm of her hand up, she screamed, "*Do not touch.*" She was extremely tired at this stage.

When Daddy called to collect her, there was another meltdown because she didn't want to leave. As Daddy carried her to the car, she said, "See you Friday."

A surprised Granny and Granda just said, "Okay, Doireann. See you then. Bye-bye."

23 February

Mammy called with Doireann and said she'd had a disturbed sleep last night. Then she got upset when Granny opened the kitchen blinds. She had a meltdown because of the sunlight in her eyes.

Then she went into Granda as he worked on his computer. "Granda, I saw an amborghini." But Granda didn't understand.

Mammy then explained that Oisín was always talking about sports cars, including Lamborghini cars and she was copying him.

"Come into the dining room, Doireann," Mammy called out to show Granny and Granda her new red shoes, bought in Dunnes Stores yesterday. She was wearing them with her lovely black dress.

Later, she was really happy when Granny gave her some Cheerios to eat while watching the Barney DVD. She sang along with Barney and his friends, clapping her hands and then stamping her feet and saying hooray loudly at the end of the song.

Later, as she watched a DVD showing a band playing dance music, she started dancing and moving to the music, and then Granda joined in. She handed Teddy White to Granda to dance with, and she danced with Teddy Pink.

Next, "I'm going to the toilet," she told Granny when asked what she was up to.

"You have your nappy on," Granny said.

Doireann then checked the toilet rolls storage cabinet and, seeing one was missing, ran to get a new one.

Later, they all went to Dunnes Stores, including Teddy Pink. Doireann started spitting on her dress in the car and Granny gave out, saying it wasn't nice. Granda parked in the outdoor car park in a bay for mammies and toddlers.

In the store, Granny looked at all the bargains for Granda before getting him some clothes. Doireann started spitting on her dress again in Dunnes Stores as they waited for Granny, who had gone to pay for the clothes.

Granda gave out to her in a very stern voice. She looked like she was about to start crying.

Granny and Granda then promised her some popcorn if she behaved herself. Granda took her and Teddy Pink to the kiddie ride machines outside to play in.

Granny arrived with the popcorn. "We will open this in the car," she said, and they walked quickly to the car.

Doireann wanted music in the car on the way home, and Granda put Jimmy Cricket's Christmas album on.

"No, not that song, the 'Wellies' one," she requested.

She enjoyed her popcorn, while Granda played her two favourite Jimmy Cricket Christmas songs over and over all the way home.

Her new game was to bury her head in the ground to hide, thinking she couldn't be seen. She did it in the cot, and then later, she ran into the small bedroom and lay on the floor to hide. Granny and Granda just played along. She also interacted with Teddy Pink a lot today, and Granda was called upon to give Teddy plenty of hugs on a few occasions.

When Granda left the dining room, she followed and pointed a finger at him, saying in a stern manner, "Don't close the door again."

"You're a right little bossyboots, aren't you?" Granda said and started to laugh.

She then laughed too.

Later, Granda went to the bedroom to change his clothes and locked the door behind him. Just then, Doireann came looking for Granda and cried because she could not open the door. When Granda did appear again, he was confronted with a very upset Doireann, who wanted her broken yellow crayon fixed. Granda took her to the kitchen and got the scissors and Sellotape. He carried out a first aid job on the broken crayon and handed it back to her. A few minutes later, Granda was called upon again to carry out another first aid job on another break on the very same crayon!

Lunchtime, and Doireann ate her potato but would not eat the fish, which apparently, she had devoured yesterday. It was an early lunch (12.30 p.m.), and then Granny changed her nappy. A narky and tired Doireann protested, saying her legs were sore and then her knees.

Granny then put her into the cot and read her some stories. Granda put Teddy Pink on the edge of the cot hanging by her arms. Doireann thought this was funny and looked straight into Teddy's face. Eventually, she fell fast asleep.

An hour and a half later, Granny and Granda were alerted to the sound of, "Granda, Granda, Granda."

Granda picked her up, and she put her shoes on all by herself. If you tried to help, she would scream the house down. It was the same with her cardigan. She and she only would have to put it on.

Mammy and Oisín arrived a little early to take Doireann for a walk in the park close to their house on the way home. As soon as she saw Mammy, she smiled with delight. Mammy whispered something into her ear. Next thing, she said loudly, "See you Monday and bye-bye, Granny and Granda."

24 February

Granny was in Dunnes Stores shopping when Mammy and Doireann arrived in the car park and saw Granda. Mammy wanted to phone Granny to say she was outside, but Doireann wanted to go in and find her.

"I found her. I found her," she cried out when she saw Granny.

Mammy went looking for something in the stores, while Granny and Doireann queued to pay for the newspapers at the automatic checkout.

"Doireann, you can't leave Teddy Pink there on the floor," Granny told her on seeing where she had placed her.

"She is having a rest," Doireann said.

"Someone might walk on her and trip," warned Granny, now trying to encourage her to remove Teddy.

Doireann immediately stayed crouched down over Teddy Pink, looking up and down the walkways as if to ward off any unsuspecting shoppers.

The lady behind the desk was observing all of this. "Oh, I think Teddy is awake now, after his rest," the lady said.

And Doireann immediately picked Teddy Pink up off the floor.

Afterwards, Granny, Mammy, Doireann, and Teddy Pink all went to visit Aunt Val in the nursing home and met Val's sister and niece while there. Everyone interacted with Doireann, giving her big smiles, saying hello to her, and telling her she was gorgeous. She would only let them hold Teddy Pink, and when leaving, she gave Aunt Val a big wave.

26 February

Mammy brought Doireann to the doctor this morning because one of her eyes was stuck closed. She had to rinse the eye for a few days, and if it did not clear, she would have to use the drops as prescribed. Mammy said they were up Sliabh Bhui, for a walk yesterday, and it was very cold. That was how it had happened, she believed.

Doireann was also very tired today. Granny and Granda had collected her at about 11 a.m. as agreed, in Gorey, before going to Tesco's to do some shopping. They needed to stock up with extra food, as heavy snow was expected. Doireann brought My Little Pony with her into the store. She kept asking to see Baby Bop and was told she was at home and would see her later. She drove the trolley car around the supermarket, with the help of Granda. After a while, she got out of the car trolley and did loads of twirls in her lovely black dress, up and down the aisles.

On their way home to Camolin, Doireann sang a song to Teddy Pink that Mammy had taught her, and Teddy loved it.

Pointing, she said, "There's a windmill."

Granda asked her, "What does a windmill make?"

There was silence, and Granda answered with, "It makes electricity," just before she said, "It goes around!"

Granda thanked her for helping them with the shopping.

"You're welcome," she replied.

Granda joked and said, "No problem."

And she said that Oisín had taught her to say that.

They turned off the main road, heading for Marian Crescent, and she said, "We are home now."

Inside the house, she immediately went to the bedroom for Baby Bop and Teddies White and Brown. She put Teddy White with Teddy Pink to have a talk. When Granny put Barney on, she danced and clapped to the songs. She had pasta for lunch before Granny changed her nappy and put her into the cot. Surprisingly, she asked Granny to leave, and she slept for two hours. Just before this, she had said she was not well, sneezed, and looked tired.

"*Boo*," was the sound that came from Doireann's cot; Granny and Granda went into the bedroom; she was talking to Teddy Pink.

They talked with her for a while and asked her if she had a good sleep.

"She's hungry," she said, holding Teddy Pink up.

"I have berries, cucumber, and melon slices," Granny told her and Teddy Pink.

She didn't want Granny to kiss her, saying that was for Mammy. "Can you show Mammy the fruit?" she asked Granny.

"Of course, I will," said Granny.

"I love her," Doireann said.

Granda and Doireann played hide-and-seek. Granda hid Teddy Pink, and Doireann came looking for her. Granda pointed to the cot bedcover that was raised up. She laughed when she found Teddy. Then she and

Teddy went to the kitchen, and it was Granda's turn to count to ten and come looking.

"I love pandas," she said to Granda.

Granda googled some pictures of pandas for her.

"In the zoo, I pointed to a panda," she told Granda.

Next, there was knock on the door, and she ran to answer it and was very excited, knowing it was Mammy. She gave all her teddies and Baby Bop hugs, and then Granda and Granny got hugs before she left to go home.

Granda said, "I will see you on Wednesday."

"No. I will go on plane to Galway for holidays on Thursday," she said. She was reliving her Galway trip last week and even mentioned the slides and all.

28 February

When Doireann and Oisín arrived out, Granny and Granda were told there was no school for Oisín today because of the snow. It was freezing cold, and Met Eireann issued a "red alert" for parts of the country because of the expectant heavy snowfall, blizzard conditions, and freezing temperatures. Oisín made some small snowballs when he arrived in the front garden but soon came in after slipping twice in the icy conditions. He was wearing a lovely woollen hat with the Dublin GAA colours that his school friend's Granny had knitted.

They both had Cheerios for their breakfast, but Oisín said he was still hungry.

"You can have one of the rolls I made," said Granny.

"There's the floor. Have a roll on that," said a laughing Granda.

Doireann showed Granda all the food Mammy had made and put into a plastic container for her. She put it and her diamond-shaped cheeses into the fridge, before sitting down to have one of Granny's cheeses, followed by her mozzarella—which she managed to pronounce herself.

She ran into the bedroom to get Baby Bop and then went back for the teddies and Snowy. She then watched the Barney DVD on the telly, while Oisín watched some children's programmes on the big telly in the sitting room. Granda showed him how to use the two TV remote-controls.

"You are staying with us tonight, Oisín," Granny told him.

"Does Mammy know?" asked a delighted Oisín.

"Yes."

He was told not to tell Doireann.

Granny made some toast for Oisín. Doireann had her popcorn and gave some to Oisín. Granny gave Oisín some jelly babies, also. When the snow started to fall, they all went out to the back garden and threw snowballs at each other and took some photos. When it got a bit too cold, they went back in, but Oisín stayed put, wanting to build his snow fort.

After lunch, Granda helped Oisín with his fort and got him a large empty bucket and shovel to gather the mounds of snow that he had raked up for him. Doireann slept through all of this and only woke up when Mammy and Daddy called. Daddy and Oisín played with the snow across the road for a little while. Oisín was then of two minds, whether to stay or not. He agreed to stay when Granny and Granda promised to have him back home in Gorey early in the morning. Because of the forecasted blizzards and heavy snowfalls tomorrow, people were warned to be off the streets by 4 p.m.

Oisín played a game of Ludo with Granny and Granda. First prize was a scratch card and €3. Second prize was €2. Granny got all her discs home first, with Granda a close second. Oisín was not too pleased. Granny gave her scratch card to him, but he won nothing. They then watched a bit of telly before watching a DVD about Mohammed Ali, which Oisín really enjoyed. He went to bed at 10.30 p.m. after he finished his cup of hot chocolate with marshmallows and then a bread roll.

CHAPTER 7

The Beast from the East / Red Alert

1 March

Granny and Oisín were up at eight o'clock, followed by Granda, one hour later. It was very cold outside (-1.5 degrees) and was to be cold all day. The country was on red alert from 4 p.m., with forty centimetres of snow expected, along with high winds and blizzard conditions. People were being warned to stay indoors for twenty-four hours.

Granny and Granda drove to Tesco's in Gorey (10.30 a.m.) before dropping Oisín off at his house. Granny wanted to stock up with bread and milk mainly. It was just like shopping on Christmas Eve, as the place was packed and very noisy. The bread and milk were disappearing off the shelves as quick as lightning.

On the way into the shop, Oisín asked Granda where his team, Chelsea, would finish in the league table. Chelsea was currently lying fifth, below Man City, Man United, Liverpool, and Spurs, in that order.

"Fourth, directly below Liverpool," he teased, knowing Oisín supported Liverpool.

"We have some good players, like Salah," he said.

"Oh, I'll be having salad for my lunch today also," joked Granda.

Then, Oisín talked about Neymar coming to Liverpool, and Granda told him that Neymar had a problem with his metatarsal.

"What, he's gone to Arsenal!?" panicked Oisín.

5 March

The beast from the east arrived, along with storm Emma, as forecasted. Granny and Granda didn't have Doireann on the Friday because of the adverse weather conditions. Daddy dropped Doireann off today, at 2.15 p.m., and both Mammy and Daddy collected her at 4.30 p.m.

Granny and Granda brought a very excitable Doireann outside to see the snowman they had built at the weekend. Using Granny's iPad, they took lots of photos and videos. Granda took photos of Doireann standing beside and holding the snowman's hand. These were similar to photos taken of Oisín in 2009 and 2010, when he was about the same age. These were the years when there were very heavy snowfalls all over the country, with temperatures dipping as low as minus ten degrees.

Doireann started to throw snowballs at Granda, encouraged by Granny, of course. When it got too cold, they went indoors.

Doireann kept visiting Granda in his room, as he worked at his computer. She wanted to see her cousin Eddie in Cambodia on Facebook. When seeing Eddie's brother Richie, she said, "Richie is my cousin also."

Granda showed her lots of photos of her Cambodian cousins on Facebook.

Mammy's birthday was on 2 March, and Granny and Granda could not get to see her. She was delighted with the photo collage birthday present that Granny had made for her. They were photos of her as a little girl holding her Daddy's (Granda's) hand on the Bray promenade. Beside that photo was a photo of Doireann holding Granda's hand on the same promenade.

7 March

Mammy and Doireann arrived out to Granny and Granda's house at 9.30 a.m. Baby Bop was looking out the dining room window, waiting for Doireann. Startled, after catching sight of Baby Bop, she pursed her lips, saying, "Baby Bop." She showed Granny and Granda her temporary inhaler, which the doctor had prescribed for her cough. She was wearing lovely red tights with her lovely purple dress that had pockets. She loved pockets and was quick to put her hands into them and show them off.

Granda was handed Teddy White to hug, after she went and got both teddies from the cot. She brought Granda back to the bedroom to get Snowy, while Mammy and Granny chatted. Then she ran out of the bedroom as fast as she could toward the dining room and then into the kitchen, screaming, with Snowy not far behind, making a scary loud noise.

A little while later, Snowy surprised her, when he appeared all of a sudden, right up against her face and said, "*Boo,*" which caused her to giggle.

"I can't do it," she said, handing Granny the Barney DVD case to have it opened.

"It's hard to remove," Granny acknowledged as she handed the disc to Granda to insert into the telly.

Doireann didn't want anything to eat, having had plenty of Weetabix for her breakfast this morning. A little while later, she asked Granny for toast and milk. Granny cut the toast into fingers.

"What are you doing today, Doireann?" Granda asked, but she didn't know. "We are going to sleep all day," joked Granda.

"Noooooooooooooooooooooooooooooo," she said, shaking her head.

Then, Granda told her they were going to the library, and she was very happy with that and smiled.

They left for Gorey Library soon after and brought Harry the Horse (a small furry fridge magnet) along for the ride. In the car, Granda had to play Jimmy Cricket's Christmas song "Santa Bring My Wellies Back to Me" over and over on the drive to Gorey.

As they descended downwards into the Gorey Shopping Centre underground car park, Granny and Granda were told by Doireann, that they all had to say out loud, "*Wheeeeeeeeeeeeeeeeeeeeeeeeeeeeeeeeeeeeeeeeeeeeeeeeeeeeeeeeeeee.*" This also had to be repeated later, as they left for home.

After parking the car, they went and said hello to Noddy and Minnie, who were sitting in their car just inside the shopping centre's magic doors. Next, Doireann pressed the lift button for floor number one. As they were about to exit the magic doors leading to the library, Doireann battled hard not to put her coat on.

She walked on the short walls past a packed and busy courthouse towards the library. They looked at the paintings, including one of coloured hands just inside the library doors. Doireann loved one that depicted a pink flower. As they entered the main entrance to the library, two mammies with their little girls were chatting. Doireann just stood there staring, as she has a habit of doing, just like her mammy did when she was little. Soon, she proceeded to the children's books section. Granny sat with her to read books, while Granda went to have a quick read of the newspapers first, before taking over from Granny, who wanted to get a book herself.

Shortly afterwards, Doireann and Granda went looking for Granny and passed by two young female students, who were obviously studying. They both gave Doireann a big smile. Having located Granny, they headed for Dunnes Stores to get peppers, tomatoes, mushrooms, and some cans of tuna. Doireann walked down the steep stairs, holding the rail with one hand and Granda's hand with the other.

"One step at a time, Doireann," Granda said.

"Hold the rail," she told Granda, showing concern for his safety.

She played with the kiddie ride machines before heading into the shop. There, she swung on the steel barriers surrounding the automatic tills, while waiting for Granny to finish. She then helped Granny put the food into a plastic bag, and off they went.

"Doireann, will you mind Granny while I use the toilets, and I won't be too long?" Granda said as he headed for and took the lift for the first floor.

When Granda appeared back out, Granny and Doireann were already on the first-floor waiting. "She wanted Granda," Granny said sarcastically.

They had a Mexican standoff on the lift as they descended to the ground floor. Doireann and two other 2-year-olds just stood eyeing each other up, without uttering a word, as kids do. They then, travelled down the travelator.

Doireann, freely offered to hold Granny and Granda's hands, and continued to do so at the end of it. "I want a swing," she demanded.

Of course, "a swing" turned magically into many swings because of her magical powers of persuasion, until Granny and Granda were forced to lay down their "well-used arms", if you'll pardon the pun, and surrender.

"Where's Granda's *black* car, Doireann?" Granda said, emphasising the colour with a big grin, seeing it was surrounded by many other black cars.

With a bit of encouragement—a nudge nudge and a wink wink and a pointing in that direction sort of thing—eventually she shouted out, pointing her finger like a gun, "*There it is!*"

And Granny and Granda said, "Well done, Doireann, well done."

They speedily readied themselves to evacuate the building, pronto.

During the car journey home, Granny got loads of belly laughs from Doireann. The two of them were tugging at the blue cloth and Harry the horse. Doireann had great fun and laughter.

When they arrived home, Granny returned a missed phone call from Mammy, who informed them that her car brakes were poor this morning, and she had taken it to a garage. The mechanic told her not to be driving the car because the brake pads were badly worn and very dangerous. Granny and Granda offered to collect Oisín from school later and drive him and Doireann home to Gorey.

Granny had to keep reminding Doireann to eat her lunch before changing her nappy and putting her down for a nap. She would not sleep, and Granny was forced to take her out of the cot and sat her down on the dining room sofa. She watched a DVD about Winnie the Pooh and Tigger as she ate some toast that Granny made for her. Later, she drew a picture for Mammy and then played with the yellow toy barking dog with flashing eyes. It barked—bark, bark, bark—and barked and so on, until she got fed up with it.

Next, she came looking to see what Granda was up to. When Granny came looking for her, she tried to shut the bedroom door to keep Granny out.

"You are not to do that," Granny complained. "I need to know what you are doing."

Granda showed her the Facebook photo of her Cambodian cousin Eddie, who was wearing his shark hat.

"That's not him," she said.

"It is. Look. He is with his mammy, your Auntie Selin," Granda said and then showed her more photos.

She got into Granny and Granda's bed and switched on the radio and Granny pulled the blankets over her, saying, "Doireann is asleep now."

"That's good," said Granda—before she was up like a light, saying, "I'm awake now."

With that, she ran to the dining room, where the yellow toy barking dog with flashing eyes got all excited and started to bark—bark, bark, bark—again.

A while later, she ran into the main bedroom, pursued by Granny, who was trying to put a clip in her hair. Then she lay on the bed with Granny and pretended to be asleep. She pretended to snore, causing Granny to laugh. It wasn't long before they were back out in the dining room dancing around, as the yellow toy barking dog with flashing eyes continued with his merry dance also.

The time came for them to pack-up and pick Oisín up from school. Doireann struggled to put her wellies on and Granda offered to help.

"*No! I do it!*" she screamed.

At the school, Granny went in to collect Oisín. Doireann and Granda sat waiting in the car, parked at Saint Catherine's Church (Church of Ireland) in Camolin.

"Come and sit in the back, Granda," she said.

"Ah, we won't be here long enough, pet," Granda told her.

Looking in his rear-view mirror, Granda observed her playing with one of her wellies. There were white lines running across the blue welly. Pretending it was a ladder, she used her fingers to climb (crawl) up it. "I made it; I made it," she said excitedly.

Oisín and Granda talked "footie" (football) for a while on the way home.

Then, "Granda, how would you know it was raining cats and dogs?" Oisín asked.

"How?"

"You would see poodles on the ground," he said, and they all laughed.

"Why did the bird go to the doctors?" Oisín asked again.

"Why?"

"To get tweetment," he said, and they all laughed again.

"What would a pig use to treat a cut on his leg?" Granda asked.

Silence.

"Oinkment," Granda told them, as they drove into their estate, to be greeted by Mammy and Kafli, their cat.

Mammy was getting new brake pads fitted to her car that evening.

9 March

Doireann arrived at the hall door showing off her new shoes and lovely dress with two pockets.

Granda said, "And I love your navy-blue tights."

"No, Granda. They are leggings, not tights," Granny told him.

"No, Granny. They are tights," Doireann corrected Granny.

Mammy said that Doireann was not sleeping great due to all her coughing at night. She was very chesty, tired, and not in good form at all. And now she was also upset because she forgot to bring Teddy Pink today.

When she asked to go back home with Mammy, Granda said, "We have some popcorn for you later, Doireann," to get her mind off Teddy.

As soon as Mammy left for work, Doireann immediately asked for her popcorn, and Granny and Granda agreed to let her have it then because she was not well.

"I want to go to my house," she demanded.

"There is no one home; Mammy is working," Granny told her.

"Mammy lose me," she said.

Granny and Granda didn't say anything.

"Mammy is calling for me," continued Doireann.

At one stage when she was screaming and shouting at Granny, she said, "I don't like you."

Granda told her not to talk to Granny like that, and of course, her lip dropped, as if she were about to start crying. She was like a little demon today.

Earlier, she took her lunch from the fridge and ran to the dining room to show Granny.

"Doireann, you can't leave the fridge door open like that," Granda said angrily.

She ran back, and next there was a loud bang, after she had slammed the fridge door shut "accidently".

Granda called her back to explain, "You are not to shut the fridge door like that. You could break it."

She then walked towards the fridge, opened its door, and closed it very gently as Granda looked on in amazement at the cheek of it!

Granda put Barney on and, thinking it was the wrong one, went to change it.

Doireann screamed, *"No!"*

Granny and Granda informed Doireann of their proposed visit to Auntie Val today. She wasn't too keen, preferring to go home and sleep instead.

"You can have a sleep here," Granda suggested, but this was ruled out straight away.

Then Granny promised her ice cream after the planned visit, and the mood changed tenfold. The reminders to Granny and Granda about that ice cream were tenfold also. Off they went to visit Auntie Val in the nursing home, and Doireann brought Baby Bop along also, to take into the nursing home.

The nursing home carer moved Val from the activities room to the sunroom, where they could all have a chat as she drank her coffee. Doireann was eyeing up Val's biscuits, and eventually she was given one. Delighted, she nibbled away at the Lincoln biscuit. Another visitor, who was sitting with a small group just up from them, went and got Doireann a lovely chocolate roll, and we thanked her. Doireann enjoyed that too, as the evidence clearly showed. Her hands and face were covered in chocolate when she was done. Granny got some tissues to remove the evidence.

Doireann, having being very quiet up to then eventually started to talk to everyone she met. They stayed about forty-five minutes in all. Granda brought Val back to the activities room before they left. Auntie Val had given Doireann another biscuit, and she was delighted. As they left, Granda thanked the lady for the chocolate roll, adding, "Doireann will probably be in ahead of us the next time"—to the sound of much laughter.

On the way back home, Doireann mentioned the ice cream. And Granny sang, "I scream ice cream. We all love ice cream."

A little while later, Granda teased, "Eh, eh, we have to get, eh, eh, what was that in the shops, eh, eh, for Doireann, on the way home, eh, eh?" And before she answered, Granda declared, "Bread." And Granny agreed with him!

Doireann immediately said, "It's ice cream," causing Granny and Granda to laugh out loud.

"We are only joking, pet," she was then told.

They parked at Cartons Daybreak outlet in Camolin, and Granny went in.

"Sit in the back," Doireann told Granda.

And he did—until Granny arrived back with a tub of ice cream. She then had a huge smile on her face.

"You can have your lunch first," Granny told Doireann.

"No, the ice cream."

"Okay, have half the ice cream and then your lunch," reasoned Granny.

"No. Ice cream."

She sat at the kitchen table, with the tub of ice cream and a spoon as happy as could be.

She still looked very tired and told Granny she wanted to sleep. Granny tried to settle her in the cot first and then tried the small bed. Then it was back to the cot again, but she just would not sleep.

Granda went in and read her three stories. And when he finished, she wanted to get out and said, "I want Granny."

Granda lifted her out of the cot to let her sit with Granny and watch the big telly in the sitting room. She was very moody and had two big rosy cheeks, which was usually a sign of teething.

With Daddy in County Mayo for a Stag Weekend, Mammy arrived with Oisín and said she planned to watch a movie with the kids that night.

"What time is the Ireland v Scotland rugby match tomorrow?" Mammy asked Granda.

"At 2 p.m.," he replied and told Oisín that the Man Utd v Liverpool match was at 4.30 p.m. on Sunday.

Oisín's football match had been cancelled for the forthcoming weekend, due to the heavy snowfall the week before.

Doireann went to Granda and asked him for a kiss bye-bye as they readied for home. When he gave her a hug, she insisted on a kiss. Granda gave her a kiss, thanked her for visiting Auntie Val, and said, "See you Monday, pet."

"No. Friday," she said.

"This is Friday," Granda said to a, by now, confused-looking Doireann.

Looking up at the wooden fly-type creature with wings—four dangly legs, a big head with big teeth, and a leprechaun-type hat and aptly named

Mick—hanging in the hall, Doireann shouted up, "Bye, Mick," much to Mammy's surprise and amazement.

As all three of them left the house waving their hands, Granda waved back and said, "Missing you already," causing Oisín to laugh out loud.

11 March

Daddy, back from his Westport, County Mayo stag party, called with Oisín to give Granny her Mother's Day present from Mammy, Gary, and Richard. Mammy stayed at home with Doireann, who was not well today.

13 March

Mammy dropped Doireann over at 2 p.m. and went for a meeting in Oisín's school with Daddy. Doireann was at the doctor's that morning and was prescribed antibiotics for an infection. She got very upset when Mammy left and started to cry, saying she wanted her Mammy. It was hard to console her.

"Would you like some popcorn, pet?" Granda asked, but she didn't answer. "Perhap Teddy Pink would like some," Granda continued.

She asked Teddy Pink and then went to find the popcorn with Granny.

Granda blew up a balloon for her and she was delighted with it. "I'm happy now," she told Granny. Granny got her to tell Granda that also.

Mammy arrived back as Granda and Doireann were playing with the balloon, punching it to each other on either side of the main bed.

Soon after, Daddy and Oisín called, and Doireann grabbed Daddy's hand, saying, "Come on, meet my friends. Granny and Granda are my two friends."

And then she told Granda, "I like your new shoes," adding, "Mine are pink." She held them up for Granda to see. Earlier, she told Granny she liked her hair.

Doireann was too sick to go to Granny and Granda yesterday and only spent an hour with them today. Mammy told Granny that she is very clingy because she is not well. Mammy smiled when Doireann started to dance while doing all the actions to some DVD music on the telly. She gave Granda a big hug as she left with "her" balloon.

14 March

Doireann waited in Daddy's car outside Granny and Granda's house and asked him where they were. He told her they were in the gym. Daddy said she woke at about 6 a.m., and they left her to sleep on until eight o'clock. Before he left for work, Daddy said she had lost her appetite and would not eat her Cheerios for breakfast this morning.

"I came back, Granny," Doireann announced and then told Granda the same with a big happy smile on her face.

Granny gave her porridge and berries, which she enjoyed while watching the telly.

"Granny, give Teddy Pink a hug," she said before giving Granny a hug herself.

Then Granda got a hug.

Granda lifted her up onto the bed to see the rain and the wind blowing the trees. "It's lovely and cosy in here," said Granda as he gave her a big cuddle. Then Granda blew into her hair. "That's what the wind does to the leaves and the branches on the trees," he told her. Granda continued to blow into her hair a few times as she looked outside, and this caused her to giggle and giggle at the wind blowing her hair.

"Granda, I lost the balloon."

"I'll get you another one later, pet," promised Granda.

Later, he brought her to the sitting room, where he blew up a balloon and handed it to a very excited Doireann. She hopped, skipped, and jumped out of the room with the balloon, and Granny helped her write a huge letter "D" on it. Then Granny got her to sit down to read her a new book she got in a charity shop. The book was called *Dora the Explorer Music to Go*, and it played music as you read the stories.

Granny changed her very wet nappy when she said she was tired in preparation for a nap. She would not go asleep when put into her cot, though. Granny had given her plenty of water to drink through the day because of the antibiotics. Granny even read her four stories, but she kept saying, "I'm awake now," much to Granny's annoyance.

On the way to the small bedroom to read the music book, Granda asked her, "Do you want to sleep?"

"No. Teddy."

"In the cot?" continued Granda.

"No. On Granda's shoulder." About five seconds later, she said, "Teddy [is] awake now."

After Granda sang along with the music in *Dora*, she then wanted to go to Granny, who was watching her soaps on the telly.

Next, she went into the dining room to put her socks and shoes on and had to show Granny and Granda when done. But as she struggled putting her socks on, Granda remarked, "It's a hard life," which she then repeated. Then as she struggled putting her shoes on, she turned to Granda with a grin, saying, "It's a hard life, Granda."

Next, Granny played a game of hide-and-seek with her. It was Doireann's turn to hide, and she ran into the dining room as Granny counted to ten. Then the toy car started playing music, which gave the game away for Doireann, causing Granny and Granda to laugh. For her next go, she hid in the same place!

Earlier, Granda joked with her and said, "Isn't Granny great?"

She nodded her approval.

"But she's not your great-granny," he continued.

"She is a great Granny," Doireann insisted.

Granda spotted a lovely big pheasant in the back garden and fetched Doireann. He put her standing on the bed to look out the window, and she got really excited at the size of it. It ran down the garden, having being disturbed by them looking out the window.

Doireann had her lunch and a pepperoni. Granny had to change her nappy again because she had done a poo just before Daddy called. Granny had to take her leggings, socks, and shoes off because the nappy was a pants-type one. Then, when Daddy tried to put her coat on because it was raining very heavily, Doireann screamed the house down. He could only manage to put the hood of the coat on her head, with the coat now acting as a cape. They then had a massive search for her soother and eventually found it under Snowy.

"I will mind your balloon," Granda told her. "And you are to give Oisín two big hugs from Granny and Granda."

It continued to rain heavily all day and into the night, with heavy gusts of wind.

16 March

Daddy took Doireann out of the car when Granny and Granda pulled up behind them after their early morning gym. Holding Teddy Pink up for them to see her, Doireann said a big hello and then had to show off her new dungarees. She pointed to the lovely fancy flowers all over them. Granny and Granda told her she looked gorgeous. When inside the house, she immediately looked for the musical book *Dora*. On a different occasion, Mammy had mentioned that Doireann loved *Dora*, and when Granny saw it for sale in her favourite charity shop, she had to get it. Baby Bop, Snowy, and Teddies White and Brown were only second fiddle now. Doireann played Dora's music and clapped and danced at the same time.

Daddy was in a hurry, and Doireann gave him a hug, saying, "Bye, Daddy."

She named all the days when Granda told her there were seven days in a week.

"Teddy Pink is tired, and she is asleep on my shoulder," she said.

When Granda suggested using the shoebox (that held his new brown shoes) as a bed, Granny went and got it. Doireann put Teddy into the shoebox and covered her up with a blanket. "She isn't well, and I don't have the thing," said Doireann, referring to a piece of equipment from her toy doctor set, as she lifted Teddy up to talk to her.

She then put Teddy into the high chair, wrapped her up in a blanket, and said to Granny and Granda, "She is warm now."

She then sat up on a chair beside Teddy. Next, she went and got her some (imaginary) food. She fetched the wastebasket from the bedroom, calling it the tower. Placing the blanket over the top, she sat Teddy on it. Granda lifted Teddy up, turned the basket the opposite way up, put Teddy back on it, and said, "Now, she's sitting on her seat."

Later, Granda sat Teddy into the shoebox and drove it around like a car as Doireann looked on and smiled. She then had some oatcakes to eat as she sat and watched the RTÉjr station on the telly. Granda sat on the chair beside her and "dozed off"!

Later, they went to the library, and Granny read some books for Doireann, while Granda read the newspapers. Doireann visited Granda at one stage before running back to Granny. Then Granda took over from

Granny and read more stories for her. When they left the library, she walked on the small wall again, opposite the courthouse. They took the lift to the ground floor, and Granny went into Dunnes Stores to get some things, while Granda looked after Doireann as she played with the kiddie ride machines.

When Granny finished her shopping, she held Doireann's hand as they all travelled down the travelator to the ground floor, out to the car park, and over to the car. They repeated the, "*Wheeeeeeeeeeeeeeeeeeeeeeeeeeeeeeeeeeeeee eeeeeeeeeeeeeeeeeeeeeeeeeeee,*" done earlier on the ramp as they drove for home.

Doireann was very tired on the journey home.

It was much later, when they learned, that her coughing, had woken the whole house up at five o'clock that morning. Daddy had to go into her at six o'clock. Granny and Granda would have kept her at home had they have known this.

She started to doze in her car seat, which was directly behind the driver's seat. Then suddenly and out of nowhere she shouted, "Granda has big ears!"

Granda laughed and, without turning around, offered his hand to her for a high five. Safe in the knowledge that Granda's big ears posed no threat, she then fell fast asleep. Granda drove past the house and on towards Enniscorthy and back to let her get a good long sleep. She was soon joined by Granny.

When they got back to the house at about 1 p.m., Granda stayed in the car with Sleeping Beauty, while Granny went inside to prepare the lunch.

Fifteen minutes later, she woke. "Where's Granny?" she asked in a state of panic and looking confused after her very deep sleep.

It was as if Granny had just vanished or had been gobbled up by "Big Ears" perhaps! Granda brought "the little morning grouch" into the house for her lunch. She didn't have any lunch with her today, so Granny gave her porridge with fruit as requested. This was followed with slices of toast and butter.

Mammy, Oisín, and his friend called to collect Doireann. She asked Granda to mind her balloon again. Granda was surprised when Mammy said that Oisín, whose football team was top of the league, had a match the following day.

"On St. Patrick's Day?" said a very surprised Granda.

They discussed the forecasted sub-zero temperatures and a forecasted "mini beast from the east" storm for the weekend before Mammy et al. left for home.

CHAPTER 8

Dr Jekyll and Mr Hyde

21 March

Doireann observed Granny and Granda arriving home in their car as Daddy spoke with a neighbour on the road. She gave them big waves, while holding a packet of crisps and two walnut whirls. When Granny suggested she should not eat them now, she got upset and started crying. Granny gave her some Marietta biscuits, while offering to chop up the walnut whirls for her later. She looked for her musical book, *Dora*, and Granny sang the songs for her. Then she watched the children's TV channel in the dining room. Granda went to the sitting room for half an hour's power nap.

That morning, Granny and Granda took her to Camolin Playground, where she had lots of fun on the slides, the see-saw, and the swings and in the tree house. She played with Teddy White on the slides also. Then other mammies came into the playground with their children. Doireann just stood watching but would not engage with any of them.

After an hour, they drove home. Granny gave her another biscuit as promised to coax her out of the playground. She then had a triangle segment of cheese. There was a major meltdown when Granny tried to change her very wet nappy. Granny talked with her to calm her down and agreed to let her change her own nappy, after Doireann said that Mammy and Daddy let her do it. Granda asked her if she was all right then, and while nodding, she gave Granda a hug and cuddled into him.

"I'm hungry," she said, after asking to watch the telly.

"What do you want for lunch?" Granda asked her.

"Sausages."

She didn't eat all her lunch. When Granny took her into the cot for a much-needed sleep, there was another meltdown. She resolutely resisted, refusing to sleep, and Granny had to take her back to the dining room.

When Granda came and sat beside her as she watched the telly, all he got was a groan. Noticing how pale she looked, Granny said, "I think it's her ear, because she keeps rubbing it."

Mammy was then updated when she telephoned Granny during the day.

Doireann searched for her small ball, and Granny found it under the dining room sofa. They all played with it for a while, and then Doireann fetched the balloon, and they played with that.

Then she was over at the kitchen drawers. "What are you looking for, Doireann?" Granda wanted to know.

"The colour pencils."

When Granda found colour pencils in the toy storage basket under the dining room TV, she insisted, with a slight whiny voice, "They are in the drawer."

On closer inspection, she was proven right. Granda found the red and green pencils in the drawer. She made a few squiggles on a Jotter, and then Granda wrote her name as she watched before she squiggled over this also. Mammy phoned to say Daddy would be collecting her. Granny hurried her along to get ready and tried to get her to put her socks, leggings, and shoes on. All Doireann would say was, "No, no, no."

"Is *no* the only word you know?" Granny asked her.

"No."

"Is it yes?" continued Granny.

"No."

22 March

Granny and Granda were doing the weekly shopping in Tesco's and bumped into Doireann, Oisín, and Mammy. A delighted Doireann pointed and said loudly, "There's Granny," and darted to give her a big hug.

Oisín wanted to see Granda, who was reading his newspaper in the car. Granda spotted him sneaking up from behind his parked car and was ready to defend the big, "*Boo,*" using his own big "*Boo.*"

It was lashing rain, and Granda got Oisín to sit inside the car. They talked footie and about his training being called off due to the heavy rain. Now lying second in the league, with matches in hand, they would be league champions if they won three out of their five remaining games.

Mammy arrived out at the car to get Oisín, but more importantly, it was because, "I want to see Granda, also," complained Doireann.

"Hiya, Da," Mammy said.

"Well, hello."

"Oh, and hello, Doireann, and hello, Teddy Pink," he said.

He then gave Doireann a high five as he said bye-bye to the three of them.

Daddy was working in Galway.

23 March

Doireann got out of Mammy's car wearing her new sunglasses and waved to some of Granny and Granda's neighbours when they drove past. She then saw Granny and Granda driving in and waved at them also. And when they got out of their car, she showed them that she had brought Teddy Pink today.

"Where's the sun?" she asked, her arms outstretched.

Now in the house, she went for Baby Bop, Snowy, and the teddies first, before fetching *Dora* to play the music. "Granny, press one of the buttons," she instructed, referring to the book. And when the music started, she became animated, pretending to sing the song.

Mammy said she'd woken up at five o'clock that morning but hadn't been taken out of her cot until 7 a.m.

"Bye, Mammy," Doireann said at the open hall door, while moving Teddy Pink's arms from side to side.

Although she had Cheerios for her breakfast at home, she now had a big bowl of Granny's porridge with fruit and then some toast.

"Can I bring Teddy Pink to the playground?" she asked.

"We are visiting Oisín's school today to support their Daffodil Day fundraising events," Granny told her. "And on the way home afterwards, we will bring you and Teddy to the playground," continued Granny.

She and Teddy Pink sat down to watch some telly until they were ready to go. Granny and Granda put their best clothes on for the occasion and not to let Oisín down. They parked the car in Camolin Celtic's car park, just up from the playground. Doireann walked on the wall, holding Granda's hand, for the rest of the way.

It was now the school break time, and Oisín was playing football with his schoolmates in the grounds. There were other people in the school class rooms, doing face-painting and (fake) tattooing. There were small items for sale, including toy chicks. There were raffle tickets on sale. There were many prizes also.

Granda beckoned one of Oisín's classmates over to paint Doireann's face.

"I don't want it," she said in a sulky voice and just wanted Oisín.

They went outside just as the school bell was ringing and saw all the school children, including Oisín, standing in their lines, preparing to return to their classrooms. Oisín had come over to them briefly, and Doireann, still sulking and now moaning as well, wanted to be with him. Granny and Granda went back into the school ahead of the school children.

Oisín joined up with them again and organised getting a fake tattoo on Doireann's arm. She didn't want it, and another meltdown followed. She didn't know what she wanted and was screaming and crying. They took her outside because of the racket she was making, and Oisín followed behind. He wanted to go home with them, but they told him he had to stay until school finished.

Doireann was uncontrollable by now, and it got worse as they neared the school gates. Granda lifted her up to carry her, and she continued to scream and cry. Passers-by seemed to give sympathetic nods as they went past, and Granda wasn't sure if it was for Doireann or for him! Just as they approached the turnstiles that brought you out onto the main footpath, she was still crying for her brother and started to cough. As they got close to the car, her cough got worse, and next thing, up came every ounce of horrible green mucus phlegm—onto and all over poor Granda's clothes.

The mucus ran from shoulder high all the way down his good Marks and Spencer coat and onto his good corduroy trousers and down to his socks. Granda was literally destroyed and fuming and had to remove his coat on this cold day, for fear of upsetting all the other passing sympathisers' stomachs.

Granny took her to the playground, as promised, while Granda went home to change his clothes. When he returned to the playground, Doireann was having such great fun. Dr Jekyll and Mr Hyde then came to Granda's mind!

Later, when back home, Granny gave her two Marietta biscuits. Because Granny would not give her a third one, she said, "I want to go home," in a whingy voice, while seated on her toy car.

"You won't be allowed to drive that car on the road; you'll have to wait till Mammy comes," Granda told her.

Her head dropped, and her sulky moany mutterings continued.

Granny switched on the telly, and this seemed to satisfy her. Granny got Granda's mucus-ridden clothes ready to scour. Doireann sat on Granda's chair at the table and watched videos of herself and Granny and Granda on the iPad. Then Granny gave her some notepaper to do some "works of art" with Granny's biro. Then she was moved to her own chair and given noodles for lunch.

After lunch, she was released from her chair, where she let on to be a dog and started panting with her tongue hanging out.

"What's your name?" asked Granda.

"Kelly."

Kelly then watched some telly again and looked for her high chair to climb into all by herself. Once she was in the chair, Granda locked her straps, much to her disdain.

"I don't want this," she said as she grabbed the closed straps.

After a while, with her arms outstretched and looking at the closed straps, she proclaimed in a moany voice, "I won't be able to go home now." Then she told Granny she wanted to go for a sleep. She went into Granda, and with hands outstretched, she told him that Mammy usually put her into the sheet (the sleeping bag). Granny said she would make up one for her.

Doireann changed her own nappy with Granny in attendance. "Did you change that nappy all by yourself, Doireann?" asked Granda.

"I did," she replied, rather proudly. She then took off towards the dining room, saying, "Come on, Granny."

As she passed by Granda, he again asked, "I thought you were going for a sleep?"

"No. I'm not," he was bluntly told.

"Why are you not going for a sleep?" continued Granda.

"Because I am not tired."

Her nose had to be cleaned a lot today, and she looked pale again. She watched the telly with Granny and then with Granda and then by herself, standing closer to the telly to leave Granda on his own.

Mammy called and a delighted Doireann ran to greet her. She got the balloon and wanted Granda to play with her, while Mammy and Granny chatted. Mammy got ready to leave. Doireann said, "Goodbye, Granda. I am going now," as she shook his hand.

"Where are you going?" he asked.

"I am going home."

"What is Granny and Granda going to do? Are you going to leave me with Granny, all on my own?" joked Granda.

She came close to Granda, and said, "I will call you tomorrow."

She asked for help with putting her jacket on, and Granny obliged. Then she put her shoes on by herself and collected Teddy Pink and her balloon. Granda had said she could take the balloon home to her house.

24 March

Mammy phoned Granny to say her car wouldn't start. She needed to drive Oisín to his football match in Camolin. They had been to Arklow's bird sanctuary this morning. Later, Oisín told Granda they had fed two swans in the pond. Doireann wanted to pet them, but Mammy said no, you can't. Daddy was still in Galway.

Granda drove to Gorey to bring Oisín to his football, and as he drove into Sean Lios estate, Gorey, where they lived, Oisín ran into the house to pick up his gear bag as Mammy and Doireann looked on. Oisín was into Granda's car in a flash, and Doireann just stood there with her soother in her mouth, looking like Maggie Simpson. Looking rather confused, as events were happening at lightning speed, she said, "That's Granda's car."

"It is Granda," Mammy said.

Granda then opened the car window and waved at her, and she waved back, still looking confused at what was unfolding in front of her little eyes. She would never have experienced this before. Mammy told Granda she really appreciated this. Granda asked her about the car, and she said that Daddy would be home later on that evening and would sort it.

As Granda drove to Camolin, Oisín said on more than one occasion, "Thanks for this, Granda."

"Sure. I wouldn't want to see you miss your football."

To this, Oisín replied, "I haven't played a match in three weeks."

"Has Doireann still got a runny nose from her cold?" asked Granda.

With a big grin on his face, Oisín said, "I hear Doireann snotted all over you yesterday, Granda." And he laughed profusely.

"Oh, it was more than just snot. It was green and clear phlegm on my overcoat and all the way down and onto my corduroys as well," Granda said grumpily.

"Oooooooh." Oisín squirmed, while laughing even more at the thoughts of it. He told Granda about his friend, who brought artificial slime into school one day, and he let Oisín hold it. Oisín threw it, and it went down the inside of his friend's shirt, and from the sound of the moans and groans, he definitely didn't like it.

His friend's Mammy would collect Oisín after the match.

It was about fifteen minutes into the match as they arrived at the grounds, and Oisín just grabbed his gear bag and WAS out of the car as quick as you could say presto, while thanking Granda.

"You better score a goal for me now," Granda shouted after him.

Mammy texted to thank Granda again and to say they won the game 3–0. He didn't have a great game but had great fun with his pal afterwards.

28 March

Granny and Granda left their house to collect Doireann in Gorey as agreed for their day out in Bray. As Granda filled up his car with fuel at Cartons Daybreak forecourt on his way out of Camolin, Mammy phoned

Granny to say she would be leaving for Camolin soon. She had a hair appointment in Kilkenny, so they rearranged the collection point, making it more convenient. As they met up, Doireann hopped out of Mammy's car, holding up Teddy Pink for all to see.

Granda started guiding her towards his car, when she got upset, saying, "Mammy is getting a CD for me."

They waited until Mammy produced the CD and said, "Doireann likes song number three on the CD."

Granda strapped her into the car seat. She gave Mammy a big hug after she left a bag of overnight items that included pyjamas, overcoat, and a duffel bag. "Bye-bye, Mammy," she said loudly as Mammy returned to her car.

Mammy and Daddy were attending a wedding in County Kilkenny and would be staying in a hotel overnight. Granda played her favourite song on their way to Bray.

"Again, Granda; again, Granda; again, Granda," she demanded, each time the song ended and would get very impatient if Granda was too slow.

"Doireann, Granda has to keep his eye on the road while driving," Granny told her firmly.

Eventually she wanted another song played but didn't like it. So, Jimmy Cricket's Christmas "Wellies" song was requested over and over and over and over, until she got fed up with that one. Granda had to fast-forward to another one of her favourites.

"I had banana for breakfast," she told Granny.

A concerned Granny phoned Mammy.

"She had rashers, egg, and toast for her breakfast and then had a banana in the car on the way out," Granny was informed.

After about thirty minutes into their journey, Granny gave Doireann a packet of Tayto Snax. When she had eaten about 75 per cent of them, she said, "I'll keep them for later." She would not let Granny mind them.

Some five minutes later, she scoffed the lot.

As Granda drove through Bray town, she said loudly, "There's a zebra." And sure-enough there were lots of posters on lots of poles depicting a zebra.

Rather than pay the €3 per day parking fee along Bray Promenade, Granda parked his car on Newcourt Road off Putland Road, just up from the promenade, where there were no parking meters. They took the buggy out of the car boot and eventually managed to convince Doireann and Teddy Pink to sit in it. They walked towards the playground.

Doireann had great fun, climbing up to a platform that allowed her access a slide and go down again and again, lots of times. She played on almost all of the playground equipment before they left for a little walk before lunchtime.

Granny gave her a surprise—a little chocolate rabbit.

"What's in it?" she asked Granda, when, after eating the rabbit's chocolate head, she shook it. She couldn't see into it.

Granda turned it upside down, and one of the Smarties inside got stuck in the neck.

"Eat more chocolate, Doireann," said Granda and this allowed him to release all the different-coloured Smarties onto a paper tissue.

"Wow," she said, as she ate them one by one.

She and Granny waited at the promenade while Granda went to get his car. When Granda arrived back, he was fuming.

"What's wrong?" asked Granny.

"I just got a parking ticket for €40, and I cannot understand why," complained Granda. "I couldn't see any 'no parking' signs. And some locals, even a young Garda on a bicycle could not understand it either," continued Granda.

It was a bit of a setback, but Granny and Granda didn't want to spoil Doireann's day. "I will have to enquire about it, later," Granda said.

They drove up to the free parking area just below Bray Head that overlooks the Irish Sea and the promenade to have their lunch. They took Doireann out of the car seat and let her sit on the back seat with Granny. When they finished their sandwiches that Granny had made, they went for a small walk, taking the shoulder bag containing Doireann's drink and a flask, tea bags, milk, and cups. They sat at a picnic table. While she had her milkshake, Granny and Granda had a cup of tea. They watched all the dogs pass with their respective owners. There were loads of them, all of different shapes and sizes—the dogs that is! Granda held Doireann up as she glanced over the bridge railing to see the oncoming DART train below. She got all excited as it exited the tunnel below, heading for Greystones.

She started to moan as they continued a walk on the pathway, around a small bend covered in on either side. Then it was as if the whole area just lit up. Right in front of them was a fantastic panoramic view of the Irish Sea, the promenade, Dalkey Island, Howth, and a shoreline full of hills and houses, stretching as far as the eye could see.

"Wow, what is this place?" Doireann said loudly, and a passing young couple thought this was very funny—hearing this little madam talking like an American visitor.

Then, very excited again, she grabbed Granda's hand to walk down some steps to a perimeter wall and examine the view more closely. Granda pointed to all the amusements, shops, hotels, and big houses along the Bray promenade below. "There's Dalkey and the island, where your Mammy grew up and where Granda was born," he told her.

On hearing a rattling noise, Granda turned to see a large thin metal pole vibrating from the strong breeze coming in off the sea. Doireann was curious. He got her to hold onto the pole, while looking skywards, to feel and see it vibrate at the same time. "It's trembling with the cold," joked Granda.

Granny and Granda eventually coaxed her back to the car as she whinged and protested because she didn't want to leave. She had great fun running freely, while giggling, on the wide-open grassy surrounds and around a big tree while being chased by Granda.

Back in the car, Granda played the number three song over and over while she slept like a little baby for the whole journey. Granny stayed with Sleeping Beauty in the driveway as Granda crept into the house for a well-earned cuppa.

Granny texted Granda when she awakened from her ninety-minute snooze, to help bring the "baggage" and Doireann into the house.

Then she spotted Mammy's car parked outside and said, "I want Mammy."

And Granda had to explain to her that Mammy would be here to collect her and her car in the morning. She accepted this and played with some toys before watching the telly. She ate all of her dinner (shepherd's pie), and Granny gave her a surprise. It was another little chocolate bunny with smarties inside, which created more fun and excitement.

Granny took her out to the back garden for a little while to kick football. Next, she did some pretend shopping. "Oh dear, no bread in the shop; we will have to try another one," (in the garden overgrowth down the garden), she told Granny.

They soon came in due to the cold. Her temper tantrums had now become more intense—as had been experienced when trying to leave Bray earlier. Before bedtime and to get her to relax, Granny sat and watched the movie *Hop* with her. Then it was time to change her nappy, before attempting to put her pyjamas on. She would only wear the bottoms, complaining that the top was dirty, and she refused to wear it.

"Doireann, the pyjamas top is clean. That is only a clean stain," Granny told her.

"No, I not wear it," she insisted.

Granny made do with the top she already had on her. It was now 7.45 p.m., and Granny took her into the cot.

"It's not night-night time," she argued, "'cause it's still bright. Look." She pointed at the light coming in through the blinds.

Granda had earlier and foolishly put a tablecloth over the blinds in anticipation of such a confrontation. The clocks had only gone forward at the weekend. Eventually, Granny managed to convince Little Miss Temper Tantrum to go night-night after reading her a story.

Firstly, she had to go into Granda and give him a big hug, night-night. "Have a nice dream, eh a nice Martin Luther King, Doireann," Granda said, while reminding her of the lovely day in Bray today to keep her focused on her dream.

She had a long sleep, as did Granny and Granda.

29 March

Granny got up at about 7.40 a.m. to check on Doireann, who was just awakening. About fifteen minutes later, she wanted to see Granda, who was still asleep. She woke Granda up as she ran into the bedroom, announcing, "Granda, I had a dream."

"Was it a Martin Luther King?" Granda asked her, and she just nodded.

"Teddy Pink fell, and I picked her up and gave her a kiss," she told him.

"That's great. And was Teddy Pink happy?" he asked.

She nodded, and Granda then said, "That's a lovely dream."

A little while later, she said, "I want to tell you a secret." And she whispered into Granda's ear, "My Mammy is coming this morning."

Granda said yes, nodding too.

Granny was making their porridge, and Doireann joined Granda, who was sitting up in his bed now. He showed her how to turn the radio on, increase and decrease the volume, and select the radio stations. When she managed to switch to a different radio station, she said in a loud and excited voice, "I did it. I did it."

Granda had his breakfast in bed, and she looked on in amazement, seeing this for the first time. As she followed Granny out to the kitchen, Granda asked, "Are you having porridge as well, Doireann?"

"Yes."

"With berries," Granny added, and Doireann gave a lovely, contented smile.

Later on, Teddy White visited Granda to say hello as he read his newspaper. And then Teddy, moving his right arm from side to side, said bye-bye. Then Teddy Brown visited Granda, and he too, waved bye-bye.

"Where's Teddy Pink?" enquired Granda.

"In the dining room," she said, and that was the end of the visits.

There was a very heavy frost during the night. With the central heating on, Granda snuggled in beside Doireann on the sofa to look at the Barney DVD on the telly while Granny got dressed and ready. She changed Doireann's nappy and put her shoes on, without any objections, while she watched the telly. Then she called Granda over to watch the dancing musicians on the DVD, as she did all the actions and movements. Then she went and got Baby Bop to dance with Granda. She started to laugh and giggle when Baby Bop gave her loads of hugs, cuddles, and tickles. She was disappointed they had to cancel a visit to Camolin Playground because of the hailstones.

Granda lifted her onto the bed and held her hand while she looked at the hailstones in the back garden.

"Snow," she said.

"No. They are like tiny snowballs but are called hailstones," Granda told her.

They decided to visit Gorey Library instead, and on their way to the car, heavy rain fell. Doireann was giving out because Teddy Pink got drenched, and then she refused to sit in the car seat. As Granda stood waiting to strap her into her seat, he got drenched also. Granda ordered her into her seat, or they weren't going; and she quickly obeyed.

Granda removed his dripping wet coat and drove the car, while Doireann now enjoyed her two Marietta biscuits. They parked in the Gorey Shopping Centre open car park, near to the Dunnes Stores entrance and ran from the car. Granda wanted the heavy rain to remove all the muck and dirt from his car.

As they sauntered through the main corridor, Doireann observed and commented on almost everything that came into view. They had to dash across the area in front of the courthouse to the library because the rain was now bucketing down. Doireann had a temper tantrum when Granny and Granda tried to get her to put her coat on before they ran the "gauntlet" to the library.

Entering the library doors, she had a peep in the hallway to the right, where lots of voices were coming from. It was some meeting, of no interest to her. She headed for the children's section with Granny as usual, and Granda headed over to the newspapers section. Granda had a quick visit from Doireann before she legged it back to Granny. Then Granda took over from Granny and read the *Mr Mean, Miss No Good,* and *Chloe and the Goose*" stories to her.

It was not too long before they had to run the gauntlet again—and through all the puddles this time—as they headed for the car.

"I'll fetch the car and meet you in the basement car park," Granda told Granny.

He actually met them where Noddy and Minnie had their car parked. Doireann refused to leave, and Granda had to lift her out of Noddy's car. As they walked out, she protested vigorously, while swinging her arms and angrily retorted, "I am coming!"

"You are coming, because I said you are," Granda told her.

Next thing she spurted out something that could not be understood, except for the word, *Mammy,* in a real fit of rage and temper. She was having the last word!

Back home, Granny gave her a milkshake. Then a battle ensued because she wanted more Marietta biscuits. After an emergency meeting at the UN General Assembly (sort of), an agreement was reached. Doireann would get one and only one biscuit.

Next, she was playing with her teddies and borrowed Granny's phone. Then she wanted the radio remote control to use as a phone. The three teddies, Pink, White, and Brown all had mobile phones up to their ears. Then she phoned them and said, "Hello. Doireann here," which was followed with some mumblings.

Earlier Granny had done a pigtail for her, and Granda took some photos. They didn't have a hairclip and Granny promised to buy some, to have them spare, as Doireann's lovely curly hair kept getting into her eyes.

Granny was boiling an egg for her. She was in Granny's arms when she reached out to touch the pot and burnt her fingers very, very slightly. It could have been a lot worse but for Granny's quick reaction. Granny was not happy with her, though. She screamed when Granny ran her fingers under the cold tap. Her fingers were all right; it was more the fright than anything else.

Doireann had that egg and then had another. She only ate the white of the egg and not the yellow—just like her mammy when she was little.

Later she watched the rest of the *Hop* DVD with Granny as they waited for Daddy to collect her. Mammy had gone straight home, as she was not feeling well. Granny and Granda said their goodbyes to her and Daddy.

CHAPTER 9

The Codebreaker

1 April

It was very cold (between four and six degrees) on this Easter Sunday, and Granny and Granda, were visiting Oisín, the birthday boy, who was 11 years old today. Granny said to Mammy over the phone, "We are running a bit late this morning."

"Is that because you are getting slower?" joked Mammy.

"Granda couldn't find his false teeth," Granny joked back.

"Are you serious?" Mammy asked, sounding alarmed.

When Granny started laughing (Granda doesn't have false teeth), Mammy said, "Ah April Fool's!"

Granny and Granda arrived at their house, and as soon as the hall door opened, they sang, "Happy Easter to you. Happy Easter to you. Happy Easter to Oisín. Happy Easter to you"—to great amusement and laughter.

They gave Oisín his birthday card and present, and he showed them the football boots he also got for his birthday. Noticing the similarity between the birthday cards and knowing she'd got her cards on sale, Granny joked, "Buy one for €1 or get three for €2"—to lots of laughter.

While in the kitchen having a chat, Doireann asked Granda, "Have you got my Easter egg?"

Granda laughed.

Mammy had told her that Granny and Granda were on their way to visit them, and she could not understand why she didn't get her Easter egg. They told her that, because there was nothing for the other kids visiting her house at the time, both hers and Oisín's Easter presents (Oisín's was a massive bar of Aero, and Doireann's was a chocolate bunny with Smarties) were in a bag Mammy was minding for later.

Doireann whispered to Granda, "Okay. I leave it for later."

Smart girl our Doireann, as she knew she could have bunny and the Smarties all to herself later!

Granny and Granda then left to give Aunt Val her Easter egg before going to Bray for the day. Granda had to pay the €40 parking fine he got in Bray last Wednesday. Apparently, you cannot park parallel to a solid white line in the centre of the road—only a broken white line. On that stretch of road, it begins and ends with a solid white line, interrupted by a broken white line in the middle, which Granda had just missed!

10 April

Mammy phoned Granny for a chat. Doireann didn't want to go to crèche today, saying she missed Baby Bop so badly. Then she hid under the bed, kicking and whinging. Mammy asked her to dress herself, and she did. As they headed out the door, she gave Mammy a hug saying, "Sorry, Mammy."

Last Wednesday, she didn't want the dinner Mammy had made for her and had started screaming, shouting, and giving out, storming around the house. Daddy and Oisín couldn't calm her down, and Mammy said, "Just leave her. She will calm down eventually."

Mammy told Granny, "I remember being like that also. Gary and Richard would be looking at me."

Next thing, Doireann just shoved her dinner away, and it went all over the table as she continued with her temper tantrums. When she did eventually calm down, Mammy picked her up and sat her on her lap. She ate the dinner and wanted more.

11 April

As Mammy talked to Granny on the phone to say Daddy would drop Doireann out to them early, she, overheard the conversation, ran to the phone, and said, "Hi Granny," jumping up and down excitedly.

"Baby Bop and the teddies are waiting to see you," Granny informed her.

"I'm bringing Teddy Pink to see you."

She gave Granny a big hug at the hall door as soon as she arrived, and when Granda looked for one, he was handed Teddy Pink to hug instead.

When she entered the hall, Baby Bop, Teddy White, and Teddy Brown were all waiting there to greet her, as Granny had told them that she and Teddy Pink were on their way. She got all excited and showed them Teddy Pink and gave them all lots of big hugs.

Granda showed her the Facebook photos of her new Cambodian cousin, Rosie, in her mammy's arms. There was also a lovely photo of a bunch of flowers, sent to Mammy from her school in Phnom Penh, where she teaches. Doireann sat on Granda's lap, as he read out Uncle Richard's (Rosie's daddy's) message about her new cousin, Rosie. She studied the photos while eating her favourite blueberries. Next, she wanted the Barney DVD on and sat and watched it.

Granny and Granda talked to her, as they all sat on the sofa. Granda gave her (sore?) leg a little squeeze. Earlier, Daddy had told them, she woke around 1 a.m., saying her leg was sore.

"Don't touch my leg," she snapped.

"Why?" Granny enquired.

"Because he'll break it," she moaned.

"I love your ponytail," Granda told her.

"It's a plait," he was bluntly told.

"Who made it?" he asked.

"Mammy."

She took her lunch out of the bag, and the noodles were still hot. Then, as she took out the melon slices and some other fruits, she said, "Mammy made them."

She wanted to go to the playground.

"It's too wet," Granny told her.

Begrudgingly, she agreed to go to the library instead.

Soon after, she said she wasn't well.

"What's wrong?" asked Granny.

"My neck hurts," she replied.

She hadn't had much of a breakfast either, apparently.

Granny took her into the small bedroom because she said she wanted to lie down on the bed. No sooner had Granny done that, she was out of the bedroom in a flash before Granny, with some excuse or other. Then almost immediately, she ran up and down the dining room and kitchen non-stop, saying loudly, "Granny, look at me. I am running."

Then, while waiting for Granny to get ready, she jumped up and down on Granny and Granda's bed. Telling her to be careful, Granda, aware that he had asked her the same question before, asked her again if she knew what an accident was.

This time, she pointed to her head saying, "A bump."

"What's that?" she asked, pointing her finger.

"It's a piece of fluff," Granda said.

Next thing, she was slapping the bedcovers to shift the fluff, until it vanished off the bed. She found the tiny spec of fluff again and continued with her new game, until it was, as she described, "all gone", and couldn't be found.

Granny and Granda were ready to go out to the car, but Doireann acted up, not wanting to put her shoes on. Eventually, they coaxed her to put them on, with the help of Teddy Pink. "You have the shoe on the wrong foot," Granda pointed.

"Okay," she said in a moany voice, and then louder she said, "I can put them on."

Then they battled to get her to put her coat on, while encouraging her to take just one teddy to the library. Another emergency meeting at the UN General Assembly was called (sort of), which resulted in the following truce: Baby Bop and Teddy Brown agreed to stay behind and mind the house, with Teddy White minding the car. Only Teddy Pink would accompany Doireann to the library, with Granny and Granda following close behind.

In the car, Granda played "Pretty Woman" for her over and over and over as usual. Then, when fed up with that, she wanted the other song. "Downtown" by Petula Clarke, was then played over and over, until they arrived at Gorey Shopping Centre. As they drove down the ramp to the basement car park, they all screamed the usual, "*Wheeeeeeeeeeeeeeeeeeeeeeee eeeeeeeeeeeeeeeeeeeeeeeeeeeeeeeeee.*"

Granda explained the markings for the different parking bays to her. Theirs was for parents. Pointing to the smaller image, she said, "Doireann," referring to herself. Then Granda explained the image for wheelchair users.

"I don't hate you anymore," she said to Granny.

"I didn't know I had been hated at all," a rather surprised Granny responded, to which she and Granda had a right good laugh.

They paid a quick visit to Noddy and Minnie before getting the elevator to the first floor. They paid another quick visit to the kiddie ride emergency car on the first floor. Then she bluntly refused to wear her coat as they headed towards the exit doors. She would only wear her coat like a cape, putting the hood on her head and leaving the rest of the coat flailing.

No sooner was she on the small wall, she wanted to put her coat on because she was cold. The strong breeze didn't help either.

Next, using her magic powers once again, she opened both the outer and inner library doors with her arms outstretched. Observing the activities just inside the doors first, she then ran in through the library door and ran to the kiddies' section. As Granda read the newspapers, she approached, looking for her soother, which was in his coat pocket. She then happily darted back to Granny with soother in her mouth. When Granny went to change her library book, Granda sat down beside her to read some books she had selected before he was barricaded in. Granda was completely surrounded by the round portable plastic pouffe-type seating before being rescued, when she prised an opening.

She moved one of the seats out of the way and beckoned Granda. "Quick, Granda, out here, come on, out here."

Granda felt liberated, just like Nelson Mandela before him.

She pretended to yawn, and copying Granda, she even covered her mouth with one hand.

Armed with a new book, Granny was ready to "hit the road".

"Noooooooooooooo, I am not going," moaned Doireann.

Granda started walking towards the door, telling her, "Teddy White is waiting in the car. Now come on and take Teddy Pink with you."

She did and they took the lift to the ground floor, and then they walked down the travelator and out to the car, where Teddy White was sitting and waiting patiently.

As they listened to "Downtown" again while driving to Camolin Village, Granny received a phone call from Mammy, who wanted them to pick up some books for Doireann in the library. Granny told her she was too late, as they were now near to home.

"Have you got the little gadget thing—you know, the thing we took with us?" Granny asked Granda. She didn't want to mention the word *soother*. You have to get used to deciphering coded messages like this, especially in emergencies. The emergency here was they only had one soother, and now they didn't know where it was. Mentioning the word *soother* would mean Doireann would want it. And when she wanted it, she had to have it. And if you didn't have it, it was time to hit the mattresses.

Now, grinning and holding the soother aloft, a voice from nowhere proclaimed, "I have it." It was Doireann, the codebreaker! There were plenty of laughs all around.

Back in the house, they had more battles with the codebreaker. Granny, after trying to change her nappy, ended up saying, "You can do it then."

It was lunchtime, and Doireann said, "I don't want noodles."

Granny told her, because she was good in Gorey today, she was given a Marietta biscuit.

"I want more," she insisted.

"You will get one more biscuit after you eat your noodles," Granny told her.

Doireann stuck her heels in initially but conceded in the end. Granny wasn't losing this battle. She ate all of her noodles but without the bib.

It was a continual battle all the time. She didn't want to sit in her chair, and now she didn't want to wear her bib. At one stage, when she stood up on the chair, Granda said, "Sit down, because it's dangerous."

She continued to stand and stare at Granda.

He stood up, and she knew he was angry because immediately she sat down but still wanted to protest and said, "Oh, Granda, I don't want [you] anymore," with each and every word emphasised and uttered in a very, very angry tone.

Later, as she sat on the sofa with Granny watching a DVD, Granda ran past, and she gave him a big smile. Then she stood up on the sofa, and Granda told her to get down, and she did.

Granny took her out to the back garden, and they headed down the garden. She had her (broken) mobile phone up to her ear, taking a pretend call, saying, "I am with Granny," and mumbling the conversation as she walked.

When Mammy and Oisín called to collect her, Mammy went back outside, because she forgot something.

"Right, I am going now," said Doireann as she passed by Granda, who jokingly said back, "I thought you were staying here for good."

With arms outstretched, she responded angrily, saying, "I am going to my mammy. I want Mammy."

"Will you go with her and hold onto her hand, because she is acting up a lot today?" Granny asked Oisín.

They had only exited the hall door when Mammy appeared back and asked her to go back inside. Doireann obviously had other plans and started to roar, kick, and scream in protest. Mammy had to pick her up and carry her into the house, where she started a "sit-down protest". She continued with her sit-down protest on the floor, as well as crying.

Before they left for home, Mammy told how, the other day, Doireann had called her Ma (Dublin for Mammy])

13 April

Doireann and Daddy were having a little stroll when Granny and Granda arrived home and parked their car. Doireann had seen them waving, and she started running after them, saying, "Daddy come on."

She showed them Teddy Pink, who had been waiting also in Daddy's car for them to arrive.

Daddy gave her her pink shoulder bag.

"My smoothie," she reminded Daddy, who then fetched it from his car.

She then showed them the lovely free-flowing black dress she was wearing for today as they headed indoors.

As she gave Daddy a hug, Granda asked, "Are you going with Daddy?"

"No; with yous," she replied, and off into the house they went.

She immediately went for Baby Bop, who was in the cot. She had to wake her up first. Granda brought Teddy White and Teddy Brown into the dining room for her.

"Snowy, Granda," she said, her shoulders shrugged.

Granda brought Snowy into the dining room as well, after finding him hiding on one of the bunk beds in the bedroom.

Granny gave her a kiss, and she moaned, saying, "You hurt my lips."

Granny thought her lips were red. Granda gave Granny a kiss, and she gave them a big smile. Then she went and got Baby Bop and gave her a big kiss on the lips.

"Can I have porridge?" she asked, as she sat in her high chair watching the DVD *Alvin and the Chipmunks*. "Can we go to the playground?"

Granny said, "Yes, when we have finished our breakfast."

"What happened to your lips that they are sore?" Granda asked.

She climbed up onto the red chair and stood looking into the dining room mirror.

"What are you doing? That's dangerous," said Granda.

"I have to do it to see my lips," she said, while continuing to look into the mirror.

Then later, she said, "Granny, Teddy [Pink] would like a biscuit."

With hands outstretched, Granny said, "All gone."

"Maybe next week," Doireann suggested.

"Where are you going, Doireann?" Granny asked.

"I want to see Granny, no Granda."

He was working on his computer, and she gave him a little hug and then went off. Granda then went in and sat beside her as she watched Barney. Granny started to sing along. "You are not to sing. Leave Barney to sing it," Granny was politely told.

Granny had given her three hairclips. As she watched Barney, she had them between her lips. "They are for your hair, not your mouth, so take them out," Granda told her.

Granda got the "stares" from her, and about two minutes later, she said, "Don't talk to me like that."

Next, she removed the folded pillowcases lying on a chair beside the washing machine in the kitchen and threw them onto the floor. "You can't do that, so pick them up," Granny told her.

"They must be on the floor," Doireann insisted. She would not remove them and ran out of the room. Granny had to pick them up.

Eventually, she turned the telly off herself and was ready for the playground and went looking for Granda. She did not have a coat with her today, so they put a track end top on her instead. Granda asked Granny if she had the s-o-o-t-h-e-r, spelling the word rather than naming it, making it difficult for the codebreaker.

"I have the baby one," the voice in the background said.

"What are we talking about?" Granny asked her.

"The soother," she said with a big grin.

On the way out, she cleared away the many small stones, right down to the last one, while Granny and Granda stood patiently until she had finished. She got into the car seat and, after closing the seat belt herself, moaned, "It's too tight."

Granda loosened it for her before driving to the playground up the road.

She had great fun, as she had the whole playground to herself. She managed to climb into the tree house all by herself, while bellowing, "I did it; I did it," before sliding down the slide. "I did it; I did it," she bellowed yet again and again down the slide. Then over to the bigger slide, and down she came. Then she got her (small) football and ran around kicking it loads of times.

"We have a Lionel Missy," Granda announced.

She sat on the see-saw, and Granny sat on the other end.

"Get off; you are not to use the see-saw. Get off," Lionel Missy ordered.

"I'm tired. I want to go home," she complained after about an hour.

"Okay," said Granny.

And then she ran around on the grass, just outside the playground pen.

After a while, Granda said, "We are going home now, Doireann. Come on. We are going to the car."

"No, I want to go into the playground," she whinged.

"Okay. Two more goes on the slide, and that's it," Granny said firmly.

She continued to run around on the grass.

"Okay, let's go," said Granda.

"I don't want to," she whinged and walked towards the playground gates. "Keep walking towards the car," Granda told Granny. She then thought about following them but stopped and continued to whinge and protest.

"Don't look behind. Just keep walking and get into the car," Granda said.

She sat on the pathway outside the playground while they sat into the car. The distance between them was about a ten-seconds walk. Next thing, she ran towards them, visibly upset. Granda ran to meet her, gave her a huge hug, and said, "We were only sitting in the car until you came, pet."

She quietened down as soon as she got into the car.

Back in the house, Granda had a cup of tea, while Doireann had a smoothie. Granny gave out to her when she deliberately spilled some of the smoothie onto the floor.

"Here, put the carton and straw into the bin, please," Granda said to her after she finished her drink.

Then, she went searching for the music book, *Dora*. But shock and horror, it couldn't be found.

"Maybe you took it home with you, the other day," Granny suggested.

"No, I didn't Granny," she insisted.

"*Dora. Dora. Dora!*" shouted Granda. "Did you knock on the *door-a*, Doireann?" continued Granda as he drank his tea.

Granda was ignored, and when Granny found the book, it was happy days. Granny sang the songs alongside Doireann and Dora. Granny wanted to change her nappy, but she said no. She started messing with the hall door handle until she was told to leave it alone.

"Mammy's coming," was her moany reason for being at the handle.

"She is coming but not yet," Granda told her, adding, "Granny can change your nappy because I don't think you can."

She then took the nappy from Granny, saying, "I will do it," and she did.

She had some pasta, beetroot, and toast for lunch and washed it all down with an orange juice, spilling some on her dress. She wouldn't eat the sausages or trees (broccoli), swinging them around instead.

"You will fall from that tree," joked Granda.

"I don't like it," was her reply, even though she had eaten it on many previous occasions.

Granda was sitting at the table eating his lunch.

"Granda, you have a big mouth," she said. Then she stood up on her chair and put one foot on the table.

"Sit down, that's dangerous," Granda growled.

Standing and looking straight at Granda, "No," was her defiant response.

When Granda put her sitting down, she got up on her knees. Granda told Granny as he sat down in the dining room. She got down off her chair and followed Granda, saying, "I don't like you, Granda, when you give out."

Granny and Granda showed her photos and videos on Granny's iPad. She loved looking at them, especially the ones taken in Cambodia.

Later, as Granny played with her, she stopped, to move her hair away from her eyes. Then she immediately pulled the hair back over her eyes in a playful manner. Granny pulled more of her hair over her eyes. Doireann removed the hair then. They did this a few more times. She did everything opposite to what Granny did.

Next, Granda played football with her. He passed the ball to her, and then he would throw it and she had to catch it or try to.

Later, she went to Granny, signalling with her hands, as she said, "Bathroom, we need more," and Granny knew it was toilet rolls.

"How many do we need?" asked Granny.

She tried to answer by signalling with her fingers.

Granny asked, "Three? No. Two?"

"Yes," she said.

Granny got two toilet rolls for her to place them in the small storage cabinet beside the toilet.

16 April

Granny and Granda had just finished their workouts in the gym and were getting changed for a swim, when Mammy phoned Granny, saying, "My car won't start. Could you collect Doireann at the house instead and drive Oisín to school on your way home, at the same time? Daddy went to Galway last night."

They abandoned their swim and immediately drove to Gorey. Mammy was playing with Doireann and Oisín in the front garden as they arrived.

Mammy had to walk hurriedly to work. Oisín was a minute early for school! Mammy later told Granny about the new car battery costing €130.

Granda admired Doireann's lovely new red shoes. When they arrived in Camolin, one of the neighbours also admired her lovely shoes, as did Teddy Pink. She was so delighted, with a big smile on her face, that she skipped, hopped, and jumped up the pathway to the hall door. She immediately went looking for Baby Bop and the teddies and brought them out to meet Teddy Pink, who was sitting on the black sofa in the dining room at this stage, resting.

After his breakfast, Granda had to rush off for a ten o'clock appointment with his doctor in Gorey.

"Where are you going, Granda?" she asked as he prepared to leave.

"I have an appointment with my doctor, and I won't be too long," Granda told her.

"What's wrong?" she asked, looking a little concerned.

"Ah, it's just my annual pass-fit test, pet."

"But, what's wrong?" she kept asking.

Granda thought he should have just said he had to go to Gorey for a message. "Doireann, when I get back, we will take you to the playground, okay," Granda said, and she nodded.

Later on, as soon as she heard the hall door opening, she darted from the dining room with Granny behind her asking, "What is it, Doireann?"

"Are you fixed now, Granda?" she asked.

He just nodded and laughed.

While Granda was away, she played with the miniature cars, done some drawings, and then got Granny to wrap up Teddy Pink and put her down asleep. Granny told Granda that she then got bored and wanted to go outside.

"No, not until Granda arrives back," Granny had insisted.

She whinged and moaned, went into the small bedroom, and lay down on the bed for a while. Granny said she had to change her nappy also.

Soon, they were in the playground as promised, and Doireann was up and down the slides, climbing up into the tree house and then on the swings, playing hide-and-seek with Granny, and literally running all over the place, while Granda prepared his car for an NCT car test in Enniscorthy the next day.

It was a lovely sunny day but windy. Doireann darted up from the playground and asked, "What are you doing, Granda?" as he removed the hubcaps from the wheels as part of the preparations.

Granda explained what he was doing and why before she, none the wiser, darted back to Granny for more fun in the playground.

When Granda arrived in the playground, after finishing what he was doing, he heard her shouting, "Look, Granda," as she bombed down the big slide.

She fetched a Camolin Celtic football left on the grass patch outside the playground because it was burst. Lionel Missy then did her dribbling skills all over the playground. Next, she laughed and giggled at Granny as she chased her around the equipment, without being caught.

Now near to lunchtime, they got ready to leave for home, when a very tired-looking Doireann, said, "I want to stay."

"I'll race you to the car, and I bet I'll beat you," said Granny.

She took off out the gate as fast as she could run, making it to the car first, and loudly proclaimed, "I won."

During the three-minute drive home, she nearly fell asleep.

She sat in her high chair having her lunch, while watching the DVD *Alvin and the Chipmunks* on the telly. Granny went outside to hoover Granda's car, while he sat at the kitchen table to have his salad lunch.

"What are you doing sitting at the table, Granda?" she asked.

"I am writing notes," Granda told her, and little did she know that they were these very same notes the reader is reading right now.

She ate her buttered bread with a banana and drank lots of water. When she was removing the shells from her boiled eggs, Granda asked in a surprised voice, "Did you lay them yourself, Doireann?"

"Mammy made them," Granda was politely told.

Then she ate her two boiled eggs, the white part only. Next, she was looking at Granny's retirement photo, featuring her sitting with her work colleagues and Mammy. It was on the small shelf above the dining room stove. "There's Mammy," she pointed.

"Yes," acknowledged Granda.

As she continued to look at the photo, he asked her, "Now, where's Granny?"

She turned away from the photo, looked Granda straight in the face and said, "In the loo, Granda." And she was!

Later, there was a knock on the dining room door. Granny opened it and the postwoman was there delivering a bookmark. Then there was a *knock, knock* the second time. The postwoman handed Granny a book this time. There was another *knock, knock*. "There," said the Postwoman, handing Granny her iPad now. Then the postwoman wanted them all back again.

Mammy called for Doireann and waited for Oisín, who was walking down from his school. Doireann went to Granny upset. "What's wrong, pet?" Granny asked.

"I need some popcorn," she was told.

"I'm sorry, but the popcorn is all gone," Granny said.

She had another smoothie instead, and Mammy promised her a choc-burger ice cream after her dinner.

Off they all went, with Oisín hiding a few jelly sweets that Granny had given to him, unbeknownst to Doireann. Oisín thanked Granny and Granda for bringing him to school that morning.

CHAPTER 10

Kidnapped (Sort of)

18 April

Granny and Granda parked in the driveway after their usual early morning gym. Mammy's car was parked outside but with no sign of anybody. They brought their gear bags and the bin in and opened the curtains. And then Doireann appeared outside with Daddy. She was eating some creamy, crunchy biscuits a neighbour had just given her.

Granda was offered some but declined, saying, "Thanks anyway, pet, but I am going to have my breakfast now."

To this she replied, "You're welcome."

She was wearing her lovely red shoes, red pants, and purple dress.

"Aren't you lovely—the most gorgeous girl in Ireland," Granda said.

"No. Granny is," she said.

She went and got Baby Bop and the teddies out of the cot, where they had slept overnight. "Can I watch *Alvin and the Chipmunks*?" she asked as she sat into her chair.

Then she asked for milk, and Granda poured some into her special cup. He pressed the beaker lid firmly and handed it to her.

"The lid is wrong," she complained.

Granda had to remove the lid and reposition it before it was acceptable. "Here, there you are," he said as he handed the cup back to her.

"Thank you," was the reply from Madam.

He took some photos of her watching the movie, and when it ended, Granny was requested to put it on again, for Madam's second viewing.

Handing her some toast, she had just made, Granny asked, "What did you do in crèche yesterday?"

To this, Doireann replied, "Nothing. Can we go to the playground?" she asked Granny.

"No. It's too wet. Would you like to go to the library, instead?"

"I want the playground," she demanded in her moany that's-not-fair voice.

Granny decided to play hide-and-seek with her. She ran into the main bedroom as Granda worked on the computer. "Over there," Granda said, telling her where to hide.

Granny came into the room looking, and Granda talked to her for a few minutes.

Then, Doireann jumped up from where she was hiding, saying, "I am here-earrrrr."

"Have you got a wet nappy?" Granny asked as she ran off, saying, "It's cold."

Granny attempted to change it, but she resisted. "Doireann, the library will be closed by the time we get there, and there's no point going," Granny said angrily.

"Okay then," she reluctantly agreed.

She put her own leggings on the wrong way around and refused to correct them. She ran into the kitchen and lay on the floor in protest. Then she did not want to go to the library and sat up at the table to do some drawings instead. Granny continued at trying to convince her that the library would be closed unless they went then. Doireann kept drawing and singing away to herself and not listening. Granny and Granda decided to ignore her.

After a few minutes, she got down from the chair and put her socks and shoes on. "I want to go to the library now," she said, looking in the hall for her jacket, but it wasn't there.

Granny pointed to where it was in the kitchen, and when she put it on, she proclaimed, "I did it. I did it."

She went into Granda, all dressed up and ready to go, and asked, "What are you doing?"

"I am writing a story about you," Granda told her.

She ran out to Granny saying loudly, "Granda is writing a story."

Granny said, "Tell Granda to stop writing, because we are going now."

She ran back into Granda, "You are to stop writing now."

"Okay, pet," said Granda.

On the way to Gorey, they got her to sing "Lady in Red", because she was wearing her red shoes and red leggings. She sang some of the lines, over and over.

As Granda drove down the Gorey Shopping Centre basement ramp, "*Wheeeeeeeeeeeeeeeeeeeeeeeeeeeeeeeeeeeeeeeeeeeeeeeeeeeeeeeeeeeeee*," was the clarion call from all and sundry.

Granda parked in one of the family bays. Then, Doireann magically opened the electric doors. They used the travelator that took them up to the ground floor. Doireann was going to step onto the other side of the travelator, but stopping her in her tracks, Granny and Granda explained the dangers to her. They got the lift to the first floor after she pressed the button. Next, she ran to magically open more electric doors, before running past the courthouse towards and into the library and down to the kiddie's section.

Granda read *The Irish Times* before taking over from Granny, who wanted to look for some books for herself. Doireann handed Granda a tiny book about clothes to read to her. Then he read *Little Miss Tidy*, *Mr Topsy Turvey*, and a book about two girls who lived in a doll's house. This was done once she had rearranged the cylindrical plastic seating of varying colours.

Later, they left the library, to use the lift for Dunnes Stores, as Granny needed to get some groceries. Just before this, Doireann wanted to run down the wheelchair access ramp that ran parallel to the Courthouse building. "*Wheeeeeeeeeeeeeeeeeeeeeeeeeeeeeeeeeeeeeeeeeeeeeeeeeeeeeeeeeeeeee*," she'd scream, while running down the sloped surface and then back up again.

Granny took charge, while Granda went to use the toilets on the first floor of the shopping centre. He returned to learn that Doireann had had a major meltdown. Having reached the end of the ramp, she decided to make good her escape, with Granny in hot pursuit. Granda was given the full story, on his return. "It was terrible. It was like she was being kidnapped, with all her screaming, kicking and crying—as lots of [courthouse] people looked on," said a visibly upset Granny.

They sat and waited on a seat inside the shopping centre, while Granny used the loo. As Granny shopped in Dunnes Stores, Granda remained outside in the main foyer to guard the "hostage", as she joyfully played in the various kiddie ride machines. Next, she checked out the exit chutes on the slot machines containing various types of sweets but found nothing. She helped herself to a paper bag and later deposited it in the bin, after crumpling it up.

Back in the car, she refused to get into her seat and didn't want to go home.

"We have to go home because it's nearly lunchtime," Granny reasoned with her, but she was not for moving. She just sat beside Granny in the back seat with a moany-looking face on her.

"Granda will get into trouble with the police, if he drives with you like that," Granny told her.

She wouldn't budge, so Granda said, "Okay, we will just sit in the car and do nothing."

And that was exactly what they did—nothing.

Then she attempted to climb into the front seat but had second thoughts and sat back down defiantly. Granny had bought some oatcakes in Dunnes Stores. "Would you like an oatcake?" Granny asked her.

"Yes."

"Well, you have to get into your seat."

"No."

"Well, no oatcake then," Granny insisted.

Eventually, she got into her seat, and Granda strapped her in. Then Granny gave her one oatcake and off they drove, doing a big, "*Wheeeeee eeeeeeeeeeeeeeeeeeeeeeeeeeeeeeeeeeeeeeeeeeeeeeeeeeeeeeeeeeee,*" up the ramp and home.

Granny and Doireann played tug of war in the back seat with Granda's small blue cloth on the way home. As they passed by the playground in Camolin, she said, "I want to go to the playground."

"Another day," Granny promised.

"Now," insisted, a very moany Doireann.

But Granny and Granda stuck to their guns and drove home for lunch.

When she finished her noodles and broccoli, Granny took her out to the back garden to play football. It was lovely and sunny now. By the time Granda arrived out, Doireann had been playing with all the stones surrounding the fuel tank, and now they were all over the yard.

"We can't leave them like that," Granda told her as he started to gather them together and deposit them back to where they came from, while she protested and gave out.

Next, as Granda sat on the bench. She sat with him, getting down off the bench and back up again. Then she said she wanted to sleep on the bench. Next, she was awake and got down off the bench and continued doing this over and over.

Pointing, Granda said, "Look at Granny's beautiful flowers and the different colours, Doireann. You have yellow, white, purple, red, and pink ones."

She wanted to go closer and look at them.

"The grass is wet," he told her.

But she continued with her "protest march".

"Put your hands on the grass," he said.

And realising it was wet, she immediately checked her shoes. "They are wet," she complained. She walked off the grass and removed her shoes.

"You can't walk around in your stocking feet," Granda protested.

But she insisted on taking off her wet leather shoes. Granda took them from her, dried them with some tissue paper, and handed them back so she could put them back on again. Granny came to Granda's rescue. She got the little buckets and watering cans from the shed for Doireann to play with. She sat on the cold slabs and put lots of stones into the buckets and then out again.

When Mammy came, she ran to give her a hug. Granda took a photo of Granny, Mammy, and Doireann, all sitting at the garden table.

She asked Granda, "Have you finished drinking?" and pointed to his green metal gym bottle.

Earlier, when visiting him at his computer, she tidied up a plastic bottle and this green bottle on one of the shelves near Granda's workstation and asked, "What's the green bottle?"

He unscrewed the cap and showed her the straw inside it.

"What's it called?" she continued.

"A container," Granda said as Granny took a fit of laughing.

20 April

Granny and Granda spotted Doireann walking down Norrismount with Daddy and beeped loudly as they drove towards their house. She started to run, to show them her Everest and Skye pyjamas top.

In the house, she asked for Baby Bop, and Granda brought her to the cot to take her out. He showed her how to open the bedroom door by pulling down the handle and pushing the door open. Then he was instructed to bring the teddies and Snowy out. She opened a press door in the kitchen, asking, "Anything here?"

"All gone," Granny said. Granny offered her an oat-cake.

"No. I don't like them."

"You had one the other day," Granny reminded her.

"I don't like them," she insisted. "Can I have the DVD?" she asked, referring to *Alvin and the Chipmunks*. At the beginning of this film, there is no sign of Alvin and the chipmunks.

"I don't like this," she complained.

Granny fast-forwarded the DVD until Alvin and the chipmunks appeared, and then she was contented. As she sat and watched, there were all different expressions on her face because of the different film animations. Then she stood up while watching it. Next, she said she was tired and wanted her soother. She sat up on the chair, and Granny squeezed an orange to make a juice drink for her. When she drank some, she exhaled with a deep breath of pleasure. Another juice drink followed, thanks to Granny. Then the soother was back in her mouth.

"I'm scared. I want to go home?" she said.

"There's no one at home. Anyway, what are you scared of?" Granny asked.

"Ah, nothing," was her response. "My back is sore," she complained.

Granny rubbed her back for three seconds.

"It's okay now," she said. She had her pyjamas top off and now wanted it back on. Granny offered to help. "No, I do it," she insisted. She couldn't locate the sleeve for her other arm and moaned and groaned.

"Look for it," Granda told her, and then she found it.

There were more moans when she couldn't pull the top down. Just as Granda was about to help her, she managed it.

She picked up Saturday's *Irish Times* sports section and said she was going to read the paper. Spreading it on the floor, she started talking, pretending to read out loud what was in front of her. Granda took a photo of this.

Later, Granda asked, "Can you take up the papers from the floor please, Doireann, in case Snowy slips?"

She collected up the newspapers and gave them to Granda to read, and he thanked her. They all got ready and then drove to Bolger's Hardware Store in Ferns to get a new coal shovel. Granny stayed with Doireann outside in the car park, so she could play with the plastic toy house on display. When Granda came out of the shop, he was invited over to "her" house for a cup of tea. She actually wanted Granda to enter this tiny house.

"Can I have my cuppa outside, Doireann?" Granda pleaded.

And she brought it out and put it on a wooden table, also on display.

Granny and Granda enjoyed their cups of tea before they all headed back to Camolin.

Granda's car tyres needed air. He drove to Cartons Daybreak forecourt and asked Doireann if she wanted to help, but she preferred to stay put. Then Granda dropped her and Granny off at the playground. She ran off as fast as she could to beat Granny to the playground gate. Granda drove home to begin his first grass cut of the year. It had been such a long winter that, all of a sudden, the grass was growing quickly, with everyone complaining. Granda stopped mowing the grass and tried phoning Granny but could not get her. He drove up and met the two of them, walking down from the playground.

Doireann was having a meltdown because she did not want to hold Granny's hand as they walked down through Camolin Village, with cars and trucks whizzing past. Granda pulled into a driveway and got her into the car. He tried to explain why Granny wanted her to hold her hand and the dangers out there, but he might as well have been talking to a wall. She was obviously very tired and now even more so, after her exploits in the playground.

"Doireann decided she was walking back to the house," Granny told Granda. "I wanted to phone you but couldn't manage it, as I had to watch her and try to hold onto her hand," Granny continued with her complaint.

When they got home, Doireann sat watching the movie again, with the soother in her mouth and with a grumpy look on her face. Granny changed her nappy after chasing her around the house. She then wanted to go out to the backyard without her shoes on, and Granny said no. She didn't like the noise of the mower and was frightened of it. She played with her metal buckets and watering cans, putting the stones in and then out in the lovely sunshine, with Granny in attendance, as Granda cut the grass.

Earlier, Granny told her she wanted to use the loo and to wait by the door. She wanted to go in with Granny. Leaving the door ajar, Granny told her to wait there. Next thing, she was beside Granny to inspect the toilet rolls storage cabinet and said, "Okay, we don't need anymore," and went back out.

Mammy arrived and chatted to Granny for a while before leaving for home with Doireann. Granda continued cutting the grass. Later, Mammy phoned Granny and confirmed they were moving from Gorey to Camolin, having agreed to rent a house there.

23 April

Granny and Granda were late arriving home after their gym today. Mammy, Doireann, and Teddy Pink were all waiting at the gate. Doireann showed them her lovely long flowing dress with red, yellow, sky-blue, black, and blue flowers. She wore it with a red hairband, silvery shoes, and red leggings. Oh and, of course, she was wearing her red jacket, as it was chilly this morning. Teddy Pink gave them kisses and hugs.

As soon as they got inside the house, Doireann went and got Baby Bop, Teddy White, Teddy Brown, and Snowy from the bedroom. Later, she wanted Mammy to take Teddy Pink home, saying, she was tired. Mammy and Granny suggested putting her asleep in the cot, and Granny got a blanket for Teddy.

"Can I wear your lovely dress?" joked Granny.

"No, it won't fit you," Granny was bluntly told.

Mammy laughed as Doireann modelled it. Granda took photos of her, making sure he got the front as well as the back of her lovely dress. She walked Mammy to the hall door as she left for work and gave her a big kiss and a hug, saying, "Bye-bye, Mammy." And she closed the door after her.

Earlier, Mammy had told Granny and Granda that Oisín was delighted they were moving to Camolin. She also told them that his team had won the league and they all got ice cream, minerals, and crisps for the celebrations.

"Granda, I had ice cream," Doireann said.

"Did you?" asked a surprised-looking Granda. As she nodded, Granda continued, "And did you like it?"

"Yes," she said, while continuing to nod her head. "Granda, did you get your hair cut?" she asked.

"I did."

"I cut Granda's hair," Granny told her.

"She didn't eat a whole lot this morning, and I'll take her to the doctor later," Mammy informed Granny. "Her digestive system is not great, judging by her poos, with little white lumps in it."

Granny said she would be observant today when changing nappies.

Doireann then had Granny's porridge and fruit while sitting in her high chair watching the *Hop*, a movie about a rabbit. She had to wait for her berries to thaw first though.

Later, when they decided to go to Gorey Library, Doireann had to bring Teddy Pink and her sunglasses, even though there was no sun today.

"Do you have the other thing with you?" Granda asked Granny before they left, meaning the soother.

"I'll have it" (Give it to me), said the codebreaker, her hands outstretched in the back of the car. She then (pretend) phoned her Mammy at Curves in Gorey and asked, "Where's the sun?"

"Well, where is the sun?" asked Granny.

"In Curves," she was told.

Granny continued, "You tell your mammy and daddy that you are our ray of sunshine."

Doireann had held Granny's hand as they left the house, so Granny wouldn't fall. The car was parked on the road.

Stopping at the gate, Granda asked, "What do we look and listen for, Doireann?"

"Cars and none coming," she answered.

"Well done and good girl," Granda said.

"*Wheeeeeeeeeeeeeeeeeeeeeeeeeeeeeeeeeeeeeeeeeeeeeeeeeeeeeeeeeeeee,*" was the clarion call again today as they entered that basement carpark.

They were lucky to find one empty parking bay, as the car park was packed today. They used the zebra crossing to get to the magic doors, while explaining the safety reasons why to Doireann. Granda put Teddy Pink sitting on the travelator handrail as they headed up to the ground floor. Doireann quickly grabbed Teddy Pink while still holding onto Granny's hand as they neared the top. Then she pressed the up button to call for the lift. She used all of her magical powers to open all the closed doors that confronted their speedy advance towards and into the library.

Just inside the library foyer, they admired an artwork of a well-decorated May-bush, before heading to their usual areas in the library. With Granny's permission, she ran up to Granda, only to run back again.

Doireann got shy at times. Whenever a stranger or one of her own peer groups appeared on her travels, her head would drop as she inched past; or she could just stop, dead in her tracks. On the lift earlier, a stranger had spoken to her, but she'd just stared and said nothing, as if sizing the person up. She, like her mammy at that age, would sometimes stand and stare at people, especially people from her own age group. Last week, an Asian couple were on the elevator with their little girl. She was around the same age as Doireann and wore a lovely Chinese-style red dress, full of frills. Well, Doireann just stared and stared. She said nothing but continued to stare at the little girl's dress, even when getting off the lift.

Granny read books to her, and both of them even looked at and listened to books that made loads of different animal sounds. Granny got her to name all the sounds, and Granny would then repeat the sound.

After a while, Granda sat with her while Granny searched for a book for herself. Granda read Doireann's chosen books aloud. There was a story about Spot the dog, who was ill, and another about Peppa Pig, who got a Dinosaur balloon from Grandpa Pig.

It wasn't long before she was doing the "*Wheeeeeeeeeeeeeeeeeeeeeeeeeeeeeee eeeeeeeeeeeeeeeeeeeeeeeeeeeee,*" with Granny supervising once they had exited the library.

Granda visited the loo, and when he returned, poor Granny was on her third lap with the sprinter. Next, they used the steep stairs down to the ground floor, and Granny went to Dunnes Stores, while Granda stayed outside as Doireann played in the kiddie's ride machines.

"Can I go to Granny now?" she asked.

And in they went and helped Granny pay for the bread and milk.

When they decided to use the travelator, Doireann refused to hold Granny's hand.

"Okay, we will use the lift instead," Granda said in a firm voice.

She immediately agreed to hold Granny's hand.

"Bye, Noddy," she said as they headed out through the magic doors towards Granda's car.

As they exited the car park, up the ramp, they all screamed "*Wheeeee eeeeeeeeeeeeeeeeeeeeeeeeeeeeeeeeeeeeeeeeeeeeeeeeeeeeeeeee,*" as usual.

When back home, Granny said to Granda, "I'm going in to change [clothes], so watch over her."

"Doireann, we're getting a new Granny, because she's said she's going to change," joked Granda.

No response.

"Ah sure your Granny is great, but she's not your great-granny," continued Granda. "Imagine having a great-granny and only a Granda," he pondered, sure he might as well have been talking to himself, such was the *deafening silence*.

Doireann had blueberries and toast to eat with an orange juice when they arrived home. Later on, she would only eat a bit of her lunch. Granny had a battle trying to get her into the small bedroom to change her nappy, as she kicked and screamed. Then Granny tickled her and got some laughs.

Watching *Hop* again, she smiled at Granda when he sat next to her high chair to give her some company for a little while. "Where's Baby Bop?" she asked Granda.

And when he handed Baby Bop to her, having fetched her from the cot, she gave her loads of loud hugs and kisses. Then she dropped her soother onto the floor, and looking down at it from her high chair, she groaned with a whingy-moany sound.

"Do you want your soother?" asked Granda, in a whingy-moany voice back to her.

She grinned at Granda.

After lunch, Granda went for a snooze in the sitting room, and after about thirty minutes was suddenly awakened by Doireann's loud singing in the kitchen with Granny. Before this, they had built a tent, using a blanket hanging over the kitchen table, and she then wanted poor Granny to crawl into it.

And it was poor Granny again, when she had to change her nappy for a second time, which warranted a gasping rush to speedily open a window or three this time round.

Mammy phoned Granny to say she was running late.

A little while later, Doireann got a burst of energy, when Granny, pretending to be a monster, chased her, screaming, from the dining room onto Granda's lap in the sitting room. Then she got down off Granda's lap but couldn't go any further, as he'd locked his feet tightly together, preventing her.

"I did it; I did it," she shouted after she'd wriggled free from Granda's clutches.

Granny and Granda had to repeat that exercise over and over.

"I want to take Mick for [a] walk?" she asked, looking up at him dangling from the fuse-box cabinet in the hall.

Granny handed Mick to her, and holding the string, she got Mick to hop along the floor. She was just full of energy at this moment. Granny got her to sit down, while reading her a story from the *Dora* book as the music played.

Granda was looking out the sitting room window, passing some time, when Doireann arrived in. "Can I see Mammy coming?" she asked, now wanting to stand up on the sofa to reach the window.

"No, it's too dangerous, and I'm not looking to see Mammy coming," Granda said firmly.

She had now eaten the triangular-shaped cheese she got from the fridge. "Can I have another one?" she asked.

Granny got one to open for her. She loved those spreadable cheese sections.

Next, she said, "Come in," as she invited Granny to crawl into her tent.

Then she went and got some of her books, one at a time, before sitting on a cushion to (pretend) read. "Here," she handed Granny a Winnie the Pooh book to be read to her twice as she knelt on her knees.

Knock, knock, the hall door sounded.

Doireann was up in a flash, running to the door, loudly proclaiming in an excited voice, "Mammy is here."

It was Mammy and Oisín.

"We are moving to Camolin," Oisín told Granda.

"Ah that's brill. I'm delighted for you," Granda said back.

Covering her mouth with her hands to hide what she was saying, Doireann loudly said, "We have to go now, Mammy."

"What? I thought you were staying for the rest of your life," joked Granda.

"No, I am going home," she insisted, still covering her mouth with her hands. She repeated the exercise a few more times.

As she stood at the hall door, Granda approached her, covered his mouth with his hand as she had done and loudly asked, "Where are you going?"

She moved close to Granda's ear and whispered, "I am going home."

They gathered up all of Doireann's things. Granny informed Mammy that her poo was okay and outside in the bin if she wanted to inspect it. She didn't!

Granny and Granda stood at the hall door saying, "Byeee," while Teddy Pink waved one of her arms back at them as they headed for Mammy's car.

CHAPTER 11

I Didn't Hurt Her Ears

25 April

Daddy had Doireann in his arms as Granny and Granda drove onto their road after an early morning swim and gym in Arklow. As soon as Doireann saw them, her legs starting kicking frantically to get down. She ran into the driveway, saying, "Teddy Pink is at home."

"Ah, is she tired?" Granda asked.

"Yes."

"Who made you that lovely plait in your hair?" Granny asked.

"Mama," she replied, before running into the bedroom to get Baby Bop. "*Boo,*" she shouted and started to laugh, having just frightened the life out of poor Baby Bop, who had been fast asleep. Granda then helped to take Baby Bop out of the cot and brought Teddy White, Teddy Brown, and Snowy out to the dining room as well.

"Don't let Snowy frighten me," she said, meaning she didn't want a chase.

Snowy gave her a huge kiss instead.

"Can I watch the telly?" she asked,

Granda put her sitting in her high chair. Granny gave her some toast.

"I want butter," she demanded.

"I did butter it," Granny told her.

She insisted she wanted butter. Granny complained that the butter had melted into it and promised that, in future, she would wait until she was ready to eat her toast before buttering it. Granny put more butter on her toast. Granny squeezed an orange to make a juice drink for herself, out of eyesight of Doireann, or so she thought.

"I want an orange juice," was the next order.

This was followed with a cup of milk and Weetabix. Granda took some photos of Doireann's new method of resting her feet, rather than dangling her legs, while sitting in the chair. He then took a selfie with her as she leaned her head into his, saying, "I love you, Granda."

They promised her they would take her to the playground that morning. The sun was shining, but the forecast was for showers, thunderstorms, and hailstones. Then Granny gave her a new football she had bought in Gorey the day before. There was a massive look of excitement on her face as she ran, saying, "Look, Granda."

"Wow, that is a lovely football," Granda told her.

"Come on, Granda." And she kicked the ball.

They both kicked it back and forth to each other.

"Let's bring it to the playground later," Granda suggested, and she agreed.

"What colour is the football, Doireann?" Granny asked.

"It's lellow." Doireann pronounced yellow /lellow/, just like her big brother, Oisín, had when he was little.

"What colour are the spots?" continued Granny.

"Red."

As Granny got ready, Granda said to Doireann, "It might rain when we are at the playground."

She asked, "have you got a [an] umbrella?"

"Very good idea, Doireann. I have a big umbrella in the car boot," he said.

As they waited for Granny, Doireann crawled, real fast, past Granda, stopping at the sitting room door with her fingers crawling along and saying, "The spider is coming."

Granda got noisily scared as he moved backwards with the spider in hot pursuit, until Granda could go no further and stopped. Then the spider started to talk and crawl up Granda's leg, saying, "I am going to bite you."

She and Granda took the yellow football, Teddy White, and Granny to the playground by car. Once the car was parked, Granny, Doireann, and Teddy White headed for the playground gate, while Granda reattached the sun visor to the window beside Doireann's car seat. Later, as dark clouds approached, Granda walked speedily up to the car and took the large umbrella out of the boot. There was still sunshine about, and Doireann had great fun on all the equipment, running here, running there, and playing football with Granny and then with Granda a while later.

"Granda, look at Doireann. When she is not happy about something, her arms and head drop down. Then her shoulders go up, her fists are clenched, and she walks funny," said a very observant Granny.

They decided to move, as the clouds got darker. And after about five minutes, when they were back at the house, it started raining.

Doireann sat up in her high chair, eating her strawberries that *her* mammy had prepared for her. When she was opening the fridge door to get the strawberries out, Granda's foot accidently hit the door as he passed by, causing it to slam shut. She got a big fright, and immediately Granda gave her big hugs to console her, saying, "Sorry, pet. That was an accident. Are you alright?"

Then, as she opened the fridge door again, it hit Granda's knee. "Sorry, Granda," she said, now obviously concerned.

"Thanks, pet. I'm okay; don't worry," Granda assured her.

When she finished her strawberries, she helped herself to three sections of her favourite spreadable cheese. She had her lovely pink watch with her today. "It's beautiful, Doireann, and you should take care of it," said Granda. "Make sure not to lose it, so you'd better 'watch' it," he joked.

Granny read some of the new books she got for Doireann in a charity shop in Gorey the other day. Then Doireann played postwoman, delivering letters to Granny before it was Granny's turn to be postwoman. Granda left some old envelopes at the hall door letter box, which Doireann then delivered to him. They fell onto the bedroom floor, having been pushed (thrown) through an imaginary letter box.

Granny had to chase and catch her, to change her nappy. As she did so, she asked Granny, "Do you love me?"

"Of course, I do. Do you love Granny?"

"Best of pals help each other," she told Granny.

For lunch, Doireann had a salad with beetroot for starters and then pasta with a boiled egg. When she removed her bib, she just flung it to the floor, and Granny gave out to her. Granda changed the radio stations to some music. Doireann liked it and moved to the music while in her high chair. She and Granny had planned to go out to the back garden after lunch, but the rain came, and there was disappointment all round.

Granny gave her colouring pencils and paper to do some drawings. She went to Granda to show him the pencils and the pencil box, asking, "What does it say?"

Granda read it for her "Twelve colouring pencils," emphasising the twelve again and then counted, "One, two, three, four, five, six, seven, eight, nine, ten, eleven, twelve," and finished with a "Wow! Will you draw a picture for me?" he asked her.

"No, for Mammy."

"Ah, fair enough," said Granda as she went back to Granny with a hop, skip, and a jump, while holding on to her new colouring pencils.

When she tired of drawing, she sat on the dining room sofa, and Granny read her *Winnie the Pooh and Tigger* Too, a book she got for her the day before.

Granny went to the loo when she finished reading the book. Granda sat beside Doireann.

"You read the [same] story," Granda was told.

As he read it in an animated way, she looked up at him. And when Granda looked at her, she said, "You are too loud."

Granda then started to whisper the story, and when her face showed displeasure, he read with a quieter than loud voice.

Knock, knock, the hall door sounded.

Granny went to answer the door, with no movement from Doireann, who simply asked, "Who is at the door?"

As soon as she heard Mammy's voice, she hopped up and out of the sofa, running to give Mammy a big hug. "I thought Daddy was coming," she said, followed with, "We are going home now."

"I thought you would stay for ever," joked Granda.

"I have to go home to Teddy Pink, and I will bring him with me the next day," she told Granda.

27 April

Granny and Granda were in the gym when Mammy phoned to ask if we could meet her and Doireann at Tesco's, as Daddy was dropping Oisín to school. Granny phoned Mammy as they were leaving Arklow, but Daddy had not yet returned. Doireann's car seat was in his car. Granda drove to their house instead and waited there, until Daddy arrived back. It was raining heavy, and Doireann's coats and one of her wellies were in Daddy's car also. Mammy and Daddy had to go to Dublin today, and Granny and Granda offered to mind Doireann for a little longer, until they got home (4 p.m.).

Doireann gave them a big wave from the porch as they approached the gate. Then, as Granda gave her a big hug and thanked her for the big cheerful waves, she stood, bent sideways with her head looking downwards.

Granda searched the floor area and said, "Well, look at those beautiful gorgeous new shoes. Who bought them for you?"

"Mammy," she said, looking as proud as punch.

The reason they needed the wellies also was because Doireann did not want to get her new shoes wet. Granda had to carry her to his car, followed by a shoe inspection because of the falling rain. They were okay, as Granda had protected them from the rain with his spare hand.

She had a bottle of bubbles in her hand. "Where did you get that?" Granda asked her.

"Mammy."

"Aren't you very lucky? You must be the only person in Ireland, with a great Mammy and a great Granny," joked Granda.

Daddy arrived with the car seat, one wellie, and three coats. They loaded up the car with the one wellie from Daddy and the one wellie from Mammy! Granda made sure he had Doireann's grub for the day, her shoulder bag, a coat, Teddy Pink, and Granny.

They arrived in Camolin and parked on the road outside. Before they got out of the car, Granny told Doireann to put her wellies on. As she put the second one on, she started to moan, and Granny tried to push it on for her. But no, it had to come off. When she took her soother out of the boot, they all laughed. She then put her coat on before advancing onto the small puddles for a dance and a jump or two.

In the house, she wanted her strawberries and then her smoothie. She got Teddy Pink to give Granny and Granda hugs and kisses. "How are you today, Teddy Pink? Doireann left you at home on Wednesday for a well-earned sleep because you were tired," Granda said.

Teddy Pink didn't talk, as sometimes she got very shy and would only talk to Doireann. Granda handed Teddy Pink back to Doireann, who had been observing everything. She gave Teddy a big hug and a smile. She then thanked Granny and Granda for taking care of her.

Later, when she went to take Baby Bop out of the cot, she held onto the side of the cot but couldn't reach in. Granda moved Baby Bop slightly over and nearer to the side, allowing her to reach Baby Bop's ears. After she pulled her out by the ears, they headed for the dining room.

Granda had a little smirk on his face and said, "Oh, me ears."

"*I didn't hurt her ears,*" she roared.

Now laughing at her response, Granda said, "I am only joking."

Granda brought the teddies out to the dining room to sit with Teddy Pink and Baby Bop. Snowy tried to catch Doireann, but she was rescued by Granny, who wrapped her arms around her real tight as she screamed. Next, she held tightly on to Granny again when Snowy came face to face with her.

The *Alvin and the Chipmunks* DVD continued to roll to the end during all the excitement. She watched some telly as they got ready to go out. Because it was still raining, they cancelled their planned trip to Arklow and decided to visit Gorey Library instead.

Granny wanted to use up another free €10 Dunnes Stores shopping voucher that Tesco's were accepting. So, they went there first. Granda dropped Granny and Doireann off outside the shop, where the kiddies London bus ride was parked before driving to a parking bay. When Doireann had travelled to all of her busdestinations, she parked the bus up. She then got into a Trolley-car, to drive around the shop. After their shopping, she decided to put in another shift, driving the London bus.

Granny was in attendance outside the bus depot as they waited for Granda to arrive with the car. It was still raining and icy cold. Wanting to help, Doireann offloaded the bread, like bags of coal, and dumped them into the car boot.

Next stop was the Gorey Shopping Centre basement car park, which was almost full up again. "*Wheeeeeeeeeeeeeeeeeeeeeeeeeeeeeeeeeeeeeeeeeeeeeeeee eeeeeeeee,*" they all screamed before finding a parking bay.

There was the usual visit to Noddy and Minnie before they had a walk up the travelator, with Doireann holding Granda's hand. "How do we get there?" she asked, now mindful of her surrounds, as she looked skywards towards the first floor from the ground floor.

"There," said Granny, pointing to the lift. Granda pointed to the call button with an up arrow on it. When Doireann pressed it, a surrounding red light lit up.

On entering the lift, an excitable Doireann was about to send them back down again, until Granda swiftly intervened and directed her finger towards the one button, away from the minus one button.

When they exited the lift, Granny showed Doireann the travelator below and said, "Look where we are now," so as to give her some sense of direction.

They exited the magic doors and headed for the library. It was Teddy Pink's turn to use her magic powers and open the automatic outer and inner library doors, with outstretched arms. Granda had a quick read of the newspapers before meeting up with Doireann in the kiddies' section to read her a book.

She had other ideas and pulled a musical farm animal book from under a pile of books in front of them. She then proceeded to play each and every sound for everyone in the library to hear, whether they liked it or not. The animals would have their say today!

They soon left for home, after Granny got herself a book and an Australian DVD for Doireann, called *Blinky Bill*. Teddy Pink obliged once again by magically opening the library doors.

"*Wheeeeeeeeeeeeeeeeeeeeeeeeeeeeeeeeeeeeeeeeeeeeeeeeeeeeeeeeee,*" screeched Doireann as she ran up and down the long ramp at the courthouse.

First, it was her and Granny. Next, it was Granda's turn to stand while she ran down into his arms. Granda would then chase her back up and into Granny's arms. Her reaction during the chase depended on her mood on the day. She would either protest, giggle, scream, or give everyone in the vicinity a rendition of all three as she ran.

As they headed for Granda's car, she was reluctant to leave the shopping centre

Granda said, "It's lunchtime now, Doireann, and I am going to have one of your boiled eggs, yum, yum."

"*No*," was her emphatic response.

This distracted her, and Granda continued. "Now, where would Granda's car be, eh?" he mused.

"There it is," she pointed and was delighted that *she* had found it.

She slowly got into the car and then slowly got into the seat, holding Teddy Pink. "*Wheeeeeeeeeeeeeeeeeeeeeeeeeeeeeeeeeeeeeeeeeeeeeeeeeeeeeeeeeeeeeeee*," they all screamed as they drove up the car park ramp.

As Granda drove home, Granny and Doireann, threw the small blue cloth at each other in the back and then would pull and drag on it to get it back, with lots of giggles and laughter. They had done this earlier that morning, and Doireann loved it.

When back home, Granda switched on the kitchen radio, to get the RTÉ 1, one o'clock news.

"Turn it off. I don't want it," Doireann said.

Granda ignored her and left it on.

Later, she ran to Granda as he sat working on his computer and said, "I'm having rashers for lunch." Granny decided to treat her to a few fried rashers to have with her Mammy's lunch.

She laughed when Granda put the empty circular cheese box on his head before putting it on her head. She didn't like her "favourite" spreadable triangle cheese sections today.

She was tired today and Granny hoped she would fall asleep while watching *Blinky Bill*. It was full of Australian lingo, and she just gave up watching it instead. At one stage, as she watched *Blinky Bill*, Granda ran past her, without a response. When he ran back past her, she gave Granda a big smile.

It wasn't long before there was a major meltdown, though. She had put her nappy on back to front, and when Granny tried to fix it, Doireann got herself into quite a temper. Now staring at Granny, while pointing her finger with a scrunched-up face, she shouted, "You get out of here right now," and then ran to open the bedroom door.

"You are not to speak to me like that," Granny told her.

She still had a blistering temper and continued her rant, but whatever she was saying, Granny couldn't understand it. Granda eventually succeeded in reaching the battlefield, using his commando-style movements up through the hall, only to encounter fierce resistance at the coalface, until the bombardment fell silent. A negotiated settlement followed, whereby, firstly, Granny was allowed to approach and defuse the explosive device (the nappy) and, secondly, Granny brought her outside to play football now that the rain had stopped.

As Granny kicked the ball on the ground, she said, "No, no, Granny, not like that," and showed Granny how to kick it out of her hands, the way Gaelic football is played. They came back into the warm house after a little walk down the garden, as it was getting colder. Granny read *Winnie the Pooh and Tigger Too* for her. Next, she got her colouring pencils to do some drawing for a while.

There was another meltdown when Granny took her in for a nap. "*No, no, no,*" she screamed, so that the whole of County Wexford would hear her cries and pleas for help—in the hope that someone would rescue her. Granny persisted and managed to quieten her down, but it wasn't long before she was back up, running all over the place. Granda read *Winnie the Pooh and Tigger Too* for her also. But a little bit into the story, she got bored and, instead, wanted to play with the round cardboard cheese box, putting it on her head and letting it fall off over and over.

Then, Mammy phoned Granny to say there was an overturned truck on the M50, and they were at a standstill. Granda read a whole book called *Brave Bitsy and the Bear* for her and had just started singing along with the songs in *Dora* when she stopped him after the first song.

Granda asked, "Do you want any more books read?"

"We can play a game," she said.

"What game?" asked Granda.

"You teach me," she said. In other words, she wanted Granda to invent a game for her.

Granda went and got some balloons, and she selected the pink one. He blew it up, stretching it first, and knotted it to keep the air in. Then he kept blowing up other ones, only to let them fly around the room, causing her to laugh out loud. She asked for a balloon to blow up and took the navy blue one. She copied Granda by stretching it and stretching it until the head became detached from the main part. There was silence as she looked up at Granda, who started to laugh.

"Sorry, Granda."

"That's all right, pet. Here, there's another one."

They then punched and kicked the two fully blown-up balloons for what seemed like ages.

Later on, Granda took her in to watch a children's programme on the big telly in the sitting room, until Mammy and Daddy arrived (5 p.m.). She wanted to take the balloons home and Granda gave them to Mammy to take to the car. They had to hurry away to sign a lease contract for the rented Camolin house.

28 April

Doireann, Teddy Pink, and Mammy paid Granny and Granda a quick visit this morning. "I am not staying," Doireann told Granny. Granny and Granda gave her a big hug and were shown Teddy Pink, who had to get a hug also. Mammy was delivering some things to Granny.

"There's a big dog poo in the garden on the stones, and I nearly walked into it," Mammy said.

Granda went to the shed and got a shovel and a cardboard box to remove the dog poo, to the overgrowth at the bottom of the garden, with a promise that, if he found out who the dog owner was, he would return it back onto his or her doorstep with pleasure. Later, a very disgruntled Granny sprinkled pepper around the front garden also.

Doireann showed off her new red leather shoes and her fancy clothes. Mammy was taking her for a walk, while Oisín played a football match in Camolin. They said goodbye to Granny when exiting the front door.

"We'd better say goodbye to Granda," (he was down the garden) Mammy told Doireann.

"There's no need," she said, waving her hands in the air and obviously eager to proceed with the promised walk with Mammy.

Granda gave Teddy Pink a hug at the side gate, having come up from the end of the garden before they left.

30 April

Doireann was holding Daddy's hand as she walked on a neighbour's wall. "The baby lamb was crying," she told Granny and Granda, as they returned home from Arklow.

Daddy had phoned the owner of the field where the lamb was caught between two hedges. It had separated from its mammy and all the other sheep and little lambs. Granny and Granda said they had heard lots of *baa baas* during the night.

"I didn't bring Teddy Pink," she told Granda as he admired her lovely red shoes.

"Was she tired?" enquired Granda.

"Yes."

As soon as she was in the house, she went and got Baby Bop and the teddies and brought them out to the dining room. "Leave Snowy there, on the bed," Granda was ordered. She put her yellow sunglasses on and then put them on Baby Bop for Granda to take some photos with his mobile phone.

She'd had Weetabix for her breakfast but was still hungry. Granny made porridge, put some fruits in it, and gave it to her as she sat watching *Blinky Bill*. Her facial expressions were a combination of smiles, alarm, scared, and weepy.

Later on, there was a *knock, knock*, and Granny opened the dining room door. She was handed a leaflet and a pencil from the postwoman.

"Thank you," Granny said.

"Are we going to the playground today?" Granda was asked, and he nodded, while saying Gorey.

"Is that the one with the red thing?" Doireann asked.

And he said, "I think so" (but he didn't know what thing this was].

Next thing, she was gone, running in to watch the movie as the music got a bit louder.

When Granda took a selfie of himself wearing Doireann's yellow sunglasses, she smiled. Later, she wanted to try out her potty-training toilet seat, twice and was then reluctant to put her nappy back on.

"Right, the telly off. We are going out now," Granda announced.

"Don't turn it off; just pause it," she ordered.

Because it got a bit late, they went to the local playground instead of Gorey. When the sun went in, it was extremely cold in the playground. Doireann had great fun anyway, playing in the tree house and on the slides, the see-saw, and the swings. She and Granny played with her yellow football and chased it all over the place. There were some other kids playing there with their mammies as well.

They left to drive home, and as they got into Granda's car, Granny was singing some song to herself.

"Doireann, I want you to say this to Granny: 'We'll have to give you a penny and send you on to the next street,'" joked Granda.

"Granny, go to the next street!" she said.

Back in the house, Doireann had the popcorn she did not like the other day! Granda went outside and started cutting the grass before his lunch. Doireann would not eat her lunch that Mammy had made for her, as she was not hungry. "She had the extra breakfast" (porridge) "and oatcakes this morning," explained Granny.

She wanted beetroot and couldn't get enough of it. When Granda gave her lots of his beetroot, she gave him a lovely smile.

As she talked to Granny, she covered her mouth with her hand, because she didn't want Granda to hear. Granny asked her if she would eat such and such or such and such and so on, and every time, her response was "*No*," forcing Granny to tell her, "I have no options left."

"I am no options!" she replied. "I want to get out," she moaned, meaning she wanted to get out of her high chair.

Joking, Granny said, "Oh, it's hard getting out of the seat," which prompted Doireann to stand up, while making groaning sounds, like "oooooooh" and "aaaaaaah," before sitting back down again.

"Ah, you are old and stiff," Granny told her.

Doireann did it again for fun, with lots of hardship expressions on her face this time.

When out of her chair, she got some blankets from the bedroom and put Baby Bop, Teddy White, and Teddy Brown down for a sleep. Using a pillowcase, she lay down to (pretend) sleep as well.

When the sun returned, she played out the back and Granda continued with his grass-cutting. She loved playing with the stones and even took some home for good measure.

Mammy called to the house and had to fit the car seat that Daddy had left at Granny and Granda's house that morning. Doireann stood on the road to watch Mammy, and when Granny tried to move her to safety, there was a major meltdown. Soon after, as they were about to leave, Mammy said, "Say bye-bye to Granda, Doireann."

"Bye-bye, Granda," she shouted.

Granda walked up from the garden and gave her a huge hug bye-bye as she picked up a few more stones to bring home.

CHAPTER 12

That'll Be on Your Tombstone

2 May

Granny and Granda were late returning home from their gym and swim because of heavy traffic in Arklow. Daddy, Doireann, and Teddy Pink rambled around the area in the meantime. Daddy carried Doireann until she wanted to get down to show Granny and Granda Teddy Pink and her lovely red pants and her sleeveless top with coloured seashells and starfish. Then, she showed them her new child necklace that her Mammy's friend had given her. Of course, her red leather shoes didn't go amiss for a mention either, which Granny and Granda acknowledged as well.

She went and sat waiting on the hall doorstep, while Granda wheeled the bin up the side of the house and Daddy gave Granny Doireann's shoulder bag and grub from his car.

Once inside the house, Doireann ran to the bedroom. She lifted Teddy White out of the cot to bring to the dining room and said to Granda, "You get Baby Bop and Teddy Brown." She sat Teddy Pink, Baby Bop, and the other two teddies on the sofa, while Granny got their porridge ready, including some for Doireann, who had asked for some.

Then she did some artwork with her colouring pencils and Granny's biro. "Granda, look, I drew an aeroplane." It was obviously one of those very fast planes, because by the time Granda got to inspect it, the plane was nowhere to be seen, only some circular speed lines! Granda showed her how to draw a circle. She opted to draw a heart instead and a very good one at that. Granda drew an arrow through it.

She asked for an orange drink and Granny squeezed two oranges and put the juice into her little cup. "Can I have more, Granny?" she pleaded.

"There's no more left, and you have had enough," Granny insisted.

"There is three [oranges] still there" (it was actually five), she told Granny, who then, bluntly said, "No."

"Can I watch *Blinky Bill*?" she asked.

Granny switched it on, while Granda strapped her into her high chair. She had her porridge while watching *Blinky Bill*, and Granny and Granda smiled at her facial expressions.

"Would you like to go to Gorey Playground today?" Granny asked her.

"Is that where the red thing is?" she asked again today.

"It's the one near your house," Granny said.

With her arms down by her side, her hands moving, and a look of contentment on her face, she said, "Yeah, that okay."

She got out of her high chair with Granny's help, put her shoes on, and was rearing to go.

"You should put your hat on," Granny suggested, referring to a bonnet-type hat.

She went to the set of drawers in the hall, fetched her red woollen hat instead, and put it on her head. Granda put her red coat on, and Granny got her football.

On their way to Gorey playground, Doireann announced, "We forgot Teddy Pink."

"She is minding the other teddies and Baby Bop," Granny told her and continued, "We are very pleased with that, because when she stayed at home on Monday having a rest, they all missed her."

Doireann accepted that. They parked near Gorey Rangers FC and walked up the narrow laneway close by, leading to Gorey Park and the playground. They avoided using the other entrance near to Doireann's house in Sean Lios estate, in case she wanted to go home with no one there. She would not hold Granda's hand, wanting to hold Granny's hand instead as they crossed the road to the laneway. She did hold Granda's hand as they twisted and sidestepped up through the laneway to avoid all the disgusting dog poo that seemed to be everywhere.

They reached the playground eventually, where there were lots of other kids and Mammies. She was really enjoying herself, so much that she said to Granny, "We are having a great day."

It was very windy and cold, but the sun was shining brightly, and the forecasted rain had not yet arrived.

After Granda had explained why some of the playground equipment was for older kids, Doireann insisted on trying them out. "They are not for you, Doireann."

"I want to try; I can do it."

Granda had to guide and hold on to 'Miss Fearless' as he and Granny fretted.

They played with her yellow football for a little while only, as the grass was still very wet after the torrential rain the night before. The wind was blowing the ball all over the place as well. On their way back out of the park, Doireann had to try and climb various trees, with Granda in close attendance.

Next, she was over at the skateboarding section, admiring all the different slopes. She held Granda's hand as they went in to look around. "Can I walk down there?" Miss Fearless pointed.

"No, it's too dangerous," Granda advised.

As they headed out to the car, she said, "I want to slide down the slide."

"It's not a slide, Doireann," Granda told her.

She moaned and groaned saying, "I want to do it."

"No. We are going home now," she was told by both Granny and Granda.

They decided to exit by the main entrance and not the laneway, with Granda walking ahead of Granny, who was now holding Doireann's hand.

At the car, she refused to get in and complained, "Granda wouldn't let me go down the slide." Next, there was a major meltdown. She kicked and screamed as Granny tried to get her into the car. Granda just lifted her up and put her in the back seat. Crying loudly now, she reluctantly got into the car seat. She was still crying and now moaning as Granda fastened her straps.

As they drove back to Camolin, she continued to moan, while mentioning the (skateboard ramp) slide.

"If you had an accident in there, we would get into trouble," Granny said, trying to reason with her, adding, "Anyway, Mammy and Daddy wouldn't allow it either."

"Yes. They would. They have before," she argued.

"Well, we have to see what Mammy says later," Granny told her.

She did not let up until they neared home and said, "Teddy Pink will give me a big hug and make me better."

When inside the house, she went to Teddy Pink for a big hug.

Later, while having lunch, she said, "Granda wouldn't let me go on the slide."

To this, Granny told Granda, "That'll be on your tombstone!"

Doireann gave Granda a piece of her pineapple, and he gave her some of his beetroot. At one stage, as she and Granda exchanged scrunched-up funny faces at each other, she said, "Don't let the food spill down your clothes now," just like her Mammy would say.

Then Granda sang, "Doireann is the best, best. Doireann is the best, best. La-la-la-la, la-la-la-la."

She wanted him to sing it over and over again, before singing it herself. Then she sang "Mammy is the best, best. Mammy is the best-best." And next it was, "Granny is the best, best" and so on.

When she was let out of her high chair, she went to the press, looking for another cream cracker, which she then sat eating at Granda's bedroom door as he worked on his notes. Then she went into the small bedroom and shouted out, "Granny, I'm doing a poo."

Granny changed her nappy. After this, she helped Granny put the old nappy in the bin and then when they came in, she was singing, "Granny is the best, best. Granny is the best, best. La-la-la-la, la-la-la-la," over and over and over.

Granny offered to read her a story, but she didn't want one. Then, she said, "Read *Dora*?" and ran excitedly to get the book.

Granny had to remove Doireann's leggings for the wash because of a poo stain and offered her new ones that had been bought ages ago. She declined at first, only to change her mind when Granny showed her Minnie Mouse on them. "Granda, Granda, look," she said after running to him, to show off her new leggings.

"Oh, they are gorgeous, with all those lovely daisies. Who got you them?" Granda asked.

"Granny," she said, with a big happy smile. "Granny is the best, best. Granny is the best, best. La-la-la-la, la-la-la-la," sang Granda, and then she ran out and sang it to Granny.

Later, when passing the small bedroom, the smell was extra strong, and Granda opened a couple of windows. He then said it to Granny, who shook her head saying, "You want to see the amount? An adult wouldn't do as much."

Granny sang the songs along with Doireann from the *Dora* songbook. At one stage, Granny selected the wrong song. "What are you doing, Granny?" she angrily asked.

"Sorry, it will stop soon," Granny said, but it ran on for a lot longer than she thought.

Knock, knock, sounded the hall door, and Doireann ran to greet Mammy, who had come to collect her. "Those pants on Doireann were bought in Penney's," Granny told Mammy.

"Did you go to Penney's? My Mammy went to Penney's," Doireann informed Granny.

Then Doireann started humming a song to herself, while putting her things into her shoulder bag as Granny and Mammy chatted. Granny helped her put her shoulder bag on.

"Come in here Doireann," Granda then called.

When she went into Granda, he said, "Look at all the birdies at the birdbath, drinking water, bathing, and fluttering their wings. They are house sparrows." Then Granda named other birds that visited his garden, such as blackbirds, thrushes, robins, wrens, wagtails, and so on.

4 May

Granny phoned Mammy from Arklow to say they were running late. Mammy would pass on the message to Daddy, who was on duty that morning. A very quiet Doireann emerged from Daddy's car, with soother in mouth after Granny and Granda pulled into their driveway at about 9.15 a.m. "I haven't got Teddy [Pink] today," she groaned and then asked Daddy for her new football.

"Tell Baby Bop you don't have Teddy today, Doireann, when we get inside and show her your lovely black dress with your lovely red shoes and red leggings," Granda said as he carried his and Granny's gym bags into the house.

She followed with her shoulder bag and ball. Still very quiet, she sat on the sofa. "Granny, I have a sore leg," she said, and when Granny wanted to inspect it, she wouldn't let it be touched.

"What happened?" "I fell behind a truck, this morning. No, no. It was yesterday," she said.

"Did Mammy and Daddy put something on it?" Granny enquired.

"No," she replied and would not let them remove her red leggings to have a look.

They both gave her a big hug as they all chatted on the sofa.

"What did you have for your breakfast?" Granny asked.

"Cheerios. And have you got any, Granny?" she asked.

"No, but I have porridge with fruit."

"Can I have an orange drink and look at *Blinky Bill*?" she requested.

Granny made a big orange juice drink, especially for her, which she drank while watching the DVD on the telly.

Granny phoned Mammy to enquire about Doireann. "It was this morning she fell, and I mollycoddled her also because she is a bit of a drama queen at times. She is probably carrying it on, knowing she will get the attention," Mammy said. Mammy also thought she was coming down with a cold again.

"On Wednesday, we noticed she had a snotty nose, all right," Granny told her.

Doireann wasn't sure if she could walk the long distance of one metre from the sofa to the high chair, now facing the telly, when Granda asked her. Granda held her up from under the arms and Granny held her two legs, to carry her to the chair, like you would a hospital patient.

She kicked out, saying, "I don't like that," and wanted to be put down to walk herself. "I can't see it," she moaned, meaning the telly, as Granda strapped her into the chair.

Granda started to turn her chair around slowly, while making an engine sound. "Keep pressing that [pretend] button," Granda said to a now smiling Doireann. "Would you like to go to the library today, Doireann?" he asked.

"No. Playground?" was her immediate response.

"What if we go to the library and then to the playground on the way back?" suggested Granda.

She was out of her chair in a flash to put her shoes on. Her knee had had a miraculous recovery, although she did have a nasty scratch on her knee.

Granny noticed it, when changing her nappy and sent her out to show Granda. "Look at my knee, Granda."

"Ah, you poor girl. That must have really hurt you when you fell," Granda said, feeling sorrow for her.

"It's okay now," she said, matter-of-factly, and off she went back into Granny, who said she would put some Sudocrem on it because it looked very red and tender. Granny would inform Mammy later.

Doireann then helped Granny put the washing on the clothesline. Having packed away her soother and bubbles, she then sought assistance when packing other items into her shoulder bag. Granda duly obliged.

As she went off to get her football, Granda loudly joked, "Do you have your suitcase packed as well, Doireann?"

"*I don't have a suitcase!*" she shouted back.

She went in to check the toilet rolls storage cabinet, and when she'd found it full, Granda told her to let Granny know. She then reached up to check the hanging facecloth, before exiting the bathroom. "Granda, it's wet."

"It's okay, pet. It was only used this morning, and it will soon dry."

They stood waiting for Granny, who had gone into the bedroom to change.

"Doireann, we are getting a new granny. She is gone in to change. Oooooh, maybe she will appear as a monster," Granda joked, to an "empty audience".

Doireann busied herself, studying the artificial flowers in the hall. "I like flowers," she proclaimed.

"They are artificial flowers," Granda said and prompted her to repeat the word *artificial*, without a response. Granda, again asked her to try and say the word artificial.

"I can't," she protested.

"Okay then, just say Arthur," Granda persisted, but she wouldn't. Granda asked her one more time.

And she responded with, "I can't say Arthur, Granda."

Now laughing, Granda said, "You have just said it. Now say fishal."

"No, I can't," she insisted and then with a big grin on her face, she said, "I already said artificial, Granda."

During all the commotion, Granda never heard her say the word.

Granny then confirmed she had said the word, artificial, leaving poor Granda with egg on his face.

At the hall door, she looked upwards and said, "Howaya, Mick?"

Now pushed for time, they abandoned the proposed trip to the library and chose to go to the playground only, with Doireann's approval first, of course. As Granda's car indicated a right turn into Camolin Playground, she said, "I want Gorey Playground." This was where Granda's potential "tombstone inscription" had originated.

Granny and Granda decided a little white lie, was called for urgently. "Eh, Gorey Playground would be closed now, Doireann, as it is too late," pretended Granda, switching off the engine of his now parked vehicle with fingers crossed. "I bet I will win the race to the playground," announced Granda, on opening the car doors.

She was off like a bullet from a gun, with Granda in hot pursuit and shouting, "Hooray, hooray."

Carrying Doireann's shoulder bag, Granny had a race also—with Teddy White!

It was a lovely warm day, in line with the forecast for the forthcoming May bank holiday weekend. Doireann had great fun as usual—on the slides, the climbing ropes, the see-saw, and the spinning seat. Then it was to the swings she went. "Granda, push me. Again. Again. Again. This is great fun," she happily announced as she swung back and forth and back and forth. Next, she played football with Granny and Granda. Eventually, she started playing on the slides with another 2-year-old, once their respective "Mexican stand-offs" had abated.

They got back home at about 12.30 p.m., and Granny made the lunch. Doireann had a drink of milk with beetroot, pepper, and a boiled egg without the yellow. She left her melon for later. During lunch, she kept whispering to Granny, "Finish your lunch before Granda," as he looked on.

When Granda realised what she was whispering, he explained to her the way it was done years ago. With one hand covering your mouth, you would turn your head around to face the other person and say, "Word in your ear?" Granda got her to do it after a few tries.

She watched some more of *Blinky Bill* while eating her toasted white bread.

Later, Granny changed her nappy and took her outside to play with her two bottles of bubbles. She was moaning because she didn't have a coat with her, saying she was cold, yet it was actually warm outside. Granda joined Granny as she made loads of bubbles for Doireann to chase, catch, and burst. Because they only had one ringed bubble-making spoon for the two bottles, Granda decided to fill up one bottle from the other.

"No, I want to do it," Doireann demanded once Granda had started pouring.

The one bottle filled up quickly, but she kept pouring until she had emptied it onto the wooden bench and the ground, leaving her with one bottle full and another one empty.

Next, she wanted to play with the small buckets and water, but Granny told her, "No. It's near to going home time, and I don't have a change of clothing for you."

To this, Doireann responded with a meltdown, followed by a sulk.

Granny brought her inside and read her *Winnie the Pooh and Tigger Too* to calm her down and because she was tired.

Next, *knock, knock* sounded the hall door. Oisín arrived from school because Mammy was running late. Doireann began another meltdown and was giving out to Granny and Granda. Oisín tried to talk to her, but no joy. She flung a cushion from a chair at the table that she went to sit on.

When Mammy called, she had to hurry up and go, as Daddy was driving a van load of furniture to their new rented house in the Grove in Camolin.

CHAPTER 13

Reading a Magazine

14 May

As Doireann and Mammy approached the hall door, Granda was at the dining room window watching Doireann toddling up along behind Mammy. Then, she looked up and gave him a big smile and a wave. She was displaying her snotty nose, which Granny soon cleaned with a hanky when she stepped inside. She had her new pink toy, called Cora, with her. She did a pose when her coat was removed, standing straight, with one leg forward but said nothing, just stared pleasantly. She was wearing a new flowery dress and different pants and stayed in the one position, without speaking, until someone commented.

"Oh, Doireann, that is a lovely dress you have on. It's gorgeous," Granny said.

And off she went, smiling and delighted with herself.

She couldn't find her red pants at home and wondered where they were. Teddy Pink was left at home today. She went and got Baby Bop, while Granda took the teddies out of the cot for her. They were all put sitting on the dining room sofa, with Cora placed in between Teddy White and Teddy Brown.

"Why did they make Baby Bop?" she asked.

"They made her for you," Granda told her.

Then, she showed Baby Bop to Granny.

Granda gave her a big hug, saying, "I missed you."

"Well, I will be here for a long time now," Granda was assured.

She took her pink shoes off, as they were dirty and left them in the hall, where Granny suggested. Granda had jokingly suggested putting them in the bin.

"I'm not putting them in the bin," she said, with a little smirk on her face.

Mammy had told Granny and Granda she was not happy with her shoes. When Granda gave the teddies a big hug and then Cora, as requested by Doireann, she said, "Okay, let's do it right and don't squeeze, Granda."

So, Granda had to do it right, without squeezing too tightly.

She sat watching *Blinky Bill* while Granny and Granda had their breakfast after their early morning gym and swim. When she looked at them eating, Granda gave her the thumbs up, and she did it back to him. Then she held up one thumb, asking, "Where is my other one?"

And then she would make it appear.

This went on for ever, until she asked, "Granda, can you ask Granny if Mammy is coming?"

"Yes, Mammy is coming after work," Granny told her.

As Granda and Doireann waited for Granny to get ready, *Blinky Bill* ended, and she wanted it on again.

"No, we are going to Enniscorthy Playground now," Granda told her.

Next thing, the credits started to roll, with music in the background. Granda started dancing, followed by Doireann, who was now dancing with Cora. Granda was then given Teddy White to dance with. All four of them danced and danced to the beat of the music, until Granny came to the rescue.

She was ready to go, and off to Enniscorthy they went. Granny and Granda wanted to have a look at the gym facilities and get prices in the Riverside Park Hotel, which was right beside Enniscorthy Playground. Granda spoke with an employee there, who was a former work colleague of his, years back. They looked at the large pool from within the pool area and then viewed the gym from the reception area through glass panes.

"It's like Mammy's gym" (Curves in Gorey) "but bigger," said Granny.

And Doireann, sucking her soother like Maggie Simpson, nodded in agreement. "How do you get into that place?" enquired Doireann, meaning the gym.

A female gym member sitting close by, asked, "How old is she?"

"Eh." Pause. "Two and a half months short of 3," Granny said, having worked it out.

"She has a great use of words at that age," acknowledged the lady.

And Granny and Granda nodded in agreement as Doireann looked on.

"There," said Granda, pointing to the glass door, camouflaged within the glass-panelled partition. "That's the door into the gym, Doireann."

"I would like to go in, when I am older," she informed Granny and Granda.

They did a walking tour of the hotel outside, while teaching Doireann how to pronounce *Enniscorthy Playground* before they reached it.

She had a great time, running around this large playground and playing on most of the equipment. Granny and Granda took turns sitting with her on the merry-go-round. She would open the gates and say, "Okay, Granda," allowing him to get on board and take a seat before pushing it around. Then it was Granny's turn to sit on board, beside Granda.

Next, Granny explained to her, the hop, skip, and jump activity, using the numbers marked out on the ground. She then tried it. "No, Doireann, you hop on one leg there and then hop with your two legs here and then one leg again here and so on," Granny explained, while pointing to the numbers.

"In our day, you used your own chalk to scribble the boxed-in numbers on the road," Granda said.

Granny agreed, adding, "That was when we had little or no cars on the road."

Granda nodded in agreement. "You do it, Granny," Doireann said.

"Ah, my knees won't be able," pleaded Granny.

"Granda, will you, do it?"

And the young 68-year-old gave it a go, very timidly, mind.

Next thing, Doireann dashed along, doing her hops, skips, and jumps in a flash, while shouting, "Is that the way, Granda?"

"Oh yes, pet, very good," he said, feeling his age even more now.

During all the excitement, she proclaimed, "This is a great day."

While being strapped into the car seat about thirty minutes later, she asked, "Where's my oat biscuit?"

Granny gave her an oatcake type biscuit as promised.

Well into their journey home, she was enjoying her second oatcake, when Granda asked, "Do you like that cracker, Doireann?"

"They are not crackers," Granny corrected Granda.

"Doireann, tell Granny that your oatcake biscuit is a cracker" (meaning its brilliant).

"Ha, ha," said Granny.

"Ha, ha," mimicked Doireann. "We had a barbeque yesterday, and I had a burger," she informed Granny and Granda.

"Very nice. That's lovely," Granny said.

Later, she had her lunch, which included a pepperoni, among other things, before getting ready to go out to play in the back garden. "Can I get out?" she asked, wanting to be unstrapped and lifted out of her high chair.

Granda duly obliged, loosening the straps before noisily lifting her up and then moving sideways like a lifting crane. He stopped, moved a little bit more sideways, and stopped again to carry out inspections so as to avoid any obstructions, before moving downwards to the floor below, with a message from the talking lifting crane— "Now, there you go, pet," —to the now giggly, smiley face that was Doireann's.

Granda got the small watering can and put water into it for her to water the flowers in the pots as requested. She was in her bare feet and seemed to love the freedom of it. Granda and her then played with the Frisbee for a while. Having caught a glimpse of two ornamental butterflies Granda had fitted to the wall, she said, "They are lovely," and pointed as she stood still, while continuing to observe them. "Granda, the butterflies are beautiful," she continued.

"Shush, listen," he said into his finger that was now pressing against his lips.

They both stood listening to the birds whistling. A blackbird whistled. Granda tried to copy the whistle and sent it back. Then the blackbird whistled again. Granda did it again as Doireann smiled.

"They are lovely," she said, moving nearer to the flowers, touching a purple one.

"Yeah, they are Granny's; Granny planted them," he told her.

Because she was venturing further down the garden, they got her to put her wellies on, while singing the words of Jimmy Cricket's Christmas song, "Santa Bring My Wellies Back to Me".

Granny and Doireann were then out in the back garden, while Granda did some work on the computer.

Next thing, "Granda, we have a major nappy change alert," Granny announced as she dashed towards the bedroom, followed by an awkward-walking Doireann, requiring an urgent nappy change. The poor girl obviously felt uncomfortable, and Granda went to open a few windows, just in case.

Just then, Mammy called to the house and Granda joked, "You may go into that bedroom there and take a deep breath."

Shortly afterwards, "I'm going now, Granda, and will be back," she told him, before attempting to climb onto Granny and Granda's big bouncy bed, while Mammy and Granny had a quick chat. She kept slipping off, just as she was about to succeed.

"Here, Doireann, stretch your arm out further over the bed and grab onto the blanket, like this," Granda showed her.

Next thing, she was up and standing on the bed, delighted with herself, looking out the window to see the birds. There were none.

"Can I turn on the radio?" she asked.

Granda showed her how to change the radio stations and increase or decrease the volume as well. Next thing, Granda spotted a blackbird.

"Come here quick," Granda beckoned. They both watched the blackbird move fast around the garden, in search of worms. "There is usually a blackbird with its partner, who is brown in colour," Granda explained, just as another pair of birds flew across the garden and into the bushes.

She turned away and started to clap her hands to the Irish music now coming from the radio. Next, she was dancing on the bed. "Come on, Granda. Dance on the bed," she called.

"I can't, Doireann. It's too dangerous, and I might fall," Granda warned.

"Dance on the bed with your bum," she said as Mammy entered the room, laughing out loud on hearing that.

Mammy had to collect Oisín, and as they walked to the car, Granda ran after Doireann with the flowers she had picked earlier for Mammy.

"I will give you them when we get home," she told Mammy, who had just switched on the car engine.

"Bye-bye," said Granda, waving before heading back in doors for a well-earned cup of tea.

16 May

Mammy and Doireann were playing in the field when Granny and Granda drove in from their early morning gym and swim. Doireann crawled under the concrete fence to run and get Teddy Pink, who was sitting in the plastic basket on the back of her pink tricycle. "Look, I brought Teddy Pink," she said loudly and handed her to Granny, who gave her a cuddle. Granda also gave her a cuddle.

She then showed off her lovely clothes. Her wardrobe today was pink-spotted light blue wellies; multicoloured pants; a pink Everest and Skye top under her pink skirt-come-jacket with a hoodie that had horses, a bird, and the sun on it; and a beautiful hat. "You are gorgeous, Doireann," both Granny and Granda told her.

"I am staying a long time today," she announced.

Granda opened the side gate and brought her pink trike in to the back garden and then fetched the empty waste bin from outside before locking the side gate again.

When she saw Cora was waiting, she put Teddy Pink beside her.

"What about Baby Bop?" Granda asked.

She ran into the bedroom. "Look, Teddy Brown is on Baby Bop's back," she observed. And then she saw Teddy White on Snowy's back.

She arranged all her pals, sitting on the dining room sofa and asked Granda to take a photo. She then joined in for the photo shoot.

Stopping at the dining room door, she called out to Granda, "You can't catch me," and took off again, with Granda in hot pursuit. She ran into the small bedroom and around the cot, giggling nervously, and dashed back as fast as she could go to Mammy, who was still talking to Granny in the kitchen. A while later, Granny was heating Granda's porridge while in conversation with Doireann, who was searching for her pepperoni that Mammy had given her for lunch!

Granda decided to quickly change his trousers in the bedroom. Literally within milliseconds, Granda heard her heading for his room and quickly pushed the door over, preventing her from getting in. He then waited until she removed her fingers from the door before shutting it.

When he reappeared, back in the dining room, Granda noticed that Doireann was holding the pepperoni in one hand but had her fingers curled up in the other, while being very quiet. "Are you all right, Doireann?" Granda asked her.

"I'm all right!" she shouted, before crying very loudly.

Granny and Granda talked to her and tried to calm her down. Her fingers were okay, but she may have got a fright when the door pressed against her fingers, or she was upset and angry because Granda would not let her into the bedroom.

She came around eventually and sat and watched the children's telly. The programme was about two animated bananas holding a train set, and Doireann interacted, talking back quietly and smiling as she watched it intently. Granny and Granda had their porridge, in the meantime.

Later, when she ran past Granda's door and then went quiet, Granda asked, "Are you okay, Doireann?"

"Yes," and then she appeared around the door, holding a new nappy, saying, "I did a pee in my nappy."

"Sure, you have a nappy on," Granny said on hearing her.

"I need to change it," she protested and proceeded to do so all by herself, leaving Granny to bag the wet nappy and put it in the bin.

Granny had purposely left the toilet rolls storage cabinet low in stock. "Can you check and see if we need toilet rolls?" Granny shouted to Doireann.

On inspection, she charged back to Granny saying, "We need toilet rolls."

"How many?"

"Two," was her reply, and she was handed them to go and replenish the stocks.

"Did you tell Granda about the job you did?" Granny asked her.

She ran into Granda, saying, "I put new toilet rolls into the box."

Granda stopped working on his computer and put his arms around her, saying, "Well done, pet, and thank you very much for that. Aren't you a great helper, good girl?" he said loudly as she beamed with delight.

Next thing, she was on the bed. "Granda, do you want me to put on the radio? I know how to switch it on." And on it went. "I know how to switch it off, Granda." And off it went. "Granda, do you want to listen to it?"

"Yes." And he was made listen to it. "Well done, pet. Thank you very much and thank you again for stocking the toilet rolls," Granda said.

"You're welcome," she replied as Granny came to Granda's rescue.

In the distance, Granda could hear, "I switched the radio on for Granda."

A little while later, Granda handed her a blue Chelsea wristband to put on her wrist, saying, "Here, Doireann. You can have this."

"No, I don't like blue," Granda was told.

"What colour do you like?" Granny asked her.

"Pink."

So, Granda's effort to increase the Chelsea supporters club received a serious setback today.

"Do you want to go to the library?" Granny asked her.

"No," she replied in a kind of I-can't-be-bothered moany voice.

"Will we go to the playground, then?" Granny continued.

"Yeah," she replied, in a very upbeat I'm-up-for-that voice.

"Okay, as soon as I put the washing on the clothesline, we will go to the playground," Granny promised her.

"Enscorty," Doireann suggested, meaning Enniscorthy.

"No. It's too late for that one today. We'll go to Camolin Playground," she was told.

She helped Granny put the washing on the clothesline and noticed the toy rocket launcher in the garden that Granda had taken from the shed the day before, in anticipation that she might be interested in playing with it. She wasn't long getting to grips with it. She jumped as high as she could to land on the launching pad (airbag) to propel the rocket skywards. Granda was invited to have a go, while she took photos, using his mobile phone.

"Okay, we can play with this when we get back from the playground," Granda announced.

"Enscorty," she said.

"No, I'm sorry, but it's too late," Granny insisted and offered to take her for a walk instead.

They now had to cope with a major meltdown. "*Enscorty*," she demanded in a screaming voice, while continuing to cry.

A while later, and now a bit calmer, she realised she was going nowhere, literally. "Maybe Teddy Pink would like to go to Camolin Playground," she suggested and ran to the hall to put her new wellies on when Granny and Granda agreed.

She ate some crackers in the hall. Granny wanted her to take the crackers to the playground. While they waited for Granny to get ready, she left lots of crumbs on the hall floor. Granda got the dustpan and sweeping brush and swept up the crumbs, with her saying, "Sorry, Granda."

He said, "That's okay, pet."

Then she wanted to bring her tricycle and was told they were not walking to the playground because of the heavy and noisy traffic. She protested, and Granda offered to try and fit her tricycle into the car, while Granny held her hand at the car. Granda tried to fit it onto the passenger front seat, but no joy. Next, he tried the back seat, and again, no joy. And ditto with the car boot. He was about to bring the tricycle back into the house, but Doireann objected, and they were nearly having another meltdown. Granda decided to give it one last go. He adjusted the car's front passenger seat and managed to squeeze the tricycle in. Then he noticed what looked like dog's poo on one of the wheels, so he took baby wipes and a plastic bag with him to scrub it off at the playground.

On their drive to Camolin Playground, which took about two minutes, she complained that she couldn't move her legs, and Granda said, "It's because I had to move the front seat back to make room for your tricycle."

Once the car was parked, she was out in a flash to race Granny down to the playground gate. She had lots of fun on the children's equipment in the playground. Granny played chasing. Doireann took a photo of Teddy Pink in the spinning seat. And then Granny visited her pretend house and was invited in.

She drank a lot of water today because she was thirsty. It was sunny but cold and windy. After an hour, she raced Teddy Pink and Granny back to the car, and when inside the car, she said, "I did a lot of walking today."

When they arrived back at the house, two minutes later, she raced Granny to the hall door. There was no mention of her tricycle, with all the trouble trying to fit it into the car. Perhaps she didn't want to leave her pet trike behind in case it got lost or something.

Granda remembered that, one Christmas, Santa had brought her Uncle Gary (then aged two) an American jeep. During the early hours (3 a.m.) of St Stephen's morning (26 December), he'd started screaming for his jeep from his cot. The jeep had to be left in the bedroom next to his cot before he settled back down again! Granda removed the tricycle from the car and wheeled it around to the backyard. Then he readjusted the car seat, while counting to ten.

Granny squeezed two oranges to make a juice drink for Doireann, while she watched *Blinky Bill*. She loved *Blinky Bill* and watched it over and over. Granny extended its loan from the library by two weeks. After this, Doireann was off to France for a two-week holiday and, hopefully, would have forgotten all about *Blinky Bill*. She had some toast before sitting up at the kitchen table for her salad. Mammy phoned Granny to say she would be late calling, because she had an appointment with her doctor.

At the end of *Blinky Bill*, the credits rolled to the sound of music. She wanted to dance and invited Granny to dance with her. And then, when Granda appeared, he was invited as well. She put two towels on the ground, allowing her to slide around to the sound of the music. Then, she used the same towels to wrap around Cora.

"I want to go outside," she demanded, but Granny wasn't ready.

She insisted on going out.

"We have still to finish our lunch," Granny explained.

"I want to go outside," she demanded again.

"I want to stay inside," Granny said.

Doireann then had a meltdown. With her arms and hands outstretched and in a loud voice, she demanded to be let go outside. Granny tried to distract her, but she stormed off into the sitting room.

Granny followed her, soon after and asked, "What are you doing, Doireann?"

"Reading a magazine," was her curt response.

Granny took a fit of laughter before making herself some tea and toast to have while sitting in with her. Granny switched on one of the kids' TV channels as she had her tea and toast.

Eventually, they all went outside, after Granny put sun-blocking cream on Doireann's face, arms, and neck.

They played with the toy rocket launcher, and Doireann had great fun with it. Then she played with the watering cans and water. Granny helped her remove her wellies, leaving her in her stocking feet.

Mammy and Oisín called to collect her, sometime after three o'clock. She showed Mammy how she was able to use the toy rocket launcher. Then she took one photo each of Granda and Granny in the garden, using Granda's mobile phone.

"I will be back again for longer," she told them as she and Mammy followed Oisín out to their car.

Oisín called around to Granny and Granda's after his dinner to collect Doireann's tricycle.

"How is Doireann? Is she in bed yet?" Granny asked.

"Oh, wait and I tell you," [what had happened earlier] Oisín said. "When we got home, Mammy sat Doireann down to watch a movie in the sitting room. Next, from within the kitchen, Mammy heard a noise and went to investigate. Doireann had decided to play with the coal bucket and knocked it over. There were black stains on the carpet and all over her, from head to toe. She had rubbed it all over herself, and Mammy had to give her a bath."

"And that's the landlord's carpet, isn't it?" said Granny to a nodding Oisín.

He continued with his story. "After her bath, she did a pee on the floor. She then slipped on it and started crying. I thought it was water and picked her up and it got all over me. So, I had to have a bath too," he complained.

Granny and Granda laughed at that and apologised for doing so.

"What did Daddy think of all of this?" Granda asked.

"He's in Galway," replied Oisín.

Granda helped Oisín lift the tricycle out to the gate. "Do you want me to walk to the house with you?" Granda offered.

"Ah no. I'm all right, Granda," he said.

As he left, Granny gave him some sweets and a packet of crisps, and he was delighted.

CHAPTER 14

My Top

21 May

Doireann was up at the side of the house with daddy when Granny and Granda arrived from their workout, late this morning. She was wearing her pink shoes and ran to Granny, holding up Teddy Pink, as Granda parked his car.

"Here, give me a hug. I have to go," Daddy said to her before she darted into the bedroom for Baby Bop.

Granda carried Teddy White and Teddy Brown into the dining room for her.

"Granda, I want a photo of them," she said, and he got her to sit up beside all the teddies and Baby Bop for the photo shoot. He requested they all give a big smile and click!

"Can I take some?" she asked.

Granda handed her his phone to take a photo. "Doireann, mind where you put your hand. Don't block the lens at the back," Granda told the young photography student.

Then Granda took a photo of her standing beside Granny.

Next, she announced what she brought for lunch as she filled up the fridge. It consisted of, two boiled eggs, cheeses, a roll, and a smoothie.

"There'll be no more room in the fridge," joked Granny.

"Is that a rock and roll you have for lunch?" joked Granda.

"No, Granda. It's just a single roll," he was told in no uncertain terms.

"Did you have brekkie, Doireann?" Granda asked.

"No, I only had a little," she said.

Granny gave her a sliced-up banana, which she enjoyed while watching some children's programmes on the telly. Earlier she said, "I don't want *Blinky Bill*, just the telly." Unbeknownst to her, *Blinky Bill* was now safely back in the library again. She watched *Pablo and the Dragon*.

Realising she hadn't got her top with her; she became alarmed and was a bit upset. "I haven't got my top," a slightly upset Doireann said.

"Did you forget to bring it?" Granny asked, showing concern.

With her head now stooped downwards, Granda went and got the pink cardigan Granny had bought for her weeks ago. "Look," said Granda.

But there was still no reaction from her.

"You can bring it to wear the next day, Wednesday," Granda suggested.

A little while later, when she was looking for something else in her small shoulder bag, Granny and Granda experienced the loudest announcement of the day. "*My top!*" she shouted.

Oh, she was so happy now and showed them the pink top with a hood that had a skirt at the bottom. *Some top*, pondered Granda.

"When is your birthday?" Granda asked her.

"It's in July."

"Mine is in July as well," Granda said.

"I'll be three," she said.

"Wow, you're a big girl now," Granny said, looking amazed and continued with, "I can't remember when I was three."

"Would you like to go to Enniscorthy playground today?" Granda asked her.

With her face now lit up, she said yeah excitedly.

"Last week, we did promise we would take you there this week, remember," Granda explained.

They all got ready to go out. Doireann had removed her shoes earlier and was now refusing to put them back on. "You need to wear them going to the car," Granny told her.

She complained about her toes being sore, having dropped some DVDs on them. Then, she got angry with her pants. When Granny realised her pants were a bit long, she curled the extra length, up under the tights, and that seemed to satisfy Miss Fussy Boots. Granny inspected her toes and patted them softly, before helping to put her pretty butterfly socks on.

Doireann then decided to put her own shoes on, herself. She didn't want to put her top on, the one she'd pined for this morning. They brought it anyway, as well as a '60s pop music CD to play on their way to Enniscorthy. Granda beeped the car horn loudly at a speeding passing motorist, who was too close for comfort.

"Granda, Teddy is asleep," he was bluntly told by an irate Doireann. She then, spoke about the internet not working in their house, pronouncing the word *internet* correctly.

Later, when Granny enquired about her lovely pants, she asked, "Who got you them?"

As quick as a flash, she replied, "You, Granny!"

Granda was able to park the car close to the playground. Doireann did a lot of running up and down, as if in a race, and loved it. She climbed onto the steps and stairs leading to the top entrance of the covered-in long chute slides but knew she wasn't ready to travel down them yet because Granny and Granda had warned her not to. She was about to crawl through a very small tunnel that was at ground level but complained, saying, "There's something on the ground."

Granda used a hanky to remove the slug.

Then at the tunnel exit, she stopped. "It's wet," she complained.

Granda had to mop it up with more of his spare hankies before Madam appeared out of the tunnel.

She played on various equipment, before Granny and Granda joined her and Teddy Pink on the merry-go-round, where they all had great fun spinning it around slowly, mindful of how dizzy you got if it went too fast. Another Granny, who was helping her daughter, told Granda that her two Granddaughters were aged 4.5 and 2.8 years.

Doireann stood watching them play together, and then she wanted to join in, just as they were leaving. Moaning, she said, speaking of the younger girl, "I want to play with her."

"You can't. They are going now," Granny told her.

Eventually, she came around and played on some of the other equipment. Her last go, before they left, was on the rocking bee. Granny and Granda mentioned that her smoothie was at home in the fridge, and this prompted her to leave the playground without a fuss. They played the same music on the way back home, and it wasn't long before Doireann was fast asleep. When they parked in their driveway, Granny stayed with Sleeping Beauty while Granda went into the house to use the loo and get a cuppa.

It wasn't long before there was a changing of the guards. Granny made good her escape as Granda sat in the car, waiting for Sleeping Beauty to open her eyes. Granda took some selfies of her as she slept in the car seat and then took some more photos of his new (blade-1) haircut. Earlier she had asked, "Did you get your hair cut, Granda?"

"Yes, Granny cut it," he said, continuing with, "Is there too much gone?"

"Yes," he was bluntly told.

She had a forty-five-minute nap before Granny carried a very tired girl into the house and sat her on her lap and curled into her. Soon after, Granda managed to get a moany Doireann to sit in her high chair at the table for her lunch. She wanted her roll with butter, asking Granny to put more butter on it. She only took a nibble before it was wrapped up to be eaten at home later. Then she had her two boiled eggs, removing the shells herself and eating the white of the egg only. Next, she had a yogurt, and the cheeses followed this, in that order.

Because Granny had a doctor's appointment in Gorey that afternoon, she'd arranged to drop Doireann into Curves nearby, where Mammy would be. Granny went to get herself ready, and Doireann went into Granda to see her cousins (photos) in Cambodia. Granda opened the pictures file on his laptop, sat her on his lap, and showed her loads of photos of her two Cambodian cousins from when all the family visited them inJuly 2016.

Then she went in search of Granny, who was washing her teeth. Having located Granny, she asked, "What are you doing, Granny?"

"I'm washing my teeth," Granny said as toothpaste spurted from her mouth.

"Why, Granny?" (The whys were now back in fashion.)

"I just have to."

"But why, Granny?" she persisted.

"Go on, Doireann, keep asking Granny why," whispered Granda.

Poor Granny struggled to clean her teeth, with Captain Why Why in close attendance.

As soon as Granny became aware of what Granda was up to, she shouted out, "Granda, would you ever … go an' drive your car?"

Next thing, Doireann stood in front of Granda, saying, "Granda, would you ever go and drive your car?"

Granny removed Doireann's wringing-wet nappy and gave her a new one to put on all by herself. On their way to Gorey, Doireann looked at Granny and asked, "Granny, did you get your hair cut?"

"Yes."

"Did you get your hair cut, with your lovely curls?" Granny asked her. "I did."

When the music was played in the car, Doireann said, "I can't hear it."

Granda increased the volume, and Granny, who was sitting in the back of the car with Doireann, asked him something repeatedly, but he was unable to understand her. He was also driving in heavy traffic and showed his frustration, switching the music off and saying, "What is it you're saying?"

Granny gave out to Granda, saying the music was too loud and that was why he couldn't hear anything.

"Granda, don't talk to Granny like that!" Doireann warned.

When they got to Curves, Doireann got out of the car and gave Granny a hug bye-bye.

"Say goodbye to Granda," she told Doireann, who had increased her pace at this stage.

"Bye-bye, Granda," was the sound of her fading voice as she reached the main Curves door and vanished inside to see her Mammy.

Granda drove Granny around to her doctor's clinic for her appointment, before heading home to write this.

22 May

Mammy phoned Granny today to say Doireann was not well. She got sick during the night a couple of times, and it was all over the bed. Mammy said Doireann hadn't cried out, but she'd heard noises coming from her bed and lots of movements, as if she was disturbed. Her temperature was at forty degrees, and when she gave her some Calpol, the temperature dropped. Mammy kept her home today, and she slept a lot. She thinks she has a cold because she was feeling cold and shivery also.

23 May

Granda turned left off Camolin's main street, only to see Mammy further down the road towards the bridge, wheeling Doireann in the buggy. When they reached Granny and Granda, Doireann said, "Teddy Pink is wet."

Mammy had given Teddy Pink a bath that morning, and her bright pink coat was lovely and clean again

"I want to dry her," she said.

And so Granda put Teddy on the clothesline to dry.

After they entered the house, Granda said, "You can have these," handing her some advertising leaflets that had been dropped into the letterbox.

As she put them on the chair beside her, a little calling card fell onto the floor.

"What is it?" Granda asked.

"I don't know," she said after picking it up.

Granda got her to put her shoes on without her socks, before going outside to open the side gate and bring the empty recycle bin in. He then took a photo of Teddy, drying out as she hung from the clothesline, supported by two clothes pegs, one for each ear.

"Here, Granda," Doireann said, handing him the Frisbee to throw before he went in for his breakfast.

She followed soon after, with a little rock for Mammy.

"Can you leave that rock outside at the doorstep, for when Mammy calls?" Granda suggested.

But he got the sulk and then he got the moans, as she wanted it kept inside. They switched the telly on, to distract her, while the rock made its way back outside again.

"Doireann, do you want a banana?" asked Granny.

"Yeah."

A couple of minutes then passed.

"There's your banana, Doireann," Granny said.

"I don't want it."

"You said you wanted one," Granny responded angrily.

"I don't like it," Doireann told her.

"Why did you say you wanted one?" Granny asked, in a very firm voice.

Silence.

Granda had an extra banana with his porridge that morning.

She played with her toy phone, which could ring like a real one, and spoke to Mammy. Whenever it rang, she would answer it. At one stage, on hearing it ringing, Granny came looking, thinking it was Granda's phone, such was the similarity of the ringtones.

"Granda, I was sick," she told him.

"I know, pet. Your Mammy told us you got sick a few times, and you were a very good girl, very brave," he told her. Mammy said she was still a bit tired and not 100 per cent yet. Daddy, they thought, was working in Galway again. Earlier, when Doireann said, "Oisín was sick as well," Mammy said she was making up a story now, because he was okay.

She asked for an oatcake. Granny then had to clean up the crumbs left on the chair. Following this, Granny got her some raisins.

"Can I go to Enniscorthy?" she asked.

"No," Granny said.

"Camolin then?" she continued.

"Okay, when we are ready to go but not yet," Granny told her.

She watched *Two by Two*; a DVD Granny got in the library. Then she went with Granny to get Teddy Pink off the line. She ran into Granda, held Teddy Pink aloft, and said, "She is dry now."

"That's great news. I'm delighted," Granda told her.

Just before this, she ran to Granda and proclaimed with a smile, "I am a big girl now, 'cause Granny said."

Acknowledging that, Granda said, "You are the prettiest girl in the world and tell Granny that."

She ran as fast as she could and said, "Granny, I am the pweties girl in the world."

She forgot about Camolin Playground and asked Granda to go out the back to play football instead.

"I would be delighted to, as soon as I finish here," Granda promised. Granda was sorting his and Granny's revenue affairs out (two card-carrying pensioners) online.

Out they went to play football, and Granda was told, "Stand there, just over from me, and kick the ball."

Teddy Pink kicked it back with the help of the socks-only-no-shoes Doireann. They did this for a while until she wanted to take out the waterproof blanket and all the other teddies. Granda plucked a lilac flower for her, and she said, "I will give it to Mammy." She then secured it on the garden table for safekeeping.

Granda got the wheelbarrow out, laid the blanket over the top of it, and asked, "Would you like to get in?"

"Yes," she gleefully said and sat in the wheelbarrow, while Granda, acting like a horse, ran her around the garden. Then he took the three teddies on board—but not Baby Bop, as Doireann said, "She is too big, Granda."

Granda put Baby Bop sitting on the tabletop to watch Granda-the-Horse draw Doireann and her mates up and down the garden.

When Granny appeared out, she suggested using the four old plastic white garden chairs to make a tent. They all brushed down the chairs first, removing the old cobwebs and any loose dirt as they had been stored in a corner of the garden for a long time. Doireann used the small brush and worked really hard.

"I can't get this off," she informed Granda, who said, "That's okay, pet."

"Why is that on the chair?" she asked.

"It's an old paint mark. Don't worry about that," Granda assured her.

"Granny, you clean that one. And there, Granda, that's next," instructed our new supervisor, pointing.

Eventually they got them all cleaned, and Granny got the blankets to cover the chairs and made a beautiful tent for Doireann and all of her mates. Granda was invited into her tent and squeezed into it on his hands and knees, saying, "Ah this is brill, Doireann," to the very happy and proud owner.

Later, she made (pretend) tea for the teddies and Baby Bop. Granny then made her a real cup of tea as requested.

"Granda," she called out. "Here, I'm finished." She handed him her empty cup.

"Would that be all, Your Majesty," remarked Granda sarcastically.

Later, Granny took her into the house to make her a plait that she had requested earlier.

"Look Granda," she said excitedly after running in to show him at breakneck speed.

"Ah, that's gorgeous, pet. Wait there until I get a picture?" Granda said, and his phone camera clicked. "Your plait is gorgeous, and you are going to be the prettiest girl in the world," he reminded her again. "What are you going to be in the world?" he asked, wanting her to pronounce the word *prettiest*.

"Pwetiest girl," she said.

"What did Granda say?" asked Granny.

"I am going to be the pwetiest girl in the world," she said, with a big smile on her face.

Granny and Granda sat at the table to have their usual lunch that consisted of beetroot, lettuce, tomato, onions, carrot, courgettes, peppers, and sometimes radish. Granda would also have tuna, while Granny would have an egg or sardines. Their tea and toast would then follow that.

Doireann sat in her high chair to watch *Barney* and eat her spag-ball (spaghetti bolognaise) at the same time. Barney and his pals played hopscotch with the numbers one to ten, similar to the one Doireann played in Enniscorthy's playground. Then Barney would look for numbers hidden in his play area, while asking, "I wonder where they are?" This would encourage his pals to search for the numbers also. Doireann would hold her index finger over her lips as she wondered where the numbers were and played along, saying, "There they are," while pointing towards the TV screen when a number was located.

She and Granny went outside to the backyard again to play in the tent. Granny had to get into the tent beside her. Next, she said, "Okay, Granny. We'll run around," officiating today's outdoor activities.

She started to run around the tent, and Granny walked. "Granny, are you flying on another plane?" Doireann had asked earlier, aware that she was flying to France for her holidays sometime soon.

"I am not going on holidays," Granny told her.

When Mammy arrived, she told Granny how good Doireann was at getting her clothes ready for the holidays. She had watched Mammy rolling her clothes up and copied her.

"Hi, Mammy," she said, smiling from inside her new tent. Shortly afterwards, "I have to go now, Granda."

"Don't tell me you have to go," Granda said back.

"I have to go," she repeated.

He then said, laughing, "I told you not to tell me."

Now furious, she said, "Granda, I have to go hooim" (home).

She sat in her yellow buggy that Granny had given to Mammy. Granda helped with carrying it over the stones in the front garden area. "Bye, Granda."

He replied, "Bye, Doireann, and bye, ladies."

CHAPTER 15

I Did It, I Did It

9 June

Mammy and Doireann visited Granny and Granda after their two-week holiday in France. "Doireann, where were you?" Granny asked.

"On the plane."

"No, on your holidays?" Granny meant.

"France," she replied, rather quietly, her left shoulder raised up, wanting to hide the shy look on her face that showed a little smile.

Mammy told them that, early last week, Doireann asked, "Mammy, when are we going to Granny and Granda's?"

As soon as they arrived home from their holidays a few hours ago, she'd asked the same question. Hence, the sudden visit! She arrived over on her pink tricycle and parked it at the gate.

"Well, hello, Doireann and Mammy. It's great to see you," Granda said. He was working in the garden.

"I didn't bring Teddy [Pink]," she told Granda as he gave her a big hug and a kiss on her cheek, that put a smile on her face.

As they stepped inside the hall door, Granda said, "Will we get Baby Bop?"

And with that, she sped off into the small bedroom. Granda helped her get Baby Bop out of the cot and picked up Teddy White and Teddy Brown also, before heading for the dining room.

"We are not staying long," she told Granny and Granda. Then she gave Baby Bop a hug and passed her over to her mammy, who was talking to Granny. Granda handed the teddies to Doireann.

"Ah, Teddies," she said, giving both of them massive hugs at the same time.

"Are you going to tell Granny and Granda about your holidays?" Mammy asked her. "She didn't eat great there. She met Holly from Gorey. And she was in the pool a lot and had to get out of the pool when the thunder and lightning came, of which there was a lot," Mammy reminded her. "She managed to swim on her own, wearing floating pads and loved jumping off a little wall into the pool for Mammy or Daddy to catch her."

She went for a cycle, sitting on the back of Daddy's bicycle because Mammy felt her bike swaying when Doireann was on it. They visited a small seaside town of major historical importance and listened to the music on the streets. Everywhere closed up between the hours of 3 p.m. and 7 p.m. "We laughed at the daily weather forecasts for France, with all the thunderstorms and torrential rain," Granny informed Mammy. "And here we were, getting a heatwave."

"It was still very warm over there, and the sun would come out for a couple of hours each day," Mammy said. "Oisín had a great time and met loads of friends from Wexford and Gorey also. He played in the pool and on the big slide during the day, before enjoying great entertainment in the evenings," they were told.

"We missed you," Granda told Doireann, who gave him a big smile when he hugged her again.

"She missed you and Granny, didn't you?" Mammy said to the now bashful-looking Doireann.

"What did you have to eat in France, Doireann. Did you have snails? Eh, what are they called? Escargots, that's it. Did you have any escargots?" Granda enquired.

"No, Granda. I didn't see any snails," he was told, and that was the end of that conversation.

Doireann handed Granda a present of chocolates that had nuts in it. Granny was given a beautiful large blue shawl, that had butterflies on it. She put the chocolates in the fridge for Granda, with Granny's help, who gave her a big thank you-hug.

Then she went out the back with Granny and Granda, followed soon after by Mammy. She played with the ceramic teapot, and Granda showed her how to fill it with water. She watered the potted plants and came for more water. Then, when she got wet, that was the end of the watering.

Granda showed her, their new ornamental geckos and butterflies on the walls around the old garage door. They then went and fetched her tricycle, and Doireann cycled it around the backyard.

"Granda, will you take me to Camolin Playground?" she asked.

"Of course, I will, someday soon, I promise," Granda told her.

Earlier she was showing off her top, and Granda asked, "Where did you get that beautiful top?"

"In my room," she replied. "Granda, do you put [sun] cream on?"

"Of course, I do," Granda said. (In truth, he rarely did.)

She had a bump and bruise on her forehead, and Mammy said she had them all over, whatever she was up to. They drove over to Spain one day, but it rained. "You got to see the same rain, all the same," joked Granda.

Mammy said the local French kids were well behaved, and the workers worked very hard.

Doireann cycled over to the side gate and called out to Mammy, "Are we right?" (Are we ready to go?)

Granda helped push her tricycle over the stones to the main gate while she pedalled, and then Mammy took over. "Goodbye, Doireann."

"Bye, Granda."

Then Granda shouted after them, "See you, Mammy."

"Goodbyeeeeeeeeeeeeeeeeeeeee," was the shout, from afar.

11 June

As they left Arklow, Granda asked Granny to send Mammy a text. Could she tell Doireann we will be about ten minutes late? They arrived fifteen minutes late because of the slow and heavy traffic that morning. Doireann was sitting on a neighbour's wall, holding Mammy's hand when they arrived. "I didn't bring Teddy [Pink]," she shouted.

"Ah, is she at home?" asked Granny.

Granda lifted her off the wall, saying, "Well, I love those socks."

She picked up her pink shoulder bag, and they went into the house. Mammy told Granny and Granda they'd cycled to the river Bann (Camolin) yesterday and had a great time playing in the water. Oisín had brought his friend along also.

"Keep working hard to pay for our pensions," Granda joked with Mammy as she left the house for work.

"Granda, I am staying with you," said Doireann.

He gave her a big hug, saying, "I'm delighted with that, pet."

Granny gave her a big hug also, after she repeated the same thing to Granny on entering the room.

"Doireann, can you check the toilet rolls for us?" Granny asked.

She ran into the toilet and opened the storage cabinet, before darting back. "Yes, we need one, we need two, we need three," she said, counting with her fingers at the same time.

Granny handed her three toilet rolls, and she carefully carried them into the toilet to replenish the stocks.

"Thanks for doing that," Granda told the now proud-looking Doireann.

Later on, when Granny caught her with the sink press door open, she said, "Stay away from that press, Doireann. That's not yours."

"Doireann didn't eat much of her breakfast this morning," Mammy had said earlier, when observing her remove the pepperoni from her lunchbox to eat it, there and then.

She was just about to start into her banana when she asked, "Granny, can I have porridge with fruit?"

Granny gave her porridge.

When finished, she moaned, "Oh, I'm full, and my tummy hurts."

She drove the push-along car for a while, before asking, "Granny, where are my other (miniature toy) cars?"

"They are in your toy box," Granny informed her.

Kneeling on the sofa, she began to assemble the cars on the sofa armrest, having located them in the exact place Granny had said she'd find them. One car fell to the ground. "Granny, get that," Her Majesty demanded.

"When did your last servant die?" enquired Granny.

Granny and Granda both suggested she should play with the cars on the floor. *Bang.* Another car fell to the ground. With an expression of annoyance, she climbed down off the sofa, in search of the two cars that had fallen to the floor and sped off somewhere.

Later, she went to Granda, who was at his workstation, and said, "Granny says your tea and toast is ready, Granda."

"Thanks, pet. I'll be there in a minute," he told her.

When Granda eventually walked into the kitchen, Doireann was standing with her back to the countertop drawers as if guarding something. When Granny said, "No one is to go near it," Granda asked, "What's in the drawer, Doireann?"

"Candles, and you are not to go near them (or else!)," was the order.

"Ah, they are for your birthday cake. When is your birthday, Doireann?"

"July, and I'll be three," she replied gleefully.

"A *big* three. Wow," Granda said emphatically, which brought a look of delight to her face. Granda told her that his birthday was in July also.

"Granny, is this a new fridge?" she asked, holding the fridge door wide open in search of something.

"No," said Granny, and she closed the fridge door.

A short while later, while holding the fridge door open, again, she asked, "Granda, where is the present I gave you?"

She was obviously looking for the French chocolates she had given him on Saturday, and now she couldn't find them. Hence, her earlier question to Granny about whether the fridge was new. Now, having deciphered Granny's response (no, it is not a new fridge), along with the knowledge that she had put the chocolates into that same fridge herself only two days ago, it was now time for a more direct line of inquiry—in other words, where's the bootie? The 'detective' asked the main suspect, Granda.

Granny appeared as a witness. "The chocolates are in there," she said under oath.

Then Granda, picking them up to prove this, told the court, "There's nuts in them, and they're not suitable for you," he added, indicating the detective.

Well, this did not go down well at all, at all. The courtroom had to be cleared because of an imminent meltdown!

A kiddie's TV programme, speedily switched on, came to the rescue, diverting any such potential threats. Doireann was very tired today, and Granny suggested not taking her out but, instead, letting her watch more telly, while sitting on the sofa wrapped up in a nice cuddly warm blanket.

Earlier, Granda had shown her a video and a photograph of her new Cambodian cousin Rosie on Facebook. Doireann sent her a message that Granda wrote for her:

Hi, Rosie.

This is your cousin Doireann in Ireland, and I was looking at your video and picture on Facebook in Ireland and wished that I could be in Cambodia to meet and talk to my lovely cousin and my two other cousins, your big brothers, Richie and Eddie.

My bro, Oisín and me met Richie and Eddie two years ago, and some day we will get to meet you.

Keep sending me your lovely pictures and your clothes are really nice.

Bye,
Your Irish cousin Doireann.

I is [am] with Granny and Granda in their house today.

She then asked to go to Camolin Playground. Earlier, there had been a sulk and a moan because Granny and Granda had said they were going there, but she didn't want "that one". They stuck to their guns, and eventually she came around.

When they were about to leave the house, Doireann complained that she didn't have pants. She was wearing a dress with a nappy instead. Granny looked in her shoulder bag and found a pair of shorts that she was really happy with. Granny got her a small box of raisins, and off they went.

Getting into her car seat, she asked, indicating the seat, "Is it a new one?"

"No, Doireann. It is the same one, only cleaner now," Granny told her.

As Granda drove to the playground, the sun appeared. It was yet another warm day, as it had been for well over a week here in the "sunny south-east". Doireann raced Granny to the playground after Granda parked the car in the Camolin Sports Grounds. Another mammy was holding her little girl, who had slipped on the steps leading up to the bigger slide and banged her nose, which must have been very sore. That mammy left with her little girl soon after, leaving Doireann to run about freely, while Granny and Granda had to scrub sticky dirt off some of the equipment using baby wipes.

They were annoyed at those people for leaving such a mess for others to clean up. "You would think those parents would prevent their children from drinking minerals or eating food or sweets whilst using the equipment," Granda complained. "That's why picnic tables have been provided."

Granda took photos of Doireann on the swings and slides. She then climbed and climbed up to the treehouse, with help from Granny and then from Granda, before she twisted down a spiralled pole, again with the usual helping hands. Initially, she had difficulty coordinating her feet appropriately onto the foot holders leading up to the treehouse. Granda provided her with some "scaffolding" (learning), before she was loudly heard to proclaim to the people of Ireland, "I did it. I did it." Then she insisted on sliding down a metal pole, explaining that, "Mammy told me to hold it tight." She slid down the pole. And then, "I did it. I did it," echoed out once again.

Then she was chased by Granny until she reached Granda and clung to his leg, while breathlessly laughing. Eventually, it was time to leave for home. She raced Granny back to the car, with the winner getting a tiny pack of raisins. "Doireann gets the raisins because she won," Granny announced, as she handed the champion her yum-yum prize.

Back in the house, Granny told Doireann, "You go and pick a book for me to read to you after I've changed [my clothes]."

Granda checked on Doireann as she browsed through her books. "You are getting a new Granny. She has gone into the bedroom to change," Granda told her, as well as the wall in front of her, such was the response.

Eventually, she selected one of her many books for Granny to read to her. Granny weighed her after she used the toilet and said, "You are two [stone], six [pounds]."

"I'm two, six," she shouted as she ran to inform Granda.

"Wow, you're a big girl—two stone six pounds, eh?"

"No, I'm two, six."

Earlier, she wanted to be measured at the "measuring wall", located at the divide between the dining room and kitchen. One side was for Oisín, and the other was for Doireann. They got her to remove her shoes and stand straight, with her heels against the wall and her head level. Granny, using a DVD cover, placed it level on Doireann's head and marked the wall with a pencil. She had grown by about two inches since October 2017. Granda then took some photos, as she pointed to her side of the wall.

It was lunchtime, and Granda asked her, "What are you having today?"

"Crackers and egg."

"Sure, you are crackers anyway," joked Granda.

She sat at the kitchen table and had crackers, egg, and half a banana to eat. Before she had finished, she tried to get out of her chair, offering to eat the rest of her food anyway, but Granny said no and settled her back into the chair.

Granny then told her that Mammy had said she was going to give her a bath and wash her hair also, tonight. "I love getting my hair washed," she said.

"I'm not mad about it, but Granda likes getting his hair washed," joked Granny.

Earlier, when Granny had put a plait in Doireann's hair, she could feel the extra loose strands of hair at the end of it and complained, saying, "It's too short." Granny had to redo it, so as to tuck the loose strands back up onto the plait. "The plait is longer now, Granny," a satisfied Doireann said.

While Granny was in the loo, Granda showed her today's photos on his phone. When Granny arrived back, she had Snowy, and both of them chased her into the kitchen before she about-turned and ran screaming towards the sitting room. As Granny came up the hall, Granda asked for Snowy and whispered, "You go into her, while Snowy and me hide."

When Granny went into the sitting room, she asked Doireann, "Where's Snowy?"

"I know," she said, now full of excitement.

She immediately dashed out of the sitting room and headed towards the kitchen. Then, all of a sudden, Snowy appeared from around a corner and there was a *massive scream* as she accelerated at full speed, past him. They all had a good laugh at that.

Granny put sun-blocking cream on her, before taking her out to the back garden to play, putting water into watering cans. Granny had put Doireann's wellies on and removed her shorts also.

Mammy phoned Granny to say she was walking down to them, as she didn't have Doireann's car seat. Initially on hearing Granny's phone ring, Doireann started to get ready, saying, "Mammy coming."

Granny said, "Mammy is walking, because she does not have a car seat for you."

Doireann responded with, "What's this?" She stood, with an alarmed-looking pose.

Just then, she ran to Mammy, now standing at the open side gate and gave her a big hug. Mammy couldn't delay because Oisín was due home shortly from school.

"Granda, I'm not staying now," he was told.

Granny and Granda bid her farewell as she toddled off home with her Mammy.

13 June

Doireann and Daddy walked across the playing field opposite Granny and Granda's house. As soon as she got closer, she spotted her pals waiting for her and pointed with a smile. Snowy, Baby Bop, Teddy White, and Teddy Brown were all looking out the sitting room window in anticipation of her imminent arrival.

Knock, knock, the hall door sounded.

Granda, who had been looking out another window, went to answer the hall door. A solitary Doireann stood outside, looking up at him, while Daddy hid. "Did you see your pals in the window?" Granda asked.

"She could see them from the grass area," answered Daddy.

She ran to fetch her pals from the sitting room windowsill, climbing up onto the sofa first, and then handed them to Granda.

"When I told your pals, you were coming soon, Doireann, they leapt out of the cot and ran to the window to see you coming," Granda told her.

She carried Baby Bop to the kitchen, and Granda carried the Teddies and Snowy. "Don't let Snowy chase me," she said.

On hearing this, Snowy saw the opportunity he'd waited for all morning. He took off and was not far behind the now screaming Doireann before she leapt up and into Granny's waiting arms.

When they admired her lovely red shoes, red hairclip, and purple dress, she said, "I don't have tights today because it's warm."

Granda wanted to take a photo, but she said, "No, Granda," and continued with, "I had porridge this morning."

"What else did you have to eat?" asked Granda.

"Porridge," was her curt reply.

She ate her raisins and then wanted her lunch (mincemeat and noodles), insisting on the plastic container being opened. Granny phoned Mammy about this as she started eating the cold mincemeat and noodles.

"You will get a sore tummy," Granda warned her as she continued to eat, until suddenly, she stopped.

Mammy told Granny she hasn't stopped eating since she'd come home. Granny went to put the lunch away, but Doireann objected, screaming, *"No."*

Granny told her, "It has to be left in the fridge, or it will go bad."

To get her mind off the food, Granda asked, "Will I put the telly on for you, Doireann?"

"Baby Love?" she said, which was a Supremes CD she liked, before she changed her mind again. "No, eh, no." And then she hurried her thoughts. "The telly," she decided.

Granda showed her how to correctly hold the remote control to switch on the telly. Then with the other remote control, he showed her how to select a TV station. She sat with Baby Bop and watched the children's channel. Granny had ordered a book, on Wexford County Council's Library website ages ago. That morning, she received a text from the library telling her it had arrived.

"Doireann, will you remind me, that I have to get bread and milk in the shop when we go to the library later to collect a book?" Granny asked.

"Okay Granny," she said, with the usual nod of the head.

A little while later, she ran into Granda, who was at his workstation. "Granda, your breakfast is ready."

"Ah, thanks very much, pet."

"Granda, what are you doing?"

"I am writing a story about you," Granda told her.

Standing there with a twisted mouth and looking a bit embarrassed, she said, "You don't have to do that, Granda."

"Ah sure, you are the best girl in the whole world. And when you are older, you can read your book and say, 'My granda wrote this.'"

Then Granda asked her if she had been at crèche yesterday.

"Yes."

"Who did you play with?" he asked.

"Ava."

"What is the name of your new cousin?" Granda asked, checking to see if she remembered the name of her Cambodian cousin, who she had seen on Facebook on Monday.

"Oisín," she said.

"Oisín is your brother," Granny told her.

Granda repeated his question. "Who is your new cousin in Cambodia?"

With no answer, Granda reminded her, that she had been looking at her on the computer the other day.

Still no answer.

"Rosie," Granda answered for her and then got her to say the name *Rosie*. And when she said it, Granda said, "Good girl; well done."

Granny mentioned, she had to collect a library book, and Granda turned to Doireann and said, "We will park the car in that place in Gorey, where we can do a '*Wheeeeeeeeeeeeeeeeeeeeeeeeeeeeeeeeeeeeeeeeeeeeeeeeeeee eeeeeeeeeee.*'"

And she agreed with a grin.

After his breakfast, Granda went into his room to catch up on some work before they left for the library.

"Granda, can you mind Doireann, while I use the loo?" Granny asked.

"What are you doing?" Doireann asked Granda.

"I am working on my [computer] files," Granda told her and showed her what he was doing.

"Can I do that, Granda?" she enquired.

"When you are bigger."

"I'm bigger now," she ventured. "Can I take a photo of you, Granda?"

"Of course, you can." He picked up his phone and explained to her how it was done.

Click, sounded the phone camera as she took a photo of Granda.

"You take one of me, Granda," she said.

"Hold your face up straight. Closer. Big smile. Ah, lovely," said Granda. And *click*, sounded the phone camera.

"I am ready now to go to the library," Granny shouted.

"Okay, in a minute," said Granda. "I just want to use the loo."

They left the house and walked to the car, which was parked on the road. As Doireann got into the car, some neighbours gave her a big wave and said hello, as they drove slowly past. She went all quiet and just looked.

As they pulled away, Doireann said, "Granny, I have a present for you."

"What is it?" Granny asked and was shown a soother.

"Oh, is that for me. Thank you?" said Granny.

Granda, given the same present, thanked her as well.

Granda picked up the small blue cloth and flung it over his shoulder, his eyes firmly fixed on the road ahead. It landed on Doireann, who immediately flung it at Granny. She and Granny flung it at each other a few more times, to sounds of continuous laughter. Then Granny hid her face behind the cloth, before laying it on her head like a cap. This caused Doireann to burst out laughing. "That's funny," she barely managed to tell Granny after catching her breath.

The wind was getting noticeably louder and stronger, as had been forecasted. "Are we on a windy [breezy] *windy* [bendy] road, Doireann, or is it a *windy* windy road?" joked Granda.

There was no comment, only Granny defending her, saying, "Don't mind your Granda!"

As Granda drove into the outdoor car park close to Dunnes Stores, he had to keep slightly to the right to avoid a customer loading the boot of her car. Next thing, a car appeared around a bend, traveling at breakneck speed, causing Granda to break suddenly so as to avoid a definite collision with the oncoming car, whose very young driver sped away quickly, realising his error. "Slow down, you-idiot," Granda shouted out, mindful of his choice of words and his attentive audience.

"Oisín uses that word, *idiot*," Doireann announced, not realising the seriousness of what had happened.

"Women sitting in the speeding car got a terrible fright," Granny said.

"He shouldn't be speeding in a car park," Granda grumbled angrily.

"*Wheeeeeeeeeeeeeeeeeeeeeeeeeeeeeeeeeeeeeeeeeeeeeeeeeeeeeeeeeeeeeeeeeeee*," they managed to recite as they drove down into the underground car park and parked in a family parking bay.

Doireann took Teddy White out of the car and hugged him, saying, "I love Teddy White," before handing him to Granny to carry. They quickly visited Noddy and Minnie. "Welcome to Toyland," Noddy announced as they headed past and up the travelator.

Doireann wanted to walk on the travelator on her own, but Granda made her hold his hand. When they reached the top, Granda, pointed to the "guidelines" for kids that showed an adult holding a child's hand. When he read it out loud for her, she nodded in agreement.

She searched the sweet vendors, grouped together and opposite the elevator lifts, before taking one of the small white paper bags. "Do you want to use it as a glove?" Granda asked her.

"No," was the reply.

"Let me show you a little trick," Granda said as he took the paper bag from her.

Granda opened the paper bag and held it with one hand, between his thumb and index finger. Then with his other hand, he pretended to throw a coin in the air. Next, with the paper bag held out, Granda looked skywards for the pretend coin. *Click*, the bag sounded as the pretend coin fell into the paper bag. Granda was able to make this click sound by twisting his two fingers, giving the impression that a coin had dropped into it.

Doireann was over in a flash to inspect the paper bag. "Where is it? I can't see it, Granda," she complained.

Every time Granda repeated the trick, she still searched for the missing coin. Granda explained the trick, showing her how it was done. Then she wanted to try. Firstly, she held the paper bag upside down with one hand to drop the pretend coin into her other hand. Secondly, she threw the pretend coin up into the air and moved around while looking skywards and holding the paper bag out to catch the falling pretend coin. The tricky bit for her was getting the paper bag to click. She tried it loads of times, with Granda saying, "Practice makes perfect, Doireann, so keep practicing it."

She pressed the lift button for the first floor, before they headed towards the library, exiting through the magic doors. "*Wheeeeeeeeeeeeeeeee eeeeeeeeeeeeeeeeeeeeeeeeeeeeeeeeeeeeeeee,*" sounded Doireann as she ran down the ramp by the courthouse into Granda's arms. As she ran back, Granda plodded very noisily behind her, in hot pursuit, before she reached Granny. Screaming, she leapt into Granny's arms, now safe from the clutches of the noisy monster behind her.

Not interested in the pictures' gallery just inside the foyer's magically opened library doors, she sped down towards the kiddie's book section. Granny went to collect her book, while Granda read a book about numbers that Doireann had selected. Granny arrived back as they were on number five. Granny struggled to put the book, along with her purse, into her handbag. Doireann was using two hands to hold her next selected book, as she sat and waited.

Seeing Granny was busy, Granda, eager to get a quick read of the newspapers, offered Teddy White to Doireann, saying, "Here, Doireann, hold this until Granny is ready."

"My hands are full," he was bluntly told.

"Now, Granda, you've been put in your place," said Granny, who was now laughing, while both of them were stunned by this 2-year-old madam.

Granda did get to read the daily newspapers before Doireann arrived up to say she wanted to go.

As they left the library, Granny asked, "What do we have to get in the shop, Doireann?"

She thought for a moment before saying, "Bread and milk."

"Very good," Granny said.

"*Wheeeeeeeeeeeeeeeeeeeeeeeeeeeeeeeeeeeeeeeeeeeeeeeeeeeeeeeeeeeeeeeeeeee,*" was repeated, but only after Granny delayed Doireann's run to let an elderly lady and another mammy pass by first.

"Ready, Doireann, go," said Granny.

But she soon stopped her dash, to pull up her dress and then her nappy and then the nappy again and so on. It was obviously annoying her, and Granny tried to fix it so it wouldn't slip down. It was one of those pants style nappies, and the fact that it was wet didn't help matters either.

When they got the bread and milk, they headed straight for the car. She fell asleep on the way home. When they parked in the driveway, Granny offered to stay in the car with her, and Granda brought the bread and milk into the house. Granda went to the car after twenty-five minutes, to find both Granny and Doireann asleep. Granny then woke up and went into the house, while Granda took over, sitting in the back seat with Sleeping Beauty. He took some photos for good measure.

He was unable to contact Granny because her phone was obviously buried deep in her handbag—or suitcase as Granda sometimes jokingly called it. Eventually, when Granny did arrive back to the car, Doireann woke up after a marathon seventy-five-minute sleep and was in good form. Granny carried her into the house and laid her down on the sofa, before covering her with some blankets.

Lunch was ready soon after, and Granny carried her to the kitchen table to enjoy the rest of her mincemeat and noodles, followed by loads of toast and a cup of tea. Granny changed her very wet nappy and gave her a pair of tights and a jacket to wear because her dress got wet also.

"Granda, you are eating too much," Doireann kept saying at the table. She mentioned her birthday again and said to Granny, "It's in July."

Granny said, "Granda's birthday is in July as well."

Her response to that was, "He doesn't look very happy! Granda," she asked, "Will you take me to Enniscorthy someday?"

"Doireann, did you know, there are eight days in a week? You have Monday, Tuesday, Wednesday, Thursday, Friday, Saturday, Sunday, and Someday," joked Granda.

Mammy had arrived and was chatting to Granny. Earlier, Granny had put two plaits in Doireann's hair, and when she showed Granda, he'd taken a photo of them, saying, "They are beautiful, Doireann."

"Can I take a photo of Mammy?" she asked Granda.

"Of course, you can," he said and handed her the mobile phone.

She then showed Granda her "photography work" and asked, "Can I take a photo of Granny?"

"Of course, you can," was his reply.

A while later, Granda noticed her looking at her upside-down empty water bottle at the kitchen sink. "Is your watering-can empty?" joked Granda.

"Yes. How do you close it?" she asked.

"I am leaving it there to dry out at the moment," Granda told her. "There's water in your other bottle."

"Can I have some water, Granda?" she asked.

"Of course, you can."

He gave her the bottle, and she took a drink. "Would you like some more?" he offered.

"Just a little," she said and stood looking at Granda after taking another sip.

"Do you want more?" Granda asked.

"No, Granda. We are going now."

Granny and Granda stood at the hall door as they all said their goodbyes. A minute later, *knock, knock*, the hall door sounded. Granny answered the door and found Doireann standing there.

"Granny, it's time to take the clothes off the line. It's raining. Goodbye," she said, before darting back out to Mammy's car as Granny bellowed, "Thanks for that, Doireann."

"She has left her soother behind," Granda told Granny after he spotted it.

"Where was it?" Granny enquired.

"On the bed."

"That's my one," Granny said, meaning Doireann's spare soother that was kept in their house.

CHAPTER 16

World War III

15 June

Doireann arrived late this morning (9.35 a.m.) with Daddy. He was in a hurry and couldn't stay. "Wave goodbye. Doireann," Granda said, and she waved at Granny and Granda.

"No, Doireann. Wave goodbye to Daddy."

Daddy gave her a kiss and went out the door. She ran after him, clung to his leg, and was upset.

When Granny and Granda eventually coaxed her into the house, Granny told her, "We will take you to meet Uncle Tony for his birthday treat later."

"No," was her blunt reply, still upset and moaning.

"Let me have a look at your lovely new runners?" Granny asked.

As soon as Granda got up from his seat to also have a look, he was bluntly and rather loudly told, "Don't take a picture."

Granda "ran for cover" instead!

Daddy had told them she hadn't had a whole lot to eat this morning but had slept well. Granny made toast for her to eat while sitting at the table and having a little chat. "Where's Teddy Pink these days?" Granda asked her.

"She's having a rest."

"That's a lovely buggy you brought this morning, Doireann," Granda said, trying to keep the conversation going.

"It's a trolley," he was told.

"Oops, sorry," said Granda, as he looked for a small hole to crawl into!

She went into the bedroom and reappeared with Teddy White and Teddy Brown, before Baby Bop arrived, under her arm, next. She put the teddies into the trolley and wheeled them around. "Are they helping you with your shopping?" Granda enquired, and she nodded.

"You push the trolley, Granda?" she requested.

He did, walking at right angles. "I don't think this is for me, Doireann," Granda pleaded.

"Look, Granda, I can do it," she said, and she proudly pushed the shopping trolley around, with the teddies on board.

"Very good," Granda told her.

"I would love a trolley like yours," Granny said.

"We will get you a big one Granny," she told her, holding her arms out at the same time as if measuring the width of Ireland.

As she took the spare soother out of the kitchen press, Granda looked at Granny and whispered, "I wonder did she bring her own today?"

"Look, Granda, I brought it," she told him, holding it aloft, having just retrieved it from her shoulder bag. Granda worried, if the codebreaker now had the house wired, also!

"Ah, very good," said Granda.

"Granda, would you like a soother?" she asked.

"Yes, Doireann," said Granda, "but it would have to be a *big, huge one*," he said emphatically, observing the big grin on her face. "Then, we could all go around making sucking sounds," he suggested.

Still grinning, she said, "No, Granda."

Granny explained why she wanted to go to Courtown and meet up with her brother, Tony, for his seventy-third Birthday. They would visit a small restaurant there, for coffees.

"I don't like Tony. I don't want to go to Courtown," Doireann insisted.

"Okay, we won't go to Courtown," Granny said and walked away.

A few minutes later, Doireann had a quick change of heart. "I think I would like to go to Courtown, Granny," she said. "Granda, would you like a cup of tea?"

"Yes, I would love one," he said to Doireann.

Granda was then handed a cup of tea from her plastic tea service.

"Thank you," said Granda. "Oh, that is a lovely cup of tea," he added after a sip.

"I had a cup of tea and a cup of coffee," she said with a smile, rubbing her tummy.

"That's brill," said Granda.

When she came looking for Granda's "empty" cup, he asked her for another cup of tea.

"Okay Granda," she said, with a grimace on her face.

She then gave Granny another cup of tea also, before arriving back with Granda's second cuppa. She got Granda to finish his cuppa.

"Oh, I am full. My tummy is sore," Granda said as she collected the cups. "Are you going to wash the cups now?" he asked.

With another grimace, she muttered, "Well, I think I'm too old," or something that sounded like that.

"Can I see Rosie?" she asked, wanting to see her new Cambodian cousin on Facebook again.

Granda let her help with switching on Facebook. They both looked at Rosie's video.

"I want the other one," she demanded.

"There is no other video, only a photo," Granda said.

"It's not," she moaned.

"It is. Look," said Granda, showing her the photo, before switching back to the video again.

Granda started to read the message they'd both sent to Rosie last Wednesday. "I don't want to hear it," she moaned.

Granda sent Rosie another short message again today before logging off, while Doireann went and asked Granny to switch on the telly, where she sat and watched a children's station until they were ready to leave.

Soon after, they headed out the door, but Doireann started to moan again, saying she didn't want Courtown. She kept it up in the car, and Granny told her, "I have made arrangements with Tony, and we are going."

She continued moaning and groaning. "I don't want to talk to Tony," she said.

Granny told her, "Okay, you don't have to talk to him."

Next it was, "I don't want to talk to you, Granny."

"Right. Don't talk to Doireann, Granny, and I won't either," Granda said as he drove along quietly.

A while later, her attitude changed, and she became a little bit more sociable.

They collected Uncle Tony at his house and drove the short distance to Courtown village and parked next to the Pebble Stones Restaurant. Granny had gone into Tony's house to warn him what to expect from the little monster, who was safely "chained" in the back seat of the car. She held Granda's hand as they walked towards and into the restaurant, with Granny and the "invisible Tony". Granny and Doireann each choose a chocolate and marshmallow cake called Rocky Road. Granny had coffee, and Doireann had a juice. Tony had a cappuccino and a sponge cake with cream. Granda had a coffee only. Teddy White didn't have anything at all. Granny put two candles, a number seven and a number three into Tony's cake and lit them. Doireann blew them out twice for Uncle Tony. Granda took some photos, and eventually Doireann came around and started talking to the now "visible Tony".

They dropped Tony back to his house afterwards, where Doireann gave him loads of waves and blew him loads of kisses from the safety of the car. She was very much like this with strangers. And if she didn't want to talk to someone, she wouldn't, no matter who it was. While in the restaurant, she sat on the very large window-sill and enjoyed looking out. On the way home, they visited the Lidl store in Gorey to return an unopened box of unwanted knee bandages. Granda took a photo of Doireann as she shopped with the store's toy shopping trolley for children.

"Granda takes photos all the time," said Granny when back in the car.

Doireann responded, "He shouldn't because his battery won't work!"

As they continued their journey home, Doireann said in a moany voice, "I want to go back to Courtown and see the big boat." This was a very large boat on the side of the main road into Courtown.

Ignoring that request, Granny and Granda encouraged her to sing the "Doggie in the Window" song instead.

Back home, she moaned again when told it was time for lunch but ate all her noodles and mincemeat, anyway. Granny was surprised at this because of the big Rocky Road cake that had passed through her mouth earlier. Granny gave her a small box of raisins as promised, while she and Granda finished their salad lunch at the table also. Earlier, she had asked for some popcorn, and Granny had to make it for her. Granny then took her out to the back garden to play with the water until Mammy arrived, to collect her.

A couple of hours later, Mammy and Doireann arrived back to Granny and Granda's house, just before 6 p.m. "I'm on a sleepover," Doireann announced as she stood holding Teddy Pink, who was wearing a dress Doireann had worn in Cambodia in July 2016.

She put Teddy down for a sleep in the cot and, later, went in to sing her a song. She then went searching for her grand-uncle Tony's birthday candles to show Mammy. "Granny," she called from the bedroom, after taking Teddy out of the cot.

Granny went into the bedroom.

"Look, Granny," she said as Teddy crawled on the floor like a little baby.

After running around for about twenty minutes, she said, "I want to go out and play."

"It's cold outside," Granny warned.

"I want to go out," she persisted.

Granny said, "Okay, only for a short while then."

No sooner was she outside than she wanted to go back into the house, saying, "I'm cold."

Granny put on a DVD, *Barney the Dinosaur*, to get her to relax before bedtime. Then, just before bedtime, she said, "Granny read *Hissing Hattie*" [Ladybird] and *"Winnie the Pooh"* [Disney].

While Granny was reading the books to her, Granda appeared with his back scratcher. It had a small hand on a long pole that Granda called "the long arm of the law". Having shoved the pole up his sleeve and hidden his own hand, Granda held out the small hand and said, "Doireann, do you want to shake Granda's hand?"

She got a terrible fright, and Granda apologised immediately.

Granny continued reading her the stories. It wasn't long before she went into the sitting room to say night-night to Granda.

"Listen, pet. I'm sorry for giving you a fright," he said.

She replied, "It's all right, Granda."

Granda gave her a big cuddle and said, "You are the best girl in the whole world. Have a good sleep now and pleasant dreams. Night-night now, and night-night, Teddy."

"Night-night, Granda," Teddy said as Doireann helped her move her arm at the same time.

There was an immediate silence.

Oisín arrived for his sleepover also, at about 10.30 p.m. He had been at his Daddy's fortieth birthday party in Gorey.

"That was a great match earlier, Portugal v Spain," Granda told Oisín.

"Hold on," Oisín said. "I bet it finished '2 – 3' to Spain," he predicted.

"No, it was a draw, 3-all, and Ronaldo scored a hat-trick," Granda informed him as Oisín's head fell into his hands.

"What were the goals like?" he asked.

"The first was a peno" (penalty), "and the second was from a cross into the box. The third goal was pure magic, from a free kick on the edge of the penalty box," said Granda. "Ronaldo took it, and the ball went over the wall and dipped into the corner of the goal. A superb goal," he added.

"Sure, Messi is much better and will score better goals than that," insisted Oisín, letting it be known where his loyalties lay!

They watched the end of a movie called *The Flag*, starring Pat Short, and Oisín got lots of laughs from it. He then watched the highlights of an earlier game between Egypt v Uruguay. "What was the result, Granda? I don't want the score," said Oisín.

"Uruguay won," Granda told him.

Oisín was not impressed with that result and not happy, that his favourite "Liverpool and Egyptian" player, Mo Salah, was left on the bench for that match. (For the record, the score was 0 - 1.)

Before he retired to bed, Oisín told Granny and Granda he'd enjoyed the party and had pizza; as he drank his cup of milk. "Granny, are you going to tell me a [bedtime] story," joked Oisín.

"I am not," said Granny. "Now get into bed and sleep. And good night," she said.

"I hope you have a nice 'Martin Luther King [dream]," Granda suggested.

Granny then sneaked into the now fast asleep Doireann to attach the plastic chain to her soother and pyjamas.

16 June (the following morning and World War III)

"Granny, Granny," sounded the quiet voice of Doireann at 6.45 a.m. Or was it Teddy Pink calling?

Granda went into the bedroom and, seeing it was Doireann, lifted her out of the cot. He carried her into Granny and Granda's bed, where she nestled in between them with a big smile on her face. Granda then went to get Teddy Pink out of the cot, but Doireann said, "She is asleep." So, Granda had to cradle Teddy Pink as he carried her from the cot. He then gently put Teddy in beside Doireann, mindful she was still fast asleep.

"Ah, what's Granda at?" Granny asked.

"Did you have a Martin Luther King, last night?" Granda asked.

She nodded. "Teddy Pink had a dream about Doireann," she said.

It wasn't long before she got up with Granny and went into the kitchen to have fruit. She visited Granda, who was still in bed. "Did you have your brekkie?" he asked her.

"No."

"What are you having?" he continued.

"Porridge."

"Oh, porridge with fruit?" asked Granda.

Off she went. And next thing, World War III broke out. Doireann told Granny she wanted fruit with her porridge.

"No, you will get a pain in your tummy," Granny warned.

When Doireann told Granda she hadn't had brekkie, she forgot to mention that she did have fruit, though.

Eventually she ate her porridge and then sat to look at the telly. She moved her chair up close to the TV and, in a kneeling position, stuck her face right into the screen.

"That is dangerous. You will damage your eyes," Granny warned her, but she persisted.

Oisín got out of his bed and tried to talk sense to her, but she wouldn't listen.

Granda got up and as he entered the dining room, she still had her face stuck into the TV screen, while telling Granny, "I can see it better like this."

"Doireann, you are not to talk back to Granny like that. And do as you're told, or I will switch off the telly," Granda warned her.

As she held her face downwards and her lower lip upwards, there was silence, until Granny said, "Ah, Granda."

"I mean it. I will switch off the telly if you don't do as you're told, Doireann," Granda insisted.

Problem sorted, and she sat back, away from the telly.

They then had your normal brotherly/sisterly spats.

Later on, Oisín sat on the bed with Granda, and they talked about different things. They were soon joined by Doireann, who sat on the other side. Granda put his arms around them both and gave them big cuddles. When they got bored, they left.

"Ah, Oisín, leave that for Doireann," Granny told him, meaning her TV seat.

While Doireann sat at the kitchen table finishing her breakfast, Oisín sat in her TV chair, and she was not having it. She continued to kick up until he moved.

Later, Granda went into the dining room, only to see her and Oisín sitting side by side on "her" TV chair, watching the telly as if nothing ever happened. Mammy phoned Granny for an update, and said she was on the way over, and it was okay for Oisín to walk home then.

Doireann didn't want to go for a wash and screamed and kicked, but Granny made her. When Granny had finished giving her a wash, she darted all over the house with her little Hello Kitty ball and a magic bouncy ball with flashing lights. Next, she played with her larger yellow ball with the red polka dot spots. Lionel Missy wanted to play outside, but Granny told her it was too wet.

"I want to go out," she insisted with a moany voice.

"Let her go out and find out for herself," Granda suggested and opened the back door.

So, with bare feet, out she went and agreed it was wet.

"Is the grass wet?" asked Granda, seeing the obvious.

She put her hands on the grass and decided then she wanted to go back inside.

A while later, she came looking for Granda and found him at his workstation. "What are you doing, Granda?" she asked.

"I am writing a story about you," he told her.

Marching off in anger, she said, "I don't want that."

"What is Granda doing?" asked Granny.

"He is reading a story about me," she replied.

Granda went and said to her, "You told Granny I am reading a story about you when I am not. I'm writing a story about you, and it goes like this." Granda started to read his story. "'Once upon a time, a little girl called Doireann and her bro, Oisín, came for a sleepover with Granny and Granda, and when they went to bed there was peace in the world. The next morning, World War III broke out. I think I will have to call you Donald and your big bro Trump," joked Granda.

There was no reaction.

When Mammy called to the house, she said she had enjoyed the party. She spoke about the noise of the traffic outside on the main street in Camolin, saying it was continuous every day and into the weekends. "The sooner the new M11 bypass is opened the better," she said.

Mammy and Granny helped Doireann gather up her things.

"Granda, we are off now."

"Ah, are you going now?" Granda asked, and Doireann just nodded.

18 June

Granny and Granda didn't go to the gym this morning and sat around waiting for Doireann to arrive. She was very late, arriving with her Daddy at 9.45 a.m., in her vest on this cool morning.

She sat up on the sofa and started to look at a book. "Is that a new boook, Doireann?" Granda asked.

"It's not a boook; it's a book," Granda was bluntly told. "My shoes are dirty, and Daddy said it happened in the forest," she said.

Daddy was hurrying off as she said goodbye.

She told Granny she had had her breakfast this morning when asked but continued with, "Can I have a banana?"

"We've no bananas, Doireann. Sorry about that," Granny said.

Granda was at his workstation now and, on hearing the conversation, started to sing, "We have no bananas today," over and over.

"What's Granda saying?" Granny pretended to protest, within earshot of Doireann.

"Stop saying that," said a very angry Doireann as soon as she appeared outside Granda's room, staring in at him with a face like a bulldog chewing a wasp.

They all agreed to go to Enniscorthy playground later as soon as Granda cut the small patch of grass out the front. "I will put a top on Doireann," said Granny.

"No, I don't want to [it]," she told Granny angrily.

"Doireann, its cold and you can't go like that," Granny insisted.

"I don't want to," she retorted.

"Okay, don't wear it, and sure we'll stay at home then," said Granda with a shrug of his shoulders.

"I will wear it, only to Enniscorthy," she then offered.

"That's that sorted then," said Granda.

A while later, Granda sat beside Granny, handed his phone to Doireann, and asked, "Take a photo of us?"

Click, sounded the camera as she pressed the button.

Because Granda was the only one in the photo, he handed her the phone again, saying, "Here, Doireann. Try to get the two of us. Hold it up and wait until you see the two of us."

"Can you see the two of us?" asked Granda.

"Yes," she said as she clicked the button and handed the camera to Granda.

"Now, can you take a photo of our heads?" Granda laughed on seeing the two headless creatures in front of him.

"No. I don't want to," she told him as she stood with her lip pursed up and face bent down. There ended the photography lesson for the day.

Granny and Doireann played with some toys, including the little miniature cars, until Granda arrived back in after cutting the grass. "Are we ready to go?" he asked.

They both started to get ready.

"I'll see you there," Doireann said as she sat pushing her toy car.

"Are you driving yourself, Doireann?" asked a surprised-looking Granda.

"Yes," he was told.

"Okay then."

"Can we bring the football, Granda. Can we play football there?" she enquired.

"Yeah, bring your football," Granda told her.

"Granda, put your top on," she reminded the now bare-chested Granda, who had just removed his sweat-soaked T-shirt.

"I will in a few minutes, Doireann. I am still very hot after mowing the grass," Granda explained.

"Granny, what's that on Granda's back?" enquired Dr Doireann.

"It's a little mole," the doctor was informed.

"Has Granny got a drink [to bring]?" she asked Granda as he hurriedly recorded these notes on his laptop.

"Maybe you could remind Granny," suggested Granda.

Then she took a photo of Granda, but it was her shoes that came out. She called them her princess shoes. "Can I sit in your [workstation] chair?" she asked.

"Of course, you can."

"Granda, can you spin me around?" she continued.

As she then sat comfortably in the swivel chair, Granda wheeled it out of the carpeted bedroom and onto the wooden hall floor, before giving it loads of noisy spins. She had a huge smile on her face, enjoying every minute of it.

"Granda, you are now starting something she will want all the time," warned Granny.

Doireann took some more photos before they were all ready to go. They headed off out to the car and drove to Enniscorthy.

"Where's Enniscorthy?" she asked.

"It's in Wexford," Granny said.

As Granda drove the car, a fierce farm smell of sewage seeped into the car, even though the windows were all closed, with the air conditioning running. It came from a farm animal transporter truck with extract fans, and sure no wonder the smell was so strong. Opening the car windows made the smell worse.

They took an immediate left turn to the playground and got rid of the smell at the same time. Doireann had a great time playing on the playground equipment.

After about an hour, they left for home. "Did you sing Happy Birthday to Daddy yesterday?" Granny asked her.

"No."

"What age is he?" continued Granny.

Silence.

"Is he 140?" suggested Granda.

Then Granny let on she had just remembered. "Oh, that's it. He's 40," she said.

Then this idiot of a driver was heading straight for them, having overtaken another car. It was as if they weren't there at all. Granda literally sat on the horn as he drove past.

"What happened?" asked a startled Doireann.

They explained what the other driver had done and why it was so dangerous.

"If he had hit us, I would have been very sad!" she told them.

Granda then sounded a few more beeps when there were no other cars on the road, much to her delight and excitement.

"Can you touch the sky, Granny?" she asked.

"No."

"Can you, Granda?"

"No."

"My daddy can," she said.

"He must be a skyscraper," suggested Granda.

"What's he saying?" she whispered to Granny. "Granda is silly," joked Doireann.

"What?" joked Granda back.

Granda started to sing, making up the words to his song as he went along.

"Sing the doggie one," she wanted.

"How much is that doggie in the window?" sang Granda.

"Louder," she said, with Granny objecting.

Granda roared out a few words of the song, before suddenly stopping. There was silence in the car, before Doireann started to laugh.

Earlier, at the playground, Granda had had occasion to ask her, "Who is the terrible rebel?"

"I am," she'd proudly told him.

When back home, she sat up at the table and had her lunch with Granny and Granda. She had spag-ball and then tea and toast. She was obviously hungry after her workout in the playground. She loved running, and Granda took a few photos of her in her stride.

Granda finished up his lunch quickly and went to cut the grass out the back. Granny stayed with Doireann as she watched the telly. Granny sat with her at one stage because she said she wasn't well.

"The sun is out, and it's nice in the garden," Granda said on entering the house to use the toilet.

"Okay, let's go out," Doireann suggested.

But Granny was hesitant because of the mower noise, which Doireann didn't like. "I will lower the noise of it," Granda suggested. Then, Granny agreed to take her out and play hide-and-seek, while Granda mowed away.

Then Mammy and Daddy called, and Granny let them in the side gate. Doireann continued to play with Mammy and then Daddy, before leaving soon after.

CHAPTER 17

Neenah, Neenah, Neenah

20 June

Granny's text to Mammy read, "We will be twenty minutes late home from the gym."

Mammy and Doireann arrived over to Granny and Granda's house at about 9.30 a.m. Mammy walked on the road, watching Little Red Riding Hood (Doireann) trudge through the wet field opposite the house. Her wellies had flashing lights as she walked.

"I didn't take Teddy Pink," she told Granda, as she entered the house.

"Where is she?" Granda asked her.

"She is resting." As she struggled to remove her wellies she explained, "They are stuck."

"Do you want a hand?" Granda asked.

She nodded, and Granda "gave her his hand." And when she held on to it, he laughed out loud. Granda removed her boots and asked, "Where will I put them?"

"In the hall."

"Okay."

A little while later, Doireann came to find him. "Granda, your toast and tea's ready," Doireann told him as he worked at his workstation.

"Ah, thanks very much, pet," he said.

As Granda tried to pass her, she said, "Don't stand on my toes, Granda."

"I won't," he replied.

Then she dashed off ahead of Granda, shouting, "Bet you can't catch my toes."

"That's a lovely pigtail, eh, sorry, plait, Doireann. Is it a David Platt?" Granda asked her, referring to a former England footballer.

"No, a plait," he was bluntly told.

She sat up at the table also to have her tea and toast that Granny had made for her. Looking at Granda's toast, she said, "Is that too much?"

"No, I have a bigger mouth," Granda told her. "Did I tell you, the outside" (sensor-controlled) "light kept going on and off lots of times last night? Also, because of the strong winds, the dragon" (a wooden ornament) "was swinging back and forth setting off the light sensor?" he informed her.

"Where, Granda?" a now very interested Doireann asked.

Granda opened the back door and pointed to the dragon and the light.

Every time she was in the kitchen after this, she would say, "I can't see the dragon."

Eventually Granny put her standing on a chair, held her hand, and pointed the dragon out to her. She still could not see the dragon. Granny took her outside and lifted her right up to the dragon. "Now there it is," Granny said.

"Ah, I thought it was a bird, Granny, in the tree," she said.

"Ah, no, pet. And there's the light and the sensor also," Granny told her.

"What is a sensor, Granny?" she enquired.

Then Granny thought about the other light sensor for the light in what they termed the cubbyhole off the kitchen and took her back into the house. There, Granny was better able to explain what a light sensor was. "You know when you have to wave your hand for the light to come on?" Granny started to explain.

Before she could finish, Doireann indicated she knew. In other words, the "penny dropped".

"Granda, she wants to look at the teddy, eh no, the telly, when you have finished eating," Granny informed him.

"You can look at me instead," Granda offered.

"Which is better, Granda's face or the telly?" Granny asked her.

"The telly," was her immediate reply.

Granny showed her some new books she'd bought in a charity shop the other day and then had to sit with her to read one. "Only one, Doireann, because I have some work to do," Granny told her.

When Granny finished reading the story, she wanted another, and Granny protested at first but then gave in. When Granny finished the second story, Doireann said she wanted to watch some telly and turned the rocking chair around. She shouted out, "I can't hear it."

"I know," said Granny, a little annoyed at her attitude. "I have the kettle switched on. And because it's noisy, it's hard to hear the telly right now," she explained. Granny then increased the TV volume for her.

Earlier, Granny and Granda had said to her, "We have to go to Tesco's and the library later."

"Noooooh," she'd said, with her head bent. "I don't want to."

"Well, Granny, maybe she can help us with some shopping. And when we go to the library, we can do the, '*Wheeeeeeeeeeeeeeeeeeeeeeeeeeeeeeeeeeeeeeee eeeeeeeeeeeeeeeee*,' as we park the car and do the other, '*Wheeeeeeeeeeeeeeeeee eeeeeeeeeeeeeeeeeeeeeeeeeeeeeeeeeeeeeee*,' at the library," Granda had suggested.

Just then, she got out of her chair and was talking to Granny. Granda ran up and sat in her rocking chair and started rocking it.

"It's going to fall," Doireann said as she looked sternly at Granda.

"I am only playing with you, and sure you are my best girl," Granda told her as he gave her back the chair to watch Barney on the telly.

Barney was singing, and Granda started dancing, moving his hands at the same time. "This is what I showed you the other day, Doireann," Granda said.

"That's not music, Granda," she protested, meaning pop music, as Barney sang, "One, two, three, four, five, six, seven, eight, nine, ten."

Later, Granda took photos of the two measuring walls—one designated to her and the other to Oisín to record their steady growth. Grabbing a hardback book, she asked for the pencil and wanted Granda to measure her again.

It was time to head into Gorey, and she turned the telly off; put her red shoes on, without her socks; grabbed her red jacket; and off they went. She had Granny's shopping bag, and Granda asked her, "Is that yours, Doireann?"

"No."

"Is it mine, then?"

"No, it's mine." She was making sure Granda wasn't getting his hands on it.

"We don't have Teddy [White]," she said when they were about halfway into their journey.

"It's too late to go back for him now, Doireann, and sure he'll be there for you when we get back home later," Granda told her.

They were singing songs with their own made-up words, when she said, "Sing the doggy one," and Granny obliged.

Then Granda sang the words, "How much is that doggie in the back seat, the one with the lovely red dress?" as they parked in Tesco's car park.

Then, she got into a trolley car, powered up by Granda. As she drove around the store, she spotted big posters of Tinker-Bell and got out of her car to give her hugs on a couple of occasions.

"She is not giving me hugs," Doireann protested after her last hug and as she climbed back into the trolley car on their way to the automatic pay area.

From there, Granny lifted her up because she wanted to deposit Tesco's blue tokens into the various charity containers near the exit. As she drove her trolley car back to the trolley parking bay, they passed Mammy's car in the car park. Granny and Granda said nothing, and Doireann never noticed it.

Because she would want to stay with Mammy, they drove from Tesco's car park to the Gorey Shopping Centre, doing their usual, "*Wheeeeeeeeeee eeeeeeeeeeeeeeeeeeeeeeeeeeeeeeeeeeeeeeeeeeeeeeee,*" as they entered the underground car park, where they parked in a family parking bay.

Before they left the car, Granny changed Doireann's very wet nappy. Then they visited Noddy and Minnie, just in time for Noddy's, "Welcome to Toyland" announcement and before heading for the travelator.

"That one is for going down," Doireann told Granda as she pointed.

She held Granny's hand as they all travelled on the "up" side. She grabbed some empty sweet bags from the sweet vending machines on the ground floor and handed them all, bar one, to Granny to mind. They travelled up to the first floor on the lift, and then she did her trick with the empty bag. Granny and Granda had a go at this trick also.

"*Wheeeeeeeeeeeeeeeeeeeeeeeeeeeeeeeeeeeeeeeeeeeeeeeeeeeeeeeeeee,*" shouted Doireann by the courthouse on exiting the magic doors by the doctor's surgery, on the first floor. Halfway down, she loudly proclaimed, "My nappy is staying on," to the uninvited audience, on a break from court proceedings. She ended up in Granda's waiting arms. Next, she ran back up to Granny, with Granda in hot pursuit, until she was rescued by Granny's outstretched arms.

She then opened the magic doors to the library, saying with her lip up and head down, "I don't want to read a book."

Granny said, "That's okay. I want to get a DVD, and Granda wants to read the newspapers."

As Granda sat reading *The Irish Times*, Doireann sat down with Granny in the kiddies' section, reading books!

She paid Granda a visit.

"Do you want to stay with me?" Granda asked her.

"No," was her curt reply, and she ran back to Granny.

"Granda, are you ready to leave?" she asked, having been sent by Granny after she got the DVD.

"*Wheeeeeeeeeeeeeeeeeeeeeeeeeeeeeeeeeeeeeeeeeeeeeeeeeeeeeeeeeee,*" she shouted again on exiting the library.

She then had a walk on the small wall, surrounding a water feature, for the public to sit on. She stopped momentarily to appear as if she was holding up that part of the building overhang above her with her hands. Next, she walked on the wall towards Dunnes Store's first floor entrance doors, with Granda holding onto her tightly, because it was not for walking on. Then as they entered the lift, she stared at a lady, who also got on the lift.

"Oh, I love your red dress and red shoes. You're beautiful," the lady told her.

Doireann gave her a massive grin.

They exited the lift in the basement and headed out to the car.

"Well, I love your dress wear," a former work colleague of Granda's told her as they passed each other.

That made Doireann as proud as punch.

She beat Granny and Granda in a race to the car, while "holding Granda's hand".

In the car, she asked for the soother, saying she was tired. As they drove through Camolin Village, she said, while looking out the car window, "That's my house, Granny and Granda."

And before she knew it, they were at Granny and Granda's house. It was now 12.45 p.m. She wanted to go outside to play.

"After lunch, Doireann. It's lunchtime soon," Granny told her.

So, she watched the telly instead.

When Granny called her for lunch, she started moaning and whinging because she wanted to watch the telly while having her lunch. Granny insisted that she sit up at the table, but the protests continued.

When Granda switched off the telly, Doireann, with face flat down on her TV chair, started crying—as if the world she knew had ended.

"Okay, Granny, leave it. If she doesn't want her lunch, she must not want to play outside after lunch," Granda said.

She had a think about this, and eventually Granny coaxed her to the table, where she ate all of her lunch.

Later, Granny took her outside to play in the cold. Granny then brought her into the house to get a cardigan. As they both searched for a cardigan in Granny's wardrobe, Doireann found new pink pants that had been hidden by Granny. She had bought them in a sale for Doireann for a later date.

"What's this, Granny?" she asked excitedly.

"They are for you when you are ready," Granny told her.

"Can I see one?" she asked. Granny took one out. And when she didn't put it back exactly like the rest in the packet, Doireann started to whinge and demanded it be put back exactly like the others.

"Do you want to try it?" Granny asked.

And after she tried it, she took it off and put her nappy back on.

Granny put the packet away, and off they went outside with their cardigans on.

Mammy called and joined them out the back for a short while, before heading home to let Oisín in, as Daddy was in Galway.

"Are you off, Doireann?" asked Granda.

With her soother in her mouth, she nodded.

"Am I getting a hug?" he asked.

She handed her jacket to Mammy, gave Granda a hug, and prepared to leave. She then dropped her wellies.

"Take them smelly wellies away," joked Granda.

Mammy then decided the wellies were better left with Granny and Granda, and she handed them to Granda.

"Will they fit me?" he asked as he pretended to put them on his big feet.

"No, Granda, not with your shoes on," Doireann said as she laughed out loud. "They are mine," she then reminded Granda.

"Okay, pet. Goodbyeyeyeye," said Granda loudly as they vanished on exiting the front gate.

22 June

Mammy and Doireann arrived over to Granny and Granda's house at about 9.35 a.m. Doireann was wearing her lovely summer shorts and T-shirt. She took her shoulder bag and hoodie from Mammy, who was holding them in her hands. Then she flung the hoodie onto the floor and began rummaging through the shoulder bag, looking for her cookies to show Granny. Mammy picked the hoodie up off the floor and was about to say something to her when Granda asked for the hoodie, and he then flung it onto the floor.

Doireann was not pleased. "Granda, don't do that," she complained.

"You did it," said Granda.

"You shouldn't do that, Granda," she continued to complain as she picked it up off the floor.

"Okay," Granda said, "now put it on the sofa."

And when she did, Granda thanked her. She was then informed they were going to Courtown today.

"We won't see Tony?" she asked.

"No, not today," Granny told her.

"Some other day," she continued, and Granny agreed.

She didn't know when to eat her cookies.

"At the playground in Courtown," Granny suggested.

"No not there," she replied.

"Have them in the car on the way," Granda suggested.

"No, not in the car," she said and then mused for a bit, before making up her own mind. "I'll have them at the playground!" *she* decided.

"Would you like some brekkie?" Granda asked her.

"I had Cheerios and toast," she replied, with a whingy moany voice.

"That's okay then. And why are you whinging?" Granda said back, in a whinging moany voice, also.

"Granny do you speak like that?" Granda asked.

Doireann stood up straight. "I don't speak like that. I talk nicely," she stated loudly.

Granda acknowledged that she did talk nicely, and the whingy moany voice was put to bed.

"Can I look at the pictures [on the iPad]?" she asked Granny.

"As soon as I have my breakfast," Granny told her.

"I want to look at them," she insisted.

"You can't," Granda said, and so as to distract her, he encouraged her to go and get Baby Bop and the teddies. "They want you. I can hear them calling," Granda told her.

Out of eyesight of her, Granda called out, "Doireann. Doireann. Doireann," in a low voice.

Off she went into the bedroom, only to arrive back almost immediately holding Baby Bop and Teddy White.

"What about the other teddy?" Granny asked her.

And she went off again to fetch Teddy Brown.

"And Snowy too?" joked Granda.

"I don't want Snowy," she said, angrily. "I want a cover; it's cold?" she added.

"Get a blanket. You know where they are," Granda said, and she did.

Next, she switched on the (pretend) engine on her toy car to do some (imaginary) shopping and drove to Granny the shopkeeper.

"What would you like?" the shopkeeper asked.

"Mmm, sausage," she said.

"How many?"

"Two," she replied.

And as she took off, Granny called out, "What about the money for them?"

She handed the shopkeeper some money, who then handed her the change.

But she put her hand up and said, "No," and drove off.

Then she arrived back at the shop. "What would you like this time?" asked the shopkeeper.

"Apples and tomatoes."

The shopkeeper handed her the apples and tomatoes and asked for payment.

She said no and continued to say no every time Granny the shopkeeper looked for payment.

As she drove off, an alert Granda shouted out, "I will get the Gardai." Granda the police car took chase; his siren switched on. "Neenah, neenah, neenah," sounded the siren as it hotly pursued the thief, speeding through the dining room highway.

Doireann just looked behind and kept going.

A while later, Granny offered, "Will I put your DVD, 'The Magic Test' on for you, Doireann?" It was an episode from *Ben and Holly's Little Kingdom*.

"Yes," she said as she sat into her telly chair to watch it. "Are you ready, Granny?" she asked.

"Nearly there," said Granny as she struggled to play the DVD.

Granny and Granda then set about getting ready for the Courtown trip, which would include a quick visit to Tesco's on the way.

When ready to go, they all got into the car, Doireann with her cookies, and off they went. She wanted her soother and took Granny's bag to get it. She couldn't find it, and Granny asked her for the bag so she could get it for her. Doireann continued to search Granny's bag and groaned for a long time, until finally Granda's patience ran thin. "Will you ever take the bag from her?" he asked Granny.

She handed the bag to Granny, who found the soother for her.

"It's a baby one, Granny," she said.

"It's the only one I have. Your mammy didn't drop yours over," she was politely told.

First port of call was Tesco's to get Granda's correct prescribed medication, instead of the generic type he had been given the other day.

Doireann wanted to go into the shop with Granny but was told it was a quick visit only. As she started to cry and whinge, Granda told Granny to keep going. She seemed to accept this as she and Granda sat in the car parked in the set-down area. Granda opened the windows, as the car was very warm from the strong sun, even though the temperature was only fifteen degrees.

"Close the windows, Granda," she said.

"Okay pet," said Granda, but left them open a tiny bit.

"Granda, can I play with the bus?" she asked.

"Okay, come on," he said, getting out of the car and then holding the car door open after opening her safety belt.

She clambered out and ran over to the kiddie ride London bus parked outside Tesco's.

A few minutes later, Granny emerged. "Right, let's go to Courtown," she said, having just returned from the shop.

Doireann got out of the bus and ran to the kiddie ride Noddy machine, which was parked close by.

"Doireann, come on. We have to go," Granny protested.

She then got down off Noddy's car and ran to another kiddie ride boat and bear machine downstream.

"Doireann, come on. The playground will be closed," Granny pretended angrily.

"I want to give the bear a big hug," she replied, before proceeding to give him loads of hugs.

They eventually got her into the car, and off they drove again towards Courtown, with Granda checking the petrol prices at each petrol station as he passed.

"I want to go to Enniscorthy," she said.

"We are going to Courtown," Granny told her firmly.

She started crying and protested, saying, "I want Enniscorthy."

After about five minutes of this crying, protesting, and sobbing, Granda had had enough. "Okay, Doireann, keep it up, and we will go home," announced Granda.

More protests, crying, and sobbing followed as Granda turned onto the main Courtown road from Gorey to continue the journey to Courtown Playground. Granda then pulled over to the side of the road and safely stopped the car. "Right, Doireann, you have two choices—Courtown Playground or home. It's your choice; which is it to be?" Granda said slowly and clearly so she understood and realised he was very serious.

"Courtown," was her response.

And the war had ended (for now).

Granda parked the car in the big car park near to the playground. When Granda helped her out of her car seat, she told him off in no uncertain manner with, "Granda, you are talking nice to me now!" This was immediately followed with, "Granny, you can hold my hand!" And off they walked, up to and into the playground, leaving the Spoilsport to find his own way.

She had great fun on the small slide and must have spent an hour playing on it, while mingling with all the other toddlers at the same time. One of the daddies there, on holidays from Clonmel, County Tipperary, told Granda his little boy was 4 years old. Doireann wanted to do everything the 4-year-old was doing, and so Granny and Granda had to keep a close eye on her. She insisted on sliding down the fireman's pole, and Granda had to hold her as she slid down.

"Granda, I want to do it myself," she demanded.

"Okay." He guided her, while holding her a little bit as she stepped across from the platform to grip onto the pole with her two hands. "Now wrap your legs firmly around the pole also," he advised her, using his hand to prevent her sliding down until she was ready. "Now slide down slowly, by easing your grip," Granda told her before removing his hand.

It wasn't a smooth landing, as she came crashing down to earth at lightning speed—or, as Billy Connolly would say, "She hit the ground like a dart!" Because she hurt her cheek, the playground was instantly flooded with tears.

Granny and Granda tried to console her with loads of hugs and cuddles, but the firewoman wasn't having it. All she wanted to do was leave, before eventually calming down. Next, she tried the slide again but nearly toppled over because she pressed her rubber shoes hard against the slide, halfway down it.

"Don't do that. It's too dangerous," Granny told her, now panicking.

"Mammy lets me," she said, now in floods of tears once again.

"I will ask your mammy later, and if she says yes, then okay," said Granny. "But you are not to do that, you hear," an irate Granny reminded her again.

"You have to listen to what you are being told. Look at what happened when you would not accept my help on the pole, deciding to do it yourself," Granda tried to explain.

She continued with her sit-down protest on the slide, wanting her own way. As soon as she decided to go for it, by attempting to slide down again, Granda just lifted her off the slide.

Granny carried her, crying, back to the car because she was tired. Granny and Granda just ignored her cries.

"They are all going now," she said, when looking back at the playground.

"Yes," said Granda. "It's lunchtime now." Granda drove past the Pebbles Café, where they had celebrated Uncle Tony's birthday with coffees and cakes. "There's where we were the other day with Uncle Tony." Granda pointed. Then they headed for home.

They had the general chit-chat in the car. And when they arrived in the driveway, Doireann removed her princess shoes and walked to the hall door in her stocking feet. She helped Granny put the washing on the clothesline. Then she went into Granda to have a look at the photos he had taken earlier with his camera. As he was downloading them onto his computer, she sat there smiling, while eating her raisins at the same time.

Shortly afterwards, Doireann called out, "Lunch is ready, Granda." And they all sat at the kitchen table, including Teddy White. She had put Teddy White into her "old" chair and fed him some (imaginary) food when Granny moved him closer to the table, next to Doireann.

Granda put his old garden hat on Teddy's head.

"Don't do that," she told him as she removed it.

When she wasn't looking, Granda put an old red facecloth on Teddy's head. As soon as she spotted it, she removed it and flung it at Granda. Again, when she wasn't looking, Granda removed Teddy from his chair as he walked past. She nearly jumped with fright when checking what was then an empty chair.

"Graaaandaaaa," she said slowly and sternly.

After lunch, Granny moved Teddy White and his chair away from the table. Doireann wanted it put back as she again sat up at the table saying, "Granda, put the cloth [the red facecloth] over Teddy."

Then Granny changed her very wet nappy, before taking her out the back to build a makeshift tent.

"Granny, I have a poo," she said to Granny about five minutes later.

"Sods law," Granny moaned.

After Granny again changed her nappy, Doireann put her new pants over it.

Next, she called out, "Granda, do you want to see my tent?"

"That's a lovely tent," said Granda, while refitting a blanket cover dislodged by the wind.

"Let's take a photo of it," she suggested and took one of Granda as well.

"Did you see Granny's trees [stumps], she painted?" she asked Granda.

"No," Granda pretended.

"Come on." She beckoned. "I'll show you."

"Ah, they are lovely," said a very surprised-looking Granda. "What colour is that one, Doireann?" he asked.

"Lellow."

"And that one?"

"Blue."

"And that one?"

"Green."

"Very good, Doireann. You certainly know your colours," he proudly told her.

Granny arrived back and took over from Granda, who went to watch the last quarter of the World Cup game between Costa Rica and Brazil. Brazil won 2-nil, scoring both goals in the sixth minute of the eight extra minutes allocated.

Doireann came back into the house and said, "Goodbye, Granda. I'll be here again."

"Ah, goodbye, pet. See you soon. And hello Mammy," replied Granda.

"Hiya, Da," she said, after rushing in the through the side gate, as she was in a hurry.

213

CHAPTER 18

The Ragged-Trousered Philanthropists

25 June

Mammy texted Granny to say they were running late. She also sent a photo of Doireann in the car after their day of adventure in Clara Lara Adventure Park, County Wicklow, the day before. She was covered in muck from head to toe. It was too late when they arrived home and decided to bathe her that morning. Snowy, Baby Bop, Teddy Brown, and Teddy White sat patiently, looking out the sitting room window, waiting to see Doireann walk across the field opposite Granny and Granda's house.

"I was with a friend yesterday in the water," a smiling Doireann told Granny and Granda, when she arrived.

"We bought an annual family ticket; it works out far cheaper," Mammy said. "And the kids loved it."

"You have big teeth," Doireann told Granda.

"Have I?" growled Granda, just like a dog.

"Yes Granda, like a tiger," she said.

Then searching the fridge, she asked, "Granny where's the present" (the chocolate bought in France)?

"I've eaten it," replied Granda.

She laughed, with a blow from her lips, because that was funny.

Later, she was looking for Granny's present (a scarf) in the wardrobe, and Granny told her to wait.

"Doireann, can you close the [wardrobe] door please?" Granda asked her. And as she did, he explained how it stayed shut, because of the metal piece latching onto the magnet.

Then Granda brought her out to the fridge magnets. He got her to hold a metal key near to a magnet to see how it worked.

"In one ear and out the other," remarked Granny.

"It's just a bit of education for her," Granda responded.

"Granny, can we go to Enniscorthy [Playground]?"

"No, not today, but maybe on Wednesday. Go and ask Granda," Granny suggested.

"Granda?"

"Yes, petal."

"Can we go to Enniscorthy?"

"Eh, not today, pet. On Wednesday," he replied.

She left the room with her head down, and Granny asked her, "What did he say?"

"Granda said no."

"Did he say Wednesday," enquired Granny.

No answer!

"Granda, did you tell Doireann we can go on Wednesday?"

"Yes, I did," he said.

Earlier, Granda told Doireann that Granny needed to get some paint in the shop. "Can I help her?" she asked.

"Of course, you can."

"Granny, Doireann wants to help you get the paint. And isn't that very nice of her?" Granda announced.

"After we get the paint, we will go to Camolin Playground," Granny told her.

"Can I paint the ladybird?" she asked, referring to a tiny garden ornament.

Granny thought for a bit and then said, "We've no red paint."

"Use the pink paint," Granda suggested.

"Ah, you can't paint it pink; ladybirds are red," Granda was told.

215

Granda then helped Doireann remove her furry friends from the sitting room window. Earlier, Mammy said Doireann could see her friends from the field. As soon as Granda got Snowy down off the window-sill, she took off, running as fast as she could and screaming as loud as she could towards the kitchen and into Granny's waiting arms, with Snowy in hot pursuit. Poor Granda held on for dear life as Snowy dragged him along also.

At 10 a.m. this morning, the temperature was twenty degrees, which was not the norm for Ireland. A foreign national once remarked to Granda that how you know the summer has arrived in Ireland is that the rain gets warmer. A Dublin woman talking on the radio once said that there's two days she loved in Ireland, Christmas Day and the "summer"! The heatwave was continuing, and Granda changed into his shorts and a T-shirt. He was still wearing his socks and slippers when Doireann arrived.

Pointing and laughing, she said, "Take them off, Granda."

Granda put his sandals on, and she liked them.

Granda took some photos, and then Doireann got in on the act. She photographed the ornamental ship on the hall table, her soother, the orange-coloured flower, and the artificial flowers in the hall and then Granny and Granda.

She put Granny's sun hat on and said, "Look I'm a farmer," and then did a funny walk.

She couldn't reach Mick. Granda lifted her up to unhook Mick and take him for a walk. When she had finished, Granda had to lift her again to re-hook him.

They went to get Granny's paint and stopped at the front gate first, in case the postman, now parked on their road, had any post for them. But he didn't. Before continuing their walk to the car, also parked on the road, they got Doireann to check for any oncoming traffic, and there was none. Granda strapped her into her car seat and drove towards Bolger's Hardware Store in Ferns.

"Where are we going?" she asked.

"Bolger's, Doireann, where it's bulging with paint, and you'll know it when you see it." Granda laughed.

They parked inside the main gates at the front of the store, as usual. It was now 11.30 a.m., and the temperature was 23.5 degrees and rising.

Recognising the store, Doireann went looking for the toy house she usually played with, but it wasn't there.

"It must have been sold," Granda told her, before Granny called them over to where the house used to be to choose a paint colour from the colouring charts affixed to the wall.

After choosing Moroccan red, Granny invited Doireann to help her paint the ladybirds (big and small) as soon as they get back home. "But you will have to change your clothes first," Granny said in a stern voice.

"Come on, guys, and go inside the shop," Doireann said to Granny and Granda.

Inside, she sat at a children's picnic bench. "Come on, Granda. Sit down." She beckoned.

"I won't fit," he said.

"Yes, you will," she insisted, and he was made to sit at the table.

The seat creaked "in pain" because of the heavy weight!

Next, she got up onto an extended sun chair-come-bed, saying, "I'm at the doctors."

They were on the road home again after Granny paid for her paint.

Doireann was all excited about helping Granny to paint the ladybirds. She preferred doing this, rather than going to the playground.

Granda parked in the driveway.

"I'm getting out Granny's side. Come on, guys. Let's go," she said.

They looked for the tiny ladybird among the stones in the front garden on the way into the house. Granny eventually found it lying on its back.

Granny replaced Doireann's dress with a large old white vest. She ran into the sitting room where Granda was having his cup of tea and a slice of toast. "Granda, look at me," she said as she stood with her vest tied up at the back.

"Oh, you look lovely. You are an artist now, so tell Granny," Granda said as he tried to finish his elevenses.

She ran to Granny. "Granny, I'm a[n] artist now."

Granny agreed.

Granny got her paintbrushes out, removed the lid from the can of paint, and stirred the paint, with Doireann in close attendance and observing everything. Then the moment arrived, and Robert Tressell's

Ragged-Trousered Philanthropists (a reference to Granda's most favourite book and bible) were at it, hammer and tongs.

Granda sneaked out and took some photos of the two budding artists. "You're doing a great job, Doireann," said Granda.

"It's a great day for painting," she replied.

And Granda agreed. As he left them to write his notes for this book, he joked loudly, "Keep up the great work now, and you are very good for letting Granny help you."

"You're welcome," was Doireann's reply.

When the painting finished, Granny brought her into the house and told her not to touch anything until she'd cleaned her hands. Granda told her that she was wearing a real artist's dress, and they would keep it for her.

Granny said, "isn't it lucky I put it on her?"

Doireann proudly showed Granda her red hands, and she didn't seem to mind, which was in total contrast to this morning's episode, after she'd arrived with Mammy.

Holding her bucket and spade, she'd complained, "The spade is dirty." Mammy and Granny had tried to explain to her that it was a stamp mark and not dirt, but she wasn't having it. And World War IV broke out. Mammy had taken the spade to the sink, ran water over it, and dried the stamp mark.

When Granny removed the artist's artist-dress, she ran into the small bedroom.

"Doireann, your pants are in here," Granny called out, but she still ran into the main bedroom to check that the pants were not in there before running back to Granny.

Before putting her dress back on, Granny changed her nappy and promised her she could put a pair of new pants over the nappy. She then darted off, with Granny in hot pursuit. "Where are you, Doireann?" Granny asked.

"Can we play football?"

"Not now, Doireann. It's nearly lunchtime," she was told.

Granny then put her dress back on her. She watched some TV until Granny had the lunch ready, and they all sat at the table. Doireann had spaghetti but only ate some of it, saying she was full. Just before this, she had eaten two oatcakes. She wouldn't wear a bib, and the spaghetti was going everywhere. Granny and Granda had their usual salads for lunch.

Doireann got down from the table and didn't want anymore and went and sat on the sofa.

"Would you like your boiled egg, Doireann?" Granny asked.

"No."

"Would you like your yogurt?" continued Granny.

"Yes," she replied, before sitting on Granny's chair at the table. Then she put yogurt in her mouth, as well as everywhere else.

Granny was using wipes to clean up after her. Granda scrunched- up his face at her when she looked at him. She responded in kind and then stuck her tongue out at him. Granda laughed.

"Granny, you do it to Granda," she said, and she did.

Poor Granda was now under attack from two monster faces and surrendered.

Daddy phoned Granny to say he was collecting Doireann at 1.30 p.m. Previously unaware of this arrangement, they now hurried to have her ready. Daddy arrived at 1.40 p.m.

"Goodbye, Granda," she said.

Granny and Granda both said, "We will see you on Wednesday. Goodbye now."

And off they walked across the field, opposite the house.

27 June

Doireann arrived with Mammy just after 9.30 a.m., and when Granda opened the hall door, she held up Teddy Pink, saying, "I brought Teddy today."

"Ah great, because I haven't seen you for a long time, Teddy," Granda told her.

She then went and brought Teddies Brown and White and Baby Bop out of the bedroom to see Teddy Pink. Teddy Pink gave each of them a kiss. They all sat on the sofa, listening to Mammy, and Granny and Granda chatting.

Aware that she got sick a few times yesterday, Granda asked, "Are you better today, Doireann?"

She just nodded and then said in a whingy voice, "My knee was hurting."

Mammy said she had fallen coming out of the house earlier.

Then, holding her soother in her hand, she said, "A snot got on this."

"Well, we didn't want to know that," said Granny back to her.

Mammy said she cleaned it in case dirt got on it.

Doireann had Cheerios for breakfast and drank water.

"What else did you have for breakfast?" Granny asked.

"Melon," she said and gave Granny a huge smile.

Granny put the washing on the clothesline that morning, while Doireann went to inspect the tree stumps Granny had painted. She sat on a good few of them, trying them out.

Back inside the house, she decided to put Granny's sun hat on. Granda wore her cap and took a selfie. Granda took a photo of Baby Bop wearing Granny's sun hat, and Doireann asked Granda to take a photo of her with the teddies. She showed Granda her bottle of bubbles that made a noisy blowing sound when you made bubbles. She laughed at the sound, and when Granda laughed, she laughed even more. Then she said to Granny, "That's not blowing; that's a fart noise." She explained to Granda how to blow the bubbles. When it made a noisy blowing sound again, she said, "That's a fart, Granda."

"Ha, ha. Okay, Doireann," Granda said.

Granny told her to ask Granda if they could go to Enniscorthy Playground today and her shoulders dropped, obviously because of what had happened on Monday. "Granda, can we go to Enniscorthy?" she asked.

"Well, Doireann, on Monday we promised you we would go on Wednesday, and that is today. And yes, we will go to Enniscorthy," he told her.

She ran to Granny, who asked what he had said.

"He said yes," said a delighted Doireann, who was now hopping and dancing around the place.

Granny said she wanted to get the salad ready for the lunch first and leave it in the fridge. So, she put Barney on for Doireann to watch in the meantime.

A black van pulled up outside Granny and Granda's, and a man dropped some large tree plants into the field opposite. As he carried them towards the main road end, they realised they were for the community's "homecoming" celebration, from 6 to 8 July 2018. A lot of people who had moved away from Camolin in years gone by were expected to visit for the event. This was also around the time for the local Catholic Church's annual "Pattern Sunday", when the community remembered their loved ones who had passed.

Off they went, as promised, to the Enniscorthy Playground.

"Where are we now?" Doireann inquired.

"We are on the road to Ferns," Granda told her.

"But where are we?" she asked.

"In Ferns now, Doireann," Granda said.

A little while later, as Granda continued driving, she asked, "Where are we now?"

"In Scarawalsh," Granda replied.

"But where are we on our way to Enniscorthy. But where are we?" her questioning continued.

"In Scarawalsh, Doireann," Granda said, emphasising the name

"I don't want Warawalshe," she complained loudly.

Granny and Granda laughed.

"Where are we?" she persisted.

"We are nearly there, Doireann," Granda told her.

Just then, they had to take a different route because there was gridlock on the main road, past the graveyard and right into the town. It was 11 a.m., and they figured there was probably a funeral. They drove up towards Pettitt's, past the newly upgraded St Aiden's School, past Doyle's pub, over towards and past Enniscorthy Library, and then down a few side roads.

"This is not it," she complained.

"We will be there soon," Granda tried to assure her.

"But this is different," she insisted.

"We know, but we are heading for the playground. Wait and see," Granda continued, trying to reassure her. Then, in an attempt to distract her, Granda sang, using the tune to "How Much Is That Doggie in the Window" and his own lyrics. "How much is that girl in the back seat, the one with the curly hair?" Granda then included some other variations, before she started singing herself, using her own made-up words.

Granny and Granda congratulated her.

Granda said, "Well done, Doireann. That was lovely. Did you 'word' that yourself?"

She just sat there, pleased with herself.

They eventually reached their destination, having to drive in the direction of the '1798 Enniscorthy Museum'. "There's the hotel. I want to go there when I'm bigger," she said, pointing.

"Okay, maybe you will get a job there," Granda suggested.

They parked the car in the playground car park, right next to the Riverside Park Hotel.

There were other kids playing and having great fun in the playground. Doireann wanted to try out the enclosed big slides, even though she had agreed that morning to wait until she was bigger. "Would you go in it, Granda?" Granny asked.

"Eh, I think I would get stuck on the way down. So, who would rescue you, Doireann, if you got stuck?" asked Granda.

She just laughed at that and continued with her pleas and demands.

"No, Doireann. When you are bigger," Granny kept insisting.

"Can Teddy Pink go in it?" she asked.

"What if she gets stuck going down it?" Granny warned.

Then realising that both she and Teddy were not allowed to use the big slides, she went to play on the other equipment and had great fun on the swings, the spinning machines, the see-saw, and climbing equipment, as well as generally running all over the place.

The time came to leave. "Only one more thing, Doireann. We have to go now," Granny announced.

It was an extremely hot and sunny day. Granny had to keep fixing Doireann's dress under her bum, before allowing her to sit on the now roasting hot equipment. When she finished her "last" go and they headed for the exit gate, she took a different direction, running to another machine.

Granda grabbed a hold of her hand and said, "Come on now. We told you that was your last."

Granda had the car air conditioning on full blast because of the intense heat and because Granny didn't want Doireann falling asleep in the car on the way home.

As soon as they arrived back in the house, it became very obvious that Doireann, rather than wanting to fall asleep, had been plotting her next move on the journey, instead. "I want to go down the big slide," she demanded.

"When you are bigger," Granny reminded her.

"I am bigger. Look," she responded, her arms stretched upwards.

"You can ask Mammy and Daddy, okay," Granda suggested. Well, if looks could kill, Granda fretted because of the look she gave him before he spurted-out laughing at the idea of it. She was just like her Mammy, at that age, *determined*.

Granda stuck his tongue out at her and made an ugly face.

It wasn't long before she got great fun giving as good as she got.

"Your lunch is ready, Granda," she shouted.

"Okay, pet. I'll be there in a minute," Granda shouted back.

"Look at my top, Granda," she said, when he arrived out into the kitchen for his lunch.

"Oh, that's lovely, what's her name?" he asked, of the image on her top.

"Anna," he was told.

"Well, wait and I'll take a photo of Anna."

"And me Granda?" she said.

"Of course," he said, before clicking his phone camera. "Now, here, Doireann. You take a photo of me?" he said and handed her the phone.

"Okay, Granda, for your 'puter" (computer)." *Click.*

"Ah, that's brill. And thanks, Doireann."

Later, Granda told her, "It's com-puter," emphasising the first syllable. "You say, *com* … puter," he told her in a clear voice.

When she got it right, Granda congratulated her, saying, "Good girl. Well done, pet."

"Granny, Doireann is very good with her words," Granda announced, and Granny gave her a huge smile.

They all sat at the table for lunch. She only wanted three crackers, a segment of spreadable cheese, and a cup of milk. Then she asked to sit on her high chair at the table and wanted the plastic tabletop belonging to it also. Granny was making Granda toast and tea after he finished his usual salad lunch of lettuce, tomatoes, onions or spring onions, radish (when in stock), peppers, courgettes, carrots, beetroot and tuna.

Then Granda took Doireann outside to play with her bubbles, until Granny was ready to come out. She giggled as she chased the bubbles.

"It's your turn [to run]," she told Granda because she wanted to make the bubbles.

"Granda, is there anymore paint left?" she enquired next.

"No. I think it's all gone now," Granda pretended.

"Did you see the ladybirds you painted?" Granda asked, so as to distract her.

She went over to inspect her masterpieces, just as Granny appeared on the scene.

"Eh, I told Doireann, there is no more paint left," Granda warned Granny.

Granny agreed, in such a loud voice, that it was brought to the attention of not only Doireann but also the whole of Camolin and the surrounding countryside! All painting was now off the menu for the foreseeable future.

Later, Granny called Granda over when Doireann's nose started to bleed as she was changing her nappy. Granda wiped her nose and pinched the top of it. It stopped bleeding, and they took her inside to rest a while.

Granny read from one of her storybooks, the one about the cat that got lost. Granny searched two pages of the book, looking for the fat cat. "Where is the fat cat?" Granny asked Doireann.

Granda was walking past at that very moment and stuck his belly out and spoke like a cat, "Meow, meow."

"Ah, there's a fat cat," Granny scoffed.

"Where?" asked Doireann as she looked around.

"Just ignore Granda," Granny told her.

Later, she approached Granda in the sitting room and whispered, while holding her index finger against her closed lips, "Granny is asleep."

They sneaked into the dining room as Granny (pretend) snored. Granda, holding Snowy up, in front of Granny's face, got him to loudly say, "*Boo.*"

Granny then said, "Granda, if I don't get my sleep, Doireann will give out to me."

During the whole day today, when Doireann was talking or giving out, she did so in a whingy moany tone. Whenever Granda copied her whinge, she would either smile or give out if he did it for too long. She got Granda's phone and took photos of Granny and then of Granny and

Granda together. Then Granda took a selfie of all three of them, with Doireann in the middle.

"You're the piggy in the middle, Doireann," Granda said, and she giggled.

Then Granda took a photo of her piggies (toes), and she laughed.

Daddy called to collect her today and had to carry her to his car, as she refused to put her shoes on.

29 June

Doireann arrived over to Granny and Granda's house in her buggy today. She was moody and very tired, and the intense heat was getting to her. Mammy had given her an ice pop to bring and a smoothie.

"Doireann is going to help us with the weekly shopping today. We normally do it on a Thursday evening, but Granda had a FLAC" (Free Legal Aid) "appointment in Dublin yesterday evening," Granny informed Mammy.

Mammy told them she'd phoned Wexford County Council to get the pedestrian lights fixed in the village in time for the Homecoming Festival, beginning in a week's time.

Doireann had Teddy Pink with her and went looking for the other teddies. Granda carried Baby Bop for her but left it in the hall and went to get Snowy. Doireann went into the hall to get Baby Bop, and when Snowy suddenly appeared from out of nowhere, it caused her to scream and shout, saying, "Don't frighten me." She immediately ran and hid under the kitchen table, the very same table that her Mammy and her Granny played under, when each of them were little. She came out when Snowy had retreated, to sit in her buggy. When Snowy appeared again, she jumped out of her buggy and shouted, "No. Get out," and wrestled Snowy to the floor.

Later on, she helped Granny put the bedsheets into the washing machine before going out to the back garden in the lovely sunshine to play. She ran around the garden singing, and then they played football with the small ball. Granny brought her into the house to change her wringing wet nappy before they headed for Tesco's in Gorey. They went to get a shopping trolley-car in the car park. But as they arrived, there was another mammy taking the last one.

"It's okay," Doireann said, and they went into the store to get one there.

When she discovered that they were all gone too, she was not a happy bunny, emitting the usual whinges and moans. Granny got a normal trolley. She refused to sit in the front of it, wanting instead, to sit in the main basket. Then her bum hurt because the wire mesh was cold. Granda laid out a shopping bag over the mesh, and she sat back on it, only to stand up almost immediately, pointing and saying excitedly, "The house, the house. Look, the house."

This was the same type of house she'd played with outside Bolger's Hardware Store in Ferns but bigger.

"Okay, we will have a look at the house," Granda said.

It was on display on the shop floor. They didn't have to ask her if she wanted to play in it. She was out of the trolley before you knew it and dashing down towards it. "You'll have to shop on your own, while I keep guard at the princess's house," Granda told poor Granny.

Doireann had a great time playing with the house. She was in and out, in and out, opening windows, opening doors, shutting windows, shutting doors. When she opened the hall door, she said to Granda, "I'm in my backyard now!"

Teddy was with her during all of these activities. Granda showed her two individual water taps (moulded on the side of the plastic house). She then got herself an imaginary drink of water.

"Come on in, Granda."

"Ah, sure I wouldn't fit into your lovely house, pet. Thanks anyway," he informed her.

Then she had an uninvited visitor—a young boy whose Mammy was left waiting outside also. She and the young boy interacted well, albeit for a short time only, until the visitor left to help his mammy with her shopping.

At one stage, the windows were opened, and Teddy Pink came flying out onto the floor. "Ah, Doireann, poor Teddy; she will get injured doing that," warned Granda.

She picked Teddy up, took her back into the house, and this time put her out the window gently and onto the floor. Other times, Teddy was put out into the back garden and then to the side of the house. When she had difficulty closing a set of windows, Granda showed her how. The left-hand side window, with a plastic rim on the side, had to close first and so on. Later, she could not open the window because she had forced it in too far. She opened all the windows wide and came outside.

"It's very hot today, Doireann, isn't it?" said Granda.

"Yes, it's hot," she replied, and off she went about her business.

Granda stood guard on the shop floor as she tended to her (Tesco's) house and enjoyed every minute of it.

She was totally oblivious to the world around her, lost in her own world. At times, she would try to force open the hall door the wrong way, and Granda would have to show her how it opened out, all the way. At one stage, Granda thought she would take the hall door off its hinges with a snap as she attempted to exit the wrong way. Sometimes, she would leave the house and play with a slide for toddlers, just up from the house. Other times she would look out the window and say, "Hello."

"Well, hello," Granda would say back to her.

Then he asked her for a wave and then a queen's wave; and with that, she moved her hand from side to side.

Now outside again, she asked, "Granda, have you got the key to the hall door?"

"Here, these are my keys," he told her.

And off she went to open the hall door. She arrived back a short while later and handed Granda back his keys. Next, she was trying to slide down the toddler's slide in reverse, and Granda told her not to.

"But I want to," she demanded.

"No, Doireann, you can't; it's too dangerous, and you will hurt yourself," Granda warned.

"Why not?" she continued.

"Doireann, turn around and slide down the correct way," a by now angry Granda told her.

"I can't, I have a poo poo," she blurted out.

"Just abandon the slide. We will be going home soon. Granny will be finished with the shopping shortly," Granda told her.

She continued to whinge and moan.

"You can have that ice cream we promised you as well," pleaded Granda. Because of the intense heat, and if she was good and helped them with the shopping, Granny and Granda had earlier promised her a big ice cream.

Eventually, she went back to play in the house. Next, she was out of the house and pushing the swing chair next to the slide. Then, Teddy Pink wanted a go and was put into the seat. She pushed the swing for Teddy for ages. Next, she spoke to Teddy, lifted her out of the swing and brought her back into the house.

When Granny arrived back, Doireann didn't want to leave. Granda mentioned to Granny that she did a poo poo and needed a nappy change. He told her to pay for the shopping first and call them when she was ready. Then, "Doireann are you right. Granny is waving at us to come," Granda told her.

"No, I want to make a cup of tea," she said in a whingy voice.

"Doireann, will you come on?" he demanded.

There were more whinges, with her saying, "I want to make a cup of tea for Teddy."

"Okay then. Hurry up," she was told.

Off she went, into the house and started talking to Teddy and so on. Then she came out of the house, and Granda started to walk towards Granny, and she followed—until she was distracted by coloured pens, pencils, cases, and other things on some other shelves. She had to go over and touch them.

"Come on, Doireann. They belong to the shop," was his final call.

As they walked to the car with the sun beaming down, she saw a trolley car, and Granny helped her into it for the short distance to the car. Next thing, she moaned because she had to leave the trolley car behind. When she got out of it, Granda pushed it to one side. Then, they had a huge whinge from her. "No, not there, Granda. There." She pointed.

"I can't park it there; it will block people," he told her, before lifting her moany self into the car seat.

"Where's my soother?" was her last request.

They stopped at Cartons Daybreak outlet in Camolin to get a tub of ice cream, as promised, and Granny got out.

Doireann said, "I want music."

Granda played the CD she liked. It was loud, and he lowered it.

"I can't hear it," she said.

228

"You can hear it all right, because I can," he said and left it as it was.

Traffic began to build up because of roadworks opposite The Pike Inn Camolin in the village. All they could think off was Doireann's ice cream, now in the boot, with the heat. Luckily, they got moving after about five minutes. Granda pulled into the driveway and told Granny to leave the shopping, as he would look after it and said, "Doireann needs a new nappy."

With all the shopping in, Granda left all the car doors open to freshen the car and closed them all again later. He opened up some windows in the house again because of the heat, and then when Granny finished changing Doireann's nappy, the second one that morning, he had to open a few more windows because of the "you know what".

Doireann was out from the bedroom in a flash. "Where's my ice cream?" she called out.

She opened the fridge, and Granda licked his lips, saying, "That was a lovely ice cream."

"No, Granda. Where is it?" she demanded.

He opened the freezer, and she had a big smile on her face. She sat up at the table, and Granda took the lid off and got her a spoon. "It's still too cold," she said.

"No, it's not," he said and took a scoop of ice cream with the spoon and put it into her mouth.

"Mmmmm, that's lovely," she said, and continued enjoying it all by herself, until she had had enough.

She couldn't finish it, so Granny put it back into the freezer for later. She had her watermelon, though. They all had their lunch at the table, with Doireann preferring to sit in her high chair again.

She asked Granda later, "Can I see my cousins again?"

"Okay wait. Now here you are, Doireann," he said, handing her the iPad to watch the videos. She sat up on Granda's lap to watch Uncle Richard's video clip of her cousins Richie and Eddie having a great load of laughs at Eddie making fart sounds. Then she sent Eddie (with Granda's help) congratulations on his second semester certificate that he displayed in one of the pictures. "Well done, Eddie, and congratulations. You are in a great school, and I wish I could go to that school. I [will] be starting in about two years. Lots of love from your cousin Doireann in Ireland. I is [am] looking at you in the picture now," was her Facebook message.

Then, Granny read some books to her, *Big Bear Hug* and *First Stories for Girls*. Then Doireann played with her pet toy dog, with flashing eyes and sunglasses that barked non-stop when switched on.

Granny then took her outside for a while. She came into the house to ask, "Granda are you coming out?"

"Yes Doireann, in a couple of minutes," Granda assured her.

Granny then inquired, and she said, "Yeah, he is coming."

Granda arrived out, and they were playing with the toy rocket launcher. Doireann said, "Come Granda. You, do it?" And this went on for ages.

She enjoyed running to get the fired rockets after they dropped from the sky. Eventually, Mammy and Oisín arrived, about thirty minutes late because of the roadworks in the village. Oisín joined in with the rocket launches, eventually managing to send one over the very high trees into the neighbour's garden. He went around to fetch it, asking the neighbours first.

Granda set up the water hose, just to top up the birdies' baths. Doireann wanted to do it, and Granda let her water the lavender bush and flowers next to it, instead. Of course, she then seized the opportunity and started trying to hose down everybody with that mischievous smile of hers. Granda bent the hose pipe to stop the flow of water. She didn't understand why the water stopped and Granda asked her to look at the nozzle to see if there was water. She did and Granda opened out the bend momentarily, allowing water to spurt out and up into her face. Her lovely pink hat got wet also. There were bated breaths all round, but she saw the funny side of it and decided to try her luck and wet someone else.

Oisín arrived back with the rocket from next door and went to have a go at the water hose, when she chased and drenched him, with big laughs. Oisín then got the water hose and turned it on her. Well, the screams from her could be heard for miles, and then she started crying.

Mammy said quietly, "Oh, she can give it but won't take it."

They explained to Oisín that she was only a child and didn't understand. Oisín took his dripping wet shirt off. He had a hurling match that night; and so Mammy had to leave immediately. Off they went to Mammy's car, parked outside.

CHAPTER 19

Granda's Birthday

2 July

It was Granda's birthday today, and as soon as he answered the knock on the hall door, Doireann was there and handed him his birthday card that she had made herself.

Granda gave her a big hug, saying, "Thank you very much for that beautiful card, pet."

She then handed Granda a birthday card from her brother, Oisín, that he had made. It read, "A happy sixty-ninth birthday, Granda. Love, Oisín."

Granda joked with Doireann and said that, when he saw Oisín, he would ask him for his sixty-eighth birthday card and then laughed. It was actually Granda's sixty-eighth birthday today! Oisín was participating in the Kellogg's-sponsored GAA Cúl sports, in Naomh Padraig's GAA Grounds, Camolin, all week. He had been on his summer holidays from school since Friday last.

Mammy told Granny and Granda that earlier, when she'd told Doireann it was Granda's birthday, she'd asked if she could have some of his birthday cake. Mammy explained to her, saying, "Granda's tummy is not well, and he won't be having cake." Well, the tears had flowed, and she was broken-hearted.

Granny immediately said to her, "You can have one of my homemade muffins later on, and we'll put a candle on it."

That put a huge smile back on her face.

"We also bought ice cream to have after lunch," Granny told Mammy, well out of earshot of both Granda and Doireann. "It is a surprise for Granda, and I will tell her when it's near lunchtime." Granny knew that she got very excited on such occasions, just like her Mammy used to.

Doireann was wearing a new pair of shoes and objected to Granda taking a photo of them. She ran into the kitchen and hid under the table, saying, "I can see you."

Next thing, Teddy Pink was introduced, and she went with Granny, to get Baby Bop and the other teddies.

"Granda, wear my hat. I want to take a photo of you," she said and handed him her pink hat.

Then, she put the pink hat on Teddy Pink. With a surprised look, she asked, "Where's Teddy?"

"I don't know," pretended Granda also.

She then removed the hat from Teddy and said, "There she is."

Next thing, Teddy White went missing. Then it was Teddy Brown's turn. Finally, Baby Bop went missing under the hat, only to be magically found when Doireann removed the hat, on each occasion.

When Granda switched on the TV and Thomas the Tank Engine appeared, she immediately said, "I don't want that."

Granda searched for another kiddies' channel, without success.

"Mind, out of the way," she said to Granda as she pushed her TV chair around to face the telly, before settling into it with the soother in her mouth.

Granny put a Barney DVD on, and when the singing and dancing started, she got out of the chair and got Granny up to dance with her. Later, she looked through all of Granda's birthday cards, with Granny explaining who they were from. She wanted to go to the playground.

"Well, Granda and I are not up for it today," Granny told her.

Granda suggested they go outside and play in the garden in the sunshine.

"Can we go to Enniscorthy?" she asked.

"Not today, but we will go another day. Wednesday?" Granny said.

"Mammy says you are the best, and I love yous," she told Granny.

Granny then gave her a big hug, saying she loved her too.

When she gave Granda a hug, he said to her, "I love you too; you are the bestest."

She pointed to the telly saying, "Look, Granda," as the band played the dance music.

Granda pointed to the guitarist and said, "Look, he is playing a guitar." He then said to Granny, "You know earlier, I showed her a banjo on the telly, and she thought it was a guitar, until I explained the difference. She is very clever because the banjo is like the guitar, and well done, Doireann," he said loudly, so Doireann could hear him. "Say banjo, Doireann."

"Banjo."

"Good girl and well done again," Granda proudly told her.

She and Granny went outside, to build a tent, using the old garden chairs and some blanket covers. The wind started to blow the covers away, so Granny put a heavy weight (stone) safely on the chair to keep the blankets in place. Just before that, when the wind blew the blankets off the chairs and onto Doireann's head, she held her arms and hands out, complaining about what had just happened. Granny speedily refitted the blankets while Doireann fetched a stone.

"Oh, you got one as well," Granny acknowledged and thanked her.

"You're welcome," she replied.

Granny brought her toy tea set out and Doireann made lovely cups of tea, with milk and sugar. Then, they all had another, and after that, they had another. All Granda could think of, with a smile on his face, was Mrs Doyle of *Father Ted* fame and decided to mimic her with, "You'll have a cup of tea, won't you. Sure go-wan, go-wan, go-wan!"

Granny had used one of her Christmas tablecloths for the tent. "Granny, you use that for the table," Doireann said.

"It's old now, and there's a stain on it that I cannot remove," Granny assured her.

When she entered the house for a break, Granda called out to show her the Facebook photos of her cousins on a beach in Cambodia that Aunt Selin and Uncle Richard had posted. Then she went to Granny, who had the *Dora* musical book. She and Granny sang along to the songs. Next, Granny took her outside again, to play in the garden.

Granda was in the toilet when Doireann came back into the house again to ask, "Granda are you coming out?"

"Yes, pet. I'm going to put my shoes on first," Granda told her.

Granda arrived outside to see that the rocket launcher had been set up.

"Granda, you are not to do it too hard" (Don't jump too hard on the rocket launcher pump), she ordered.

"Okay, pet. I will be careful."

"Come on, Granda. Are you reading a story about me?" she asked as she beckoned him over.

"I am *writing* a story about you," Granda said, emphasising the action.

"Granda, send the rocket, and I will find it," she said.

"And again, Granda?"

"And again, Granda?"

Each time she would return the rocket from the overgrowth.

"I will try," she said and jumped on the launcher, sending the rocket skywards.

"Ah, very good, Doireann. Well done," Granda said.

"Now you, Granda."

Her next request was, "Come on. We will go for a walk." And off she went, with Granny and Granda behind.

She decided she wanted to continue to the very end of the garden, where it bordered with a farm. Granny went down the slightly deep incline with her, and on their way back up, Doireann said, "Granda, this is a mountain."

Granda went to help her finish the walk up, but she about-turned and walked back down again. When they returned the second time, Granny said to Granda, "Doireann didn't like it; there was a bee, and she said that bees sting."

She happened to be wearing her "Easter bonnet" hat just then because of the strong sun. "Do you have a bee in your bonnet?" joked Granda.

She looked strangely at Granda and said nothing. Later, when back indoors, she told him, "Granda, we are going to have a small cake, but it's going to be a [sur]prise, okay."

Granny had just told her about it and to keep it *quiet*! Granny had then told her not to mention the ice cream, after showing it to her in the freezer as soon as they went into the house. She went into Granda and said, with finger pointing and with a strict stare, "You are not to go near the fridge, okay, Granda!"

"Oh, okay, pet. I won't go near the fridge," he promised.

She then asked Granda if he wasn't well.

"Yeah, Granny and I are not well," Granda told her. "Our tummies are not well, just like what you had last week."

"Did the sick come?" she continued.

"Granny did get sick, yes," he told her.

She went to Granny and asked her if she was all right.

Next thing, she decided to have a rest on Granny and Granda's bed; she removed her shoes and dumped them onto the floor.

"Okay, Doireann, lunch," Granny called out.

"No, I want to rest," she shouted back.

"Ah, come on, Doireann. There'll be no surprises," Granny reminded her.

"Okay, I'm coming," she said, now hurrying.

"Do you want your high chair, Doireann?" Granny asked.

"Yes."

"Doireann, do you say hi to your high chair?" joked Granda.

"I don't want to say that," she protested angrily.

She had beans and toast for lunch. After a while, she said, "I don't want them; I want something else."

Mammy had told Granny that she liked the beans. Granny got her some cheese triangles.

After lunch, Doireann called out, "Granda, your birthday."

He arrived in the kitchen to find two small cakes, with one candle in each for his birthday. Doireann blew out the candles for Granda and choose the pink cake for herself. "Granda, would you like some ice cream?" Granny asked.

Granda said loudly, "Yippee! That's great!"

Doireann asked Granda if he was excited.

"Of course, I am," he told her.

After they finished their ice cream, Granda thanked her for a lovely birthday party and thanked Granny also with a big hug for a lovely birthday and for the present, cake, and ice cream. Granny took Doireann outside again, and she played in her tent. Then she wanted to do a run around the garden with poor Granny.

Next, Granny sang "Ring-a-Ring-a-Rosies, and We All Fall Down" for her.

Then she ran around the grass like an athlete. When they came back into the house, Granny changed her nappy before letting her watch some telly.

"Can Teddy sit with me?" she asked.

"Yes," said Granny.

She watched *Paw Patrol*, and when it was over, she started to whinge, because she wanted to watch it again. Granny tried to explain to her that we do not have a television set-up like hers, where you can select programmes over and over again. She continued to whinge and give out and then wanted her soother. She was obviously very tired. Granny took her back outside to the fresh air, to play, while Granda went for a little snooze. He was still feeling the effects of that horrible tummy bug.

Mammy called to collect Doireann. "Happy birthday, Da," she said as she handed him a present and a card.

"Ah thanks, pet; you shouldn't be wasting your money," Granda (Da) said.

She went out to the back garden and brought Doireann in to get ready to leave. As they chatted, Oisín called to the house and said, "Happy birthday, Granda."

"Thanks, Oisín. You were early with the birthday card," joked Granda.

His face was now scrunched up because he didn't understand.

"I'm 68 and not 69, ha ha," Granda told him.

Oisín grinned as he pointed to his Mammy, who then said, "I know. Thatwas my fault."

Granny and Granda and Doireann told Mammy about the muffins with the candles and that Doireann had blown them out for Granda.

"Did you enjoy the [GAA] football, Oisín?" Granda asked.

"Yeah, and my friends were there also."

"How many were at it?"

"There were 108."

"Wow. That's a lot," said Granda and continued with, "You will probably play for Wexford someday."

"Ah, I'd prefer the soccer," he declared.

"Yeah, well, play the two games, and you never know. Look at Kevin Moran, who played for the Dubs" (Dublin) "and went on to play for Man Utd" (Manchester United) "and Ireland," he advised him.

Oisín asked, "Is there a cake for me?"

Granny went to the freezer and took out the three remaining cakes. Then there was a battle, after Oisín stated, "If Doireann is having another one, then I am having the remaining two."

"What about me?" Mammy interjected. "We need to share," she insisted.

Granny went back to the freezer to get some more cakes from another lot she had hidden away.

Doireann was behind her and asked, "What are you getting Granny?"

Oisín said something, and Doireann started crying, which then led to her screaming in a fierce rage. Mammy took them quickly out of the house and into her car. Granny and Granda called out loudly from the hall door, "Goodbyebyeeeeeeeeeeeeeeeeee," while waving and laughing at the same time.

Doireann waved back and looked totally exhausted.

3 July

Mammy phoned Granny to ask if she could visit Aunt Val in the nursing home today. They both collected Doireann at the crèche first. After their visit to Aunt Val, Mammy dropped Granny home. On the way home, Doireann, on seeing the large four-in-a-row game that Granny had just bought, asked, "Granny, can I play that?"

"Yes, Doireann, when your Uncles Gary and Richard arrive over at the weekend," she said.

As Granny got out of the car, Mammy got out too, to hand Granny the game.

"Can I come in too?" Doireann pleaded.

"No, I am not staying," Mammy told her.

When Granny looked in the car window to say goodbye, Doireann was bawling her eyes out.

4 July

Doireann wasn't in good form today. Granda was in the shed looking for some materials for his shed gutter downpipe project, when Granny called out, "Doireann is over to see you, Granda."

Daddy had dropped her over at about 10.10 a.m. that morning. She went into the shed, eating a freeze pop.

"Hi, Doireann. Who gave you that?" Granda asked.

"Mammy did."

"And your lovely dress," remarked Granda.

"It's a skirt, Granda", she responded, in such a loud voice that the metal shed roof shook.

"Oh, sorry, Doireann. Sure, what does Granda know, wha?" said Granda in his Dublin accent.

Now back in the kitchen, with the shed locked up, Granda said, "Granny, that's a skirt Doireann has on and not a dress."

"I know," said Granny.

When Granda took a photo of her and her skirt, she held up the little bow. He asked her, "what do you call that?"

"A bau," was the way she pronounced it.

Granda said, "It's a bow, isn't it?"

As she nodded, she repeated it.

"It's a golden bow," continued Granda.

She then shouted, "No, Granda! It's a bow!"

"Okay, Doireann. It's just a bow," agreed Granda.

She wanted to play in the garden, but Granny said, "Not yet. We are not ready."

As she ran to get Teddy Pink, Granny said, "Doireann has a new teddy today, Granda."

Moaning, she said, "It's not a teddy."

Granny then corrected herself. "Oh, okay. It's a tiger."

Doireann corrected Granny, telling her it was a lion.

"Has the lion got a name?" Granda asked.

Moaning, she replied, "No."

Granda took a photo of the no-name-yet lion anyway.

She covered up the lion, saying, "Don't take a photo of him, Granda."

"Okay."

She continued talking in a moany voice and said, "No photos today."

Granda agreed. He showed her an old photo of Snowy. "Who is that with Snowy?" he asked.

She studied it and said, "Mammy."

"No," said Granny.

She studied it again. "Granny," she then said.

Granny acknowledged it and told her the photograph had been taken forty-two years ago in Canada. "Snowy is a granda too," joked Granda.

"Are you okay, Granny?" Doireann asked because she wasn't well the other day (nor was Granda).

"Yes, I am okay today," replied Granny.

"Granda, are you better?" she continued.

"Oh, much better today. And thanks for asking," said Granda.

And next, the manoeuvre! "Can we go to Enniscorthy?" she asked.

Granny laughed, saying she knew what was coming.

"Okay because, on Monday, we promised we would take you on Wednesday," Granda declared.

"Can I play in the garden?" she asked.

"No, Doireann. We have to get ready for Enniscorthy," Granny reminded her.

With her head bent down and speaking in a whingy voice, she said, "I want to play in the garden."

"Okay, so you don't want Enniscorthy then," Granda said.

"No," she said.

"She doesn't understand," Granny said.

"You can play in the garden after Enniscorthy," Granda suggested.

"No, I want the garden," she insisted.

"You can watch some telly until we are ready," Granny offered.

Still whinging, she then said, "I want to play with my toys here."

Granny took her to the dining room to let her play with her toy cars and tractor. She called out for Granda. Granny told her he was busy.

"I'm writing your story, Doireann," Granda yelled back.

"Oh no," she protested.

A while later, she wanted to know, "Are we going?"

"In about ten minutes," Granny told her and continued with, "Tell Granda, we will go in ten minutes."

"Granda are you ready?" she asked.

"Eh, not yet, Doireann."

And having heard what Granny said to her, Granda said, "I'll be ready in about ten minutes. So, can you tell Granny that, pet?"

"Granda is ready and said something that was hard to understand!" Doireann then informed Granny.

Granny kept on at her and wanted to know what Granda had said.

"He will be ready in two minutes," she fibbed.

Granda burst out laughing and shouted, "I said ten minutes, ye little scallywag."

"I'm not that," she responded.

Granny, now also laughing, agreed and said, "You are Doireann; isn't that, right?"

And she nodded in agreement.

Granny then read her a story called *Tinkerbell and the Secret of the Wings*, and she listened intently.

Eventually, they headed out to the car to go to Enniscorthy Playground.

While seated in the car, Granny asked, "Where's your soother, Doireann?"

"I don't have it, Granny."

"It must be inside the house," Granny said because she could not locate it in the car.

"I don't want it, Granny," she said.

"But you will want it," Granny insisted.

"I don't want it," Doireann persisted.

"Ah, here, I'll go and look for it," said Granda, who was now about to explode.

Now much louder, Doireann roars, "*I don't want it*!"

Granda found the soother, where Doireann had dropped it, on the telly chair. Granny put it into her bag. They then left for Enniscorthy.

"We're here now," Doireann proclaimed.

"No, we're not, Doireann," Granny said.

"We are," she insisted.

"Doireann, this is only Ferns, and we still have a bit to go," Granny explained.

A little while later, she asked, "Are we here yet?"

"No, Doireann. This is Scarawalsh," said Granda and continued with, "You can't say the word *Scarawalsh*, Doireann, can you?" Granda just wanted her to pronounce the name.

"Don't say [I can't say] Scarawalsh, Granda," she retorted, putting Granda in his place.

Granda took the back roads to the playground to avoid any hold-ups in the main town.

Driving past St Aidan's National School, Doireann announced, "We are here now."

"No," said Granny.

"Where are we?" she asked.

"In Enniscorthy," Granny told her.

"We're here then," she said, meaning the playground.

"Well, it's the outskirts [of Enniscorthy], Doireann," Granny tried to explain.

"But where is it?" continued the playground enthusiast.

Granda said, "This is Enniscorthy, and it's In Enniscorthy."

Granda had to negotiate a detour due to road works, and eventually arrived at a full carpark at the Enniscorthy Playground, by the river Slaney, which was now packed with kids also. As Granda dropped them off, Doireann asked, "Where are you going, Granda?"

"I am just going to park the car, Doireann. I won't be long," Granda assured her.

Luckily for Granda, a hotel guest was just leaving, and he parked in that spot. There was another parking bay out of bounds, as a driver had taken up one and a half parking bays, which irked Granda. When Granda entered the playground, Granny was sitting beside Doireann, who was having her smoothie drink. Granda put his hat on her head because of the strong sun, but she just flung it to the ground, saying in a moany voice, "I don't want it."

Granny said to leave it and put the hat in her bag. Mammy normally put sun factor cream on Doireann before arriving at Granny and Granda's house in the mornings but forgot to do it today. Doireann played on the usual playground equipment. Granny and Granda stood guard, especially whenever she climbed up something. She really enjoyed herself, as there were many kids there this time. Other times, she would have it all to herself.

The zip wire that whizzed along an overhead wire, when pushed, was very popular. Doireann was told it was for older kids, but she still had to climb up the steps to the platform and "size it up". Next thing, the zip wire seat hit her on the head on its return, and she started to cry, more from the fright than anything else.

Granny held her in her arms as she cried, until she was back on the platform to size it up once again. She put Teddy Pink and "Tiger-Lion" on the large circular spin-around seat and pushed them around with the help of Granny.

When Doireann had asked Granny for the tiger, Granny had replied, "It's a lion; that's what you said it was."

"It's a tiger!" Doireann insisted.

"Does he want a name?" Granda asked.

"Teddy," she replied.

"Ah, okay, Doireann. It's Tiger the Teddy; you have two teddies with you today," Granda announced.

Granny got her to sit on the large circular spin-around seat before pushing it. At one stage, when she fell off, she could not stop laughing, as she lay prostrate on the rubber surface. She was now in great spirits. She ran about for a little while only.

The intense heat, along with the continuous sunshine got to her, and she soon tired. Each time, when Granny and Granda suggested they leave, she complained, saying, "I want to try another one," meaning another piece of playground equipment.

Granny would say in a stern voice, "Okay, one more and then we are going."

Granny found herself repeating the same thing over and over, all to no avail. Continuing to ignore Granny, Doireann started to run along a designated wide-open space within the playground.

"Start walking towards the gate, while keeping an eye on her," Granda said to Granny. He then called out to her, "We are going now, Doireann."

"Wait for me," she shouted back.

"Come on," Granda said in a hurried sounding voice.

"Wait for me," she shouted again, unknowingly attempting to achieve a new world record in athletics, such was her pace. She got the message.

"We have to find Granda's car," Granny suggested.

"There it is," she pointed.

Granny gave her some water to drink. "It's very hot in the car," she said.

Granda opened all the car doors before he strapped her into her car seat.

"Can I have the soother?" she asked.

"I knew that would happen," Granny proclaimed.

Granda drove the car, with the air conditioning on full blast and the windows wide open, until the a/c was nice and cool. Then closing the windows, Granda started to sing (using his own words) songs that Doireann knew.

"It's my turn," she announced and went, "Lalalalalaa lalaaa lalalala," and so on.

"That was lovely," Granny said.

Then Granda picked up the small blue car towel and flung it over his shoulder in her direction.

She picked it up and flung it at Granny, who was sitting beside her as always, while giggling at the same time.

When she wanted Tiger the Teddy, Granny said, "Sorry, but I cannot reach it."

The teddies were on the floor, and Granny had her seatbelt on. Doireann got angry and started to whinge, demanding them. Granny emphasised, "No," evoking more ructions in the back of the car. Granda started singing, "I am a happy person today, ha ha, ha ha. And Doireann is a moany person today."

"*Don't do that, Granda!*" she roared.

"I can sing if I want to," Granda told her.

When they arrived home, Granda helped her out of the car seat. She picked her teddies up off the floor and said, "You are being nice to me *now*, Granda," with a very distinctive emphasis on the word *now*.

Granny changed her wet nappy, and then she immediately headed for the fridge to have her strawberries. Granny gave her blueberries also. She wanted five berries. Granny counted the berries, using Doireann's fingers. "One, two, three, four, five" and threw in an extra one, making it six.

Doireann insisted she wanted five berries, and Granny counted the six berries and even gave her another one, making it seven. She was still not happy and had a face on her that would stop a clock. *A right little tearaway, ha ha*, mused Granda.

She loved her fruit, which was great and a credit to her mammy for encouraging her to eat fruit since she was a baby. Earlier, she ate a small box of raisins, also. Then she had some nuts and pitta bread, with tea.

"Are you finished, Granny?" she asked.

"Have you finished? Is the proper way to ask," Granda told her. "Doireann, say it like that," he asked?

"Granny, have you finished?" she asked.

"No, Doireann, not yet."

"I'm finished," she said.

"You should say, I have finished," Granda, the teacher, told her.

She still had her tea to finish, and as she started to drink it, Granny declared, "There's butter and everything else in the tea."

"Yuck," said Granda.

She must have dunked her pitta bread into the tea.

After lunch, Granda was told by Doireann, "Follow me."

She needed help getting blankets for the tent that Granny was going to resurrect for her again today at her request. Granny got the three large blankets out. Using a bedsheet, Doireann put it over Teddy Pink and Teddy the Tiger as they lay on the dining room floor.

"Are you taking them out to the tent?" Granda asked.

"Shush, they are sleeping," he was bluntly told.

Granny built the tent, while Doireann set up the rocket launcher in case of an attack. She ran towards the kitchen door to get Granda to come out. Seeing her running, Granda opened the bedroom window, from where he was working at the same time as Granny shouted, "Wait, Doireann. Granda is busy."

Doireann opened the kitchen door anyway and ran into Granda's room. "Granda, are you coming out?" she asked.

"Yeah, I'll be out in a couple of minutes," Granda assured her.

"No, Granda, now," she insisted in a whining voice.

"Doireann, I will be out in a couple of minutes," he repeated.

"Granda, stop reading about me."

"I am not *reading* about you."

She stood there sulking and continued to demand that he come out at once. Granda sent her out to Granny, and the crying got louder, so Granny brought her back into the house.

Eventually she calmed down and went outside again. Granda arrived out, and Granny went to use the loo. Doireann loaded a rocket onto the launcher and jumped on the pump, sending the rocket sky-high. "You're next Granda and don't do it too high," the sergeant major ordered.

"Okay [yes sir], Doireann," he said and sent his rocket a distance far shorter than the sergeant major had done.

"Okay, Granda, [let's] race to get the rockets," was the order.

Granda pretended to run, mindful that his superior must win!

Ten minutes passed and the ammunition was running low, when Mammy appeared, up by the side of the house. As Granda opened the side gate's combo lock, Doireann peered through the small gaps. Seeing Mammy, she excitedly said, "Hiya, Mammy."

"Hiya, Doireann," came the reply, just as Granny arrived back out.

She showed Mammy what she had painted with Granny last week. Mammy had a good look at the newly painted ladybirds and admired her work. "Now, Mammy, I'll show you the coloured flowers that Granny did" (grew) and brought her to them. Then, she showed her Mammy the painted tree stumps.

"Who did them?" Mammy asked her.

"Granny."

"Ah, they are very nice; they are lovely," Mammy said.

CHAPTER 20

A Promised "Picnic"

5 July

Granny travelled to Loughlinstown Hospital with Granda. He had to have a small medical procedure done. Mammy and Daddy collected Uncle Richard at Dublin Airport around the same time. He was on a visit from Cambodia. Richard et al. arrived at Granny and Granda's house at about 4 p.m.

Later, he handed out various gifts from his family. Doireann was delighted with her Cambodian shoulder bag and a couple of different types of "lucky" elephants. Aunt Selin also sent her a beautiful lady's gold-coloured metal ornament box, with double mirrors inside. It had an elephant engraved on the outside of the cover lid.

Doireann then played the singalong game, "Ring-a-Ring-a-Rosie, and We All Fall Down" with Mammy and Granny. Richard loved it, as his daughter's name was Rosie. Granda, Mammy, and Doireann had to play the game also. She wouldn't play with Richard and was very shy and stand-offish as she always was with strangers. But when she was leaving with Mammy, she gave him a lovely big wave bye-bye.

9 July

Doireann walked across the grass to Granny and Granda's house with Mammy. When Granda opened the hall door, she said, with her hands well animated, "I didn't bring teddies today, Granda."

"Ah, are they tired?" he asked.

"Yes."

"Doireann put them asleep before leaving the house," Mammy told Granda.

"I saw the spiders," she said.

Mammy explained, "We had to be careful when stepping through the gap in the concrete fence [surrounding the grass] so as not to disturb the spiders' houses."

"I have a smoothie, and you are not getting it," she told Granda with a beautiful big smile on her little face.

Granny came to the hall door, and Doireann handed her a stone she had chosen from the garden. "Is Rishie [Richie] here?" she asked.

"Yes. He is asleep at the moment," Granny said.

After Mammy went off to work, she made Granny and Granda tea with her toy tea set. Later, Granny went out the back to play with her and her toy skittles. Each time she readied herself to roll the plastic ball, the wind would blow the plastic skittles down first, much to her annoyance. Happy days!

They decided to play with the Connect 4 game instead. Granny went in to talk with Richard now that he was up. Granda stayed with Doireann and played with the skittles again. Next, they played with the rocket launcher. Granda positioned a chair down the garden. They had to try and land the rockets on it. Her first two attempts were successful, but she missed on the third go. Granda kept repositioning the chair for her after each miss, until she got tired from fetching the rockets and bored with the game.

"Will you come to my house, Granda, to play?" she asked.

"Of course, I will," he assured her.

"I will bring all my friends," she told him.

"Well, Doireann, I think you will have to ask Mammy first," he suggested.

Granda and Doireann sat down for a while, and then she said, "I want to go inside."

"Will I put the telly on for you?" he asked her.

"Yes."

She sat and watched Peppa Pig, before watching Barney with all the singing. Earlier, Granda had shown her a lovely picture of two macaws, perching on a tree branch in Brazil, on his computer screen (Edson Vandeira / Getty images).

"Granda, can I have some of your water?" she asked.

"Of course, Doireann."

After she had some water, Granda asked, "Do you want more?"

"No thanks."

Then Granny made Granda a cup of tea.

"Can I have one, Granny?" she asked. Doireann struggled to sit up on the chair. "Move that," she told Granny.

"Where's your manners, Doireann?" Granny reminded her.

"Please," she said.

Granny removed the cushion, allowing her to sit up on the chair.

"Are you not drinking your tea, Doireann?" Granda asked.

"I'm waiting for my toast," he was told.

"You are getting toast. Oh wow!" joked Granda.

"And my tea is still hot," she added.

Granny put more milk into her tea.

"I am drinking like you, Granda," she said.

Then she and Granda started to hide their faces from each other behind some of the bottles on the table.

"I can see you, Granda," he was told, and he hid his face again and again, until she got bored with that game.

Granny gave her her toast, and she ate some of it.

"I want to see what's on" (the telly), she said as she hopped down off the chair to have a look.

She started to sing along with some of the songs then. Later, she danced like all of Barney's friends on the telly, including Baby Bop. Next thing, she darted out of the room towards her cot to fetch Baby Bop. At one stage during the morning, she went looking for Granda.

"Are you all right, Granda?" she asked, showing some concern.

"Ah, I'm fine," he assured her.

Granny had told her that Granda had hurt his toe.

"Is your toe better now, Granda?" she asked.

"Yes, much better." And he gave her a big hug for her concern and told her he loved her very much.

Off she went, with a smile as big as a Cheshire cat.

Later, she went to Granda, followed by Granny, to ask him to open the circular Happy Cow box of triangular cheeses. Granny said, "When I pulled the string to open it, it just snapped, and she wouldn't let me carry on with it anymore."

Granda twisted the "sealed" cover in a circular direction to loosen it. He then showed Doireann the lid and said, "Here, you try and open it."

She did and marvelled at all the little triangular cheeses, inside.

"Do you want one?" Granny asked her.

"No."

"Well, put them back into the fridge; that's where the happy cows like to be in this weather," Granda told her.

Later, she helped Granda put new fresh water into the three small birdbaths in the garden, after he emptied the filthy water out and cleaned them. They filled a small grey (toy) watering container from the outdoor tap to transport across the garden to the birdbaths. It took forever and a day. Then they had a look at all of Granny's lovely flowers, and Doireann admired the lovely pink ones. Granda asked her to name the colours as he pointed.

"Red. Blue. Lellow. White." And some others.

Pointing to a purple flower, Granda said, "That one looks blue, but the colour is purple."

Then Doireann noticed a bee flying in and around some of the flowers.

Granda explained, "That's a bumblebee, and it's getting its food from the small lavender flowers."

After observing the bumblebee for a while, she said, "I love bumblebees." Then she spotted a white butterfly and watched it hover around a plant, landing sometimes and then hovering around again. She and Granda then went off down the garden, in search of more bees, butterflies, and flowers. She pointed to a dandelion, and Granda said, "That's a weed."

They saw loads of dandelions down the garden among the overgrowth. Granda walked on one of them by accident, before he was warned. "Don't do that, Granda," she snapped.

"Oh sorry," he said.

She pointed in the direction of the grass, which had now turned to hay because of the heatwave that year. She wanted to know what the little flowers were.

"Oh, they are daisies," he told her.

"I love daisies," she said.

As Granda continued to venture further down the jlong-overgrown section towards the lower half of the garden, he was ordered to go no further. "Stop, Granda, there's bees," he was warned. She was having a "bee in her bonnet" moment! Granda mused.

Granda pointed to the thorny bramble bushes and warned her about them. "That's where blackberries grow, but don't touch those thorns, because they will hurt and scratch your skin."

Then Granda showed her the nettles and explained how they give you a terrible sting that will last for a long time.

Now, back inside the house after their horticultural venture, Granny asked Doireann to replenish the toilet roll stock in the bathroom. When she finished that task, she took some photos using Granda's phone. Next, she picked up her own phone (a redundant one) and made some (pretend) phone calls, while, at the same time, interacting with Granny. Then, she took some (pretend) photos of Granny before it was Granny's turn to take some of her. The emphasis, during this photo shoot was on their respective smiles.

Later, when the Barney DVD ended, she immediately asked, "Can we go out in the garden?"

"Hold on a minute," requested Granny.

"I am going out myself."

"Doireann, I told you to hold on a minute," Granny said sternly.

When Granny was ready, she took Doireann out to the garden to play skittles again. Next thing, Granny was marching behind her on the paths between the flower beds. The sun came out, so they both came in for their sun hats. Doireann didn't have a hat with her today, so Granny lent her one of hers. Once back outside, she removed the sun hat!

Mammy arrived at about 2 p.m. with Oisín. Doireann and Oisín played hide-and-seek in the back garden for a while, before Oisín came in, complaining of the heat. He was attending a tennis camp in Ferns all week, and it was for ninety minutes each day.

When Doireann came in, she was all animated as she asked Oisín, "Are you not finding me?"

Oisín said nothing.

She repeated this over and over, until Mammy stepped in and asked him to play one more game with her before they headed off, and he did.

As they headed out to Mammy's car, Doireann had the green football, and Oisín, the white one.

"I want to stay here," Doireann told her Mammy.

10 July

Granda's twin sister, Aunt Phyllis, called to the house to see Richard. After their lunch, Oisín arrived over and parked his bike up the side of the house. "Mammy will be over soon," he informed Granny and Granda.

Knock, knock, the hall door sounded.

"Can you open the side gate for the buggy?" Mammy asked Granny after she answered the hall door.

Doireann was in the buggy, and when Granny opened the side gate, Granda noticed that she had been crying. "Did you enjoy crèche today?" Granda asked her.

"Yes. No," she replied.

"Did something happen?" he asked.

"A little boy hit her at crèche, today. I am going to complain about that type of behaviour later today," Mammy said angrily.

Doireann showed Granda her "Seaside Dominos" that Mammy had bought for her. Aunt Phyllis then spoke with her and gave her hugs. Aunt Phyllis gave her and Oisín some money. Then she handed money to Richard for his children back home in Cambodia. Before Granda left to drop Phyllis home and then visit the 'Famine Frave' with Richard in Enniscorthy, he used his phone to take some group photos.

Mammy asked, "What are you going to do with all these photos, Da?" because Granda had been taking a lot of photos of late.

Initially, he wanted to make a large photo album but later decided to write this book instead and might produce an album, albeit an amateur one, of all the photos at a later date.

Granda drove Richard back to Mammy's house after Enniscorthy, where they stayed for about forty minutes. Granda tickled Doireann at one stage, and she then told him to tickle Oisín, and he did. She crawled over on the floor and tickled Granda's toes through his sandals as he stood talking. She tickled his toes a few times and got great giggles as she did so.

"Your Mammy used to massage my feet when she was little," Granda told her.

Then she ran up and down the living room lots of times, non-stop.

"Do you want to play dominoes with me?" she asked Granda.

"I will play tomorrow. So, make sure you bring your dominoes over to the house with you," Granda told her.

She nodded in agreement. She lifted Oisín's hurley off the sofa and called it a racket.

"It's a hurley, Doireann," Granda told her.

"No, it's a racket," she insisted. After talking to her Mammy, she said, "It's a hurl, Granda."

"Okay, Doireann," he said.

Kafli, the cat, came into the house and walked over to Doireann, who was spreadeagled on the carpet. As Granda and Richard left to go home, Kafli was ahead of them as they went to open the hall door.

11 July

Granny phoned Mammy to inquire about Doireann being dropped over early as planned this morning. It was getting late, and they had to drive Richard to Bray for the DART. Daddy was running late and arrived over at 10.25 a.m., before he dropped Oisín in Ferns for his tennis camp. Mammy was down in their Kilkenny Curves today. Doireann looked upset, as if she had been crying.

"Are you all right, pet?" Granda asked.

Daddy said, "Ah, she banged her head," which explained the bump on her head.

She seemed a bit disorientated, not knowing whether to stay with Granny and Granda or stay with Daddy.

"Give us a kiss before I go?" Daddy asked.

"No," she said and pulled away from him. She was moaning and still obviously upset over her accident earlier.

Granda beckoned her over and gave her a few hugs. She seemed happy with that.

Next, she was stand-offish with Uncle Richard and not saying anything, just staring, as she always did with new strangers.

When Daddy and Oisín left, Granny and Granda hurried to get going, packing the prepared picnic items into the picnic shoulder bag and gathering up a few other things to bring on their day out in Bray.

"I want to bring Teddy," Doireann told Granda. "I left Teddy Pink at home," she realised.

"Ah, is she resting?" Granda asked.

She nodded her head and ran towards the cot. "Here is Teddy Brown," Granda said, as he lifted him out of the cot.

"No, not that one, Granda," she said.

As he continued his search, he eventually found Teddy White hiding under Snowy and Baby Bop.

"There he is," she said, giving him a big cuddle when Granda handed him over.

Granny spoke with her in the back of the car and sang a few songs with her as usual.

"Where are we going?" she gently asked.

"Bray," Granny told her.

"Where's Bray?" she asked.

"Eh, eh." Granny was now lost for words.

"It's near Greystones," Granda said.

"Oh, Greystones," she said, as if she knew where that was!

That ended that conversation.

"Is this Bray?" enquired Doireann.

"No, it's Kilpedder," Granda told her.

Richard was enjoying the journey up. It had been years since he'd last been home from Australia. He now lived in Cambodia and was visiting family and friends for three weeks.

As they drove on the new M11-Wicklow bypass extension, Granda indicated where Jack White's Inn and Lil Doyle's were in the distance. They used to pass these landmarks on the old N11 on their way to Brittas

Bay Beach, County Wicklow, from Dalkey, County Dublin, when they were little.

"Oh, it's closed," Richard said of Lil Doyle's pub and restaurant.

"It's because of the bypass," Granny told him.

A while later, Granda pointed to the Beehive Pub and Restaurant and said to Richard, "When you were all little, we would cheer for Roisín" (Mammy) "as we passed by the Beehive because she had performed Irish dancing in that place on one St Patrick's Day with her Dalkey Irish Dancing Class."

"This is Bray," an excited Doireann announced as Granda negotiated his way through heavy traffic down the main street.

"Yes, you're right," a surprised Granny said.

"Where is the water?" she asked, meaning the Irish Sea.

Granny interjected with, "Hold on. We have to drive there yet."

As Granda drove towards the DART station, he got held up, with the traffic build-up and because the barrier for the DART train crossing was closed.

"Look, Doireann, there is the water." Granny pointed.

"Can we go there now?" she wanted to know.

"As soon as we drop Richard off," Granda said. "There's the DART, Richard," Granda told him.

"It's a long one," he replied.

"Yeah, they have lengthened them now, with more people commuting into Dublin," Granda updated him.

They dropped Richard off at the DART station entrance and drove back around towards the seaside and promenade. Richard was meeting up with his friend Ian in Dublin. He was travelling down from Portadown in Northern Ireland.

"Will we see Richard again, Granda?" Doireann asked.

"Of course, we will, pet," Granda assured her.

Granda paid the full daily parking charge of €3 this time!

They headed for the playground, which was full of kiddies, along with mammies, daddies, and grandparents at their beck and call. Teddy White was left in the car. Doireann had a great time on the slides and swings and just generally running around. When walking on the snake, Granny would name each alphabet letter that she stepped on one at a time. She mainly played on one slide, where she could climb up steps made of rope. She would then sit there waiting her turn to slide down. Then she would stand up, run to the rope steps, and climb up again and again and again. She wouldn't talk to the other kids, just stare at them, observing everything, just like her Mammy did when she was little. There was a cold breeze coming in off the sea, which felt a lot colder each time the sun went in.

After about an hour, Doireann saw some kids being given bread to eat. "I want some food," she said to Granda.

"Go and ask Granny," he told her.

"It's only 12.30," Granny said.

"I want food," she insisted.

"Let's go and park in our usual spot," Granda suggested.

They all walked to the car. As they neared the car, there was a meltdown. She was uncontrollable, and they could not understand what she was saying. She even screamed as they tried to put her in the car. Granny asked her to calm down and explain her problem.

"I don't want to go home," she cried out and was now sobbing.

"We are only moving to another place, not far away that you've been to before, for our lunch," Granda explained, trying to assure her.

This immediately generated another major meltdown, as she complained, saying, "We are to have a picmic."

Oops, Granda had said *lunch*. "Ah Doireann, we are going to have a picmic; I am sorry for saying lunch when I had indeed promised you a picmic," said an apologetic Granda.

The war ended at 12.45 p.m., now that they had reached a peace agreement, involving the promised picmic and not to go home just yet. They parked in the car park, just below Bray Head.

Granny located a vacant picnic table with beautiful panoramic views of the Irish Sea. Realising they forgot the blanket they would normally use as a tablecloth, Granda hurried back to the car to fetch it. Doireann helped Granny stretch the blanket all the way across the table before they laid out all the goodies. She sat beside Granny while Granda went back to the car again, this time to get his phone and take a few photos.

She ate some of her mammy's homemade banana bread, Granny's cupcake, some of Granny and Granda's crisps, and two Marietta biscuits with butter sandwiched between. This was all washed down with a cup of tea for good measure.

Granny said, "Next time, we won't show her the goodies until she eats her mammy's food first."

Granny and Granda had cheese and onion sarnies with their cups of tea. The sun came out also, which made for a lovely picnic. Granda put the picnic bag and blanket back into the car boot, and when he returned to the picnic table, Granny and Doireann were both pointing towards the sea. Granny had spotted a boat out in the sea. Doireann, being smaller, couldn't see it. So, Granny told her to stand up on the seat.

"Granda, look at the boat. Stand up on the seat," she beckoned.

As Granda neared, she said, "Look, Granda, a boat in the sea. Ahoy there," she called out loudly. She decided she wanted to walk up towards the top of Bray Head, climbing the many, many steps.

"Doireann, I am not able for this," complained Granny, but she just kept climbing away.

After about twenty steps, Granda said, "Doireann, we are getting you a lolly pop, and we need to go to the shop now before they are all gone." She immediately about-turned and headed back down.

Granda reminded Granny about Doireann's promised freeze pop.

"It's called a please pop, and I don't think they will have them," said Granny.

"Doireann, don't worry. We will get you a pop. That will please you," joked Granda.

Before heading back to the car, they let her run down the slightly steep walk that leads to a big open grassy space of grass for picmics. There was hardly anyone there. Only one table was full of young teenagers having something to eat. She loved dashing down towards and around a big wide tree at the end of the wide-open space. Next thing, she darted, full steam ahead, towards a cliff edge, with Granda in hot pursuit.

Granda held her hand and showed her how steep it was at the edge of this massive open area. Granny explained how dangerous it was as Granda inched closer to the edge to let her see for herself.

When they turned around to go back up, Granda said, "Okay, Doireann, let's run."

And with that, she was away in a flash, determined to beat Granda.

Granny let her run around for a bit more, before they headed for the car and drove back down to the prom. The prom was getting busier, so they decided to avoid it and drove straight to Tesco's in Bray town.

Before going into Tesco'swith Granny, she said, "You are not coming, Granda." And even when Granda pretended to cry, it made no difference. So, Granda sat back in the car, writing his notes.

They arrived back in no time.

"They don't do singles," Granny complained. "We have to go to the garage shop next door."

Then Granny told Granda that Doireann was moaning about her legs being sore when they were in Tesco's. "I am not carrying you," Granny had to tell her in no uncertain fashion.

When they arrived back from the garage shop, Doireann was doing a hop, skip, and a jump as they approached the car. They had a Loop-D-Loop for Granny and some other special lolly pop for Doireann. They then left for home.

When they finished their lolly pops, Granny said to her, "I want you to lie back and get a sleep like me."

"Granny, Granny," she whispered.

"Doireann, I thought you were going asleep," Granny said.

She carried on for another while, until Granda put some music on. Doireann fell fast asleep for the whole journey home.

Then Daddy phoned, wanting to know what time they would be home, as he had to do an errand in Gorey.

"It'll be about forty minutes," Granny informed him.

Granda parked in the driveway, and Granny decided to stay with Doireann until she woke up, which occurred ten minutes later. Doireann then watched a bit of telly, until Granny phoned Daddy, letting him know that they had arrived home. Five minutes later, Daddy and Oisín were at the hall door for Doireann, but she didn't want to go, moaning in protest.

"Is Richie here?" asked Oisín.

"Ah, no. He is in Dublin until tomorrow meeting up with his friend," Granda informed him.

When they left, Granny and Granda went to the gym to try and keep in touch with their workouts.

CHAPTER 21

They Are Lazies

18 July

Oisín headed home after his breakfast. He had stayed overnight in Granny and Granda's house because Uncle Richard was returning to Cambodia the following day. Mammy arrived over with Doireann later that morning. She had to hurry away to drive her Spanish student to his school and drive Oisín to his football camp. Granda was getting washed, and Granny put the Barney DVD on for Doireann.

"Hello, Doireann. It's great to see you again, and you have lovely clothes on today," Granda told her when he arrived in the dining room. When he gave her a hug, she put her arms around him.

"Did you choose those lovely clothes yourself?" he asked.

"No, Mammy," she told him.

"Well, aren't you the pretty one. Let me take a photo of you." *Click.* "And now one with Granny." *Click.*

She then explained, in an animated fashion, the different coloured clothes she was wearing. "My pink dress goes with my tights, and that goes with my shoes," she said and did a twirl for good measure.

"Did you enjoy your holiday last week?" Granda asked.

"Yes. There were two playgrounds, a little one and a big one. Granda, you wouldn't be able to sit on the [toy] car seat, because you would break it," she said as she laughed out loud. She went to her shoulder bag and took out her soother.

"She gave that soother to Mammy earlier before she left the house," a very surprised Granny informed Granda, now wondering how it had made its way back into her bag. "Mammy is trying to cut the soother out," Granny added.

Doireann danced to the music and sang from the Barney DVD. Then she watched the music DVD and danced to it also.

Granda sat at the kitchen table eating his porridge.

Doireann pointed at him and asked, "Is your porridge hot, Granda?"

"Yes, a bit hot, Doireann," Granda informed her.

"Blow on it," he was told.

And he did, before putting a spoonful into his mouth.

As he was about to take another spoonful, he was reminded, "Blow on it, Granda."

He did as he was told.

"Hold hands under it, Granda," she advised, referring to the spoon. "And don't let it spill."

"I am holding the spoon over the bowl. Look," Granda told her.

She continued to observe Granda's behaviour as he ate his porridge. Granny made toast for her.

"Can I go out after this, Granny?" she asked.

Granny was cleaning the dishes.

"I will take her out as soon as I've finished," Granda offered instead.

"Can I get Baby Bop?" she asked.

"Yes," Granda said and went into the cot to fetch Baby Bop and the teddies for her. Snowy was left in the cot to rest up today. Granda had still not finished his breakfast.

"Mind your breakfast doesn't get cold, Granda," she told him.

Uncle Richard appeared in the dining room, but Doireann said nothing. He picked up Teddy Pink. "Is this Pinkie Bear?" he asked her.

But she just stood silent, observing the big, tall Uncle Richie. Later on, while sitting at the table for lunch, she said, "You're the best granny."

"That's nice, Doireann," Granny replied.

Granda was standing close by. "Eh, and Granda is the best granda as well," she said.

Granda looked at the little box on the table and asked, "What's that, Doireann?"

"They're raisins," he was told, as she grabbed them and ran off, saying loudly, "They're mine, Granda."

She allowed Granny to remove her very wet nappy, once Granny agreed to let her wear, only her pants. Later, while out in the garden, she quickly ran into the house and said to Granny, "I need to do wee-wee." And then announced to the world on her return that she had done a wee-wee.

"You are a big girl now," Granda proudly told her.

"Yes, I am big now," she proudly agreed.

Out in the back, once again, she played with the tent, the skittles, and the bins and buckets. She watered some flowers and then ran up and down the garden a lot. Granda took photos with his phone. He then cleaned the three birdbaths and filled them with water from the water butt, conscious that a hosepipe ban was in operation, due to the current heatwave. Richard went for a jog, doing his warm-ups across the road first, and Granny swept the kitchen floor. Using the feathered duster, Doireann swept the hall and then the carpet in Granda's bedroom, where he was now working on his book.

"Would you like the radio on Granda?" she asked.

As he jotted down all of this activity, he nodded first and then said, "Yes, pet."

The radio was switched on and, "Is that okay, Granda?" he was, once again, asked.

"Yes, pet. And thank you very much for all of this," Granda said.

"You're welcome," came the sweet reply.

Next thing, with a giggle, she was rubbing Granda's back, saying, "I am 'sweeping' your back, Granda."

"Okay, Doireann," Granda said.

They played more of the same games in the garden after lunch. Later on, Doireann kept saying, "I'm not shy now. I'm not shy anymore," and so on. She was referring to Richard and her interactions with him a lot more. Down the garden, as Richard chased her and Teddy Pink, she off-loaded Teddy, to get away faster. Richard picked Teddy Pink up and went in the opposite direction, away from her. He then started to run as she took chase, and as he sped up, running around the makeshift tent, she started giggling as she tried to catch him, getting closer and closer. Next, the rocket launcher was set up, and they all had a go at launching the rockets. Then they played with the Frisbee, and after this they played with the four-in-a-row game, placing the discs into the slots.

Earlier, as Doireann and Granda went for a walk down the garden, she held Teddy Pink and cradled her as she walked and muttered some words. On their return, she said Teddy was tired and Granda held Teddy. "No, Granda. That's not the way to carry Teddy," he was told.

Granda held Teddy up to his shoulder.

In a much louder voice now and with her hands outstretched, she said, "No, Granda, not that way."

Granda handed Teddy to her, allowing her to show him how to cradle Teddy Pink. Then she again handed Granda Teddy Pink to cradle properly, and he did.

Now, over at the back door, she was close to where some cobwebs were. "Mind, Doireann, there are spiders' webs there," Granda warned.

"I don't like spiders, Granda," she replied.

"Ah okay, pet. That's okay," Granda assured her.

Then she searched for one and pointed to a web, with something on it. "That's not a spider Doireann; it's a dead fly," Granda told her.

"How did he dead], Granda?" she asked.

"Ah, I don't know. Come on. Let's walk again," said Granda, not ready to give a lesson on wildlife.

Granda sat on the bench.

"Would you like a cup of tea, Granda?" she asked.

Granda headed for the kitchen door, saying, "Oh, okay, Doireann. I will fetch your tea service."

"No, Granda, not that," he was told. She pointed to the yellow ceramic teapot and cup, now used as a garden ornament. She brought over the cup, with water already in it.

"There you are, Granda."

"Ah thanks, Doireann," said Granda as he pretended to take a sip. "That was lovely."

"Can I finish it?" she asked.

"Oh, well, okay, but be careful, as the water is dirty," Granda warned.

She took a pretend sip like Granda had.

"Do you want to pour the rest, on some flowers?" asked Granda.

She then went and poured the water (tea) on the flowers.

Next, she asked, if she could pick a flower for Mammy.

"Which one do you, want?" Granda asked.

She approached the flowers and pointed towards the only two pink flowers in the garden.

"Well, Doireann, you better ask Granny first," Granda suggested.

Mammy and Oisín called to collect her. Oisín was a bit upset because Richard was going back home soon. They stayed for about thirty minutes because Doireann was having such fun playing. Richard asked Oisín around later in the evening after dinner, as it was his last night in Ireland.

As they were about to leave, Doireann remembered the flower for Mammy and ran with Granny to the pink flowers. She then changed her mind and pointed to the flowers by the back wall. "The red one, Granny," she said.

Mammy took it and put it into her hair first, before putting it into Doireann's hair. They all told her that she looked gorgeous before they left for home.

19 July

Mammy, Doireann, and Oisín called over to say goodbye to Richard and to give him some presents for Selin, Richie, Eddie, and Rosie. Doireann showed Granda the small paper bag she was holding and said it was for her cousins and baby Rosie. She took the big bag of chocolate buttons out to let Granda see it.

"Oh, that's brill," he said.

Mammy had another bag with the other presents. And then Richard put them into his suitcase. There were hugs all round and goodbyes, except for Doireann, who got upset and refused to give Uncle Richard a hug when he said he was leaving. She did not want him to leave. Mammy then, promised to let her play for a little while across the road, just to get her and her sad-looking face to leave.

When Granda started to take a few photos, with his mobile phone, Doireann loudly said, in an angry voice, "No more photos, Granda."

Mammy then left to get to Oisín's football camp, for 10 a.m.

20 July

Granny answered the knock on the hall door to find Doireann standing there in her raincoat. "It's raining," she said.

Mammy had Teddy Pink stuffed down her top because Doireann had told her to. She was concerned about Teddy getting wet. Pointing to the blue Chelsea jersey that Granda was wearing, she asked, "Why are you wearing that?"

"I support Chelsea football club and not Liverpool, who Oisín and Daddy support," Granda informed her.

"I have cookies," she told Granda, pointing to her shoulder bag. "I want them."

Mammy opened the little packet for her. She stuffed a couple of cookies into her mouth, while Mammy and Granny chatted. "You're lazies" (ladies), Doireann announced, her mouth full of cookies.

"They are *lazy*," joked Granda. "Are they biscuits you are eating?" he teased.

"No, Granda, they are cookies."

"Oh, okay. Who cooked them cookies then?" he asked but was ignored.

"Would you like some, Granda?" she asked.

"Ah, no, pet, and thanks for asking."

Then, she cleaned the kitchen floor with the small brush and pan.

"Bye, Mammy," she shouted. "Bye, Mammy. Byeeeeeeee, Mammy," she shouted again as Mammy and Granny continued to chat at the hall door.

"Bye, Doireann," Mammy said back as she left for work.

"Granda, can you put this together?" she asked, holding out the small pan and brush.

"Let me show you how you put it together," he suggested instead.

After his demonstration, he invited her to try it. As she attempted it, Granda encouraged her. "Well done, pet. Now press down hard." He pointed to the brush handle. "And clip it in," he said as she snapped the pan handle in place. "Ah, well done. You're great."

"Can you put it back to where you got it from, now, pet?" he asked.

Just as she put it back into the cubbyhole just off the kitchen, Granny arrived and said, "Thank you, Doireann," and then asked, "Did you have breakfast?"

"Yes."

"What did you have?" asked Granda.

"Porridge."

"Oh, just like me. And did you have toast?" Granda asked.

"No."

"I did. Ha ha," joked Granda.

And she gave him a lovely smile back, knowing Granda was teasing her.

"You had cookies, though, didn't you, Doireann? And Granda didn't," Granny said.

Doireann nodded in agreement. She went to the fridge and took out the round cheese box, full of triangular cheese sections. "Can I have one, Granny?" she asked.

"Yes."

"Can you help me open one?"

Granny opened it for her.

Leaving the dining room, she asked, "What is Granda doing?" and went into his room, where he was at his workstation writing these notes.

"Hiya, Doireann," said Granda.

"Look Granda," she said.

"Brill, you have some cheese. Do you like that cheese?" Granda asked her.

She nodded yes and then followed Granda into the dining room, until he managed to escape from her, once again.

"Granny can you switch on the telly?" was Granda's SOS. She sat and watched Peppa Pig. Earlier, she'd asked Granny, "Can we go to Enniscorthy?"

"Well, it's raining," Granny reminded her.

"When it stops raining," she persisted.

"It will be very wet, Doireann," Granda interjected.

"But I told Mammy."

"We will take you there next week. Promise," said Granda and opened the back door to show her the wet garden furniture and other wet things outside.

"But when it stops," she pleaded.

"Ah, sure, Doireann, it will take all day for it to dry," Granda explained. That finished that conversation.

Thomas the Tank Engine came on the telly. "I don't like this" she shouted.

"Okay," said Granny on entering the room, irritated by her attitude.

She wanted the TV channel changed to some other children's programme.

A while later, Granny and Granda were chatting by the workstation. Doireann arrived in to see what was happening. She had already said she didn't want to go to the library today. Granda asked her again, and she said no, with an animated moan. Granny said she just had to get some things in Dunnes Stores and left it at that.

"Would you like to do a, '*Wheeeeeeeeeeeeeeeeeeeeeeeeeeeeeeeeeeeeeeeeeeeeeee eeeeeeeeeeee,*' and then say hello to Noddy?" Granda suggested.

Silence.

Granny then said, "She is tired."

"Well, hello, tired," Granda said, offering her his outstretched hand.

Granda got the (I-hate-you) stares.

Granda logged into Facebook and then asked her, "Do you want to see your [Cambodian] cousins playing football?"

She sat up on Granda's lap to watch the video that Uncle Richard had posted. "Who is he?" she asked.

"He's the coach," Granda told her.

"Who are they?" she asked of the other young children in the photo.

"They are your cousins, Richie and Eddie, with their school pals."

Pointing to the one girl in the group, she asked, "What's her name?"

"Ah, I don't know that, Doireann."

She then looked at the photos of the children holding their completion certificates, before watching another video of the children chasing the adults, trying to snatch coloured rags from their hands.

She then went into Granny and told her she didn't like dinosaurs.

"I wouldn't like to see one in our garden," Granny said.

Doireann made a big screeching noise and told Granny it was like a tiger. She made the same noise again. Granny told her that as soon as the film—a funny cartoon called *Two by Two* about the animals travelling to and boarding Noah's Ark—was over, they would go out to the back garden because it had stopped raining. "The garden is still wet but not as wet as earlier," Granny told her.

When Granda asked Granny for the name of the film for his notes, Doireann told Granda that it had stop raining. "We will go outside when the film is over," Granny reminded her.

When the film was over, they went out immediately. "Granda, I want to get the things," she said as she stood at the closed shed door.

She carried the bucket out with the skittles and ball, as well as the discs for the Connect 4 game. Granda got the metal buckets and placed the skittles on them.

"Where's the other ball?" she asked.

"Inside, Doireann. I will get it," Granda offered.

The games they played, involved attempts to knock the skittles off the buckets and lobbing the skittles into the large bucket. Then she ran up and down the garden before Granny built an obstacle course for her, using the skittles. She also had to touch the twirling pendants hanging from the clothesline as she ran past. Teddy Pink had to clap her hands each time she completed the obstacle course. She would remind Granda to prompt Teddy to clap her hands. Then she held Teddy Pink between her teeth, saying, "Look, I have a cub," and Granda quickly took a photo. Other times, she would run to Teddy Pink and give her a big hug, or she would just talk to Teddy.

To coax her in, for her lunch, Granda promised to come out and play again after lunch, and she accepted this. She only ate a bit of lunch and got down from the table, saying, "I am ready to go back out now."

"Get back up to the table and eat some more. We are not going out until we have all finished our lunch," Granny told her.

She had spag-ball and would only eat the spaghetti and not the mince. She wanted to watch Barney and sat up in her TV chair. Granny gave her some Cambridge bread with butter. At one stage, she dropped her bottle of water, spilling it on the floor. Granny mopped it up. Then Granda mopped up some more of the water that Granny had missed.

"Thanks, Granda. And I'm sorry," Doireann said.

"That's okay, pet. You only dropped your bottle. You didn't spill the water intentionally," Granda assured her.

Granny turned the bottle upside down, and when no water came out, she couldn't understand why the floor got wet. Granda explained, "When the bottle fell on its head, the cap closed shut, but some water did leak out just before the cap closed."

When Barney and his pals started singing and dancing with their arms moving, Doireann was up and out of her chair, copying them. Next, poor Granny was dragged into the fray. Then, all of a sudden, Granny said, "Doireann, don't move. Stand there and don't move; you must have wanted to go to the toilet, and you should have said something."

As Granda was writing these notes, he could hear the hairdryer on. So, God knows what got wet, and he wasn't asking. When Mammy had called to the house earlier this morning, she'd proudly proclaimed that Doireann wasn't wearing a nappy and she had asked to go to the toilet before they left the house. Later, when out in the garden, Granda had reminded her to tell them if she needed to go to the toilet.

After Granny finished with the hairdryer, Doireann arrived back out, looking for her small dingy cars to play with. Because she never played with them anymore, Granny and Granda had given them to Richard to take back to Cambodia for his kids. They had been lying at the end of Doireann's toys box. You'd wonder what drew her back to the cars then?

Granda quickly made up a story. "I moved them somewhere and will have to look for them but not now," he pretended.

To get her mind off the cars, Granda asked, "Will you tell us when you want to go to the toilet, pet?"

She nodded in agreement. She had asked Granny for a nappy, but Granny told her, "You don't need one. Just tell us if you want to go to the toilet."

Granda then assured her it was an accident and not to worry and that she was a big girl now. Later on, she gave Granda her soother, saying, "I don't need that now, because I am a big girl."

Granda went to her toys box and, seeing some small figures of people and animals, suggested building a shed for these figures with her building blocks. Granda started putting some blocks together, until Doireann said, "I will do that, Granda." This kept her busy for a while and took her mind off the cars.

What if she reminds me about the cars again? thought Granda, deciding he would have to buy new ones for her.

She wanted to go out, but Granny said, "You can't because your shoes are outside drying."

"Perhaps she could play outside B-A-R-E-F-O-O-T-E-D because it's warm and dry now?" Granda suggested. Granda had been mindful to spell the word *barefooted*

Doireann asked, "What are you saying, Granda?"

Granny agreed to take her out and Granda explained to her what he had been talking about. "Do you know what barefoot is, Doireann?" he asked.

"No, Granda."

Pointing to her bare foot, Granda said, "It means you have nothing on your feet, and they are bare."

Off she went with Granny. Next thing, she was back in, running to Granda, asking, "Can I have your phone, Granda? I want to take a photo of Teddy Pink."

Teddy Pink was now sitting up on the big old empty plastic paint bucket. She took the photo and immediately returned the phone, saying, "Thank you, Granda."

"Ah thanks, pet. You're very good," Granda told her.

"I took a photo of Teddy."

"Ah brilliant; and was Teddy happy?" he asked.

"Yes," she said, before running out to Granny again. She loved being out, running around the garden.

Mammy called and got her ready to go. "I want to go on the (ride-along) car," she said and hopped on it. She wouldn't put her pants or shoes on, and Mammy had to carry her to the car parked outside.

Granda shouted, "Bye-bye, lazies."

And Doireann waved with a big smile as Mammy laughed.

CHAPTER 22

S-C-A-R-E-D of the D-A-R-K

23 July

Granny texted Mammy to say they would be home at about 9.20 a.m. from the gym. After they arrived home, Mammy phoned Granny (at 9.45 a.m.) to say she would be over with Doireann, in about five minutes. She had sent Daddy to Gorey for something for Doireann's lunch and didn't think he would be so long. Granny said she could have made up something for her.

Mammy, Doireann and Oisín arrived over at 9.50 a.m., and because Oisín was now in a hurry to get to his football camp, Mammy didn't hang around. There were some quick hugs for Doireann, and off they went. Granda took a photo of Oisín in his new Irish rugby jersey before he left. He then took photos of Teddy Pink and Tiger Teddy for Doireann.

Granny asked Doireann, "Did you have your brekkie?"

"Yes."

"What did you have?" Granda asked.

"Cheerios."

"Did you sing, cheerio, cheerio, cheerio while eating them?" continued Granda as he did a little dance.

She looked at him strangely.

Now holding Teddy Pink, Granda got her to sing cheerio, cheerio, cheerio, moving her arms to the music at the same time. Doireann laughed at this and got Tiger Teddy to do the same. Then Granda held on to both Teddy Pink and Tiger Teddy, as they waved their arms and sang cheerio, cheerio, cheerio, with him. Doireann loved it and laughed, studying their every move.

She drank her smoothie; watched some children's programmes on the telly; and then watched Peppa Pig, which she loved. Granny's questions to Doireann fell on deaf ears because she was so engrossed in Peppa Pig.

Later, she talked about jumping on the bed and how you could hurt your head. "Always hold hands out," she told Granny.

Next, she talked about being in Clara Lara, an adventure park in County Wicklow yesterday and asked, "Have yous ever been there?"

"We used to take your mammy and your Uncles Gary and Richard, there when they were young," Granny told her.

"Granda, I got sick yesterday," she said.

"Up there?" Granda asked, meaning in Clara Lara.

"No."

"Where?" Granda had another go.

"When we got home. But I was all right after it," she told him.

"Did you have your dinner," Granda enquired.

"Yes."

When Mammy arrived to collect her as usual, she was surprised at this news, after Granny and Granda had informed her.

"Doireann wasn't sick yesterday!" Mammy told them.

Doireann went into Granda as he was writing his notes and asked, "Did you leave the teddies on top of my chair, Granda?"

"Yes, I did," he replied with a big grin on his face.

A while later, as she sat watching the telly, Granda lay Teddy Pink and Tiger Teddy on their bellies on top of her chair, looking down at her. Then Granda went and took a photo of Teddy Pink. She took a photo of Granda holding the two teddies and then asked, "Can we feed the ducks today?"

Granda told Granny, who in turn told her that we should not be feeding the ducks at this time of the year. She then agreed to go to the library in Gorey, and Granny told her to sit on the toilet before they left to see if she could do a wee. As this was a "no-nappy day", Granda suggested to Granny that they bring some spare nappies, just in case.

Doireann noticed she had left her red jacket behind last Friday. She wanted it taken down off the coat rack in the hall to bring it—in the sweltering heat (twenty-four degrees).

After she went to the loo, she jumped up on the weighing scales, as usual. She ran to Granda, saying excitedly, "I am 2 stone 6 [pounds]."

"You are a big girl now," Granda told her, and she nodded in agreement. "You are going to be a big girl and a pretty girl; and you are the prettiest girl in Ireland," continued Granda.

Next thing, she ran back into Granda again. "Would you like a cup of (pretend) tea, Granda?" she asked.

"Oh, yes, Doireann. I would love one."

"How many sugars?" she asked.

"I don't take sugar," Granda informed her.

She had difficulty with this and looked at Granda strangely.

"I never take sugars," Granda assured her.

Off she went, only to return a few seconds later. "There you are, Granda," she said, handing him his cup of tea. "I put my own special sugars in it, Granda," she told him.

"Oh, well thank you very much," Granda said. Granda took a little sip from the small plastic cup of tea, as she stood and watched.

"Go on, Granda. Take more," he was told.

Granda did and said, "That's beautiful, Doireann. And thank you very much. You make a lovely cup of tea."

Next, she called out, "Granda, we are going to 'hit the road' now."

Granny had told her to say that to Granda.

When they went out to the car, Granda called her and asked, "What am I doing now?" as he bent down and hit the road with his hand.

She thought for a moment and then said, "You are hitting the road."

"Now, when you said, we are going to 'hit the road', that had a different meaning. It meant, we are going to leave and head up the road," Granda explained.

Granda threw Teddy Pink into the car seat ahead of Doireann. She climbed over Teddy and said, "Teddy will sit on my lap."

"And lap it up," joked Granda.

"Where did we get Granda from?" joked Granny.

"In the house," was Doireann's innocent reply.

Granny and Doireann both had some fun in the back of the car as Granda drove. He threw the blue cloth over his shoulder in Doireann's direction. She, in turn, threw it at Granny. Teddy Pink was now a pretend tiger, with Doireann making screeching tiger sounds.

"When is your birthday, Doireann?" Granda asked (knowing it was this coming Saturday).

"July," Granny answered. "It's on the twenty-eighth."

"No," said a concerned Doireann. "It's twenty past eight," Granny was told.

She spoke with Teddy Pink and asked her if she wanted to go to the library. The answer must have been yes, because as soon as Granda parked in Gorey Shopping Centre's underground car park, Teddy Pink got out of the car with her. "Teddy always holds my hand."

She also held Granda's hand, letting go as soon as they reached the doors. She and Teddy ran over to Noddy, who was sitting in his car. "Welcome to Toyland," said Noddy as they both sat into his car.

Next, they took the lift to the first floor, after Doireann pressed all the right buttons. Their first visit on the first floor was to Daniel's racing car, parked over from the doctor's surgery. On their way over to the library, Granda asked, "would Teddy like to walk on the wall?"

"Yes, and I will hold her hand," Granda was told.

"No, you won't. You'll hold my hand and carry Teddy Pink in your arms," Granda immediately told her.

Handing Teddy to Granny, she stretched her arms up high to touch the granite overhang above her by the water feature. "Look how big you are getting," Granda told her.

She walked the rest of the wall, going up as far as the library wall, until she could go no further.

"Try and push that wall out of your way," joked Granda.

She grunted, while attempting to push it. "No good, Granda. It won't move," she said.

"Come on, and I'll help you down," offered Granda.

She ran to magically open the library doors. Inside the library, Granny sat with her in the kiddies' section, while Granda went to read the newspapers. About thirty minutes later, Granda heard the pitter-patter of tiny feet. Doireann had arrived to check on him. "Is Granny reading you stories?" Granda asked.

While nodding her head, she asked, "What are you doing?"

"Reading papers, eh, newspapers," he told her.

"Very good. Newspapers," she said and ran back to Granny.

Then Granda went and sat with her, while Granny went looking for some books for herself. Granda read a book that had paper windows, and she loved looking behind each one.

Sensing a toilet visit was imminent, Granda asked her, "Do you need to go to the toilet?"

Her head nodded, and they immediately looked for Granny. "Granny, she needs to go to the toilet, *now*," Granda warned.

"Okay," said Granny, handing Granda two books, Doireann's shoulder bag, and Teddy Pink to mind.

"Doireann didn't like the toilets because it was dark with blueish-purple lights. I stayed there [in the cubicle] with her, and she was okay then," Granny informed Granda.

Just before this, Granda had been reading a newspaper, next to the reception desk, inside the library. Doireann came dashing in, proclaiming in a very loud and cheerful voice for all and sundry to hear, "Granda, I did a wee."

"Oh, that's great, Doireann. Well done," Granda said quietly.

"Can I do a, '*Wheeeeeeeeeeeeeeeeeeeeeeeeeeeeeeeeeeeeeeeeeeeeeeeeeeeeeee*'?" she asked as they exited the library after Granny got the books, she had been looking for earlier.

"Okay, Doireann. Give me Teddy and your shoulder bag," Granda said and then went to the end of the wheelchair ramp, beside Gorey Courthouse.

She took off, charging down towards Granda and immediately turned around, shouting, "You won't catch me Granda." She ran as fast as she could back up the ramp and straight into Granny's outstretched arms. She wanted to do it again.

"I have a please pop" (a freeze pop) "at home for you," Granny said.

"Oh, lovely. I will have that," Granda said.

"No," Doireann shouted. "It's mine."

"I'm only joking, pet," Granda assured her.

Off they all hurried, with Granny visiting Dunnes Stores first for bread on the way. Doireann played on the kiddie ride machines, with Granda in attendance, while they waited for Granny. Pointing to the Irish tricolour on the wall, Granda told Doireann it was the Irish flag. "Now, can you tell me the colours?" he asked as he pointed to each one.

"Green. Lellow."

"No, it's white next, Doireann, and … orange," Granda told her.

Granda got her to say the colours again, as two ladies passed by with big smiles on their faces. Using his mobile phone, Granda took photos of her and Teddy Pink playing in the kiddie ride machines.

Granny and Granda never put money into these machines. They would, instead, encourage her to play on them and use her own imagination. Her favourite machine was the Disney princess coach. Whenever she arrived at the imaginary castle in her coach and as soon as she stepped down from it, she would give a royal bow.

When Granny arrived back with the bread, she ran to the elevator instead of the travellator, to access the underground carpark. They all had to do the usual, "*Wheeeeeeeeeeeeeeeeeeeeeeeeeeeeeeeeeeeeeeeeeeeeeeeeeeeeeeeeeeeeeee,*" as Granda drove up the ramp and out of the carpark.

She took the soother, saying, "I'm tired."

At home, she sat up at the kitchen table and enjoyed her freeze pop while Granny prepared lunch. She then ate her olives and crackers with milk and requested some music. Granny played a CD, and the song "Baby Love" came on. Whenever the follow-on song was about to play, she would protest, saying, "I don't like that." So, "Baby Love" had to be played over and over and over.

"Granda, when I finish my lunch, can I go outside?" she asked.

"Yes, okay, Doireann."

"I love Granny and Granda," she said.

And Granny said back, "And I love you, Doireann."

"I love Granda too," she said.

"And I love you also, pet," Granda told her.

"I miss Baby Bop," she said, and off she went to the bedroom to fetch her.

"What are you doing, Granda?" she asked on her return.

"I'm writing notes about you," Granda told her as he took the opportunity to quickly write some notes while sitting at the kitchen table.

She scrunched her face up, as if to say, why?

Granny then joked, "Is it about me?"

"*No*," Granny was loudly told. "It's me," Doireann said. "You've a statue," she said to Granny, pointing to it on top of a kitchen cupboard.

"That was my mammy's; it's Our Lady," Granny told her.

"We don't have a statue. Eh, we do have a statue," she corrected herself.

"What is it?" Granny asked. "I don't know; Oisín has one," she said.

Granda said, "When you're trying to identify a statue, Doireann, just ask, 'Is statue?'" (Is that you), joked Granda.

She was left looking at Granda in a funny sort of way.

Granda took her outside and lifted her up to put a peg back onto the clothesline that had fallen off. "Look, Granda, a butterfly," she said, pointing.

"What colour is it?" asked Granda.

"It's white."

"Let's see where he lands," he said.

"He is not going to land, Granda."

"He has some yellow on his wings," Granda informed her. "Will we look for bees, Doireann?" he asked.

"No. They sting," she said and ran to the rocket launcher. "Can you take this out, Granda?" meaning for him to assemble the launcher.

"Okay, Doireann, put the rocket in," he told her when he had the launcher in place for blast-off.

"Your turn now, Granda," she said. And each of them took turns.

One of Granda's rockets went very high, and as it dropped from the sky, it fell through some large trees and bushes, but luckily it landed in their garden in some overgrowth. Granda went to fetch it, and she said, "Be careful, Granda."

Next, she made Granda a cup of tea in the yellow ceramic teapot. Then she watered the flowers in the flower beds. Out came the watering cans and buckets so they could be filled with water and then transferred to the various buckets before the flowers in the ground were watered. She turned the outside tap on and off as required. Granda was made to hold different buckets or watering cans under the tap for her to fill.

"Granda this is not working," she complained. She couldn't get the water to flow from the large watering can into the tiny one.

"Come on, and I'll show you." Granda got her to hold the watering can handle at the very end, so as to tilt the can. She pointed its nozzle over the tiny container and got the water to flow into it.

Granny came out and gave Granda a break. Granda continued with updating his notes.

Mammy called to the house, at about 2.20 p.m., having been in Kilkenny today and went out to the back garden. There was no sign of Doireann or Granny for a little while, until they heard, "Hiya, Mammy," from down the garden.

Doireann came running up to give Mammy a big hug and a kiss. They went into the house, gathered Doireann's things, and left for home.

25 July

Daddy and Doireann were waiting at the gate when Granny and Granda arrived home from their early morning gym and swim. Doireann held up Teddy Pink for Granny to see as Granda took the gear bags out of the car boot. Daddy walked her to the hall door and asked for a hug before leaving. He told Granny that she was tired because she'd had about three hours less sleep last night. Spelling out the reason, Daddy said, "She was S-C-A-R-E-D of the D-A-R-K." He didn't want to draw attention to it.

"Granny, I was scared of the dark last night," Doireann, the code breaker, said, as Daddy listened on.

Granda pointed to her runners and said, "They are the same as Granny's." Out came Granda's mobile phone to take some more photos.

Granda went and brought the empty bin up the side of the house and into the backyard. He passed a bumblebee, crawling on the ground, possibly because it had overfed itself on the beautiful lavender flowers in a neighbour's garden, where lots of bumblebees visited. This particular bee was a type Granda, when a young kid, used to call, a red-arse bee, because he was all black, except for his red bum. Granda said to Doireann, "It's a red-bum bee, and the other ones are bum*ble*bees." Granda took a photo of it, as she wanted to study it closely when back indoors.

"Did you have Cheerios this morning, Doireann?" Granda asked.

"No. Porridge."

"Oh lovely," Granda said.

She was now sitting at the kitchen table, eating her melon, blue berries, and red and green grapes. "Who gave you them?" asked Granda, excitedly.

"Daddy did." Then she asked, "Can I go outside, Granny?"

"After our breakfast."

She then helped Granny put the washing on the clothesline.

"Doireann, did you understand what 'we are hitting the road now' meant the other day—when you said that to me? I should have explained it better to you," said Granda.

She shook her head, indicating she didn't know.

"Well, you came into me and said, 'We are hitting the road now.' This is a saying that means we were moving off—leaving or driving—to where we want to go," Granda explained. "So, when Granda hit the road with his hand, he was trying to be funny but give you the true meaning of 'hitting the road', as well. You are clever because you knew this when I asked you."

She was more interested in sitting up at the table to finish her fruit at this stage. Later, she pulled the TV chair around to face the telly, and with the soother in her mouth, she sat back, waiting for Granny to switch the telly on.

"Are you going to watch some 'smelly', Doireann?" Granda asked.

"No. *It's the telly*," she loudly and bluntly told Granda.

Earlier, Granda listened as Granny spoke to her, saying, "Granda has to get a [electric] light fitting, and he wanted to know if you could help?"

She nodded in agreement and asked, "Is it heavy?"

"No. And you can carry it for me, okay," Granda said.

She nodded in agreement again.

"Would you like some toast, Doireann?" Granny asked.

"No, just bread," she replied.

Granda asked her, "Did you say goodbye to Oisín, this morning?"

"No. He in bed," she informed him.

"Did you say goodbye to Mammy?" continued Granda.

"She in bed," was her answer.

Granny and Granda then assumed she must have had the whole house awake because of the dark last night!

Granny took her to the toilet to do a wee first before they went out. She came running out to Granda, saying, "I'm two, six, Granda."

"What's that, pet?" asked Granda.

"I am two, six," she said, before Granny reminded him, she was referring to her weight.

"Well, aren't you a big girl? Two stone, six, wow," he said, looking amazed.

She nodded and was well pleased with herself.

Eventually, they got ready to leave. "You go ahead, Granda, and take her out to the car. I have to get a towel," Granny said.

The towel was for nappy-less Doireann's seat, just in case. Granda took her and Teddy Pink to the car. Granny locked the hall door and followed soon after. They were all seated, belted up and ready to drive off.

"Do we have Doireann's soother?" Granda asked.

"We forgot it. I will go in and get it," Granny offered.

"No, I will," Granda offered instead.

"You don't know where it is," Granny told him.

"Where is it then?" he asked.

"I don't know!" she said.

Granda just got out of the car, while counting to ten.

"Take the spare one, if you can't find it," she said out loud.

While searching for the soother, Granda picked up Baby Bop and found a piece of buttered bread on the TV chair, where once a young girl called Doireann had sat. Granda couldn't find her soother and took the spare one.

When he arrived back to the car, Granny said, "Doireann is too hot now. She wouldn't take her cardigan off for me earlier, and now she wants it off."

Granda took her cardigan off and counted to ten again.

They pulled out of Marian Crescent after a lorry went by. "That's a big lorry, Doireann," Granda told her.

"It's not a lorry," was her curt reply.

"What is it?" enquired Granny. "It's a truck," she said.

They saw lots more trucks on the road that morning.

On their journey, Granny referred to Doireann's lovely dress. "Where did you get that lovely dress?" she asked.

"In my home," she was told.

"In your home? And would you have any nice clothes for me in your home?" Granny asked.

There was no response to that, so Granda asked, "Is there any nice three-piece suits for me in your home?"

This was ignored also.

Now looking at the yellow top Granny was wearing, she said, "You were wearing that the other day" (meaning yesterday). "You walking and you go past the house," she added, meaning her house.

"Did you see me from your house?" asked Granny.

"No, no. Oisín said, 'There's Granny.'" (They had seen her from Daddy's car yesterday.)

They drove to the electrical shop on the old Dublin Road, towards Enniscorthy and purchased a light fitting (€12), and Granda was only charged €10. Just after Scarawalsh roundabout, Granda turned left onto the old Dublin Road, taking this route for a reason. If he had gone the normal route, she would have recognised they were near to Enniscorthy Town and the playground.

Then, she surprised both Granny and Granda. "This is Enniscorthy."

"No, it's Ferns," Granny pretended.

Doireann didn't want to go into the electrical shop. "I was here before," she announced. She had been there only once before—and that was a year ago!

They went to a garage further up the road and got unleaded petrol at €1.42 per litre. Granny and Granda decided against going to the Lidl store, as it was getting hotter with the lovely sunshine; the temperature had risen to twenty-three degrees.

Granny reminded Doireann about her freezer pop at home.

"It's a please-a-pop," she said.

"Okay, please-a-pop," Granny agreed.

Doireann put Teddy Pink into the passenger seat before sitting into her car seat in the back. Granda strapped her into the car seat and then put the seatbelt around Teddy Pink also. As Granda drove, Doireann was trying to jump up while, at the same time, saying, "A right job, a right job," and so on. She wouldn't say where she got that from.

Granda parked in the driveway. When she got out of the car, she removed the seatbelt from Teddy Pink, after mumbling some words to her first. She then took Teddy Pink into the house. Later, Granda found her soother in the bathroom. She had to do another wee soon after they arrived back home. When finished in the toilet, she ran to Granda and said, "Granda I'm two, six."

"You are still two, six, wow; you are really big now," he told her. Then, joking, he shouted after her, "Is that two and sixpence?"

"Don't mind your Granda," said Granny, laughing.

She and Granny sat up at the kitchen table eating their please-a-pops. When finished, Granny went to the bedroom, saying, "I have to change" (her clothes).

"Doireann, you're getting a new granny; she's going to change!" Granda said. "Maybe she will change into a monster." He laughed.

A while later, Doireann had finished her cheese. "Did you clean your hands?" Granda asked. He checked and saw that she hadn't. Heading to the kitchen to get a wipe, he asked her, "Do you want a wipe?"

Holding her hands out, she nodded.

"For your hair?" joked Granda.

She looked at him as if he had three heads.

"I am only joking with you. Come on," he told her.

He handed her a wipe and explained to her how to use it properly, wiping all over her hands and fingers. Then, she put the wipe into the bin when Granda told her. Later, she showed him her two plaits that Granny had done for her. He took a photo and said, "They are lovely."

He lifted her up to let her see them in the mirror. She couldn't see properly, and so he said, "I will show you how you can see your plaits."

She climbed onto the red chair to look into the dining room mirror, while Granda held up a small portable mirror, behind her. She smiled when she saw her two plaits. Granda said, "Now, you have learned something new, and you can show Mammy and Daddy how to do that."

Next, while Granda worked at his workstation, Doireann arrived in. "Are you finished with that?" she asked, pointing to an empty cup.

"Yes, pet," he told her.

"Will I bring it into the kitchen?"

"Ah, yes, pet, and thank you very much," he said.

"There, Granny. Granda is finished his tea," she said, handing her the cup.

Later, Granny took Doireann, who was like a bag of cats then, out the back. She had her soother in her mouth, while she and Granny played with the Frisbee.

They came in for lunch, and Doireann took her lunch out of the fridge. It was lasagne, and she didn't want it. She went and sat up on the dining room sofa, sulking. Granda said, "Okay, Granny, we will have our salad, and Doireann will have nothing. What will Doireann have? Nothing?"

Granny then said, "I will heat it."

And Doireann said, "Okay."

She sat up in her high chair and clipped the straps closed herself. Poor Granda had to move her and the high chair over to the table. And as he struggled, Granny said, "All two stone, six?"

To this, Granda whimpered, "two stone, sick."

They all had their individual lunches, and Granda gave Doireann some of his beetroot because she loved it. Granny then gave her some oatcakes because she loved them also. Granny took her into the sitting room to look at the big telly, hoping she might fall asleep, as she was extremely tired.

Granny answered the hall door for Mammy and Oisín. Granda went out to the back with Doireann and Oisín, while Mammy and Granny chatted. Oisín took her for a walk down the garden, but Granda stopped them halfway down, saying, "It's a bit dangerous in the lower half of the garden, and I won't be able to see the two of you."

Anyway, Doireann didn't want to go any further. They played for a bit where they could be seen. Then Granda called them to come and water the flowers. They had great fun, especially Doireann, filling up the buckets and watering cans and then watering the flowers.

Oisín gave up and went inside for something to eat. Doireann continued back and forth, watering the flowers and jumping up and into the large red towel hanging from the clothesline as she passed it. Even when Mammy came out to get her, she wanted to continue filling the bucket and watering the flowers, back and forth, back and forth, non-stop, loving it all the while, with Mammy looking on with a beautiful big smile on her face.

Eventually, they all went into the kitchen, and Doireann wanted to know what Oisín was at. He was buttering his two Marietta biscuits to make a buttered biscuit sandwich.

"Doireann could have one," suggested Granda. And Granny buttered one biscuit and broke it to make half a buttered biscuit sandwich.

Immediately and very loudly, Doireann was not having that. "I want a proper one!" she protested loudly, and she got it.

Granny had the half one.

Granny asked Mammy if she would like to join them on Saturday down in Tramore, County Waterford, where they were going for a day out. Daddy would be walking with his father and friends in the Wicklow Hills on Saturday, which was Doireann's birthday. Mammy was having a little birthday party for Doireann on the Friday instead. Granny and Granda would only have her until 12 p.m. that Friday. Mammy was delighted to accept the offer, as she had nothing planned with the kids for that day. Granda offered to do the driving, also.

After they'd had their buttered Marietta biscuit sarnies, they left for home.

CHAPTER 23

Forty Shades of D

27 July

Doireann arrived at Granny and Granda's house with her mammy at about 9.25 a.m. She had brought her new buggy Oisín had given her for her birthday. Teddy Pink sat quietly in it. She would be 3 years old tomorrow, Saturday. Mammy told Granny, there had been real excitement and lots of smiling faces yesterday, when Doireann, along with the other "older" kids in her crèche were shown around a bigger room they would be using come September.

Before Mammy left, Granny and Granda sorted out their new arrangements for Doireann, from September next. They would be minding her for one day only each week, as she would be attending crèche for four days a week, at the state's expense. Granny asked if a Friday was okay and offered to collect her early, and she could stay until about 4 or 4.30 p.m.

"That would be great, because I could get down to Kilkenny [Curves] that day," Mammy said.

Granny told her, "We could get to do more activities with her, as we have plans, and a longer day would suit us."

Mammy knew Granny and Granda were always available anyway if she needed a helping hand, like collecting the kids from school or crèche or just minding them and so on. Mammy had arranged to collect Doireann at about 12 p.m. today but then phoned to say she had to collect Oisín at 12 p.m. in Gorey after his tennis and would be a bit late.

Granny and Granda gave Doireann her birthday card and present, and she was very excited. The present was a pink travel case on wheels. Inside the case was a tiny pink teddy, a variety of clothes, a baby bottle, and a cup. She absolutely loved it, and you could see her mind beginning to go into overdrive, preparing to go on a (pretend) holiday somewhere. Granny then read the birthday card to her, and she loved it. She was also wearing a birthday badge.

As Granda took a photo, he asked her, "What did the card say?"

"Birthday cake," she replied.

Granda laughed and corrected her, saying, "It said 'birthday girl'."

"Granda, can you clean the wheels?" she asked, meaning those on her new buggy. They got mucky when she'd wheeled it over this morning.

Granda got some wipes and started to clean them but then had to take a telephone call. Granny took over. While Granda was on the phone, Granny got the aeroplane over to France with Doireann, went to their hotel room, took all their clothes off, and got into the pool for a swim—before flying back home!

Then Gary phoned Granny. Granda took over duties when his phone call ended. Doireann took Granda and her buggy, with Teddy Pink sitting in it, for a walk down the garden and then back up again. Then she told Granda, "We have to go on holidays," before going into the kitchen to collect her travel case.

"You wheel that," Granda was told as she pointed to the buggy.

They walked out to the wooden bench, and she put her travel case on it.

"Did you give the man the tickets?" Granda asked her.

Holding her hands out, she handed the man her tickets and then climbed up onto the bench.

"Granda, sit down," she said.

"We are flying now, Doireann. Isn't that a lovely view?" Granda said as he looked out the small aeroplane window.

Granny arrived over to the flying aeroplane, and Granda told her they were flying.

"Sure, I flew to France this morning," boasted Granny.

"Have you got a hankie, Granda?" Doireann asked.

"Here is a clean one," Granda said, handing her one from his pocket.

She started to wipe her nose, until Granda took over. Holding the hankie over her nose, he said, "Now blow." And she blew. "Blow again, Doireann." He encouraged her more, and when she did, lots of muck came out of her nose. Granda got another clean hankie out for a repeat performance. "Where it all came from, I do not know," Granda mumbled as he put the hankies into the bin. "But she is good at clearing her nose," he loudly declared, so she could hear him.

"I am hungry, Granny," she said.

"Would you like some toast?" Granda asked her.

"No. An oatcake?"

They all went inside, and Granny got her an oatcake and switched on the TV for her also.

"Doireann, do you need to go to the toilet?" asked Granny.

"Yes," she replied and started to walk towards the toilet herself.

"Wait," Granny told her.

"No, I'll do it," she protested.

"You can go yourself, and Granny will be with you," Granda told her. That seemed to satisfy her.

"Good girl," Granny said when she had finished.

"Hold on, Doireann. Wash your hands."

And she did so, for Granny.

Next thing, she hopped onto the weighing scales as usual.

"You have lost a little; you are two, five something," Granda could hear Granny say. "Wait now, Doireann. Now try again. Oh, there you are; you are two, six again," Granny informed her.

"Granda I am two, six again," she repeated.

"Ah that's great, Doireann. Wow, you are certainly a big girl now," Granda reminded her.

"Granny, could you get a hankie for her, because she is trying to wipe her nose with her arm?" pleaded Granda.

"Right, Doireann. I want Mammy, who is in Gorey, to hear you blow. And again. Come on, louder than that. Good girl. That's loud enough," said Granny.

She then asked Granny to go on the aeroplane again.

Later, she went in to Granda. "Granda, I have to have a sleep because I will be having my party," she said.

"Oh yes, Doireann, and you will be nice and bright for your party, among all your invited guests," said Granda.

Because Mammy, Doireann, and Oisín would be joining Granny and Granda tomorrow on their day out to Tramore, Granda decided to present Doireann with a poem come song (to the tune of a Johnny Cash song) for her third birthday.

"When am I going home?" asked an impatient Doireann.

Granda showed her the time (11.30 a.m.) on his phone and said, "Mammy will collect you, within the hour."

As she stood there, Granda was typing these notes. He asked her, "Do you want me to read you a poem?" (It was the new one Granda had just written for her.)

"No. I don't want to hear a poem," she said bluntly and walked off.

She and Granny went out to the garden, and Granda followed later. The weather had changed. It had rained very heavily during the night. Today, it was cloudy and cooler, with more rain expected. The grass was still a bit wet, but that didn't deter Doireann from taking Granny, to her (imaginary) house down the garden. She asked Granny, "Did you get me the travel case for Christmas?"

"No, it's for your birthday," Granny told her.

"Thank you very much, Granny. Can I take it home?" she asked.

"Of course, you can. It's yours," Granny assured her.

She then took Granny to France again on holidays with her new travel case. While walking around the airport, waiting to get on the plane, Doireann suddenly stopped.

"Do we have to stop?" Granny asked.

"We have to stop. Wait here," she replied.

"Is it because there are people [queued] in front of us?" Granny enquired.

Doireann just nodded as she and Granny stood still in the empty garden.

After Granda arrived out, he was bluntly told by Doireann not to come into the house (an imaginary house built on the pathway down the garden).

"Will I knock on the door?" Granda asked.

"No," he was loudly and bluntly told.

"We are cleaning the house," Granny said.

Doireann, appeared to make cleaning movements, while standing in the same spot. "Now, you can come in, Granda," she told him.

"Okay, I will knock on the door first," Granda offered, making a *tap, tap* noise.

"Come in, Granda," she said.

"Oh, isn't this a lovely clean house," said Granda.

"We were out shopping this morning, Granda," she said. And then immediately, "Let's go shopping again."

Off they all went, further down the garden path where the shops were, all hidden among the weeds, thistles, nettles, and other kinds of overgrowth.

She went up to the shop countertop, while Granny and Granda stood waiting outside. Granda could hear her, ask the (imaginary) shopkeeper for bread and pepperoni and then she stood waiting, for the shopkeeper to return with her order. Taking her items off the countertop, she handed them to Granny and Granda.

"Did you pay for these, Doireann?" Granny asked.

"Yes," she replied and then held out her hand to count her change.

They then walked up the garden to sit at the garden picnic table. She pulled both the buggy and travel case along. "Come on, Granda. Sit at the table," he was ordered, and then she immediately jumped down from the seat herself. "I forgot to get a flower for Mammy," she remembered.

Granny helped her pick a poppy.

"What is that?" she asked Granda.

"It's a flower; it's called a poppy, Doireann," he informed her.

Before too long, she was up and running towards Granny's flowers again.

"What's up?" Granny asked.

"I need to get a pink flower," she said.

"Okay, you can pick that yourself," Granny told her.

Next, she started to talk about her party later on.

"Will there be lots there? Will your friends from crèche be there?" Granny asked.

"No, my cousins will."

Next, she was playing with Teddy Pink and then tidied up the clothes she had put on her earlier. Granny and Granda started singing the happy birthday song, and she joined in. When they got to the lyrics, "Happy Birthday to Doireann", she was startled, as she then realised it was being sung for her.

Holding up the tiny teddy that came with the travel case, Granda wondered loudly, "Is she Teddy Pink's baby?"

There was no response from Doireann.

Granny went back into the house, and Doireann put Teddy Pink back into the buggy.

"I will strap you in," she said to Teddy Pink.

"Will I help you?" Granda offered.

"No, I will do it," she insisted.

"Okay, and if you need help, just ask," he said.

Later, as she struggled, she asked, "Granda, can you do this?"

"Come on, and I will show you," he said.

Wrapping the open straps around Teddy Pink, Granda showed her how to pass one strap through the centre one.

"Let me do it," she said.

As Granda handed it to her, he said, indicating the strap, "When it's fed through, grab it and pull it all the way through."

She did that. "I can't do the last bit, Granda," she said.

"Yes, that's hard, Doireann," he agreed, before doing it for her. "Whoever designed this for kids, should be shot with toy guns," Granda suggested.

She walked to the back door to bring the buggy in. Granda showed her where to stand when pulling the buggy up the steps, and she managed it eventually. "Are you going to bring the travel case in?" Granda asked, and out she went, to get it.

"It is a case, Granda, and it is mine, not yours," he was bluntly told.

Handing Granda the little cardigan, she asked, "Can you turn this [inside out], Granda?"

She put the cardigan into the case, after Granda fixed it. Then, Granda handed her Tiny Teddy Pink, and he, too, was put into the case, and then it was brought into the kitchen. Pointing her finger at Granny, she announced, "It is my case and not Granda's and not yours. Can I bring this case home?"

"Of course, you can, Doireann. That's your birthday present," Granny assured her again.

"Can I leave the buggy here?" she continued.

"Okay, Doireann," Granny said.

But Mammy took it home anyway when she called to collect her later.

She sat at the table to have her lunch (at 12.30 p.m.), just when Mammy and Oisín called to the hall door. She ran to see who it was, and seeing Mammy, she put her head up, lips to the ready, to give her a big kiss.

Mammy was surprised when Granda told her they had flown to France and back this morning.

Granny then laughed, saying, "And I had to take my clothes off and go for a swim."

Granda sat with Oisín for a chat, and they talked about football.

"The tennis coach said, Oisín was a very good player," Mammy informed Granda.

Doireann, then kicked up and didn't want to finish her lunch, while Oisín buttered his toast that Granny had done for him.

"Take it with you, Oisín," Granny suggested, knowing Mammy wanted to start moving.

As they left to walk home, Granda offered them a lift, but Mammy declined. Oisín teased Doireann outside, causing her to scream a couple of times. Mammy gave out to him and said, "Oisín, take the buggy."

Teddy Pink had his straps on in the buggy and stayed very quiet. Doireann took her travel case.

"Oh, and by the way, we are all going to Tramore for the whole day, tomorrow," Granda told Oisín.

"Oh yeah, I forgot. I am looking forward to that, Granda," replied Oisín.

"So are we," he said back.

28 July

Doireann was officially 3 years old today. Mammy, Doireann, and Oisín called over to Granny and Granda at about 10.20 a.m. as planned.

Granda had loaded the car with the picnic and other things for their day out in Tramore. Mammy took her things out of her car and put them into Granda's car. They were on the road by 10.30 a.m., and the temperature was fifteen degrees and cloudy. The night before, there had been very heavy rain.

Daddy was walking in the Wicklow Hills with his father and friends today and had booked an overnight stay up there also. He had left at 8.30 a.m. this morning. Daddy and Oisín had sat up late the night before, watching a movie. Oisín gave them an account of the movie, on the journey. He was extremely tired today also, especially from all his sporting activities during the week. He even had football training yesterday evening, after his tennis.

Granda stopped halfway into their journey, in New Ross, County Wexford, to use the loos and stretch the legs in the lovely local park. Oisín took his football out to do a bit of kick about, while Mammy, Granny, and Doireann went to the loo. Granda stood guard at the car. Mammy let Doireann go to the playground for a while and then let her just run up and down.

Mammy said, "Doireann would not go to the toilet, because it was one of those toilets without a seat, only the steel bowl."

Doireann moved onto a small dirt track, and as she ran and ran, Mammy took some photos of her and then took some of Oisín also, playing with the football. This was where President John F Kennedy's people came from. The President's visit to Ireland had included both this area and County Limerick, which was where, in particular, the Kennedys had very close family roots. The President was assassinated in Texas, United States of America, a few months later—an event that shocked the world. Now back in the car, they drove over the big bridge in New Ross, County Wexford, which spans the River Barrow, much to Doireann's excitement.

"Oh, Mammy, we are going over the bridge," she said, giggling in delight.

"Yes, Doireann," acknowledged Granda.

They were now in County Kilkenny, and just up the road, Granda pulled into a service station to get his usual Saturday newspapers. Granny went into the shop, followed by Mammy, who wanted to get some bananas for Doireann and Oisín.

All aboard once again, they headed for Waterford City and passed by the new New Ross bypass construction site. Driving over the Kilkenny-Waterford border at Riverbank, they approached another big bridge spanning the river Suir, bringing them into Waterford City (Déise). Doireann looked out the car window in total amazement, saying excitedly, "Another big bridge."

The traffic through the city was heavy and slow. Earlier, as they played some DVDs in the car, one of Doireann's favourites was Roy Orbison's "Pretty Woman", and another was "Downtown." Just as the word *downtown* in the "Downtown" lyrics played, Doireann was ready to sing it out as loud as she could, much to her Mammy's amusement.

They played some of Jimmy Cricket's Christmas songs that Doireann also liked, even though it was the wrong season. Once they got through the city, which included an extended detour, just after the Tower Hotel, they took the road for Tramore.

"Are we there yet? Are we there yet?" asked Doireann.

"Just around the corner," said Granny.

"Park Granda, park," pleaded Doireann.

The temperature in Tramore was nineteen degrees, and there were sunny spells. They drove through Tramore town and headed out towards Newtown Cove for their picnic. Earlier, Granda had asked Doireann, "Are we having a picnic?"

"Yeaaaaaaaaaaaaaah," was the response.

They parked in Newtown Cove car park, which was full of swimmers, divers and jumpers, surfers, people fishing, and others rowing their boats, as well as other families enjoying their picnics. They set out their stall at a vacant table, only to move immediately, as the wind was very strong and blew the table blanket off the table.

They walked down some steps, onto a green bank and down towards a few more tables and seats, before reaching another picnic table. Granda walked back up to the loo, and when he returned, the picnic had started. Mammy had brought lunch for her and Doireann. Oisín was happy to have Granny's grub. They had bread rolls, lettuce, tomatoes, ham, salami, eggs, and cheese. Granda had his favourite white bread, to make his sarnies with.

The clouds got darker to one side of them. The wind didn't bother them now, as they were lower down, surrounded by cliffs and bushes.

"We should have brought the large umbrella," Oisín suggested.

"We'll be okay. The forecast is not for rain," Granda assured him.

They continued with their "picmic", with Doireann running around now and again, before getting back up at the table to continue eating.

"Those clouds are getting darker," Oisín warned.

But they ignored him.

Next on the menu, after the sarnies and salad, was tea, buns, biscuits, and crisps, with plenty of excitement for good measure. Granda looked after the tea, filling the five cups as ordered.

"Granda, I like half and half—half tea and half milk—with one sugar," requested Oisín. He was the only sugar taker.

"Okay, there you are, Oisín," said Granda, handing him his "half and half".

Mammy said, "Half fill Doireann's cup and fill the rest with milk."

"There you are, Doireann," Granda said.

Mammy wanted the teabag left in hers, as she liked strong tea. Granny and Granda, once their cups of tea were made, dived into the goodies like everyone else.

"Ah, there are no more buns left with the icing," complained Oisín.

Granda had eaten the last one, leaving the plain buns that Doireann loved. "Sorry, Oisín. I thought you had one already," Granda said.

Granny said, "He had a Marietta biscuit butter sandwich first."

Oisín ate the ordinary bun anyway and then ate some Bourbon biscuits. They had little chocolate bars then, after all of that.

As they were finishing up, the heavens opened up, rain pouring from the sky. Granda ran up to the car to get the large umbrella. As he approached the car boot, the heavens opened even more, and he got saturated. It was a good distance up, and he jumped into the car to move it a bit closer before running the now shorter distance back down, with the umbrella.

There they all stood silent, the table blanket over their heads. Because they had to clear the things off the table first to use the blanket as an umbrella; they got drenched as well. Granda joined them, and they must have looked like some sight, huddled together under the blanket and large umbrella as the rain pelted down. The stronger wind didn't help either, and Granda had to grip the umbrella firmly.

"Can we go?" Doireann asked, standing in the middle and looking up at everyone, all standing there, miserable.

"Okay, let's go," said Granda, with the rain easing off.

They manoeuvred a way up towards the car.

"Put the heat on full, Granda," said Granny, hoping to get them dry.

The ladies (or the lazies, as Doireann would say, with her mouth full) went to the loo, while Oisín and Granda dried out in the car heat. Granda's seat was ringing wet also. The rain shower passed, the sun came out again, and the wind died down.

"Can we go down the steps to where the swimmers are?" Oisín asked Granda.

"Okay, I will take you if Mammy and Granny want to take a rest," Granda said.

They wanted to go down the steps as well, and off they all went to look at the swimmers, diving and/or jumping into the water from the high diving board. They stayed there for about thirty minutes because Doireann and Oisín were enjoying it so much. Eventually, they climbed up the many steps back to the car. Nearing the top, it began to rain again. So, it was time to get to the car as fast as you could.

With everyone back, sitting in the car, breathless and panting, Granda took out the poem he had written for Doireann's birthday, called "Forty Shades of D", and offered to sing it—to the tune of Johnny Cash's song, "Forty Shades of Green".

Doireann sat silently in the back, munching on something, while listening at the same time, but totally oblivious, to the special moment:

Forty Shades of D
'Tis Doireann's birthday once again
Now 36 months old.
It seems like only yesterday
We received this heart of gold.

She runs and hops and skips and jumps
Full of life and joy.
Playgrounds are her special treat
To slide and swing real-high.

Sometimes "wheeeeeeeeeee" to Noddy
Then lift to go outside
Walk the wall towards library
Through magic doors a-wide
In kiddies' corner, lots of books
With Granny holding while
She runs to Granda to present
Her sweet and gentle smile.

She loves the garden, birds, and bees and
Flowers that are new,
Playing with the water tap
As the cows play moooosic too.

No nappy is the challenge now,
An accident or two
Its only water after all and
Not a smelly poo.

So happy birthday three, Doireann.
'Tis a very special day.
I hope you have the best of fun
With lots and lots of play.

In kiddies' corner, lots of books
With Granny holding while
She runs to Granda to present
Her sweet and gentle smile.
She runs to Granda to present
Her sweet and gentle smile.

Oisín and Mammy loved it. Mammy recorded it and played it back. Granda said, "I was breathless singing it."

"Da, I wouldn't have noticed," a beaming Mammy said.

While this was going on, Granda had given Oisín two scratch cards.

"I've won €50," Oisín shouted excitedly, only to immediately apologise with, "Oh, I didn't rub all of it." One amount was €500 and not the third

€50 required. Again, he thought the same, when scratching the other card. But alas, it was not to be, his lucky day.

They headed back, to Tramore town, which included a big hilly road they'd driven up earlier. Doireann was alerted to do the, "*Wheeeeeeeeeeeee eeeeeeeeeeeeeeeeeeeeeeeeeeeeeeeeeeeeeeeeeeeeeee,*" for all and sundry.

Oisín laughed at the word, because of Doireann's little accident in the car earlier. Mammy had to change her wet pants, after she did a wee on the car seat.

Doireann had kept shouting, "I don't like this seat. I want to get out of this seat," before Mammy realised what was wrong with her.

"Ready, Doireann," Granda said.

"*Wheeeeeeeeeeeeeeeeeeeeeeeeeeeeeeeeeeeeeeeeeeeeeeeeeeeeeeeeee,*" they all shouted as the car went down, down, down the big hill.

Granda parked down at the prom, paying the daily rate of €2. Walking into the amusement park, Doireann got very excited, doing hops, skips, and jumps as if she knew the place. "Was Doireann ever here before?" Granda asked Mammy.

"No," was Mammy's response, who was just as surprised as Granda.

Doireann must have associated this place with the ordinary playgrounds that Granny and Granda would take her to play in. Doireann loved playgrounds. Granda then remembered that they had treated Mammy to a day out in Tramore before—when they'd brought Oisín and 7-day-old Doireann along that day as well. It had been a great day too, like today. Granny handed Mammy some money for the kids to spend at the amusements, insisting it was Granny and Granda's treat.

Oisín immediately headed for the bumper cars, which he loved. When Doireann got on a kiddie's car ride, Oisín was close behind, on a kiddie's motorbike. For the rest of the afternoon, both Doireann and Oisín tried out various rides and things and had great fun. Granda went on the mini-Helter-Skelter with Doireann, and she loved it. Granda was a bit nervous on it, whenever he looked downwards at the people below. Oisín went on the Jungle River ride himself, after failing to convince Granda to go with him. Granda had done it with him, three years previously, and had sworn, "Never again."

Mammy had posted a video on Facebook of Granda and Oisín that day on the Jungle River ride, and of course Uncles Gary and Richard had a great laugh at poor Granda's expense. As well as getting wet, the jungle river ride scares the hell out of you. Doireann loved looking at it, splashing down both ramps. The last drop was really steep and when it dropped, you couldn't see a thing as you plunged down. It was very funny, watching all the other mums and dads in it with their kids, knowing what the feeling was like, especially plunging down the last drop and getting a bit wet.

Oisín then got on the Chair-o-Plane twice, and he loved it. Doireann and Oisín paid into the Minion bumpy castle. No sooner was Doireann bouncing on it than she called for Mammy to take her off it. Good enough, the girl in charge gave back the token to Mammy. Oisín stayed on it and later told Granda of all the fun he'd had on it.

Sometimes it rained, but not for long. It did get cold whenever a thick cloud passed over. Mammy and Granny only had their tops on. Granda went and got his short jacket from the car. When the sun came out, Granda had to take his jacket off because of the heat.

"We'll be having fish and chips shortly," Granda told Oisín.

"Thanks, Granda," he said, with a huge surprised-looking smile.

They all used the loos first, before heading for Dooley's chipper. Granny and Mammy did the ordering, and with a huge bag of greasy goodies, they sized up a place on the prom to eat, but it was too windy. They drove to a park just up from the town and sat at a picnic table in the sunshine and away from the cool breeze coming in off the sea. With plenty of salt, tartar sauce, and a big bottle of water, they all got stuck into their fish and chips, which were delicious.

When they finished, Oisín wanted to run down through the park to the edge of the lake. Mammy and Doireann followed, and the three of them had great fun running around, while Granny and Granda walked to the car and waited for them.

When the three athletes arrived back, Granda suggested going for ice cream cones and a walk along the prom. Granda drove back towards the end of the prom, where there were a lot of surfers out in the water. Mammy sang, "I scream, you scream, we all scream for ice cream," to the giggles pouring out from Doireann and Oisín in the back of the car.

Granda asked Oisín, "If you went into the shop and said, 'Ice cream please,' and the shop owner asked you what type, what would you say?"

"Eh, what Granda?" he asked.

"You would say, 'A loud type.'"

The laughs eventually came.

Mammy paid for the ice creams, and they sat facing the water and watching the surfers as they all licked away. Granda had an ordinary cone. Granny had a little 99. Mammy had a tub of peppermint ice cream and didn't finish it, because she didn't really like it. Granny finished it for her. Doireann had a raspberry cheesecake in a chocolate cone. Oisín had a chocolate ice cream in a chocolate cone. When they all finished, Oisín borrowed Mammy's phone and ran to the edge of the seawater to take a photo of the large waves. He then sent the photo to his daddy.

Mammy decided to put a nappy on Doireann for the journey home, afraid she would do more than a wee-wee and knowing she would fall asleep. This was when Doireann's screaming started, and Mammy had to bribe her a bit because, when she starts screaming, people run for cover. Mammy let her hold a box of Kinder chocolate sticks while she put the nappy on her.

Inside the car, Mammy opened the box and explained to Doireann that she had to share. There were six sticks—one each for Granda, Granny, Oisín, and Mammy and two for Doireann. Granda put his aside for later as they drove for home. It was now about 6 p.m. Granda drove out at the far end of the prom, avoiding the town, to access the main road to Waterford City and pulled into a garage first for a fill-up of "cheap" petrol (€1.40 a litre).

Just up from this garage, there was another garage. Pointing to it, Granda said, "That's where we stopped off to get hot water to heat the milk exactly three years ago, when Doireann was only 7 days old."

"Will I mind your Kinder stick, Granda?" Doireann offered, having spotted him putting it down earlier.

"No thanks, pet." Granda laughed.

"That's Granda's," Mammy reminded Doireann.

"I'll tell you something. There's [there are] no flies on our Doireann; she doesn't miss a trick," Granny said to much laughter.

They got through Waterford City easily, and as they progressed further home, Mammy, Doireann, and Oisín all fell asleep. Remarking on this, Granny said to Granda, "And we are the old fogies, wha'? Ha ha."

They arrived home at about 7.25 p.m., with everyone very tired. Granny and Granda helped with loading Mammy's stuff into her car as they waited for Doireann to wake up fully. Oisín was still tired after his snooze and got into Mammy's car, saying, "Thanks, Granny and Granda."

Mammy lifted Doireann out of Granny and Granda's car, and they both gave her a little kiss on the cheek; said bye-bye, pet; and thanked her for the lovely day. "See you again soon."

Granny and Granda then unloaded their car and "fell in" through the hall door and had a well-earned cup of tea.

CHAPTER 24

Bless Me

30 July

Granda was in the shed when Daddy, who was in a hurry, dropped Doireann over at about 9.50 a.m. "Granda, Grann-daa, Grannnn-daaaaa," the little voice echoed from outside. It was Doireann calling, from "outer space."

Granda looked out and gave her a big wave as she stood at the opened kitchen door. She then waved back. "It's raining, Granda," she said.

"Okay, pet. I will have to run the gauntlet, so," joked Granda.

"Stand back, Doireann, because Granda is going to dash over," Granny said.

Granda ran across the yard as fast as he could and hopped into the kitchen as Doireann stood looking, a huge smile on her face. "Hiya, pet. Isn't that a lovely dress and pants you have on today. Who got you them?" Granda asked.

"Mammy did."

"You have a great mammy," Granda told her.

"No, no more photos," she objected as she tried to hide her lovely dress with pictures of animals. "Look, Granda. There is a giraffe on it." She pointed.

"And a pelican," pretended Granda, because he wanted her to explain, what it was.

"It's not a pelican," Doireann objected in disgust.

"Well, what is it, then?" asked Granda.

"It's a parrot," she informed him.

"Is it a macaw?" asked Granda. "Ah, okay, it's a parrot," he said immediately, on observing a look of total bewilderment on her face.

Earlier, when Doireann had entered the house, she'd asked, "Who put the teddies there?"

"Ah, your Granda did," Granny told her.

Granda had put Baby Bop, Teddy Brown, and Teddy White sitting on the floor against the wall, directly opposite the hall door for Doireann's imminent arrival.

She took her food out of her shoulder bag and was now focused on her smoothie; which Granny had just picked up. "Granny, you squished it," she said, noticing it had been squashed.

"I didn't," said Granny, pleading her innocence. "It was like that, in the bag," was Granny's evidence.

Granda picked up Doireann's banana, and holding it up to his ears, like a telephone, he said, "Hello. Hello, who's there?"

Doireann laughed loudly.

Granda got her to do it and then took a quick photo.

Then she showed Granny and Granda her beautiful mirror box that Aunt Selin in Cambodia had sent to her. She got Granny to look into it, and then Granda had a go.

"Wait. I want to see me, in it," Doireann said.

And they all looked at her in it.

She told Granny and Granda that Mammy was at home. She also informed them that Oisín would be going back to school soon. Doireann sat on her toy motor car and said, "Granny, I am going to work." She started up the engine and headed towards the kitchen.

Later on, when showing her some family videos, on the iPad, Granny suddenly asked Doireann, "Did you fart?"

She just nodded.

"Does she need to go to the toilet?" Granda shouted in to Granny.

"No," Doireann answered, before searching the kitchen press and taking out the biscuit tin. "Can I have one?" she asked, realising there was something inside it.

Granny announced, "I forgot. I meant to hide the biscuits. Okay, just one; your Mammy will give out."

She took a custard cream biscuit and went into Granda. "Look, Granda," she said, showing him the biscuit.

"Oh brill, that looks nice," he said, just before a pile of large crumbs landed on the carpet. "Let's pick them up and put them into the bin," Granda suggested.

She did just that and then hopped and skipped towards the bin in the kitchen.

Earlier, Granny had told her, "We cannot go out the back because it is wet."

"Can we go somewhere?" she asked Granny a while later.

"Where would you like to go? The library?" suggested Granny.

"Okay, Granny," she said.

"Well, hold on for a few minutes. I have to change [clothes]," Granny told her.

"Ah, Doireann, are we getting a different granny? Maybe she'll be a monster," Granda worried.

Doireann, now smiling, roared a few scary sounds at Granny.

Granda put the children's TV station on for the short while, to let her relax while waiting. Someone was playing an instrument on the telly. "What's that, Doireann?" Granda asked.

After a short pause, Granda named it and got her to repeat after him. "A banjo."

She then sneezed loudly a few times, and Granda went to get her a tissue.

"Bless me," she said each time she sneezed.

"Oh, very good, Doireann," Granda acknowledged as he handed her the tissue. "Here, blow into this," Granda told her, and she did so, a few times, before clearing her nose.

"Mammy, Daddy and Oisín, heard me!" joked Doireann.

Granda laughed out loud. "That's very funny, pet. Good on ye," Granda told her.

"It's stopped raining," she said excitedly.

"Ah, it's still very wet outside, Doireann," Granda reminded her.

"Are we ready to go then?" she asked, just as the "changed Granny" arrived out of her "cave".

"Just a minute, I'll be there in a mo," said Granda.

It wasn't too long before they were on the road to Gorey Library. "Have we got the S-O-O-T-H-E-R?" Granda asked, spelling the word out for safety reasons.

"Yes," said Granny and continued with, "And I need to get some things in Dunnes Stores on our way back home."

Granda listened intently to Doireann telling Granny, all about her birthday party.

"*Wheeeeeeeeeeeeeeeeeeeeeeeeeeeeeeeeeeeeeeeeeeeeeeeeeeeeeeeeeeeeee*," they all shouted as Granda's car descended into Gorey Shopping Centre's underground car park.

They parked in a family bay, and Doireann held Granda's hand as they waited for some cars to pass. Next, they visited Noddy and Minnie, and Doireann showed them her new mirror box, before advancing towards the elevator. When they got into the lift, Granda took a photo of the two Doireanns in front of him. The other Doireann had managed to climb inside the mirror in the lift, and they were now standing, staring and sizing each other up!

After a quick visit to the racing car on the first floor, they went straight for the library doors, giving the wall walk a miss, as it was too wet. "I want to do a wheeee," said Doireann, as they passed by the courthouse.

"On the way back," Granny promised.

They went in through the magic semicircular doors, continued on into the library, and went down to the kiddie's area—where there were other kids and mammies. Doireann showed Granda where to sit, until Granny, who was returning some books, arrived. Granda went to read the newspapers when Granny appeared and read stories to Doireann.

Later, Granda took over the story-reading duties again, allowing Granny to look for more books and CDs to take home. Doireann pushed one of the circular plastic drum-type seats around. "Is that for me?" Granda asked.

"No, for me," she said, before climbing up and sitting on it.

Granda sat on a kiddie's seat "close to the floor" and reached over to pick a book for Doireann. It was a story come poem about kittens and their furs and purrs. The next book was about a day monkey and a night monkey, and it too was a story come poem.

Granny appeared and beckoned Doireann. She ran over, and Granny handed her a book about numbers and counting from one to twelve. Granny also got a DVD for her about the children's programme *Balamory*. Doireann wanted to go with Granny.

"Doireann, will you push that seat back to where you took it from?" Granda asked.

As soon as she did so, they both went to Granny.

"Do you want to give Granny a hand?" Granda asked her, holding his hand out at the same time.

She thought this was funny and laughed. Granda then got her to approach Granny with her hand outstretched and ask, "Do you want a hand, Granny?"

They all had a good giggle at that.

She had to do the, "*Wheeeeeeeeeeeeeeeeeeeeeeeeeeeeeeeeeeeeeeeeeeeeeeeeeeeeeeeeeee eeeee,*" when they left the library for home. After her third go, Granda had to chase her up the ramp and into Granny's arms for protection, before he tickled her.

They took the lift down to the ground floor, and Granny went off into the shop to get some items. Doireann went to the sweets area and took one of the free paper bags. "Is that your trick bag?" Granda asked.

She emptied out a pretend coin from the empty bag, into her hand. She then threw the coin in the air and held the bag out, waiting for it to drop back into the paper bag. All of a sudden, she needed to go to the loo.

Up to this moment, when asked if she needed to go, she kept saying no. Granda called Granny, who took her back up the lift and into the loos on the first floor.

When they came out of the toilets, Doireann said, "I can't see Granda."

"Where is he?" Granny asked.

"He must be in the car," she replied.

Granny pointed to where Granda was waiting. Doireann just smiled and then walked to the lift. Granny went back into Dunnes Stores. Doireann and Granda went to the kiddie's octopus ride machine. "It's not playing, Granda," she complained.

"Ah, it must be broken," said Granda, who had no intention of putting money into it. He started to press all the buttons, but no joy.

Next thing, Doireann started pressing buttons and the auto music came on, and she was delighted. Doireann took some photos of the buttons inside the machine also. The music was a song by Madness that Doireann loved. It stopped after about twenty seconds, and Doireann was not happy. As they walked towards Dunnes Stores, they found all the other kiddie ride machines were taken up by other kiddies.

Doireann gave the two plastic guide dog statues hugs and wanted to put money into them, after Granda explained how people can donate money to the Irish Guide Dogs for the Blind. There was one large white dog and a smaller black dog, together on a small plinth, with coin deposit slots on their heads.

"I don't have any money on me," Granda told her.

Granny had and into the shop they both went. They found her at a checkout.

"Granny, have you any money? I want to put it into the dogs," said Doireann.

Granda said, "Just give her some copper coins." And off they went to do their duty.

She put the coins into the smaller black dog's collection box. "I want to put one into this one." She pointed to the bigger white dog.

"Doireann, we can't keep putting money in; we'll have no money left for ourselves," pleaded Granda.

Granny came out, and they walked up the main foyer toward the lift.

Doireann sat down on the ceramic floor. "Look what I can do," she said, her legs wide apart.

"Very good, Doireann. Well done," Granda said and then asked her, "Will we use the travelator?" As she nodded in agreement, Granda joked, "Or will we use it now—you know, the travel now and not the travel later?"

With a little laugh, Granny said, "Ah, Granda, again."

"You have to hold Granny's hand," Granda told her after she let go, while travelling on the travelator.

Realising that Granda was angry, she quickly held Granny's hand again.

Doireann paid another quick visit to Noddy and Minnie, while Granda put the food items in the car. Then, with Doireann strapped into her seat, they did the usual "*Wheeeeeeeeeeeeeeeeeeeeeeeeeeeeeeeeeeeeeeeeeeeeeeeeeeeee eeeeeeeeeeee,*" as Granda drove his car up the ramp and headed for home.

On the way home, they played the "Downtown" over and over and over, with Doireann shouting out the word *downtown* every time.

Granny played the DVD *Balamory* when they arrived back in the house, and Doireann loved it. She ate her lunch with the help of Granny. Earlier, Mammy had told Granny that she'd had to play aeroplanes when feeding Doireann. By that, she meant putting the food on the spoon first and then flying it through the air, until it arrived at her mouth.

"I had enough," she told Granny.

"One more," Granny said.

"No," she replied.

"Then, there'll be no chocolate bar," she was warned.

Doireann had another spoonful.

She then had Granda's Kinder choc stick, the one she had offered to mind for him as they'd travelled home from Tramore last Saturday. Earlier in Dunnes Stores, Granda had promised her the Kinder because she had been a good girl. Then she asked Granny for a please-a-pop.

Granny said, "You are getting too many treats today, but I did promise it."

She had her freeze pop. Then almost immediately, Doireann said, "It's dried up outside."

"Okay, as soon as I have my tea," Granny said, meaning she would take her outside then.

"I would like a cuppa tea," said Doireann.

"Okay," said Granny.

"Doireann, do you want to hear Granda singing your song?" Granda called out.

"She is having her tea here first," Granny informed him.

Eventually, they went into Granda and listened to Mammy's recording of Granda singing the song he'd composed for her third birthday. Then Granda showed her all the photos he had taken in Tramore Amusement Park that day as well.

After this, Granny took her out to the garden, to play. First, they went on the bus down to Courtown and then got off, sitting themselves down on the tree stumps in that part of the garden. Next, they got another bus to some other place further up the garden. Doireann then ran around the garden and sat beside Granda, while Granny went inside to get some storybooks to read for her.

After the story books, she was off running again. "Hold my hand, Granda, and we will run," she told him.

Then, she was over at the buckets playing with the water. She told Granda that Granny said not to water the flowers. Granda explained to her why Granny had said that. "You don't water the plants during the day, because the sun will burn the wet leaves; you only water them in the evening."

"I can't lift this, Granda. Pour it into that one," Doireann pointed. Then she brought the teapot over to fill it from the tap. "How do I do this, Granda?" she panicked as the water flowed swiftly, and the teapot was now full.

Granda ran and turned off the tap and carried the teapot over to empty some into a bucket.

"I am all wet Granda," she said and showed him her wet dress.

"Come on in, and we will see what Granny can do while we wait for Daddy to arrive," Granda said.

Daddy had phoned to say he was running a bit late. Granny went to Doireann's shoulder bag and took out another dress.

Daddy called, and immediately Doireann said, "I got a chocolate bar."

Granny said, "Wait now," and continued to explain. "Granda didn't eat his Kinder bar last Saturday. She was given it instead after she ate all her lunch today."

She started screaming when Granny tried to help her put her dress on.

Granny said, "Where did the cat come from?"

Doireann started to laugh.

Granda was out in the shed, having cleared away the toys from the garden. Then, he was gluing the broken birdhouse.

"Bye Granda. Byeee, Grannndaa," Doireann called again, much more loudly the second time.

Granda popped his head out. "Ah, goodbye, pet. See you soon," he said back to her before she and Daddy left for home.

❦

CHAPTER 25

Lionel Missy

1 August

Doireann and Daddy called over at about 9.50 a.m. Daddy had to rush away. Doireann came into the house with Teddy Pink and her travel case. She was wearing a lovely skirt today, and Granny said, "Granda, have you seen Doireann's dress?"

"Oh, I did," said Granda as he admired it again.

"It's gorgeous," said Granny. "And it's matching."

"It isn't," Doireann retorted.

"Do you know what matching is?" Granda asked her.

Silence.

Granda explained, "Your yellow skirt matches the yellow flowers on your white top, and it also matches the yellow in your pants," which were multicoloured.

"They are trousers," she snapped.

"Oh, sorry, Doireann. Your trousers. You are gorgeous," Granda told her. "What did you have for breakfast?"

"I had porridge."

"Did you?"

"So did I," said Granda.

"Did you have berries?" Granny asked.

"Yes."

"I did, too," Granny said.

"I didn't have any berries, but did you have toast?" Granda teased.

"No."

"Well, I had," Granda proudly informed her.

"Did you see Baby Bop and the teddies looking out the window?" Granda asked.

"Did you do that?" she asked.

"Yes, I did that," Granda proudly told her.

"Well don't do that," said the little spitfire.

Her travel case was all wet, and so were her socks inside. Doireann had brought along the toy water bottle, full of water. "That's what caused it," Granny told her. "I have to give the bottle to Teddy [Pink]," she informed Granny.

"Bring an empty bottle in future, and we can fill it with water, here," Granda suggested.

Later, she went into Granda and asked, "Granda, would you like a cup of [Granny's] tea?"

"No thanks. I just had some, pet. And thank you very much for asking," Granda replied.

Off she went and sat at the kitchen table to have her tea and a Marietta buttered biscuit sarnie. "That's the last one, and you won't be getting anymore," Granny informed her. Doireann had asked for one, and when Granny had suggested an oatcake, Doireann had said, "No, a biscuit."

The tea spilt, and Granny asked her, "How did it happen?"

"It spilt itself," was her reply.

When she had finished her tea, she asked, in a whingy moany voice, "Granny, will you put *Balamory* on?"

When Granny answered with the same tone in her voice, Doireann let it be known that she did not like it.

"What's wrong?" Granda asked loudly, also in a whingy moany voice from his workstation. Then Granda went and asked her why she was talking angrily.

Doireann just stood quietly and said nothing.

"Listen, pet, Granny and Granda are only joking with you," Granda assured her.

"I am too," Doireann said.

Granda put his arms around her, gave her a big hug, and said, "We love you very much."

Then she attempted to climb into her high chair to watch the *Balamory* DVD that Granny had set up for her.

"We waited for you to visit us this morning, Doireann. The teddies and Baby Bop were getting impatient, too. That's why I let them look out the window, to see if you were coming," Granda told her. "Will we take them away from the window, now?"

"No, you do it," ordered the little spitfire.

Granda helped her into her chair and handed her the safety straps to fasten herself.

"Thank you, dear!" Her Royal Highness said.

She sat and watched *Balamory* while eating the rest of her Marietta buttered biscuit sarnie, slowly, savouring every bit of it. She asked Granny for another Marietta.

Granny said out loudly, "Granda, that's all the Marietta biscuits now. They are all gone, and I won't be getting anymore, because they are too expensive." That announcement was, in actual fact, for Doireann's ears.

Granda said back loudly, "Ah, are they all gone? Oh, dear."

Later, Doireann asked Granny for an oatcake. When handing it to her, Granny asked her, "Did you really have a breakfast this morning?"

"I need to go for a wee," Doireann called out.

Granny took her to the toilet. After going to the toilet, Granny told her to clean her hands and held her hands under the running tap.

"Now dry them," Granny said, handing her the towel.

Doireann stepped onto the weighing scales, before running into Granda, saying, in a very loud voice, *"I'm two, six again, Granda!"*

"That's great, Doireann. Two, six—wow, you are a big girl," Granda said, also again.

"Yeah." She smiled and marvelled, before darting back out of the room with a little hop and a skip.

When Granda went into the kitchen, Doireann was twirling around in her lovely skirt, while watching people boogieing on *Balamory*. Granda did (attempted) a pirouette with his hands up in the air and invited her to do the same.

"No, it's a twirl," she said.

"I know," said Granda. "I am doing a pirouette," he told her.

"No, it's a twirl," she insisted.

Granda gave up. "Here, Doireann. Do you want to put these toilet rolls into the store cabinet in the bathroom for me?" Granda asked.

She took them and placed one on each of three little shelves before closing the door.

"Well done, Doireann," said Granda.

Granda told Granny, and she thanked Doireann also.

Granda sat at the kitchen table for his elevenses (tea and one toast).

"Look, what I can do," she showed Granda as she moved to the music. She was making all sorts of moves, hopping and bopping and burning up loads of energy at the same time.

"Well done, Doireann. You are a great dancer," Granda said, with Granny in agreement.

Granny realised she didn't have her coat, and it was raining. The forecast was for rain all day. Her top was even sleeveless, but it wasn't too cold today. She had left her coat behind in Granny and Granda's house recently, but it had been returned. Granda offered to cover her with his jacket when outdoors today.

Balamory showed an Indian couple getting married and how beautiful the bride was dressed. The couple had to walk around the temple four times. Doireann asked Granny for something to dress up in, and Granny gave her a lovely shawl and a necklace.

"Oh, is it a birthday?" Granda asked, knowing full well it was a wedding.

Doireann looked at Granda and shook her head.

"The lady is getting married," Granny said.

"She is getting married," repeated Doireann to Granda, who acknowledged it.

Granda gave her a cuddle. "You are beautiful. When are you getting married?" he asked.

She didn't answer, preferring instead to watch the wedding.

"Are we going to the library, Doireann?" Granny asked.

"Yes, but I want to see it again," she replied, meaning the wedding.

"We can see it later," Granny suggested.

"No, now," she demanded.

And Granny and Granda had to wait.

Eventually they "hit the road", and Granda put his jacket over Doireann's shoulders, sheltering her from the heavy rain before they got into the car. They all sang along with "Downtown" in the car, on their way to Gorey Library.

Doireann brought the large necklace Granny had given to her earlier, when dressing up. She threw it up in the air, and it hit Granny just below one of her eyes. "Are you okay, Granny?" a concerned Doireann asked, realising what she had done.

"Yes, and you are not to throw that because you see what can happen," Granny told her in a strict voice.

She must have thought it was the same as throwing the small rag in the car. Doireann hadn't realised the consequences and said, "Teddy [Pink] is worried," even though Teddy wasn't with them.

Granny picked up on what she had just said and moved to reassure her, saying, "It's okay, Doireann. It was an accident." She gave her a little cuddle. Granny had to repeat this a few times, knowing Doireann was a little bit sad.

Granda joked, "Doireann is really soft, Granny. Let's throw her to one another."

They all laughed at that. And then Granda emphasised that he was only joking with her. After the, "*Wheeeeeeeeeeeeeeeeeeeeeeeeeeeeeeeeeeeeeeeeeee eeeeeeeeeeeeeeee,*" they took the usual route towards the library.

Doireann ran over and climbed up and onto the small wall surrounding the water feature near Gorey Courthouse. She began to walk the wall, holding Granda's hand. They came across a section that had broken away at the side, with some other parts ready to break away, also. At the end of her walk the wall, she failed to push the solid wall now confronting her out of the way, no matter how hard she pushed.

Jumping down, she ran to the library doors and headed to the kiddies' section as usual, with Granny. Granda went to the security guard to report the damaged section of the wall. He, in turn, directed Granda towards a bell on a counter to press for attention. A Wexford County Council employee appeared, and Granda reported the damaged wall, as well as a low-lying tree branch hanging dangerously at eye level. It was all recorded, to be passed on to the relevant departments.

Granda updated Granny, who was doing her reading duties as usual, before catching a glimpse of the newspaper headlines. Afterwards, Granda went back to Granny, saying, "The government is considering paying grandparents who mind their grandchildren for up to ten hours a week a sum of €1,000 a year. Here we are, having minded Doireann three days a week (totalling fifteen hours) over the last three years and now moving to one day a week (which will be seven hours). Sods law," moaned Granda.

Having initially visited the library late, they left at about 12.40 p.m. Doireann did one "*Wheeeeeeeeeeeeeeeeeeeeeeeeeeeeeeeeeeeeeeeeeeeeeeeeeeeeeeeeeee,*" down past the courthouse, with Granda chasing her back up to Granny.

As they passed the toilets in Gorey Shopping Centre, Doireann said, "I need to go to the toilet." Initially, Granny thought she was making it up but took her into the toilets anyway.

Granda had given Doireann some leaflets on fire safety that he'd picked up in the library. "They are mine, Granny. Granda gave them to me," she repeated over and over.

Later, as she sat in the car seat, she held the leaflets up, saying, "I am reading," and started to waffle on and on and on. Then she sang a made-up song, using words that just came into her head.

"That was a lovely song, wasn't it, Granda?" Granny said.

"Oh yes, that was lovely," he agreed.

When back home, she sat at the kitchen table and had spag-ball for lunch. Then she wanted more. When she finished that, she said, "I'll take more." And when Granny prepared it, Doireann got down from the table, saying, "I have had enough."

"You said you wanted more," Granny said to her.

"No, I didn't," she said.

"Yes, you did," Granda reminded her.

"Okay, just one bit," she offered. She took a spoonful, and off she went to dress up again for her Indian wedding.

Later on, she was holding Teddy Pink and sitting on her chair in her lovely clothes, staring down at Granda.

"Are you going to get married too?" Granda asked her.

"Yes," she said.

When Mammy called to collect her, there was great excitement as she showed Mammy her lovely dressing-up clothes and necklace. Granny gave her a new dress to take home with her. Granny had bought it in Gorey the other day. It was for a 4-year-old.

Mammy looked at it and said, "It would do her now."

Doireann loved it and thanked Granny.

She went into Granda and said, "I have to go now Granda."

"Are you not staying forever?" joked Granda. Then he said, "Okay, petal, that's okay."

Granny, realising they had left the rest of the spag-ball behind, ran to catch Mammy, but it was too late. Mammy was pulling away just as Granny arrived out at the gate. "I will run up [to Mammy's house] with it," said Granny, but Granda offered to drive her, instead.

After they delivered it, Granda was just about to pull away when Doireann darted to the hall door and gave Granny and Granda a big wave and a big thank you.

3 August

Doireann arrived with Daddy at about 9.40 a.m. in her new (€3) flowery dress Granny had bought for her. She gave Daddy a kiss as he left for work. She was reluctant to let Granda take a photo and objected when he took his mobile phone out.

Granda picked up Doireann's banana and, holding it to his ear, said, "Hello. Hello. Is that Mammy?" as Doireann looked on.

He took a photo later, unbeknownst to her.

Doireann went to Granda as he was eating his porridge to show off her red shoes. Granda beckoned her nearer and said, "They are gorgeous and look lovely with your red flowery dress."

Later, she showed Granda her two small pink teddies. He asked, "What are their names?" but got no response.

"Is it Teddy Tiny Pink and Teddy Yellow Pink?" (One had traces of yellow), Granda enquired.

Disagreeing, she moved her head from side to side.

"Oh, are they twins then?" Granda asked.

Her head continued moving from side to side, without a word.

Granda took a photo of the tiny twins anyway.

He switched the telly on for Doireann to watch *an episode of* "Swashbuckle." . She took the soother out from her shoulder bag, saying, "Granny, I'm tired."

Earlier, she had told Granny and Granda she tried to get out of her cot that morning.

"Why?" asked Granny.

"To see yous," she said.

"Ah, were you afraid you wouldn't see us?" Granny asked.

She nodded.

"We missed you too, Doireann," said Granda.

She took her lunch, which included a pepperoni, out of the bag. Then she moaned, "I don't like that," referring to the spag-ball. She had enjoyed her spag-ball the other day, Wednesday.

"Ah, just like her mammy," remarked Granny. When Mammy was Doireann's age, she would eat, say, beans one day and love them, and the next day, she wouldn't eat beans because she didn't like them.

The conversation would usually go like this: "I don't like them," Doireann's mammy would say. "But you liked them yesterday," her daddy (Granda) would remind her. "I don't like them today!" she would insist.

Granny left out the spag-ball to cool down before putting it in the fridge later.

On their way over to Granny and Granda's house this morning, they had seen a beautiful horse with a young rider trotting on the road outside. It was mainly light beige in colour, with a blondie tail and mane and a white face, Daddy had told them. Doireann thought it was a lion and made a big roaring sound when talking about it.

"Did you say goodbye to Oisín this morning?" asked Granda.

She moved her head from side to side.

"Was Oisín there?" continued Granda.

She nodded.

"Did you give Mammy a hug?" Granda asked Noddy, and she nodded.

"I bet you gave Mammy a big, huge kiss?" Granda persisted.

"Yes." At last, she spoke.

"I bet you love Mammy?" continued Granda.

Nodding, she said, "And Daddy."

"Of course, you do, and Kafli," Granda replied.

Again, Noddy nodded, agreeing that she loved the cat, and repeated what Granda had said. "Kafli."

Granny put *Balamory* on after Doireann requested it. "Granny, I need to do a wee," she said, and they both went into the toilet.

When she finished, Granny fixed her clothes, and she darted off. Calling her back, Granny said, "Doireann, you have to clean your hands."

After washing her hands, she got up onto the weighing scales.

"You're two, five," Granny told her and then suggested, "Hold on and we'll try again." When Granny then told her it was two, six, she ran to inform Granda.

"Granda, I still two, six."

"That's brilliant. You are certainly a big girl. And listen, Doireann, you are a great girl for telling Granny you needed to go to the toilet. That shows you are a big girl now," Granda informed her before she took off again, wearing a huge smile on her face.

Later, Granda passed by Doireann to find her twisting back and forth to the music on *Balamory* and joined in, doing ordinary dancing, well sort of. Loudly, Doireann said, "No, that's not the way."

"Oh," said Granda and changed to the way she was doing it.

Granny then said to Granda, with Doireann listening, "I told her I had the proper dress for that dance once."

"Will I put my dress on then?" joked Granda.

"No," Doireann said in a slightly angry voice. "I do it in my dress," he was bluntly told.

Earlier, she had told Granny, she wanted to go to the playground.

"Which one, Doireann?" Granny had asked.

"Camolin."

"Okay."

As she continued to watch *Balamory*, the Indian wedding came on, with lots of dancing. "I want to dress up," she immediately said.

"Not now, Doireann. We are going to the playground," Granny reminded her.

"I don't want to go. I want to dress up. Come on, Granny. It will be over," she protested.

"Sure, we can play it again," Granny said, before changing her mind. "Okay, so, you don't want to go to the playground?" Granny asked her.

Doireann then had a change of heart. "We go to the playground and dress up after."

"Dressup when we get back," said Granda. "And Granny as well, she can dress up," he also suggested.

"No," she retorted.

"Why not?" Granny asked.

"You are not dressed [dressing] up. I am. You are dressed," Granny was told.

Granda had a cuppa and a slice of toast, before going out. Doireann continued to watch *Balamory*, dancing and singing to the music and song. Granda turned the telly off and promised her she could watch it again when they returned home later.

"You can dress up, and I will dress up, also," Granda told her.

Now shaking her head, with a grin on her face, she loudly said, "You can't dress up."

Doireann went to the loo. Granny had to call her back to clean her hands, and then she weighed herself again. She ran to tell Granda, excitedly, "I'm still two, six stone, Granda."

"That's brill," he told her.

When Granny was ready to go out, Doireann ran to tell Granda and said, "We are ready to hit the door now, Granda."

"The door? Do you mean the road?" he corrected her.

"We are ready to hit the road, Granda," she then said.

"Okay, pet."

Outside, as he stamped on the road a few times, Granda asked, "What am I doing, Doireann?"

"Hitting the road," she replied.

They brought some old towels, as it had been raining slightly on and off, and the playground equipment would be wet. The sun had just come out, and it was nice and warm as well. The forecast was for sunny spells, with the temperature at twenty-three to twenty-four degrees.

"It's very hot in here," Doireann said as she climbed into Granda's car.

"Yeah, hold on, Doireann, and I will sort that for you," Granda said before opening all the windows. He then turned on the air conditioning, before pulling off once Granny had secured Doireann in her seat.

"What time is it?" Doireann asked.

"It's 11.35 a.m.," Granda informed her.

"It's eight o'clock in the house," Doireann said.

"So, we are way ahead now?" joked Granda.

"No, it's not eight, it's eighty o'clock," she corrected herself.

"Oh, it's eighty," acknowledged Granny.

They parked inside the grounds of Camolin Celtic FC, and when Doireann got out of the car, she pointed at the tractor being used to cut the grass on the soccer pitch.

Granda said, "You'll be okay," and held her hand as they walked past the tractor, towards the playground. Granda got her to wave to the man driving the tractor, but he was too busy looking elsewhere at that moment.

Doireann started to play near two other girls, playing on the equipment also while their Mammy sat at a table. She tried the slide after Granny wiped it down with a towel. She was still getting stuck, halfway down, though.

"The next time, you will have to wear pants," Granny told her.

"I have my pants," she told Granny.

"Okay, your leggings or trousers," Granny said.

Granda wiped the slide further up, where he could reach it and Doireann tried it again. This time, she made sure her dress was under her bum as she slid down, and it worked.

Then she got on the swing beside a little boy who was nearly reaching the sky as he swung back and forth. Granny wasn't pushing Doireann's swing hard enough, so Granda was called into action. "Push harder, Granda," he was ordered.

It wasn't too long, before she was calling out, "it's too high, Granda," and he was ordered to slow it down.

"I want to get off," was her next request.

So, Granda slowed the swing down, until he brought it to a full stop, and she jumped off. She went to play at something else and then got bored.

She watched the small boy and his big brother on the swings for a while and then wanted to leave.

On the way back, Doireann asked Granny, "Can I have a freeze pop?"

Granda licked his lips, saying, "Yummy."

"You can have one, Granda," Doireann offered.

As Granda drove into the driveway, now laughing, he asked, "Can I have the last one?"

Doireann looked concerned, and Granda said, "I am only joking, pet. You can have your freeze pop."

Granny asked her, "Do you want to go out to the garden?"

"No, Granny," was the reply.

Later, she went into Granda, as he worked on his computer. "What is that you have?" Granda asked.

"Raisins," she told him.

"Raisins! Where did you get them?" he asked, pretending to be surprised.

"In my house," she said.

"In your house. That's some house you have," Granda told her.

Next, Granny put *Balamory* on for her, and she dressed up for it. Just before that, Granny read her a story from *Dora*, the music book. Granda went out to the kitchen, and seeing Doireann dressed up, he told her, "You are lovely in your dress and necklace."

When he tried to take a photo, she said, "No," in a weepy-sounding voice.

She then started to sing along with *Balamory*. "Is she having her freeze pop?" Granda asked Granny.

"She already had it and her raisins. There is one there for you, Granda, a yellow one," Granny informed him.

"Granny, I need to go for wee," Doireann said.

Granny took her into the toilet. She went to the loo, washed her hands, and jumped up on the scales. She dashed out, looking for Granda, who now had a basket covering his head as he hid behind the slightly closed bedroom door. "*I am two, six,*" his big deep voice said and continued with, "*That's great, Doireann. You are a big girl now.*"

Doireann took the basket and put it on her head, causing Granda to laugh.

"Here, Doireann," Granda said, handing her an empty small-sweet paper bag he got one time in Dunnes Stores. "Now show Granny your trick," he said.

"Where did you get it, Granda?" she asked.

"Oh, I kept it safe for you," he told her.

"Thanks, Granda."

She went out to Granny and said, "Look Granny." She pretended to take something out of the paper bag, before throwing it up in the air. Then she held her paper bag out.

"Now, get the paper bag to make a noise, as if something has dropped into it," Granda advised.

She made a little noise with it, and Granny said, "Well done, Doireann."

Next, Granda was sitting, watching *Balamory* with Doireann, when the Indian wedding came on, just as Granny was putting the washing on the clothesline. When the wedding group got dressed up, she said, "I want to."

Granda went and got the dress and necklace out for her.

Next thing, she took them off and said, "I don't want it now."

Granda put the dress on over his clothes and then the necklace. Doireann gave Granda a weird look.

When Granny came in, she laughed and said, "It looks well."

Granda went and got his phone and asked Doireann to take a photo and thanked her when she did. Then Granny took a photo also.

It was time for lunch, and they all sat at the table. Granda observed Doireann mimicking something she had obviously seen on the telly. She was holding her hand up at her ear, pretending to be on the telephone. This was done by bending the three middle fingers, leaving the thumb and little finger exposed. Her thumb was okay but not the small finger.

When Granda tried to adjust her small finger, she wouldn't let him. "You have to do that, Doireann," Granda explained and demonstrated it at the same time.

"*I am*," she protested loudly, and he left her to it.

She had her pepperoni and then the spag-ball. She left some of the meat behind but ate all the noodles. She then pointed to the water bottle on the table, and said, "I want that."

"Ask nicely," Granny told her.

"I want that," she said, continuing to point

Granny said, "I am waiting for a word."

"Please," she said.

And Granny gave her the water.

She was tired and moody now and didn't want to go out to the back garden. Granny had promised to let her see *Paw Patrol* on the big telly in the sitting room. In the meantime, Granny had just finished her lunch and was making some toast for herself to have with a glass of water. She didn't want to have a hot cup of tea with Doireann beside her while watching the telly.

"Can you read me a story, Granny?" she asked.

"Okay, in two minutes," Granny said.

Then Doireann said, "I want to look at the pictures on this." She held up the iPad.

Granny, now feeling a little bit frustrated, said, "No wonder you get indigestion. Give me two minutes," she demanded.

Next thing, she wanted to watch *Paw Patrol*.

Granny, now a little angry, said, "That's three things you want. Now which one is it?"

"*Paw Patrol*."

"Okay, in a few minutes," Doireann was told.

"Where are you going now?" Granny asked her as she headed off.

"I want to get teddies," she said.

A short while later, Granny called out, "Hello, Doireann. What are you doing?"

But there was no answer.

Granny went looking for her, and when they both returned, Granny said, "She hurt her tummy stretching in to get the teddies out of the cot."

"Ah, are you okay, pet?" Granda asked as she just stood silent, with a face like a bulldog chewing a wasp.

With her toast and a bottle of water, Granny now disappeared in to watch *Paw Patrol*, with the little miss wasp chewer and I want this, and I want that, and so on.

Granda went into the sitting room, and there was Doireann sitting on Granda's seat, watching the telly. "Who's been sitting in my seat?" Granda Wolf asked.

She just sat there, watching the telly, totally oblivious to the outside world and not a care in the world. *Paw Patrol* wasn't on, so they watched some other programme instead.

When it ended, Granny asked her, "Will we go outside?"

"Yeah," she agreed.

And out they both went.

They were playing football when Granda arrived, and he played as well. Granda named her Lionel Missy.

"Who, Granda?" she asked.

"Lionel Missy, because you are going to be a great footballer," Granda assured her.

Later, she told Granda she would be a great runner. Then she ran up and down the garden and all over the place. Doireann said, "Look, Granda," as she tried to kick the ball out of her hands, like a GAA footballer. But it didn't work out.

Granda congratulated her anyway. Granda then showed her how to do a drop kick.

"Oh cool," she said and tried it, but again it didn't work out.

But Granda still said, "Well done, Doireann; it takes time and plenty of practice."

Earlier, Granda had sensed she needed to go to the toilet. Twice he'd asked her, and twice he'd been told no. Then all of a sudden, with panic on her little face, she hurriedly announced, "I need to go to the toilet" (yesterday).

Granda rushed her into Granny, but Mammy had just arrived and took over.

Afterwards, Mammy told Granny that, as Doireann sat on the loo, she'd said, "Granda isn't very good at the football, and I will have to teach him!"

Mammy and Granny joined Granda and Lionel Missy for a bit of football coaching out the back. Then, she got Mammy and Granda to play and sing, "Ring-a-ring-a-rosies. A pocket full of posies. A-tishoo! A-tishoo! We all fall down."

Next, she held Mammy's hand and ran through the towels hanging from the clothesline loads of times. She had lots of fun doing this, laughing all the while. In fact, she laughed so much that Mammy really enjoyed just looking at her having all this fun.

Doireann started to water some flowers, on her own. "Come and help me water these flowers," said Mammy. She was so excited helping her Mammy.

The time came, and Doireann closed up her shoulder bag, put it on her shoulders, and said, "I am going now, Granda."

"Okay, pet. And sure, we'll see you soon," he told her.

"On Thursday," she said.

"No earlier, on Monday," Granda said. And then realising it was the August bank holiday Monday, he corrected himself and said, "Eh, no, it'll be Wednesday next, pet."

Off they went at about 2.50 p.m., with Granda saying, "Goodbye, lazies," as Doireann waved back.

Granny and Granda had a cup of tea and spoke about Mammy's conversation earlier. She'd told them that yesterday evening, she'd had to wake Doireann up from her afternoon nap, and then she'd cried. When she'd gone to take her out for a walk, she'd said her legs were hurting her, and Mammy had been concerned. She'd phoned Daddy to come home quickly. When he'd arrived home, Doireann was running all around the place. Mammy said she was really worried and that they had taken her to the doctor a while ago about this same thing, but he couldn't find anything wrong and suggested X-rays if they wanted that. The jury was still out on that one.

The crèche staff, not having seen Doireann for three weeks later remarked on how big she had grown!

CHAPTER 26

"Will You Say Hello to Teddy, Granda?"

6 August

Granny and Granda visited Avoca Handweavers, County Wicklow, early on this bank holiday Monday. On their way home, they stopped off at Tesco's, Gorey, to use the loo. Just then, Mammy arrived there too with Doireann and Oisín to get something for Oisín's lunch, before he played his very first tennis match today.

"Hiya, Granda," Doireann said, as she got out of the car.

"Hiya, Doireann."

She ran towards him and gave him a big hug. "I didn't get to see Granny and Granda today," she said to Mammy.

Oisín came over to Granda to talk about his tennis match.

"Are you playing the same age group?" Granda asked.

"Yeah," Oisín replied.

"Are you looking forward to it?" he asked him.

"Yeah, but I am tired today."

"Why? What's up?"

"I didn't sleep last night. I just couldn't, and my back was at me," he told Granda.

"Will you be able for the match?" Granda, now concerned, asked.

"Ah, yeah," Oisín assured him.

"And how many sets?"

"Three," he was told.

"Well, enjoy it now, won't you?"

Oisín nodded.

As they talked, Doireann joined them and tipped Oisín on the belly, saying, "Come with me to the bus" (meaning the kiddie ride machine).

"It's full," he told her.

She stopped walking towards it when she saw other kids getting in and out of it.

Granda got down on his hunkers to talk to her. "What are you doing today? Are you going to watch Oisín?"

"Yes."

"What is he doing?" continued Granda.

"Playing tennis."

"What happened to your arm?" he asked her.

"I fell while walking yesterday."

"Ah, poor girl, it must have hurt you."

She pulled her arm away, saying, "It's okay now."

"No, it's not. It looks really red and infected," Granda insisted.

Mammy told Granny she was getting some Sudocrem in Tesco's, for it.

As Granny and Granda prepared to leave for home, Doireann ran to Granda again and gave him another hug. Oisín then gave Granda a hug. And Granny said, "Hey, what about me?"

Granny gave Oisín a hug and rubbed his back at the same time.

"Oh, rub my back up higher, Granny. And higher," he asked again.

A lady passing by started to laugh at that.

As they parted ways, Mammy said, "I will phone later to let you know how his tennis match went."

7 August

Granny's phone rang at about 6.40 p.m. "Hello, hello," said Granny.

"Hello, Granny. I am using Mammy's house phone, Granny," Doireann told her.

"Oh, okay, Doireann. And, how are you?"

"What are you doing, Granny?" she wanted to know.

"Well, I have just finished washing the dishes, and I'm going to dry them now."

"Is Granda there?" Doireann then asked.

"Yes, Granda is here."

Granda came to the phone. "Hello, Doireann. And, how are you?"

"I'm fine."

"What are *you* doing?" Granda asked.

"I am using Mammy's house phone."

"What else did you do today?" he asked.

Silence and then, "I have my dinner."

"Oh, you are having your dinner now?" Granda wanted to know.

"*No,*" she said loudly.

"Oh, you are going to have your dinner?" Granda assumed.

"*No,*" she said, loudly again. "I had my dinner," she explained.

"Oh sorry. You had your dinner. What did you have?" Granda asked.

"Eh, bread and bolonase" (bolognaise), she said.

"Oh lovely. Was it tasty?"

Silence.

"Was it yummy?" Granda asked, instead.

"Yeah, it was yummy, yummy. I was on the bus today, Granda."

"Ah brill. And you were in Gorey."

"Yeah," she said.

"And did you like the big bus?"

"Yeah," was the only information offered.

"Are you coming over to us tomorrow, Doireann?"

Silence. "Noooo," she eventually said. And then there was more silence.

"You will be over tomorrow, Doireann," Granda said on hearing the background conversation with her Mammy.

"Yeah, I will be over," she said.

"Will you say hello to Teddy, Granda?" she asked.

"Okay, Doireann."

"Hello," a different voice spoke to Granda.

"Ah, hiya, Mammy," Granda said. "She wants me to say hello to Teddy."

"Yeah, she is gone off to get her."

Doireann arrived back with Teddy Pink.

"Hello, Teddy," Granda said.

"Teddy says hello and how are you, Granda?" Doireann told him.

"Okay, Doireann, time to say goodbye to Granda," Mammy said.

"Granda, it is time for you to say goodbye," Doireann said.

"Okay, Doireann, goodbye. See you in the morning. I will pass you over to Granny," said Granda, who was now laughing.

"Bye-bye, Granny," said Doireann.

"Bye-bye-bye, pet," said Granny, to the sound of, "Byeeeeeeeeeeeeeeeeeeee," from Doireann.

Granny had bumped into Mammy, Doireann, and Oisín earlier that morning, and when Doireann spotted Granny from a distance, she'd pointed, saying loudly, "There's Granny!" Granny had been delighted to see them.

Oisín didn't go to his football today, as he was tired. He'd played well at his tennis match yesterday (Sunday) but was beaten. Granny mentioned to Mammy that yesterday Oisín had told Granda he didn't sleep great on Saturday night. Granda asked him what was up, and he'd said he didn't know but that his back was sore, and he was restless. Mammy said his back was sore from hurling the other day.

8 August

After her workout, Granny went to the locker room to change into her swimming togs and checked her phone while there. There was a missed call from Mammy. "Doireann must have pressed the re-dial button," Granny told Granda as they drove out of the gym car park later.

Granny returned the call.

"Maybe Doireann will answer," Granny joked. Daddy answered. "Ah, hello, I got a missed call. Was that Doireann messing?"

"Yeah."

"Ah, okay. Listen, we will be home in about twenty minutes," Granny informed him.

Mammy and Doireann arrived over at Granny and Granda's house at about 10 a.m.

Knock, knock, the hall door sounded, and Granda answered it. There was Mammy with a little scooter at the door but no sign of Doireann. Mammy was looking over to her right and grinning as Doireann hid. Realising what Doireann was up to, Granda asked Mammy, "Is Doireann not coming today?"

"I don't know where she has gone," said Mammy.

Granda peeped outside the door and saw Doireann standing close to the wall; a big smile on her face. "I was hiding," she said excitedly.

"Is this your scooter? Isn't it lovely? Where did you get that?" Granda asked her.

"Oisín gave it to me last year for my birthday."

"Wasn't he very good to you?" he said.

"Look, Granda. I can go fast on my scooter," she said.

He watched her scooting past, safely and not too fast. "Well done, Doireann. You are brilliant on the scooter," he told her, adding, "Did you know I had a scooter, when I was small?"

"Where did you get it?" she asked.

"Santa Clause brought it to me, and I used to scoot all over the place on me scooter," he said.

Doireann thought this was very funny, and she laughed. "Look at my new lunch box," she said to Granda.

"Oh, that's lovely, Doireann," he remarked.

Mammy said, "I bought it for her yesterday."

"Look at all my food in it," Doireann marvelled.

"*Wow*," he said loudly.

"I will put it in the fridge," she said.

Mammy ran to her and said, "Take the banana out first."

"No."

Mammy had to explain. "You don't put bananas in the fridge," Mammy told her as she removed it from the new lunch box.

"Okay, Mammy," agreed Doireann and then started to arrange her food in Granny's fridge.

Mammy asked, "What are you doing?"

Granny said, "It's all right. She always does that."

"What are we doing this morning?" Granny asked Granda.

"Well, I have to get petrol, for the car, in *Enniscorthy*," he said, highlighting the last word loudly so Doireann could hear him.

Doireann, then asked, "Can I play in Enniscorthy in the playground?"

"Okay then. We can do that," agreed both Granny and Granda.

"Until we are ready to go, do you want to watch *Balamory*?" Granny asked her, and she agreed.

Later, she was singing along to the TV song title, "Balamory".

Mammy had put cream on a small lump on her eyelid. The redness had reduced, but, "If it is not gone today," Mammy said, "I will take her to the doctors."

Doireann was great with her hugs today. Firstly, Granda got some lovely hugs, and when Mammy had to leave for work, she gave her plenty of hugs and a big kiss and then another lot at the hall door. Then, when she came back into the kitchen, Granny remarked, "I never got a hug." Doireann gave Granny the biggest hug of the day and then another one.

Daddy's car was in for repair until today, and they only had Mammy's car. Mammy told Granny and Granda earlier that Doireann only wanted to bring the scooter with her today. She told Mammy she was leaving Teddy Pink and Tiger Teddy at home to rest because they were very tired. Richard sent a Facebook photo of his new haircut and newly grown beard, with the Irish flag hanging up in the background. Granda showed Doireann her Uncle Richard. And as she looked, he asked, "Doireann, can you see the flag?"

She nodded.

"What flag is that?" he continued.

"The Irish flag," she said immediately.

"Well done, Doireann," Granda said proudly.

And Granny was also amazed when Granda told her that Doireann knew the Irish flag.

Doireann went to the toilet before they headed off to Enniscorthy. When finished, she came running to Granda, loudly proclaiming, "I'm two, six, Granda."

"Oh, well done, petal. That's great."

"I think there's going to be a storm," Granda said as he viewed the dark clouds on the horizon.

"What will we do, Granda?" Doireann asked.

"I think it might rain," announced Granda as he opened the hall door to have a better look.

Doireann followed him and said, "It's cold."

Granny gave Doireann her cardigan to wear.

"Granda, can you help me with my cardoring?" she asked.

When she had her cardigan on, she said, "Granda, how do I look?"

"You look gorgeous, pet. You are the prettiest girl in Ireland," he told her.

"I feel all cuddly now," she said as she rubbed the arms of her soft "cardoring".

As they left for Enniscorthy, the rain started to fall lightly, and it was very cold. The temperature was about fifteen degrees, today. Doireann wanted Granny to sing songs to her in the car.

"This old man, he played one. He played knick-knack on his drum ..." And so, on went the song.

Later, when Granny said to Doireann, "We are now in Ferns," she immediately said, "No, it's not."

"It is," Granny insisted.

"It's not," replied Doireann, refusing to believe Granny. "What is it then? Enniscorthy?"

"Doireann, it's not Enniscorthy, and you can see; it is too small," Granny tried to explain.

They drove off the main N11 road onto the old Dublin Road, just past Scarawalsh, where the large carpet and furniture store was. Granda drove into the Topaz Garage (now named Circle-K), parked the car, and waited for the very heavy shower to pass over. When the rain stopped, he filled the car with petrol.

"Doireann, do you need to go to the toilet?" Granny asked.

"Yes, I need to do a wee-wee," she said.

"Okay, we will go to the Hotel in Enniscorthy first. Is that okay?" Granny asked.

"Yes," she said.

When they arrived at the playground next to the hotel, Doireann said, "I don't need to go" (to the toilet).

"But you said you wanted to," Granny reminded her.

"Not now," Doireann argued.

Granny and Granda let her go on into the playground first. Granda used the toilets in the Riverside Park Hotel anyway, before returning to Granny and Doireann in the packed playground. Granda spoke with another Granny from County Carlow, who was on a day out with her grandkids and daughter, who lived in Ferns. "What part of Carlow are you from?" Granda asked her.

"Just outside, near Tullow."

"My father's people are from Carlow," Granda told her.

"Who are they?" she enquired.

"The Hearns'. My Uncle Gary was a butcher," Granda informed her.

"That's right," she said, "and he died very young."

"Oh, that was my cousin Gary," Granda said.

"Yes, he died suddenly, in his forties," she acknowledged.

"He had a shop," Granda mentioned.

"Yeah, he was a butcher also," she said.

"My name is Gary Hearns also," Granda said, introducing himself.

Doireann played on the equipment as they became vacant and had great fun. "Granda, I want you to hold me," she said.

She then climbed up a twisted ladder as Granda guided her.

It wasn't long before more dark clouds arrived overhead, so they decided to head home.

"Maybe Doireann, will be okay for the toilet, until we get home?" Granny suggested.

"Doireann, do you need to use the toilet?" Granda asked.

"Yes."

Granda then said to Granny, "I need to go again, and I want to report a dangerous part of the rockery wall just outside the hotel anyway."

Granny took Doireann to the loo, and Granda spoke to and showed the receptionist the danger lurking outside. When they walked back into the hotel, the maintenance man, who Granda knew from way back, was there. They had a quick catch-up before Granda showed him the part-collapsed rockery wall. He agreed, it needed immediate attention. Granny and Doireann had taken a seat in the foyer, while waiting for Granda.

They got back home in no time for lunch.

After lunch, Doireann went into Granda, as he was writing his notes. "What's up Doireann?" he asked.

"I am going to Wexford," Doireann, the bus driver said.

Granny arrived in, boarded the bus, and got down on her knees at a pretend seat. The bus driver was on the phone, talking to whoever was in charge. "What do you think of Granny, on her knees?" enquired the bus driver. She then turned to Granny and said, "The lady said you have to sit on your bum."

"Let me talk to the lady," Granny said.

"She is gone," the bus driver said and then, "Hold on," as she phoned her boss again, before passing the phone over to Granny.

Granny was told to sit on the seat, and the bus driver made sure she did, before driving the bus to Wexford.

When they arrived in Wexford, they got off the bus and went into the town (vacated the bedroom), before going out to the back garden. A while later, they went into the house, and Granny went to the toilet.

"Granda, will you come outside?"

"Okay, Doireann."

"Bring out the scooter," he was told.

"It needs a word," Granda reminded her.

"Please," she said.

"Good girl. Have you got enough room for your scooter?" he asked.

"No, actually," she replied.

"Okay," said Granda and moved the garden furniture around to make more room on the granite slabs for her. "How is that?" he asked.

"That's fine, Granda." She then took off, on her scooter, saying, "I will go on the grass. Come on, Granda; we will go to the shade."

"It might be damp," Granda warned.

But she either didn't listen or didn't want to hear. She then parked the scooter and said, "Let's make a tent."

"I think the grass might be a bit damp, Doireann," Granda again warned her.

She bent down to touch the newly cut grass and said, "No its not!"

"Oh, we'd better wait for Granny to come out," Granda suggested.

Granda took her over near to where the house sparrows were twittering loudly and got her to listen for a brief spell.

Next thing, she said, "Come, Granda, onto the bus."

Granda followed her to the patch of ground, covered with mulch, that had some painted tree stumps. "Sit here, Granda."

He sat on a tree stump, while Doireann went further up to sit on another tree stump.

After a minute or two, Granda asked, "Are you the driver?"

"No, it's the man," she replied, before running to hide behind Granny's flowers.

"Let's play hide-and-seek, Granda," she suggested.

Reluctantly, Granda got up to go and find Doireann, who could now be seen directly in front of him! As he headed in the direction of the house to "find her", she called out, "Granda."

"Yes, pet."

"I just did a fart," she said, with a laugh.

"Do you need to go to the toilet?" he asked her.

Appearing slightly startled at Granda's question, she quickly said, "No."

"Okay. I will go and try to find you," Granda said.

Granda looked in a few places for a while, before pointing to her, saying, "There you are. Come on, Doireann, and sit on the bench with Granda?"

"Okay," she said, before running up to the bench.

When Granny came back out, Granda went back in to finish his notes.

A while later, at about 2.30 p.m., Mammy called to the hall door to collect Doireann and went out the back. Doireann, seeing Mammy, came dashing up the garden, calling out loudly, "Mammy, Mammy."

"Let's do 'Ring-a-Ring-a-Rosie'," she then wanted. They all held hands and sang, "Ring-a-ring-a-rosies. A pocket full of posies. A-tishoo! A-tishoo! We all fall down." And they all had to fall down on the ground at the end of it.

The football was out next, and they had to play footie, with none other than Lionel Missy. Then it was a game of tag. Mammy ran after Doireann and tagged her. She then ran after Mammy and tagged her.

"Okay, Granda, you're next," Doireann said.

As Granda chased her, she ran onto the granite slabs, tripped, and hit the ground really hard. She got a terrible fright and screamed for the whole of Camolin. Mammy held her. Granny started talking about the women snoring the wrong way in *Balamory* to get her mind off the fall, and it worked. Doireann began to laugh at that, in between the sobs. She came around soon afterwards.

"Tiredness was a factor in that accident because she ran around non-stop in the playground," Granny told Mammy.

Doireann asked for help with getting her scooter down the steps at the front door when they were leaving. Granda helped her, and then Doireann pointed her finger at him and, in a very bossy tone, said, "You are not coming to my house, only me and Mammy."

Mammy got a good laugh at that.

Then Doireann told Granda, "You can come another day, but not now."

"Okay, Doireann," he said as she went out towards the gate.

Still pointing, when at the gate, she said, "I will lock you in."

Doireann always gets excited whenever Mammy is around.

CHAPTER 27

Balamory and the Indian Wedding

10 August

Doireann arrived over with Daddy early this morning at about 9.20 a.m. Granda answered the *knock, knock* on the hall door, to be greeted by Daddy, holding Doireann's pink buggy. But there was no sign of her. "Ah, do we not have Doireann today? I can't see her in the buggy," Granda said.

"No," said Daddy as he looked sideways towards the neighbour's garden.

"Granny and Granda thought she was coming over today," pondered Granda.

Still no sign of her.

Granda stuck his head out the door, to see a smiling Doireann holding Teddy Pink. She was hiding beside the garden owl ornament. "I was hiding," she said.

In she came as Daddy picked up her smoothie and shoulder bag from her buggy. "Here Doireann. Give us a hug?" asked Daddy, before rushing off to work, taking the buggy with him.

"Doireann, are you going to say bye-bye to Daddy?" asked Granda.

She ran to the hall door, waving, and said, "Bye, Daddy."

"Bye," Daddy said back.

"I want my smoothie now," she told Granny.

"Firstly, put your lunch into the fridge," Granny said.

334

"No," was the blunt reply.

"Doireann, come on, now," said Granny as she opened Doireann's shoulder bag, adding quickly, "Oh, it's sticky." She took the bag over to the kitchen sink to remove whatever it was. "Sticky" is Granda's pet hate, and he runs a mile from it. Granny ended up looking for a place in the fridge for the lunch box after Doireann took it out of the now non-sticky shoulder bag.

"Here, Doireann, Teddy Pink is having your smoothie," said Granda, who was holding the smoothie up to Teddy's mouth.

She looked sternly at Teddy and said, "Teddeeeeeeeeeeee," and removed the smoothie and straw from her.

"Granda, can you put the straw into the smoothie and don't squeeze it?" she asked.

Granda did that and handed it back to her. She drank it very quickly and then rubbed her tummy while looking very full. The smoothie ingredients were three-quarters of a pressed apple (48 per cent), half a mashed banana and a dash of pressed pineapple (20 per cent), a squeeze of crushed pumpkin, a splash of pressed carrot (1.5 percent), and no colours.

"What did you have for your brekkie?" Granda asked.

"Cheerios and bread."

"I bet you sang to Mammy when you were leaving with, 'Cheerio, cheerio, cheerio, Mammy,'" Granda suggested.

"*No*," she said bluntly.

"Granda, will you put *Balamory* on, for Doireann?" requested Granny.

Doireann hopped down off her TV chair, searched her shoulder bag, and said in a sad sort of heart-broken voice, "I forgot my soother."

"You can get Granny's spare one," suggested Granda.

Now with a smile on her face, she went to Granny's press and took the spare soother. Then she sat back up on her TV seat to watch *Balamory*.

"I bet you gave Mammy a big hug and a kiss this morning when you were leaving your house," Granda said.

The now nodding Doireann, responded with a, "Yeah."

"And did you give Oisín a hug?" he then asked her.

She shook her head from side to side and said, "When I get home later."

Next thing, she was out of the chair and dancing to the music.

Granny joined in and showed her how to hold her arm up in the air, telling her it was Scottish music.

"I need to go to the toilet," was the clarion call from Doireann at about 10.45 a.m.

"Hold on a minute," said Granny.

But she just darted off to the loo, with Granny then in hot pursuit.

"You are a great girl," Granda told her when she darted, past his room after she had finished, only to dart back again and declare loudly, "I am twelve, six."

"No, it's two, six," said Granny.

"Two, six," repeated Doireann, correcting herself.

"That's brill, Doireann. You are still two, six; well done."

And off she went, as happy as a pig in a little pigsty.

"We need toilet rolls, Doireann," Granda said loudly.

"She knows," replied Granny.

"How many, Doireann?" Granda asked.

"One."

"Only one?" he asked. "Sure, go and have a look," Granda suggested.

"She already looked and knows," Granny told Granda.

"Oh, I think it might be two," suggested Granda and went with Doireann to get two toilet rolls.

Granda gave her the packet of toilet rolls, and she removed two and ran to the toilet roll storage box to replenish the stocks.

"Well done, Doireann. Thank you very much for that," Granda said.

"You're welcome," came the reply.

Next thing, she ran into Granda. "Granda, look. I have two plaits."

"Come and let me see; oh, they are gorgeous. Here, stand-steady, and I will get a photo of them," Granda said. Then he gave her a hug, while saying, "You are the prettiest girl in Ireland."

"Don't take them out, Granda," she said, referring to the plaits.

"Oh, I wouldn't do that, pet. They are lovely," Granda assured her.

Soon, after that, she returned to show Granda a lovely bracelet Granny let her wear. "I think it was her Mammy's," Doireann said, not realising she was referring to her own great-grandmother.

Granda took a photo of it, and she then had to look at the photo.

"That's a gorgeous bracelet, Doireann, on the prettiest girl in Ireland," Granda told her as she ran back to Granny.

Later, Granda mentioned the bracelet when he saw Granny in the dining room.

"Oh, she is wearing it as a crown now," Granny remarked and pointed at her as she sat eating her pepperoni.

"Can I have a drink?" Doireann asked.

"Of milk?" Granny asked her.

"Yeah."

"In the small cup?"

Silence.

"In the small cup?" Granny asked again but louder this time.

"Yeah."

"There you are," Granny said as she handed her the cup of milk.

She was now glued to *Balamory* and also acting out parts of it. Granny was putting the washing on the clothesline, and Granda was having a cup of tea and a slice of toast, when an announcement was made, loud and clear, for all to hear. "I need to do a wee-wee!"

Granda opened the back door and called out, "Granny, come quickly."

She took Doireann in to do her wee-wee. There was no weigh-in this time. Earlier, Granda mentioned to Granny how pale Doireann looked.

Granny said, "Maybe it's her clothes."

"No, she is very pale looking," Granda insisted. "When Mammy was Doireann's age, she was forever getting kidney infections and running to the loo all the time," Granda reminded Granny. But she couldn't remember that.

Doireann handed Granda Teddy Pink to hold and cuddle. He wanted to take a picture of Teddy Pink. "Can I take it?" Doireann asked.

"Okay. Wait now, until I switch it on. There you are," said Granda, handing her the phone.

She held the camera up to get Granda.

"Don't forget Teddy," he reminded her.

Doireann focused on Teddy and not Granda. *Click.*

Granda looked at the photo and then got her to take another one—of both him and Teddy, this time. Then, Doireann wanted Granda to take a photo of her and Teddy, and he took two.

Granny went into the toilet, and Doireann asked Granda, "Can we go out the back?"

Granda thought they were going to the playground and waited to ask Granny, before answering.

"Do you not want to go to the playground, Doireann?" Granny asked.

With her head down, she moaned a little, while trying to make up her mind.

"We can play in the back after the playground," Granda suggested.

"Okay," said Doireann meekly.

They all got ready and left the house to drive to Camolin Playground. "You can have your freezer pop, when we get back," Granny informed her.

Granda joked, "And what about mine?"

"There is only one, for Doireann," Granny said.

"What about Teddy Pink?" a concerned-looking Granda asked.

"I will share it with her," Doireann promised.

"Ah, that's very nice, Doireann," both Granny and Granda told her.

As they approached Granda's car, Doireann pointed to the road, which was stained with a dotted line of white spots. It was as if someone had fired a machine gun full of paint from an aeroplane. "That's bird's poo," she loudly proclaimed.

"Oh, it is," agreed Granny.

"And the whole road has been splattered," remarked Granda.

Doireann assisted Granny with fastening her seat belt. As Granny struggled, she said to Doireann, "Your skirt is in the way."

"No. It's a dress," Granny was loudly reminded.

The playground was very busy, with lots of children and mammies. The sun was out, but it was a bit cool when they arrived. Then the clouds arrived with strong breezes, making it feel colder. Doireann had her cardigan on. Granda went back to the car for both his and Granny's jackets, but Granny didn't put her jacket on. Doireann had good fun, climbing up into the playhouse and then sliding down the slide lots of times. Next, she played on the bigger slide with Teddy Pink.

Later, she played with an older girl, who had her younger sister with her. She ran to the swings and then to the see-saw with another little girl. Then Teddy Pink sat into the spinning seat, and Doireann made it spin around.

Granda was then called upon, to assist Doireann, as she descended down a twisting pole from the tree house—a lot of times. At times, Doireann just stood and stared, observing other kids as they played with their siblings or friends. After about an hour, Doireann wanted to go home.

They were only in the hall door when she wanted her freezer pop. "Will you let us get in the door?" pleaded Granny.

Later, Granny switched on her iPad for Doireann to watch the videos of Uncle Richard's visit home last month. Next, Granny went to play some music.

"I don't want the song, 'Baby Girl' [Baby Love]," Doireann said.

Granny put some Christmas songs on, instead, after she had requested them. Then Doireann went to get Baby Bop but struggled to retrieve her from the cot.

"You should have asked," Granny told her after checking on her.

Now Doireann was united with Baby Bop, Granny asked her, "Would you like me to read a story to you?"

"Yeah," replied Doireann, and they took some books out.

Granny turned the Christmas CD off, leaving the radio music on instead as they sat in the dining room. Granny read a Winnie the Pooh book about an Easter egg hunt. On hearing the word, *honey* mentioned, Doireann said loudly, "I love honey."

Doireann was tired and asked Granny for a drink.

"Do you want some milk?" Granny offered.

"I want water," she said.

"Okay, Doireann."

Then Doireann got upset, saying, "I never bring a soother."

Granny cuddled her and asked, "What is wrong with you?"

She wriggled away and lay on the floor, saying, "I don't want you to do that."

"What are you doing?" Granny asked her as Doireann started to bite the sofa. "Don't eat my sofa," Granny warned.

Granda appeared and said to Granny, "Doireann was very good on the equipment in the playground, and you can see how strong and big she is getting when climbing."

"I am eating the sofa," she said, making a scoff-scoff-scoff noise, as if munching it.

Granny went to get her some water, and Granda said, "Don't worry about forgetting your soother, as that can happen, and sure, you can use Granny's one. Granny uses that at night when going to sleep," joked Granda, to a silent audience.

It was lunchtime, but Doireann wanted to sleep. Granny called out from Doireann's room, "Granda, we are sleeping. You go ahead with your lunch; it's in the fridge."

Granda sat and had his usual salad lunch, consisting of, beetroot, lettuce, red onions or scallions, tomatoes, carrots, courgettes, peppers, and tuna. Then he had a cup of tea, with two slices of buttered toasted bread. In the winter months, instead of tea and toast, Granda might have a bowl of hot soup or a cup of Bovril. He loves the Bovril, especially with some black pepper and breaks up two slices of dried bread to put into the Bovril and could be heard to joke with, "Yummy, yummy."

Anyway, Granny arrived out, saying, "She may not last" (stay asleep).

One minute later, Doireann arrived out, only to decide she wasn't ready for lunch yet and returned to her bedroom. About four minutes later, she arrived out, again.

"Did you have your sleep?" asked Granda.

She nodded and sat at the table for her lunch.

With the lid removed from her lunch box, containing chicken pieces, she then wanted to use the pink plastic knife and fork attached to the underside of the lunch box. As she struggled to remove the knife and fork, the chicken pieces fell out and all over the table. Granny picked them up and helped Doireann remove the knife and fork. Next thing, she removed the lid from the tub of natural yogurt, splashing yogurt all over the place at the same time. Granny mopped it up and asked her to be careful. She showed Granny and Granda the sharp side of the knife and they had to touch it. "It is dangerous, and I won't use that side," Doireann announced.

Next thing, the tub lid was stuck to Doireann's arm, and she held it up for all to see. Granny was called into action once again to remove the evidence. For the rest of the lunch, it was all eyes on deck as Doireann went through the menu, with Granny and Granda basically walking on eggshells. She finished her brown bread and ate some orange that Granny had segmented for her. Afterwards, when she put the lid back on the lunch box, Granny tried to take it.

"No, I will mind it," she demanded.

"Doireann, I need to put it in the fridge to keep it fresh, because Mammy will want to give it to you, later," Granny told her, knowing Mammy would want her to eat the rest of her food. Granny put it in the fridge as soon as Doireann got down from the table, saying she had finished her lunch.

She wanted the CD *Baby Love* played, and Granda obliged. Doireann started to dance around the place. Then she wanted to put Teddy Pink into the high chair. Granda had to remove the little table first. Doireann strapped Teddy in and continued dancing to the music. "Granny, look at me." Doireann did a blink-blink and then a wink-wink with her eyes. "Granda, look at me." And she then entertained him.

Then as Granda danced, she said, "That's funny," and got Teddy Pink to dance with her instead. "Look at me. Look at me," she called out, with her arms in the air as she danced up and down the dining room floor. "Look at me, Granny," she called out as she walked, taking small steps but moving fast.

Earlier that morning, before they went out, Doireann had called out and said, "Look what I can do, Granda." And she'd walked on her two heels.

"Very good, Doireann. That's brill. Can you walk on your toes?" Granda had asked.

"Yeah, look, Granda." And off she'd gone, walking on her toes.

Granny took her out the back as promised and played football, until she said, "I need to go to the toilet."

Granny brought her in. Then she did a weigh-in; ran in to Granda, and announced, "I'm two, six, Granda."

"That's absolutely brill; you are still two, six. Well done," Granda told her.

Mammy arrived at 2.30 p.m. to collect Doireann, who was out the back again, playing with Granny. They tried to play with the plastic skittles, but the wind kept blowing them over.

When Mammy opened the kitchen door, Doireann got very excited and ran to give her a big hug. Doireann ran into Granda and said, "Granda, we are going now."

"Ah, are you going, Doireann? Ah sure, okay," Granda said.

"Yeah, we are meeting Layla," she informed Granda.

"Who, Layla?" Granda said.

"It's big Layla and not small Layla. Mammy said we are meeting her," she told him.

"Are you meeting Layla later?" joked Granda.

"*Now, not later*," Granda, as well as the whole of Ireland, was informed.

Mammy was talking to Granny, and next thing, Mammy handed Doireann the bunch of flowers that Granny and her had picked in the garden earlier. Doireann smelt them and got Granda to smell them also. Standing in wait, with her shoulder bag on her shoulders and the bunch of flowers in her hand, she begged, saying, "Come on, Mammy."

Mammy collected the rest of Doireann's things and headed out the hall door. Granda said to Mammy, "You and Daddy are welcome to join us for a drink with Uncle Tony tonight."

"Ah, thanks Da, but I don't think we can make it."

"Bye-bye, lazies," Granda said.

"Bye-bye, Doireann," Granny said.

Mammy and Doireann both waved back at them.

15 August

Mammy and Doireann arrived over at about 9.45 a.m. Oisín, was still in bed; he didn't want to go to the football camp, so, he is helping Mammy all day today instead. Doireann saw Snowy looking out the sitting room window as she walked across the field with Mammy. As she got closer to Granny and Granda's house, she could see Baby Bop looking out the dining room window.

At the hall door, she showed Granda her new red phone.

"Did you see Teddies Brown and White in the other sitting room window at the side?" Granda asked.

Mammy beckoned Doireann over to have a look.

Granda said, "All your friends were looking out, waiting to see you coming."

Doireann had a new jacket, dress, and runners on. "Where did you get that lovely dress?" asked Granda.

Granny and Granda stood waiting for her to say, "In my house." But she whispered in Mammy's ear first. Then she said, "From Mammy's friend."

"You look gorgeous in that dress," said Granny.

"And with your lovely curls in your beautiful hair," said Granda.

Mammy said, "We had to stop on the way over because Doireann was making a phone call. I heard her say, 'Hello I'm on my way.'"

Doireann then said to Mammy, "I was talking to Granny and Granda on the phone."

Mammy handed Granny and Granda some unusual flowers that Doireann had picked on the way over this morning.

"Thanks very much, Doireann, for the flowers," said Granda and put them in with the artificial flowers in the hall.

"Can you check the toilet rolls cabinet in the bathroom, Doireann?" asked Granda.

She ran in and opened the cabinet door.

"How many do we need, Doireann?" Granda asked.

She held her hand up, showing Granda all five fingers.

"Oh, three rolls. Very well then," Granda said, who had checked earlier.

Doireann ran to tell Mammy as Granda fetched the toilet rolls packet in the cubbyhole. Granda let her take the three rolls out herself. Just as she replenished the stocks, Granda took a photo of her. "Thanks for that, Doireann. You are very good," Granda told her.

"You're welcome," she replied.

Mammy had to put (medical) drops into Doireann's eyes because of a cyst on her eyelid. "Show Granny how Mammy does it, Doireann," Mammy said.

Proudly, Doireann lay flat on the dining room sofa and let Mammy put the drops into her eyes.

Mammy, then asked her, "What do we do now, Doireann? You have to move your eyes up, down, and sideways, haven't you?"

After Doireann had done all that, Granda joked, "You have to say, 'Oh my god,' and put your eyes up to heaven, Doireann."

"What do you call that on your eye, anyway?" Granda asked.

"A cyst," she told him.

"Very good, Doireann. You know what it is, then?" he said.

Doireann, then had to put the drops (pretend) into Mammy's eyes, and so Mammy had to lie back on the sofa. Next, it was Granny's turn for the eye drops. Granny saw "Saturday" printed on the drops bottle and assumed it was then when Mammy had taken Doireann to the doctor. Mammy was told by the doctor that, if the cyst didn't clear up in two weeks, then the eye specialist would have to check it further. Granda made himself busy elsewhere.

Granny had to text Mammy later, when she saw that the drops had to be applied four times a day, to ask if she should do it. Mammy texted back and said yes, but if Granny wanted to wait for when Mammy called, that was okay. Granny decided to apply the drops at about 1 p.m.

Doireann showed Granny and Granda her new slippers. They both told her the slippers were lovely. Granda took a photo of them. She threw a furry toy mushroom at Granny and then at Granda. Granda let on to eat it. "Where did you get that, Doireann?" he asked.

"In my shop."

"Is it a musher-room?" joked Granda.

"No," was her blunt response.

"It's a mushroom, isn't it?" said Granny, and she nodded.

Granda put the mushroom on his head, and said, "This is my new hat." Doireann laughed, before removing it.

She gave Mammy a big kiss and said, "Go on, Mammy."

Mammy then left for work.

Granny put *Balamory* on for Doireann. And then, a little bit later, she had to dress her up for the Indian wedding. Doireann sang the songs and danced away too. At the beginning of *Balamory*, there is a big ship in the water, with dolphins all around it.

"Dolphins go very fast," Doireann told Granda.

"Oh, do they?" said Granda, looking very surprised.

She then went to the fridge for her lunch box and started eating the strawberries. Next, she decided to have some nuts.

"Did you have a brekkie?" Granda asked her.

Nodding, she said, "Yeah."

"What did you have?"

"Porridge."

"Did you have any bread?" continued Granda.

"No." She then pointed to the bottom of her lunch box and said, "There is brown bread there."

"Maybe you will have some brown bread that Granny made last night," Granda suggested.

Granny made Granda a cup of tea and buttered a slice of her brown bread for him. Sitting at the table to have it, Granda noticed Doireann opposite eating her Mammy's homemade banana bread. "I'm very thirsty Granda," she said.

"What is that you are drinking?" he asked.

"Milk."

Granny acknowledged that she was very thirsty and gave her more milk.

"I don't want the nuts in the bread," complained Doireann.

"You already ate loads of them," Granny reminded her.

"I don't want them," she insisted.

Granny had to remove each and every nut so she could eat more of her Mammy's banana bread.

"And I thought you were nuts?" joked Granda, again to an empty audience.

Granny asked, "What will we do today?" and, looking at Granda, she whispered, "Enniscorthy?"

"No," said Granda because it could rain. It was about twenty degrees today but very cloudy. They asked Doireann if she wanted to go to the library, as it might rain.

"No, I want to stay here; I want to rest," she said.

"Okay," said Granny.

Doireann went into Granda's room, and he asked her, "Do you know what I am doing?"

There was no answer as she fiddled with her new (out-of-order) pink phone.

Granda held her and said, "I am writing a story about you."

She smiled. She held her pink phone up as if to take a photo, and Granda made a face and held his arms up. "That's being funny, Granda," she told him.

"I know. Do you want me to take a fun picture of you with my phone?" asked Granda.

"No. You can't. Your phone is charging," she reminded him.

Granda said, "Hold on a minute." He left the room and arrived back with his phone, put it on camera mode, and held it up. "Right, make a funny face," he told her. *Click.* "Do you want to see your cousin Rosie?"

"Yes."

Granda switched on the broadband. Granda explained to her as he pointed to the internet icon at the bottom left-hand corner of the desktop screen after she climbed onto his lap that, when that red indicator disappeared, the internet was then ready to use. "Look, it's gone now, and I will now go to Facebook," Granda demonstrated.

They looked at Uncle Richard talking to baby Rosie and then looked at more videos and photos of her.

"We have a puter at home," Doireann told Granda.

Granda then explained, "It's computer, Doireann. And you have a computer at home; well, that's good."

"No. More than one," she said.

"Oh, okay," acknowledged Granda.

Granny entered the room and, looking out the window, said, "Look at all the birdies getting water." Granny and Granda had three plastic dishes full of water in the garden.

Doireann looked out the window, to see about a dozen house sparrows, either drinking the water or bathing in it. She immediately got down off Granda's lap. "I want to go out the back," she demanded.

Granny wanted her to put her jacket on first. "Where is it, Doireann?" asked Granny.

Granda hung it up in the hall earlier this morning. She brought Granny to the coat hangers in the hall to get her coat.

After about ten minutes, they came back in because she needed to go to the toilet. She didn't put her coat on for her second exit. It started to rain, very slightly. Granny took her in to put her coat on. Doireann got upset and started crying because she didn't want to wear a coat. Granny explained that she could get wet. Then they both went out with their jackets on to play football.

Later, Granda got ready and went out also and met Granny and Doireann walking up the garden. "Where have you been?" asked Granda.

"Oh, we have been on the bus, and then we went to the shops," Granny told him.

Granda played a bit of footie with Doireann, but when Granny told her, "You are not to put your two arms inside the one plastic armband," she started to sulk.

She was wearing a plastic band on one of her arms. Granny spent some time explaining to her, that, if she fell, she would not have the proper use of both of her hands.

Doireann left the armband on one arm and said, "I'm tired."

Granda started to play footie again. But she just said, "I want to go in." And in she went, sulking and tired. "I am thirsty, Granny."

Granny gave her some more milk.

Now back indoors, Granda told Granny, within earshot of Doireann, "She is very good to tell you when she is thirsty."

Doireann agreed with Granny after she offered to read her some stories. The books were called *Tinkerbell* and *Winnie the Pooh and Tigger Too*. With her soother in her mouth, Doireann sat back on the dining room sofa, between Granny and Baby Bop. *Grow Caterpillar Grow* was the third story Granny read for her. Granny said to Granda, "I felt like nodding off asleep myself after our gym and swim early this morning."

For lunch, Doireann didn't want much initially and didn't have a whole lot left, anyway, as this morning, she had eaten her pepperoni, strawberries, and nuts and some of the banana bread. When she wasn't looking, Granda put the toy furry mushroom into Baby Bop's mouth, like a soother.

Later, when she saw it, she took it out and just stared at Granda, knowing it was him. Granda repeated it, again, only for Doireann to remove it again, saying, "*Granda*," in a disgruntled manner. She immediately put the furry mushroom back into Baby Bop's mouth though, and said, "That's her food."

Doireann then ate cucumbers, beetroot, a little bit of Granny's brown bread, the white of a boiled egg, and blueberries. "I'm tired," she kept saying.

Before lunch, she lay back on the dining room sofa with a blanket for about five minutes. "I am finished (resting) now," she'd said and sat at the table. When she'd finished her lunch, she sat on the sofa again under the blanket and took one of the Mr Men books, to "look at". Then she went into Granda.

"What are you doing, Doireann?" Granny called out.

"I am with Granda. Granda, can I look at the videos?" she asked.

"Let's look at the videos on Granny's iPad," he suggested.

Doireann ran to Granny and said, "We are going to look at the videos on-iPad."

They looked at the videos of Richard again and then the videos of the snow and Granny and Granda's snowman. "Granny, can I have a freeze pop?" Doireann asked.

"I only have a yellow one," Granny informed her.

"I like a lellow one," she said.

"Okay," said Granny and took it out of the freezer.

"I have to put the drops into your eye. So, show Granda how we do this," Granny said, and she showed him.

Granda held her freeze pop while Granny applied the drops. Then Granda went to his workstation to write a few more notes.

"Where's Granda?" she asked.

"I think he has abandoned ship," joked Granny. "Where are you going, Doireann?" she asked.

"I want to go and see this ship," she told Granny.

Granny had a hard time explaining that one to Doireann!

Granda went outside to bring the car into the driveway. He had left it out on the road this morning, in anticipation of a journey to the library. As he got out of the car, Doireann was looking out the sitting room window, sticking her tongue out at him and giggling. She wanted to go out to the back again, and Granny obliged. Doireann put her jacket on, without any hassle, when Granda said, "It's beginning to rain lightly again."

They played tag and went for a walk, before going to the (pretend) shops to get milk and pepperoni. When the rain got heavier, they came in. Doireann had put a cloth over Teddy White's face before she went out the back. While she was outside, Granda put Doireann's Paw Patrol slippers on Teddy Brown's feet. He then put the toy mushroom into Baby Bop's mouth. Then he left all three of them with a book each to read. When Doireann saw this, she put her hands on her hips and stared at Granda. Next thing, the slippers were pulled off and the mushroom removed, as well as the books, in an animated mood of disgust.

Knock, knock, the hall door sounded.

Granda answered it, to be greeted by Oisín and Mammy. Doireann and Oisín trick-acted and fought, with the usual screams coming from Doireann and then Mammy giving out to Oisín. Granny told Mammy, about Doireann being tired, and Mammy said, "She didn't get any afternoon naps for the past couple of days."

When Oisín heard that Doireann hadn't finished all of her banana bread, he was up like a light looking for it and scoffed the lot.

Mammy told Granny and Granda, "The other day, Doireann held the phone up and said she wanted to take a selfie, and Daddy was gobsmacked." Mammy told him she knew where that came from and smiled at Granda at the same time.

Doireann then wanted some banana bread, and Mammy said, "Lucky for you, I still have some left at home."

"Do you have the car, Mammy?" Doireann asked.

"Yes, I do."

"And the car seat?" continued Doireann.

"Yes, of course, I have the car seat."

Doireann started to cry because she would have to get into the car seat.

Granda said to her, "You have to use a car seat." Then he beckoned her over for a cuddle. No way. She wasn't having cuddles and continued whinging.

Granda reminded Granny to give Mammy the eye drops. Granny got the eye drops from the fridge and handed the bottle to Mammy, and off they went at about 2.45 p.m.

CHAPTER 28

Doireann Is a Hippy: Peace, Brother

17 August

Doireann arrived over in Mammy's car today at about 9.45 a.m. It was raining, damp, and miserable.

"Hi, Granny," Doireann said after Granny opened the hall door.

"Ah, you have dressed Teddy [Pink] up in her clothes," Granny said.

Granny and Mammy started to talk. Granda was finishing his porridge when Doireann appeared around the dining room door. "Hiya Doireann," Granda called out, to a big smile on her face.

She took her grub out of the shoulder bag and put it in the fridge. Then she took out the smoothie and got Mammy to insert the special straw that came with it. As she started drinking it, she said, "Granny, I am not staying long today."

"You are only staying with us for a short while?" asked a disappointed Granny.

"Yes," was all she offered.

Doireann was in great form today, jumping all around and running. Mammy said, "She slept until eight fifteen this morning."

Doireann got her bottles of bubbles out and left them on the hall table for later. Granda went into his bedroom to hide away his medication. He always did this when Doireann was around. She followed Granda in, like a shot. "What are you doing, Granda?" she asked.

"Ah, I am just tidying up, Doireann," Granda replied. "Is your smoothie nice?"

Doireann nodded as she sucked on the straw.

"Come on. We'll go into Granny," Granda suggested, and off they both went into the kitchen.

Lately, she was like a shadow and followed Granda everywhere. Everything now was, what are you doing, Granda? Where are you going Granda? Granny, where is Granda? and so on.

"Look at my new runners, Granda," Doireann said.

"They are lovely, pet," he told her.

"Her eye seems a bit better," Granda said to Mammy.

"No," replied Mammy. "Going to bed last night, it seemed to get larger," Mammy informed Granda.

The doctor had said to give it two weeks a week ago.

"Granny had a similar cyst when she was young and had it removed," Granda said.

"Oh, did you?" asked Mammy.

As they spoke, Doireann started to complain, loudly, "Granda, let Mammy go. Granda, let Mammy go."

So, they stopped talking and Mammy said, "Bye-bye," and dashed off to work.

Doireann didn't want her photo taken. "Can I take a photo of Teddy [Pink] then?" asked Granda.

"Yes," she agreed, and he took one.

Then Granda put Teddy on Doireann's TV chair and remarked how lovely she was, all dressed up. "Doireann, will we take a selfie?" Granda asked.

"Yes, come on Granny," beckoned Doireann.

Granny, Granda, Doireann, and Teddy Pink, all sat up tightly together, and Granda took the selfie. Granda was hoping to do some notes, but Doireann was clinging to him.

Granny asked her, "Would you like *Balamory*?"

"Yes."

Granda put it on for her as she sat in her TV chair, after finishing her smoothie.

Holding her tummy, she said, "I'm very full now."

"What did you have for brekkie?" Granny asked her.

"Porridge."

"What did you have with it?" continued Granny.

"Milk."

"Yeah, but did you have fruit, like berries," Granny asked, and Doireann just nodded.

"I don't want my freezer pop yet," she said as she sat back to watch *Balamory*.

Granda quickly asked, "Would you like to have it when we come back from the library, because it's raining outside?"

She nodded in agreement.

Later on, Doireann was doing some drawing at the kitchen table with Granny. Granny got papers, colouring pencils, and pictures out for her to draw. "Can I have a drink of water, Granny?" she asked. "I am thirsty."

"Okay." Granny gave her some water in the small cup.

Next thing, Doireann went into Granda, with Granny's spare phone, which she called "the Cambodia phone".

"Oh, I like your hairband, Doireann," Granda told her.

"It's not mine," she said.

"I know, but it's lovely on you," said Granda. "You look like a real hippy." He took a few photos, of her.

Granda went to the kitchen with Doireann to see her masterpieces of artwork. There were pencils and paper strewn everywhere.

"I need to do a wee-wee, Granny," she said.

"Okay, come on," Granny said.

Doireann did a hop, skip, and a jump up the hall. When she finished, she stopped Granny from leaving, saying, "I have to wash my hands." Granny congratulated her for remembering.

Doireann then ran into Granda. "Granda, I am still six stones," she said.

Granny corrected her saying, "It's two, six."

"Brill, Doireann. That's great," said Granda.

As Granda was writing this very piece, he had Doireann and Teddy [Pink] sitting on his lap. With soother in mouth, Doireann was asking to see the "finger pad" in a moany voice.

"You mean, iPad, Doireann," Granda said.

"Yeah, iPad. I don't want to see this, Granda," she replied with her moany voice, referring to Granda typing.

"Okay, just a minute," said Granda and then stopped typing. He went and got the iPad, and Granny sat with her to look at some videos. Doireann loved looking at the photos and the videos. Earlier this morning she was pretending to throw snow, re-enacting their video footage of the recent heavy snowfall—when Doireann and Granda had thrown lots of snowballs at each other.

It wasn't too long before they gathered up their things and headed for the library. It was still raining as they got into the car. Once inside the car, Granda threw his new cloth at Doireann. It was a white cloth with large brown spots.

"This is a new cloth," she said. "Where did you get it, Granny?"

"Oh, in the shop," Granny told her.

"That is a spotty cloth," said Granda. "And we got it in a spotty shop, and the man who sold it to us had a spotty face."

Silence.

Granny must have thrown the cloth back at Doireann. Granda heard her say, "I catched it."

Granda put the music on as requested by Doireann, and it was a very slow song, on RTÉ One radio. When Granda changed stations, she said loudly, "*I want it.*" When the song had finished, she wanted other music. Granda changed to Lyric FM, and yes, she was happy with that station. That music was extremely sombre. Granny got Teddy Pink to waltz to the music, which caused Doireann to laugh and laugh. Doireann continually interacted with Teddy Pink as if she were human.

"*Wheeeeeeeeeeeeeeeeeeeeeeeeeeeeeeeeeeeeeeeeeeeeeeeeeeeeeeeeeeeeeee,*" they all went as Granda drove down the ramp to the underground car park in Gorey Shopping Centre.

He parked in a family bay. And looking at the family image on the wall, Doireann said, "There's Mammy, Daddy, and Doireann."

"That's right, Doireann. Very well said," Granda told her.

"I am bringing Teddy Pink and the spotty cloth," she said, and off they went.

On the lift, two men stood expressionless and silent, and Doireann moved closer to Granny, her head down and not a squeak.

Looking at her headband, Granda announced, "Doireann is a hippy."

There was great laughter from the two men, who could see what Granda meant.

The hippy got into the racing car on the first floor and took Teddy for a drive, after wrapping her up in the spotty cloth. Next, they headed out the doors towards the library, with Doireann preferring to take the walk-on-the-wall route. On the wall, she tipped the granite overhang above and Granda said, "Look. Doireann's head is nearly touching it now; you are getting big, Doireann."

At the end of that walk, she jumped off the wall and ran to the library doors.

"Let Teddy open the doors," said Granda.

But she just marched through, with Teddy under her arms.

Granny and Doireann went to the kiddies' section, which was busy enough with other kids and their guardians. Granda went to read the newspapers as usual. "Granda, she wants to use the loo," said Granny as they passed by.

"Okay."

Later, Granda took over from Granny, who had read a lot of books to Doireann this morning. Doireann choose a book titled *Spot and Ben* for Granda to read to her. After that one, she got a Mr Men' book. As Granda read the Mr Men book, she stood up to stare at other activity around her, so he stopped reading. Another Mammy was fixing her baby into a buggy, and Granda asked Doireann, "Is the baby asleep?"

"No. She has a bottle."

Then she was watching the other sibling, who ran up the library corridor. Next, she was looking at another family, who had just arrived. Granda waited for her to sit down before he continued reading the story.

Because it was late and near lunchtime, Granda skipped some pages, finishing the book rather quickly. Doireann never noticed, and when he got to the end, he said, "Now, there you are Doireann. Let's find Granny."

They checked they had everything with them before exiting the library doors.

Doireann wanted to do the*wheeeeeeeeeeeeeeeeeeeeeeeeeeeeeeeeeeeeeeeeeeeeeee eeeeeeeeeeeeeeee* run, with a chase from Granda as she ran back into Granny's arms. Next, she went over to the racing car again, while Granda used the loo on the first floor. When Granda returned, Doireann was just getting back into the car after leaning on it, while her (imaginary) friend helped.

Granny said, "She had a bit of bother with her car and had to phone a friend, Ellen, who came and helped her out of the mud."

Next, they headed down the lift and out to Granda's car. With everybody strapped in, Granda played a '60s music CD for the journey home. "*Wheeeeeeeeeeeeeeeeeeeeeeeeeeeeeeeeeeeeeeeeeeeeeeeeeeeeeeeeeeeee*," they all roared as they left the car park.

Raising his two fingers for the hippy in the back to see, Granda said, "Peace, sister," and explained what it meant. Granda then got her to hold her fingers up and say, "Peace, brother."

As soon as they walked into the house, Doireann went to the fridge and took her pepperoni, and Granny and Granda's lunch boxes out.

"Thank you," Granda said.

"You're welcome."

For lunch, Doireann had her pepperoni, cucumber, beetroot, sweetcorn, and brown bread, along with the milk Granny gave her. She knocked the last small piece of her pepperoni to the floor by accident.

Granda picked it up quickly and checked it was okay.

"Thanks, Granda," she said and then asked, "Is it okay?"

"Ah, yeah. I counted to seven," Granda told her.

Doireann noticed Granda was writing some notes at the table during lunch.

"What are you doing, Granda?" she asked.

"I am writing a story about you, Doireann."

That conversation ended as quickly as it had started.

Granny helped Doireann to make beetroot sarnies with the brown bread. She wanted to cut the sarnies with her plastic knife. Then she ate some of the sarnies and said, "I don't like beetroot," but then corrected herself, saying, "I don't want it."

This morning, before Mammy left for work, she told Granny that Doireann loved beetroot now. Granny said to Mammy, "We give her beetroot from time to time when she asks for it."

Doireann wanted the freezer pop that had been promised to her and was given it, as she had eaten a fair amount of her lunch. Granny packed away the leftovers for Mammy to use later. Doireann choose a brown (Coke) freezer pop, from the selection. "Granny, I will have them all."

Granny said, "You are only getting one, Doireann."

"I know, but I will get [one] another day," she said, explaining what she meant.

"Ah, okay, I understand," Granny told her.

Later, Doireann put her half-eaten freezer pop on the table to adjust the paper tissue around it, leaving a mess on the table. Granny got a cloth to wipe it up and half-jokingly said, "I don't know what I'm going to do with you, Doireann."

With a smile on her face, Doireann said, "I know, Granny. You put me in the bin."

Granny nodded in agreement.

"The bin is too small," Doireann said gleefully.

Granda then said, "We'll just have to get a bigger bin, so."

Later, Doireann went into Granda with a butterfly magnet she had removed from the fridge door. "Look, Granda."

"That's beautiful, Doireann. You like butterflies, don't you?" he said.

"Yeah," she said, smiling. "I like butterflies landing on my hands and on my nose," she continued. "Do you like butterflies, Granda?"

"Yeah, landing on my hands but not on my nose," he told her.

Later, Granda went to the dining room / kitchen area to find Doireann dancing to the song, "Flowers in the Rain". Granny had to restart it each time Doireann called out, "Again Granny, again Granny," over and over and over. Then, she danced with Teddy Pink. Then Teddy sat beside Granda. "Clap your hands," Teddy was told.

As Teddy (and Granda) clapped hands, Doireann did all sorts of twists and moves with her hands outstretched, while looking directly at Teddy. Then, when the song finished, she picked Teddy up, whispered in her ear, and then gave her a big hug.

"Granny, Teddy wants the bracelet back on," Doireann said. Earlier, she had removed her hippy bracelet to try it out on Teddy Pink. Now, she wanted it back on Teddy's head as she danced. This was her way of saying, I, want the bracelet back on my head and using Teddy as a decoy.

Doireann, holding Granny's [real] phone, was having a (pretend) conversation with someone. "Yeah, yeah, all right, yeah," the conversation flowed, with Granny, now out of the room.

Next thing, Granny's phone started ringing because of a genuine incoming call. Totally startled, Doireann immediately roared, "*Granny.*"

Granny's ringing phone was now like a hot potato in her hand. Running as fast as she could, in a state of panic, to get Granny, she shouted out, again, "Granny, Granny, your phone is ringing."

"Thanks, Doireann," Granny said, as she took the phone from a now much-relieved Doireann. "Hello, hello. Ah hello, Phyllis," Granny said and started a conversation with Granda's sister, who was unaware she had just interrupted Doireann's earlier phone conversation! Doireann wasn't bothered about that, though. She was obviously very relieved at getting rid of that hot potato from her little hands.

Later, after a visit to the loo, Doireann darted out and located Granda. "Granda, I'm two and six now," she loudly told him.

"Ah, that's brill, pet," Granda said.

Knock, knock, the hall door sounded.

It was 2.30 p.m. and Mammy was at the hall door. "*Mammmmmmeeeeeee,*" roared a fast-approaching Doireann and gave her Mammy a big hug.

Doireann went into Granda. "I am going now, Granda," she informed him.

"Ah, okay, pet," Granda said.

This morning, she'd told Granny and Granda that Oisín was going to tennis. "Doireann, do you know you can get to see a lot of tennis in Tennessee?" joked Granda. But Granny wasn't impressed and gave out.

"How did Oisín's day go?" Granda asked Mammy.

"Yeah, fine; he won his tennis match and was delighted." Mammy then spoke to Granny about Oisín and his football next season. The football manager wanted the under twelve team to be more professional this coming season, and Mammy wasn't having any pressure foisted on him at that age. Daddy was to speak with the manager and sort it all out.

Mammy also said she was talking to Daddy about sending Doireann to dancing lessons because she likes dancing. But then Mammy went off the idea, as the very young kids were being taught to dance like the older professional ones, which was not appropriate and totally out of order. Granny and Granda agreed.

Doireann forgot to take her bubbles home with her today.

20 August

Granda put Snowy into the car driver's seat and Baby Bop, wearing Granda's sun hat, into the passenger seat. In the back seat were Teddy White, sitting in Doireann's car seat, and Teddy Brown, sitting where Granny usually sits, with his seat belt on and wearing Granda's rain hat.

Mammy, Doireann, and Teddy Pink called to the house just after 10 a.m. and didn't notice the above.

Granny opened the hall door and Doireann said, "Oh, that's lovely," referring to Granny's top.

"Oh, thank you, and yours is lovely too," Granny said.

Granda took Doireann out to see the gang in the car. With a grin from ear to ear, she asked, "Why are they in there?" She walked around the car, trying to get in.

Granda unlocked the doors, letting her get into the car. She muttered something to Baby Bop, while removing Granda's sun hat.

"Look, Doireann. The teddies are in the back," Granda told her.

She handed Granda, Baby Bop and then climbed into the back. She removed Granda's rain hat from Teddy Brown and then removed the loose-only straps around Teddy White, before handing them both to Granda. She tried to remove Snowy. "He's too heavy," she complained.

"Okay, Doireann. Come around here with me," Granda beckoned her towards his car door.

They opened the door, took Snowy out, and carried them all back into the house.

Doireann had brought her shopping trolley with the toy food to Granny and Granda's house today. Mammy said, "She slept until 8.30 a.m. today."

"Will you do me a favour and check the toilet rolls?" Granda asked Doireann.

Granny had left out an empty roll on the hall table as a reminder.

Doireann ran into the toilet, opened the storage cabinet, and saw it was empty. "How many Granda?" she asked.

He counted the shelves. "One, two, three. We need three, Doireann," he told her, and she closed the door again. "Come on, and I'll show you where to get them," he offered.

They went to the cubbyhole, and Granda took the packet of toilet rolls down off the shelf and let her take out three rolls. "Don't run, Doireann. Just take your time," he said.

And they walked towards the toilet, with Granny and Mammy looking on. She put the rolls on the floor, opened the door, put the toilet rolls into the cabinet one at a time, and closed the door again.

"Thank you, Doireann," he said.

She ran back into where Granny and Mammy were still talking.

"Some words that Doireann says makes Oisín laugh because she sounds just like Granda, with his Dublin accent," Mammy said before leaving for work. She then said, "Byeeeee."

And Doireann shouted, "Bye, Mammy," as she stood at the open hall door.

Granny and Granda asked Doireann to remove her shoes so they could measure her height, at the measuring wall. The measuring wall was at the divide between the kitchen and the dining room.

"I am getting bigger," she said.

Granny and Granda agreed.

Doireann said, "My socks are wet."

"Was it, walking through the wet grass?" Granny asked her.

"No, it wasn't, Granny. I jumped in a puddle."

"Without your boots, and that's why your socks are wet," Granny informed her.

Granny got her, a spare pair of dry socks.

Later, Doireann got upset because she forgot to bring her teapot to pour Granny a cup of tea. Granny got her to improvise and explained what to do. Doireann then played with some Play-Doh. She didn't want to go to Enniscorthy, saying, "I'm tired, and I want to rest."

"Doireann, who gave you the Play-Doh?" Granda enquired.

"My cousin."

"She got it for her birthday," Granny assumed.

"No, she didn't. I did," said Doireann.

Granny and Granda were now totally confused.

"Look, Granda, I can make a circle," she said.

"Well done, Doireann."

"Can you play, Granda?" she asked.

"Yeah, in a minute, Doireann. I am just doing something at the moment."

She sat at the table, as happy as Larry, playing with her Playdoh.

Granny had to phone a Bray travel agent to cancel a Chinese Airways flight. She and Granda, had temporarily booked a flight to Cambodia last Saturday for the coming Christmas.

Granda sat with Doireann, to play with her Play-Doh. She gave him some Play-Doh to play with after he marvelled at the things she had made. "There, Granda," she said as she handed him some of her Play-Doh.

"What should I make?" he asked.

"A ball," she suggested.

"Oh, like the ones you made?" he asked.

"Yes."

"How do I make it?" he asked.

"Roll it, Granda."

When he rolled it, he then pretended it was a ball and said, "Like this, Doireann, is it?"

She laughed out loud. "No, Granda. That's a snake," she said.

"Okay, Doireann," he said and rolled it into a ball. Then Granda rolled some smaller pieces of Play-Doh of different colours, making two eyes, one nose, and a mouth and attached them to the ball he had made earlier. "Look Doireann," he said.

"That's lovely, Granda," she told him.

"That's Doireann," he told her, and she smiled. Then he showed her how to do it.

She struggled to get some Play-Doh out of a very small tub. Granda got an old toothbrush and showed her how to use the handle part to dig the Play-Doh out. Later, she used the toothbrush as a lolly pop stick and stuck a ball onto the top of it and then pretended to lick it. Granny made a man with arms and legs, and they called it the Gingerbread Man.

Next, Doireann asked to go outside, and Granny took her out. They played with the plastic skittles. And then, standing at Granda's window, she called out, "Granda, can you help, because I can't pick them all up?"

In other words, she wanted him to play with her, and out he went. He set up the skittles, and Doireann threw the ball, knocking some of them down. Then it was Granda's turn, and he kicked the small ball into the skittles, knocking down about three of them. Doireann then had a go at kicking the ball and knocked down five of them. After a couple of goes, Granda made it harder by placing the skittles in a single file. You then had to try and hit the first one to create a Domino effect. It was Doireann's turn. She said, "Look, Granny," and stood to the side, facing the line of skittles.

Pointing, Granda said, "Get down there that way because that's cheating."

She then kicked the ball from the proper place and knocked down five out of six skittles.

Then Granda went inside to have his cup of tea and some toast that Granny had made for him. Doireann and Granny soon followed, as Doireann wanted a cup of tea.

"It's a cup of Rosie Lee," she said. She and Granda would sometimes use that term, Rosie Lee. "Thanks for the Rosie Lee, Granny," Doireann said after she finished her cuppa tea, before going to the fridge.

"What do you want?" Granny asked her.

"Have you got please-a-pops?" she asked, adding, "Eh, but I don't want one now."

"Yes, for later, Doireann," Granny reminded her.

She then asked to watch *Balamory*, and Granda put it on for her, as she sat in her TV chair, eating her slice of melon. "Can I have another piece?" she asked.

"No, that's all there is," Granny told her.

"There is more," she protested.

"There's not, Doireann," insisted Granny. "That is all your Mammy gave you."

The Indian wedding, music, and dance came on. "I want to dress up," she said.

Granny complained, "You always wait to dress up when it starts." Granny rushed, to get the dress-up items for her, as she moaned with, "It's over now."

"I will start it again for you; it's okay," Granny offered, just to calm her down.

After this, it was bubbles time for her, and Granny took her outside to make plenty of bubbles. Doireann had her hippy headdress on, with the soother in her mouth as she danced and screamed, running around the garden, chasing the bubbles. Screaming was her new trait, and Granny had to get onto her for being too noisy. Then it was Doireann's turn to blow the bubbles as Granny looked on. Doireann would run after a bubble and try and get it to balance on the bubble maker stick. She had great fun, attempting this on each occasion, and when she was successful, her noisy giggles would get louder.

Eventually, Doireann came back in with Granny, who offered to read her some storybooks.

Doireann then said, "Let's go outside to read, yippee."

Granny answered with a, "Yippee," also.

They both sat at the garden bench and Granny read *Brave Bitzy and the Bear*. When finished, they went back in for another book.

"I really pushing you," she told Granny.

"You are pushing me," agreed Granny as they went back outside again.

This time, Granny read *Little Miss Wise*.

"*Granny, I have to go the toilet,*" Doireann announced loudly.

When she finished, Granny reminded her, "Come back, Doireann. Wash your hands."

Then she got up on the weighing scales. "Granda, I'm two, six still," she called out.

"Well, that is great," Granda called back.

"And she didn't need the small toilet seat either. She sat on the normal seat," Granny proudly announced.

"Oh well, that means you are certainly a big girl so, and you are a very good girl for telling Granny that you needed to go to the toilet," Granda said loudly so Doireann could hear him.

Doireann stood in the doorway to Granda's room. She had one hand on the door and the other on the door frame, with half a smile and half a smirk on her face as Granda praised her. It was like she was saying, without speaking, *I'm it now.*

She then took her shopping trolley out to the garden. Granny went shopping with her, down the end of the garden, where all the (imaginary) shops were. Just before they went out, Doireann, held her cardigan up and said to Granda, "It's inside out."

"Do you want me to fix it?" Granda asked.

"Yeah."

He corrected one sleeve, which allowed her to put it on. She couldn't zip it up, though.

"Let me show you how it's done," Granda offered.

She still couldn't zip it, so Granda showed her again. The two sides were not fully inside the zip, and she moaned because she couldn't close it. Granda put the sides into the zip, and she was able to close it. "Now, you did it," Granda said.

"I didn't do it," he was told.

"Okay, we did it," he said and then hugged her. "You will eventually learn," Granda told her.

The high achiever was still not happy.

It was lunchtime. "Granda, get out here quickly for your lunch," Doireann said after being sent, under instruction by Granny.

"Okay, Doireann," he answered.

Doireann wanted to sit in her high chair at the table, even though she had previously complained that she couldn't move her legs in it. At the table, Granda picked up Doireann's cap, which she had left on the table. Granda wore the hat, and Granny said, "Oh, Granda must be cold."

Doireann looked at Granda with a funny twist on her lips, as if to say, *what are you at?*

Granda laughed and handed the cap back to her.

"I don't want the chicken," Doireann announced and started to eat the tomatoes and some of the orange. She stuck her finger into the now peeled orange and said, "Look, Granny, my ring."

"That's lovely," Granny said. "We were at the shops" (in the garden) "today, Granda; Arklow," Granny informed him.

"Oh lovely, that was nice."

Doireann asked Granny for some of her sweetcorn, but then she wouldn't eat it. She asked for a small spoon, and Granny gave her one. "That's a tiny spoon," she said.

"I know. You asked for a small spoon," Granny told her.

"I don't want this. It's too small," she complained.

Granny took a selection of small spoons from the kitchen drawer and put them on the table for her to choose from. As Doireann was trying to make up her mind, Granda got up to get the large ladle. He then put it beside the other spoons. Doireann put her hand over her mouth as she sniggered.

"Are you laughing at me?" joked Granda.

"That is too big," she said as she pushed it away.

Doireann then agreed with Granny that they should put Granda in the bin.

When she refused to eat her olives, Granny played the aeroplane game. She put an olive on the spoon and said to Doireann, "Where are we going? Cambodia to see Richard?"

"Okay," Doireann said, and the plane (spoon) landed in her mouth.

"Where to next? Let's visit the Spanish student," Granny suggested.

Doireann said their first Spanish student's name. "Jamie."

And on went the plane to Spain and then to about ten other airports.

"Can I have my please-a-pop, Granny?" she asked.

"Okay," said Granny and then said to Granda, "We will have to put a stop to this for afters."

"What colour do you want?" Granny asked as she opened the freezer door.

"The lellow one," came the reply. She then started jumping and hopping about the place, delighted with her please-a-pop.

"Would you like a cup of Rosie Lee, Doireann?" Granda asked.

"I had one already."

Then, as Granda was about to leave the table, she asked, "Can I watch the big telly?"

"You can watch the not-so-big telly. How's that?" Granda said and turned on the small telly.

"Yeah, that's the one I mean," she said.

One of her favourite programmes, *Paw Patrol*, was on. She sat back in her TV chair, while enjoying her freeze pop, at the same time. When she finished her freeze pop, Granny gave her some bread and then more.

Granny and Doireann went out to the garden to shop again. Granny was told, she needed new runners and a dress. Granny couldn't see the proper size of runners, but Doireann found them. Once the shopping was over, she played with the rocket launcher, followed by the Frisbee.

When Mammy called, Doireann relayed the story about Granda and the big spoon and said, "We will have to put him in the bin."

Everyone laughed.

They went back into the kitchen, and Mammy gathered up Doireann's things.

Granda called Doireann as he pretended to step into the kitchen bin.

"We were only joking, Granda," she said sternly.

Granda helped Doireann down the steps, outside the hall door, with her shopping trolley, toy food, and Teddy Pink. He waved to her and Mammy as they approached their car, saying, "Goodbye, lazies."

CHAPTER 29

From a Hippy to a Punk Rocker

21 August

When Granny knocked on the door, Mammy opened it, and Doireann was all happy and excited, because Granny and Granda were taking them out that evening. In the car, Doireann said to Granny, "Granny, I love you very much."

"Thanks, pet. And you love Granda too," Granny said.

She nodded in agreement.

"And Oisín," Granny said.

And her head continued to nod.

Granny and Granda had called to Mammy's house, as arranged, at 6.15 p.m. to take Mammy, Doireann, and Oisín down to the nearby seaside holiday village, Courtown, and treat them to ice creams. It was a lovely hot sunny end to a lovely day (twenty-three degrees), and the summer was coming to an end also.

Mammy's friend made an unexpected visit just then, so they'd headed off without Mammy. Oisín was wearing his Irish FA jersey and shorts. He brought his hurley (hurling stick) and sliotar (hurling ball) with him as well and sat in the passenger seat.

Granda told him about his GAA exploits as a young man. "I played in Croke Park."

"Did you, Granda?" said a very surprised Oisín.

"Ah, it was a primary school boys' league final, and we won it, for Scoil Haroid, in Dalkey, County Dublin. I showed you that medal I got about fifty years ago, along with all the other medals and trophies that your mammy and Uncles Gary and Richard won over the years, as well," Granda informed him, while driving the car.

He also told Oisín about his involvement with the amalgamation of Dalkey Mitchel's GAA Club and Cuala Casements GAA Club, now called Cuala. Then he told him about his brothers, when they'd entered an athletic event in Dublin years ago. Together, they both brought home some great prizes (ten in all) for the house.

"What did you win, Granda?" Oisín asked.

"Oh, they all laughed when I brought home a biscuit tin that kept biscuits fresh for long periods. I came joint third in a relay race. Your mammy, when little, used to look for it—for the biscuits—when visiting her granny (your great-granny). It was just like the one Granny and Granda now have and that you and Doireann take out of the press when you are looking for biscuits."

Granny and Doireann chatted and played in the back of the car. They parked in a large car park and walked to a corner shop and ordered a choc ice for Granda and three ice cream cones for Granny, Doireann, and Oisín. The cones were very watery and started to melt in no time as they walked towards the water's edge. Doireann didn't want hers, and so they dumped it in a bin, which was full of wasps, causing them to run away as fast as they could. When the others finished their ice creams, Granny took Doireann over to a different shop to get her a different cone. Granda went back to the car to get the baby wipes for all of their sticky hands.

Later, they went into the amusements for a bit of fun. Granda looked after Oisín, while Granny took care of Doireann. Granda helped Oisín with a game of netting balls to accumulate points for tokens. Next up, he tried the motorcycle twice, coming third each time. He then traded in his tokens for something for Doireann. Doireann was on a digger and loved it, battering the lifting bucket and dropping it to the floor each time she raised it. Then she was on a horse on a merry-go-round.

After the amusements, they walked over to the sea again. As they went down some concrete steps to the water, Doireann slipped on loose sand,

and luckily, Granda was holding her hand, preventing a potentially nasty accident. In the car home, they played a CD and sang to the music.

Oisín (11 years old) told Granda about his tennis final match, coming up at the weekend and that he was playing a 14-year-old. He didn't think he could win. Granda suggested using a bit of psychology and giving the impression, before the game starts, that he had given up and was nervous and so on. "Never give up, though," Granda advised him. "Just do your best, and you never know."

Oisín swung his arms all over the place as he jived to the '60s music.

Doireann said she was tired. It was 7.45 p.m. and now well past her bedtime. As soon as they returned home, Doireann said, "Thank you for bringing me back to my house."

No one appeared to be answering the door. Next thing, Doireann said, "I know Mammy is in there," before she started kicking the door down.

Granny went to stop her when, all of a sudden, Mammy opened the door, in total shock, at what Doireann had just done. Mammy explained to her that you don't do things like that. You have to be patient. Granda had to hide his laughs at the idea of it all. *From a hippy to a punk rocker.* He giggled.

Mammy let Oisín go to watch the Camolin Celtic game, just up from their house. Both Doireann and Oisín thanked Granny and Granda for the treats that night.

22 August

Daddy and Doireann arrived at about 9.40 a.m., and when Granny answered the door, Daddy didn't know where Doireann was. "Ah, is she not here today?" Granny asked.

Then Granny looked out the door, and on seeing Doireann, said, "What are you doing there?"

She was hiding beside the garden owl, as usual.

She walked into the kitchen and saw Granda eating his breakfast at the table. He and Granny had been to the gym earlier and were not long home. "Hello, Doireann. How are you?" Granda said and gave her a little wave.

She waved back and brought some toys into the room to play with.

"Can I play with them too?" Granda asked.

But she just looked at him and said nothing.

"That's a lovely dress you have on," Granda told her.

"It's not a dress. It's a skirt," she replied angrily.

"Oh, sorry," said Granda.

Granny and Granda laughed as they told Daddy about the-kicking-the-door-down incident when no one was answering the door last night.

"We didn't raise her to do that," said a now very surprised and stern-looking Daddy.

"Ah, she didn't understand and has to learn that she cannot react like that," Granda assured him.

Discussing their evening in Courtown, Granda asked Doireann, "What were you doing last night?"

"Courtown," she said quietly.

"Did you go on the horse?" asked Granda.

"And the digger, and she loved it," Granny added.

Doireann nodded. Obviously referring to the digger, Daddy asked, "Do you want to be a builder when you grow up?"

"And kick down doors?" Granda laughed. "What did you have in Courtown?" Granda then asked her, trying to encourage her to tell Daddy.

"Ice cream," she replied, quietly again.

Daddy was working in Galway yesterday from early morning and usually got back home late. He obviously didn't know anything about Courtown last night.

"I have to go," said Daddy and gave Doireann a hug and said goodbye.

On his way out the door, Doireann said, "You have to ask to leave the house."

"Can I leave the house?" Daddy asked.

"Yes, you can leave," she said.

"Okay. Daddy has to go to work; come on in, now, Doireann," Granny said.

"I want to play with my bubbles," she said.

"Later, Doireann. It's starting to rain now," Granny told her.

"It's not raining," she said, in a moany voice.

"I am having my breakfast now. So, will I see what's on the telly?" Granny offered.

"Yes," she said and then wanted *Balamory*. Its signature tune went, "*Bala …mor …y*, what's the story in Balamory? Wouldn't you like to know?"

"Would you like some toast?" Granny asked her.

"No."

"What did you have for brekkie?" Granda asked.

"Porridge. No, no, Weetabix; me a silly-billy," she said.

"What would you like, then?" Granny asked her.

"Some berries."

Granny gave her her favourite blueberries as she sat and watched *Balamory*. When the Scottish dancing started on *Balamory*, Doireann was up out of her seat, and Granny had to join in. Doireann danced to the music, a hand in the air and so on. Later, she asked Granny if she had a soother.

"Did you not bring yours, Doireann?" enquired Granny.

"No."

Granny fetched the spare one for her.

Doireann went into Granda, who was at his workstation. "I don't want Snowy to scare me," she told Granda and asked him to bring Snowy out for her.

Granda went with her to the bedroom and handed her Baby Bop from the cot. He carried the two teddies and Snowy out. Granda pretended to catch her with Snowy as he made a scary noise. But Doireann stood her ground and firmly said, "No, Granda. He is not to scare."

"Okay, pet," Granda said and handed her the teddies and put Snowy down by the side of the dining room sofa.

Next, Granny and Doireann, played with her "seaside dominos". When Granny had to visit the toilet, Doireann called out, "Granda. Granda, will you play with me?"

"Okay, Doireann," he said and sat down next to her and played dominoes.

Granda won the first game, but she won the next ten! There were ten dominoes in the box, with eighteen missing.

"Would you like to go to the library?" Granda asked her.

"No."

"Why?" asked Granny, having just returned. "Will we bring the dominoes to the library with us?" she suggested.

"No. Can I go to Enniscorthy?" Doireann asked, striking a shy pose, expecting the worst.

Granda was about to say no because it had rained and also because it was threatening to rain again when, all of a sudden, he caught Granny's eyes, looking straight at him. "We will," her lips silently indicated.

"Okay. We'll go to Enniscorthy, Doireann," agreed Granda, but added, "And if it starts to rain, Doireann, we will have to come home."

Granny then realised Doireann didn't have a coat with her today. Doireann went to check if she did have a coat hanging up in the hall with the other coats. Granda jokingly offered her Granny's blue coat.

"No. I don't want that," she moaned.

And then Granda offered her his sleeveless jacket.

"*No. I don't want that either,*" she snapped.

She then walked into the sitting room and headed for Granda's back scratcher. "I don't want to go to Enniscorthy. Will I scratch your back?" she asked Granda.

"I thought you wanted to go to Enniscorthy," Granda said.

"No, not now," she replied and proceeded to scratch Granda's back with the back scratcher.

"Go and scratch Granny's back," he said. "Granny, Doireann doesn't want to go to Enniscorthy now," Granda loudly informed her.

"You don't want to go to Enniscorthy, Doireann?" Granny asked as Doireann scratched her back.

Doireann repeated what she had already told Granda. "I need to go to the toilet, Granny," she said.

And in they both went.

"I am still two, six, Granda," she said after her routine weigh-in.

"Ah, that's great news, Doireann," he said.

"Would you like some toast, Doireann?" Granny asked.

She nodded.

"Granda, would you like a cup of tea?" Granny asked loudly.

"Yeah, and a slice of toast please."

Granny helped Doireann put some jewellery on her head, and then she looked like Granda's little hippy again. Granny sent her into Granda.

"Granda your tea is ready," she informed him.

"Okay, pet. And thank you."

As they sat at the kitchen table, Granda said, "Doireann, isn't your granny great?"

Granny responded by repeating Granda's usual little joke. "I'm not your great-granny, though."

It was 11.45 a.m. and too late to go to Enniscorthy Playground or to Gorey Library, so Granny and Granda asked Doireann if she would like to go to Camolin Playground. It hadn't rained much, but it was very overcast, with the temperature now at nineteen degrees.

"Yes," she said excitedly, and they all got ready to go.

Granny brought an old towel with her—in case the playground equipment was wet. They had just pulled into the parking area at Camolin Playground when it started to rain lightly. They all agreed to wait in the car until the rain stopped, but it just kept coming. They drove off, having decided to chance Enniscorthy Playground. Driving towards Ferns, the rain got heavier, and so they abandoned that idea as well. Instead, Granda decided to visit Bolger's Hardware Store in Ferns. Doireann loved playing in a large toy house that was usually left on show outside the shop in the car park area.

As they drove into the car park, Doireann mentioned the toy house, but it wasn't there. "Where is it?" she asked.

"It must have been sold; sorry about that," Granda said to her. (It was later in the evening, that Granny and Granda remembered they had visited Bolger's earlier in the summer and noticed that the toy house was gone.

"Doireann can have a please-a-pop when we get home," Granny said as Granda drove out of the car park.

Doireann was a bit reluctant, at first, to accept Granny's offer—until she saw that the rain was now torrential and there was nowhere else to go, but home. Granny put her coat over Doireann, and Granda put his coat over Granny as they stepped out of the car. Doireann didn't want Granda's coat over her head, only Granny's. Granda wore his rain hat, and they bolted for the hall door.

Doireann told Granny she didn't think Mammy was collecting her today. "Daddy is picking me up," she said.

"Did Daddy tell you that?" Granny asked, but there was no response.

Granny did some drawings on Doireann's Peppa Pig Magna Doodle toy. This toy allowed you to erase your work all the time and start a new drawing. Doireann drew on it as well.

"Granny, I need to do a wee," she said.

"Okay Doireann, in you go," Granny said. "Granda, look at Doireann walking towards the toilet with a wiggle and a waddle in her free-flowing skirt," Granny called out.

Then Doireann offered the usual, "I am still two, six, Granda."

She and Granny went and sat at the kitchen table and played dominoes. After a while, Doireann said, "Oh, my brain is sore."

"What?" Granny asked.

"My brain," she said as she held her back.

Granny said, "You mean your back is sore."

"I need to do a poo-poo, Granny."

And off into the toilet they went again.

Doireann visited Granda and said, "I'm still two six."

"She did a poo," Granny told Granda.

"And a wee-wee," Doireann said. "Granda, can I take a photo?"

"Of course, you can." Granda switched on his phone camera and handed it to her.

She took a photo of Granny and Granda. Then she requested that her photo be taken with Granny and then one as she lay on the bed. Granda got her to make a funny face for the next photo. "I want to go outside with the bubbles," she said.

"Not just yet," Granny said.

"What time is it Granda?" Doireann asked.

"It's lunchtime now."

"We will have our lunch first, and outside will have dried up a bit by then," Granny told her.

"I am not hungry now," Doireann said and started to play with Granny on the bed.

Granny pretended to sleep, like Doireann, but that didn't last long.

"Granny, wake up. Come on, Granny. You have to get up," she demanded.

"Why? I need a reason to get up," Granny said.

Then Doireann, accidently banged her leg against Granny's bedside locker.

"Ah, you poor thing," Granny said. "I will get up now. Are you alright?"

She was alright and went out to the dining room with Granny and played with Snowy.

Doireann sat on Snowy, and Granny moved him along. Then Doireann got off Snowy and said, "I want to play on the" (imaginary) "slide."

"Roll on, one day a week," said today's overworked Granny. Doireann would be attending crèche for four days each week from next month, and Granny and Granda would mind her for the other day.

Doireann was now in her own imaginary playground and tried to move Snowy but with great difficulty. Granny told her, "Snowy is too heavy." But she insisted on bringing Snowy to her imaginary playground.

Next, she was on a swing and said, "I have to go now."

"Where are you going?" Granny asked.

"I am going home."

Granny heard a few grunts.

"I am home now," she said.

Granny put Doireann's lunch on a plate. She then took her and Granda's salad, that she had prepared earlier, out of the fridge. Granny and Granda had their lunch, while Doireann played with Snowy. She sat on him and lay on him and then told Granny and Granda to shush as Snowy slept. Then Snowy was dragged into the kitchen.

Granda opened the back door to let Doireann see that it was drying up, outside. "As soon as you have your lunch, we will go outside," Granda told her. Granda put Snowy back into the dining room, and Doireann sat up at the kitchen table.

She had brought beetroot and buttered bread with her for lunch. "I don't like beetroot," she said. Granda said, "You take it from me when I am having my lunch." Doireann insisted, "I don't like it."

"Will you have the bread?" Granny asked.

"No."

"Will you have Weetabix?" Granny offered.

"No."

"I know," said Granny and proposed, "You will have Cheerios."

As Granny fetched the box of Cheerios, she told Granda, "I got them for when we are babysitting Doireann and Oisín for those four days in September when Mammy and Daddy are away." Granny opened the box of Cheerios.

Doireann said, "I don't like those ones."

"Will you have an oatcake?" Granny asked her.

"Yes." Then, as she nibbled at it, she said, "I want to go outside."

"You can go out when you have had something to eat and when I am finished my lunch," Granny told her in no uncertain terms.

Granda suggested some cheese for her, but Granny said, "She won't take cheese."

"What about the spreadable rectangular cheese segments?" Granda suggested.

"Doireann, will you have the soft cheese with the cow on it?" Granny asked.

"Yes."

Doireann ate a bit; made a face; said, "Yuck"; and left it there.

"What are you going to eat, Doireann?" Granny worried.

"A banana," she said.

"I have no bananas. Will you have a pear?" Granny offered.

"No," was her blunt answer.

"I have some raisins; will you have them?" Granny persisted.

"Yes," she said and ate the very small box of raisins.

"Doireann, close your eyes. I want to take a photo of that cyst on your eyelid," said Granda.

After a few clicks, Granda eventually got a good photo of it.

Granny put toast on for Granda and went to the toilet. Granda was now standing up from the table, waiting for his toast. "You are finished now, Granda?" Doireann suggested.

"Doireann, I am waiting for my toast, and you will just have to wait," said Granda and asked, "Will I see what's on the smelly?"

"Yes," she replied and sat in her TV chair.

Paw Patrol had just started, and she was well pleased with that, as she just loved *Paw Patrol*. Granny was able to put the washing on the clothesline while Doireann watched the telly. As soon as *Paw Patrol* was over, she wanted to go out.

Granny was now ready and released the caged lioness from her cage! They played with the bottles of bubbles. Then Granda went out to give Granny a break. He made big bubbles for Doireann to chase. Then she got the Frisbee and started throwing it. At one stage, it accidently landed on Granny's flower patch.

"You're okay, Doireann; just be careful not to walk on Granny's flowers," Granda said. In a low voice only Doireann could hear, he called out, "Granny, Doireann is on your flowers." But he quickly ran to assure her he was only joking.

She was actually afraid to move, and Granda had to help her out.

"Thanks, Granda," she said.

After this, they played with the small yellow ball, throwing it over the clothesline, and then Doireann would hide it in some of the clothes. When Granny came out, she suggested playing with the big ball. Doireann ran in to get it and played football with Granda.

Next thing, she said to Granda, "I think Mammy is here." She obviously heard Mammy talking to Granny, which turned out to be right.

She went into the house and ran excitedly over to Mammy when she saw her and gave her a big hug. Then Mammy had to come outside to play footie. As Mammy talked to Granny, Doireann started to screech for attention. Mammy tried to explain to her that she was talking. Doireann got very demanding and wanted Mammy's undivided attention. Then she wasn't happy that she had to walk home because Mammy hadn't brought her car. Mammy had to carry her in the end. Doireann was very tired, and that was when she got very cranky and messy.

Mammy had a doctor's appointment for Doireann tomorrow morning regarding the cyst. Granny and Granda said goodbye as they left for home and Doireann waved back with a big smile.

CHAPTER 30

"Granda, You Will Have to Be Careful, Okay."

27 August

This was Granny and Granda's final week of minding Doireann on Mondays, Wednesdays, and Fridays each week. They had done this from when she was three months old, not to mention those extras that grandparents always helped out with anyway when called upon. They'd both survived what was termed the "terrible twos" period. They had finally agreed with Mammy to mind Doireann every Wednesday and not Friday as previously agreed, from 9.30 a.m. to 4.30 p.m.

From aged three, the Irish state paid for crèche facilities, covering 9 a.m. to 12 p.m. five days per week for working Mums. This would allow Doireann to spend a lot more time with her own peer group, which was very important.

Granny and Granda were very lucky to have her on Wednesdays, until she started attending school in August 2020. They intended to bring her to different places to let her experience more of the outdoors, not just in Wexford but also in Wicklow and Dublin. As well as enhancing her development, they would continue to have more fun with her, which was another vital part of life in general.

At about 9.55 a.m., Mammy, Doireann, and Teddy Pink all arrived over. Doireann and Teddy had walked through the field. Mammy checked her own shoes and then Doireann's before entering the house. Granda had told Mammy he'd spotted dog's poo over the fence in the field across from the house when he was cutting the grass last Saturday. Thankfully, there was a "clean bill of health".

Granda asked Mammy, "How is Doireann's eye?"

"Still the same, and the five-day supply of antibiotics she was prescribed last Friday is nearly finished. We will have to take her back to the doctor again," Mammy informed him. Mammy was concerned, as the doctor had said on their first visit that Doireann would have to have a full anaesthetic to have the lump removed surgically from her eyelid.

Doireann handed Granda a stone from the garden and said, "That's for you."

"Ah, thanks, Doireann. That's very kind of you," Granda said.

Granny was given one also.

"I love your cardigan. Where did you get that?" Granda asked Doireann.

"In the shop."

"What colour is that?"

"Lellow, and I got it in Dunnes," she told him. She was having difficulty, opening the buttons.

"Do you want a hand to open the buttons?" Granda asked.

She nodded, and Granda opened the buttons.

She removed the cardigan, and said, "I'm too warm."

"Did you say bye-bye to Oisín?" Granda enquired.

She nodded.

"Where is he going to, today?" he quizzed.

"I don't know what he is doing today," she said.

"Did you say bye-bye to Daddy?"

"Daddy wasn't there," she said.

"Oh, he must have gone to work early, so?" Granda suggested.

"Oisín is going to Tayto Park today, and he starts back at school this Friday and not Wednesday, as was previously thought," Mammy informed Granny and Granda.

Spotting her bubbles, Doireann ran to the back door and said, "Granny, let's play with them?"

"Oh, Granny has to finish her breakfast," Granda told her.

"What did you have for your brekkie?" he asked.

"Weetabix."

"Would you like some toast?" Granny asked.

"No."

Granny then asked her, "Would you like tea and toast then?"

"Yes," she immediately said and sat up at the kitchen table with Granny. "You're the best granny," she said as she ate her toast. "Can I have some more toast?"

"You are a hungry little monster, aren't you," Granny told her.

"Give us a hug?" Granda asked her.

"You didn't say, good morning," Granda was told.

"Well, good morning," Granda said and gave both Doireann and Teddy big hugs.

"My brother always makes me tea," she told Granda.

"It's Rosie Lee," Granda reminded her.

"No, it's tea," insisted Doireann. "Can I see my cousins laughing?"

Granda showed her the video of Richie and Eddie dancing. She then looked at the videos and pictures of Rosie.

"She is pretty," Doireann said.

Later on, she wanted to look at the videos again. "Can I look at [the] [i]Pad, Granda?" she said.

"Of course, you can," he said. "Where is the iPad?"

"It's in the sitting room," Granny told him.

He got it and brought it to the dining room. He gave it to Doireann, who sat on the sofa with Granny, to look at the videos of Uncle Richard again. Doireann and Granny spoke about the presents Richard and Selin had given her. Then they looked at recent photos of their family day out in Tramore, County Waterford.

"Are we going to the library?" enquired Granda.

"No, Enniscorthy," said Granny.

"Doireann, do you want to go to Enniscorthy?" asked Granda. "No. Outside," she replied, and that put paid to those plans.

"I have a necklace and it breaked", she told Granda. "Mammy and Daddy have glue," she added, before running into the kitchen. "Granny, I have a necklace."

"Have you?" said Granny, sounding surprised.

Later, Granny and Doireann were outside re-enacting one of the videos. Snowy was sitting on the toy motor car; Baby Bop and the Teddies sat on the canvas, laid out on the grass; and Doireann pushed the car with Snowy sitting on it. Then Doireann had to go to the toilet, and when she had finished, Granda was asked to mind her while Granny went to the loo. "Granda, can you come out and play with me?" he was asked.

"Okay, Doireann."

"Eh, Granny, Doireann and I are going outside to play," Granda announced loudly.

Doireann held up her arm and said, "Look at the mark, Granda."

He couldn't see anything and asked, "What happened?"

"Kafli bit me," she told him.

"Did he? Was he hungry?" Granda asked.

Her response was to give Granda confused looks.

No sooner were they outside than Doireann wanted to go back into the house. "Oh, I need my cardoring" she said and stood outside the toilet where she had left it.

"I will give it to you in a minute," Granny told her.

She stood there until Granny came out with her cardigan. She and Granny went back outside to play, allowing Granda to work on his notes.

Granda went outside and it had turned cold. He went to take a photo of Doireann.

"No," she told him, all the while continuing with her (pretend) conversation on the phone.

Granda took other photos anyway.

Doireann then said, "Goodbye," on the phone, before telling Granny and Granda she had to go now and switchedr on her (toy) car engine. She then realised she hadn't told Teddy and ran to get her to say her goodbyes. She put Teddy back on the canvas and sat into her car. Then she ran to Teddy and picked her up and held her close. "She is crying," Doireann told Granny and Granda.

Granny fetched a warm top before she continued to assist Doireann with her play-acting. Snowy, the car, the phone, the Teddies, Baby Bop, and the bubbles were all there "on set".

Granda took over from Granny and made lots of bubbles. There were large ones and small ones that blew everywhere with the wind. One even stuck on Granda's eyebrow, as he tried to make it bigger just as the wind turned in the opposite direction. Granny went in to make the salad lunches for them.

Next, it was Frisbee time. It was thrown back and forth until Doireann got tired of it. Next on the menu was the rocket launcher. "I'll do it, Granda," she said, and she launched a rocket.

"It's my turn now," Granda said and sent his rocket sky-high.

At one stage, when Doireann jumped on the air pad, the rocket didn't move. All they heard was a hissing sound.

"Ah, there must be a crack in the rocket, Doireann," he told her as he removed the rocket from the launcher. "Doireann, look down the stem of the rocket," Granda said, pointing.

"Yeah, there's a hole in it," she said.

Granda looked. "I can't see any hole; let's try it," he said.

They put the rocket on the launcher barrel, and Granda jumped on the air pad. *Puff*, the rocket headed for space, before veering towards the house and then vanishing over the rooftop. "Oops," said Granda, and he headed for the side gate.

"It's okay, Granda," Doireann assured him.

"Ah, thanks, pet," said Granda.

She stood beside Granda as he opened the side gate combination lock. Doireann tried to pull the gate inwards, but it can swing either way. Granda said, "Push it, Doireann. It's easier." And out the two went, in search of a lost rocket.

Granda walked and Doireann ran, around to the front of the house. Suddenly, Doireann roared, her finger aimed in one direction, *There it is, Granda.*"

"Ah, good on you, Doireann. Well done for finding it," Granda told her.

As they walked back towards the side gate, she said, "Granda, you will have to be careful, okay."

"Ah, okay, pet, I will," Granda said, hiding the grin on his face.

Doireann was quickly back sitting on her motor car with Teddy Pink and trying to move it with her feet. "Where are you going, Doireann?" asked Granda.

"I'm going to the shops, but I can't move it," she told Granda. "Push me."

"When did your last slave die?" Granda asked.

"Doireann, give it a push yourself; you can do it," he told her.

Then, Granny reappeared and Granda said, "Doireann wants to go shopping again." And he left them to it.

A little while later, Granny and Doireann were back indoors. Doireann was having her smoothie that Mammy had made for her. When she couldn't get the last of her smoothie out, she left it and had her blueberries instead. Granny finished the rest of the smoothie. The blueberries were still frozen, so Granny put them into the microwave to soften them a bit. The 1960's CD was playing the song "San Francisco". When she finished, Doireann ran to her bedroom to get some books for Granny to read to her.

Granda kept watching for rain, as the clouds were very thick with the odd break of sunshine. The temperature today was about sixteen degrees, and it was breezy. Snowy, Baby Bop, and Teddies White and Brown all sat on the canvas blanket on the grass, while Teddy Pink lay face-down on the grass. The rocket launcher was in between, with one rocket on the garden table, along with the two bottles of bubbles. The toy car and the Frisbee were on the grass also. Luckily, Granda had cut the grass on Saturday, and the ground had had a chance to dry out after the very heavy rain that night. As soon as Granny finished the first story, Doireann was down off the sofa in a flash and running into the bedroom to get another book for Granny to read.

Doireann said, "After this [book], I am going for a sleep."

Instead, she went into the sitting room and came back with Granda's back scratcher. Granny tickled her with it. The iPad videos were then requested and switched on again. She would watch the videos and look at the photos all day, just like her Mammy used to do.

Next, Granny and Doireann went back out to the garden and over to the shed. Earlier, she had asked, "Let's see what's in the shed, Granda."

"No, there's nothing there for you," was Granda's reply.

Now, she had convinced Granny.

They came back into the house, and Granny said, "Doireann wanted the yellow teapot that she saw in the video and thought it was in the shed, but it wasn't."

Granda whispered, "I think it might be in the cubbyhole."

"I want it kept there," Granny whispered back.

Doireann the detective obviously heard the conversation and ran into the cubbyhole, looking for the yellow teapot.

"It's not in there," pretended Granny.

She came out holding the yellow teapot and said, "Look what I found."

"That is a teapot. What you are looking for is a yellow drum," Granny told her.

Doireann asked, over and over, "Did you put it in the bin?"

"Ah, I can't remember," Granny would say. She went looking for it and couldn't find it. "We may have given it back to a charity shop," Granny informed Granda.

Granny and Granda could afford to buy second-hand toys in charity shops, and when Doireann tired of them or outgrew them, they donated them back to the charity shops. Granda looked in Doireann's toy box, but the drum wasn't there. He took out the box of cheap miniature cars. They had bought these in a pound shop as a replacement for the other cars they'd given to Richard for his kids, when he was going back to Cambodia. They'd thought then that Doireann had outgrown the cars, but not so. When Doireann resumed her visits to Granny and Granda after her two-week holiday in France, she started to play with toys that had been left to one side for a good while. She had a new-found interest in those "forgotten" toys all of a sudden. Today, she played with the new miniature cars. "Can I take them home, Granny?" she asked.

"No. Sure, you will have nothing to play with here, and you have lots of toys at home to play with anyway," Granny said.

"Granny, I need to go to the toilet," she said.

"Okay. Come on," Granny beckoned.

"Granda, I went to the toilet."

"Yes, and you are very good for telling Granny when you need to go, pet; you are getting to be a big girl now. Well done," Granda told her.

About five minutes later, she said, "Granny I need to do a poo."

"Okay, come on. That's Granda's job," joked Granny.

"No. I am okay Granny. I don't want to go now," she said.

"Okay, false alarm," Granny said, and out of the toilet, they came.

About two minutes later, Doireann said, "I think I need to go now, Granny."

"Okay. Come on," said Granny, and they headed for the loo again.

Running into the toilet, she said, "Come on, Granny, quickly."

"I'm coming. I'm coming," said Granny.

Doireann went to the toilet but had to get a change of pants also. Granny explained to her nicely that it was best not to wait in future but to go when you had to and not leave it late.

At lunchtime, Doireann had her crackers with butter and cucumber.

"Granda got a stamp on each hand for finishing his lunch." Doireann informed Granny and Granda that this stamp was used in crèches. It was supposedly used to encourage children and also to recognise their achievements. Mammy had rightly bought her own stamp device for Doireann, as one day in crèche, when she didn't eat her lunch, she didn't get a stamp like the rest in her group. So now, Doireann can have as many stamps as she wants and can give people stamps as well.

Doireann was looking for a little spoon during lunch, and Granda gave her a soup spoon. With a grin, Doireann said to Granny, "I think we have to put Granda in the bin." She started to laugh. She then muttered something like, "Granda always says jokes," adding, "I think I will ask Mammy for a Rosie Lee."

"Very good, Doireann," said Granda, "a cup of Rosie Lee."

After lunch, Granda and Doireann went outside to bring the teddies in.

Doireann said, "I want to get my phone."

"Your telephone?" said Granda.

"Telephone," repeated Doireann.

Granda got her to pronounce telephone in a real posho accent / telafouwn/.

Granda picked up Snowy and Baby Bop and asked Doireann to take Teddies White and Brown.

"Eh, I don't want to. I am coming back out to play," she said.

Granda encouraged her to go inside with her phone and said, "When we've all finished our lunch, Doireann, we will then come back outside."

"I am finished," she protested.

"Ah, we know, Doireann. But you are not going out there on your own," said Granda.

"Can I see what's on the telly?" was her next request.

"Of course, you can," said Granda.

Paw Patrol was on, and she was happy with that. After *Paw Patrol*, Granny and Doireann went outside to play with the bubbles. Later, when Granda went outside, Doireann ran to him, shouting, "Granda," and pointed at Granny's newly painted cement duck in the garden.

"Doireann, what do you shout out if something is flying towards you?" asked Granda.

Silence.

"You call out *duck* and not *quack, quack*," he told her.

They all sat on the garden bench. Doireann picked up Teddy Pink and said, "Keep away from the flies," and sat her down between Granny and Granda.

Granda held Teddy's arms, and when Teddy spoke, her voice was very similar to that of Granda's. "Look at me. I am touching the flies," Teddy said as she pressed her arms down onto the bench at the same time.

Doireann walked back towards Teddy and gave out to her. Teddy continued talking, and Doireann started to laugh and play-act with her. Teddy put her arms on Doireann's face and said, "There's a fly on your nose. I got him; I got him."

And she continued to laugh. Then, she said, "I hear Mammy."

And true enough, Mammy appeared at the side gate.

When Granda opened the lock, Doireann was delighted to see her Mammy. "She didn't want to go anywhere today, just play at home," Granda told Mammy.

"She was in good form," Granny said.

Mammy was a bit surprised, as she was very moody and grumpy this morning. Mammy had put this down to the antibiotics she was taking, for the cyst.

"Look how fast I can run, Mammy," said Doireann and took off down the garden.

"Wow, that's brilliant," Mammy said.

Doireann didn't forget her freeze pop and reminded Granny. Mammy let her eat it before they left for home.

They all said their bye-byes, and Doireann was driven home in Mammy's car, today.

Evening

Mammy phoned and asked Granny, "Would you like to come for a walk with Doireann and me?"

"Oh, yes," said Granny.

"I'll be up to you in a few minutes," she promised.

Granda had yet to park his car in the driveway and offered Granny a lift up to Mammy's first. Mammy and Doireann were walking to meet Granny halfway. As Granda drove up, they were on the footpath, opposite Parkside Camolin (Pub). Granda turned right into a driveway and got out of the car. Doireann ran up to him and gave him a big hug. Granny, Mammy and Doireann then went off for their walk up through the village and back.

CHAPTER 31

Planting Flower Bulbs with Granny

29 August

Granny and Granda arrived home from the gym, at about 9.20 a.m.
Mammy phoned Granny, at 9.35 a.m., to ask if she had any spaghetti.
Daddy had phoned Mammy to say he only had mincemeat for Doireann's
lunch but no spaghetti. Granny said she had some. Daddy and Doireann
arrived over at 10.05 a.m., and Doireann hid beside the garden owl feature
as usual. She then came into the house with another flower for Granny.
"Where's the other one for Granda?" she asked.

Daddy picked it up in the garden for her, and she handed it to Granda.
Granda gave her a big hug, while thanking her for the lovely flower. They
put them in the hall, along with the flowers that she had brought the
other day.

Daddy had to rush off and asked Doireann for a hug as he left. She was
more interested in opening her shoulder bag to have some lunch. Before
Daddy left, he told Granda he hadn't put sun cream on her, and he could
drop back with some.

"Ah no. You're okay; we have some here," Granda said.

"Daddy was silly, not to put the [sun] cream on," she said after Daddy left.

"Daddy didn't know it was going to be such a nice day," Granny told
her. "You are not having lunch now," she added before quickly changing
her mind. "Okay, you can have some berries then."

"Where is Oisín, today?" Granda asked her.

"He's at home."

"Is Mammy there?" he enquired.

"No, she's not there."

"Oh, she is gone to work?"

"No. Yoga," she said.

"Oh, yoga," mused Granda.

"I don't think so," said Granny.

Granny and Granda had earlier agreed to tell Doireann they had to go to Enniscorthy today, leaving her with no choice. It was a lovely sunny day, with the temperature between sixteen and eighteen degrees.

"Why?" she asked.

"Because Granny has to go to the shops," said Granda.

"Do you want to come straight back home or play in the playground for a while?" Granny asked her.

"Granny, do you know Oila?" asked Doireann, changing the subject.

"No."

"She is in crèche," Granny was told.

"Doireann, do you want to come to Enniscorthy?" Granny enquired.

"No," she said and added, "I am tired, Granny." She did look a bit pale, today.

Doireann went into Granda and asked, "Are you writing her?"

"Yes, I am writing your story, Doireann," Granda told her, and she smiled. Granda, then asked her, "Can you say your friend's name again?"

"Oila," she said.

"Orla?" asked Granda.

"No, Oila," she said.

"Illa?" he asked, trying to nail it down.

"No, Oila," she repeated.

"Oh, Oila," he said, with an emphasis on the "oil" in Oil-a. "And where is she from?" he asked.

"The crèche!"

Doireann went back out to Granny to get some toast and watch something on the telly. "What do you want to watch?" Granny asked her.

"Barney."

"Oh, it's Barney today?" Granny said as she inserted the DVD into the TV.

Doireann sat and watched Barney's friends, the music, the songs, and the games while eating her toast. She told Granny that Barney (the DVD) kept stopping.

Granny said, "The DVD needs to be cleaned." She ejected it and showed Doireann how to clean it.

Doireann then said, "Granny, you've a lovely kitchen."

"Well thank you, Doireann," said a delighted Granny.

When Granny put the DVD back in, it worked perfectly.

Granda asked Granny what Doireann wanted to do. "She would prefer to stay at home and play football," Granny told him.

When Barney was over and before *Oswald the Octopus* started, Granda spoke to Doireann. "Going to Enniscorthy would be too long a journey, Doireann. We could go into Gorey instead, to the library. We will play in the garden after that," Granda suggested.

With the soother in her mouth and her eyes glued to *Oswald the Octopus* on the telly, she nodded in agreement, probably just to get rid of Granda and watch *Oswald*.

Granny put her washing on the clothesline and asked Granda to stay with Doireann until she returned. When Granny came back in, Doireann asked for toast.

"More toast. Do you want water?" Granny asked.

She shook her head from side to side and said, "No. Toast?"

Granny made Granda a cup of tea and gave him a slice of toast also. Doireann had milk with her toast. They decided not to travel in the car after all. It was such a lovely sunny day, and they probably wouldn't be getting many more of these days, as the end of summer neared. Also, Doireann was very tired-looking and pale in the face. Granny and Granda told her they would not go out today and just play outside in the back garden. Granny would put sun cream on her first, though.

Granda went to the kitchen to try and locate his reading glasses and asked Granny.

"They are on you," she said, and they were!

Granny, who was making a plait in Doireann's hair, had a good laugh and said to Doireann, "Granda is going doolally."

"Look Granda," she said and showed off her plait.

"Oh, that is lovely. Can I take a photo?" Granda asked.

"No. Later," he was told.

"Okay," agreed Granda.

Granny went into the bedroom to change her clothes and said to Doireann, "I will put some sun cream on you before we go outside to play."

"Doireann, did you see your Teddy Bear friends, who were waiting for you this morning?" asked Granda.

She got up and went to her bedroom, and seeing them all animated, she giggled and then cuddled Teddy White. Snowy had stretched his head out over the side of the cot. Teddy White, who was beside Snowy, had climbed up the side of the cot and held on to the side bar, peering out. Baby Bop was sitting gracefully on the chair beside the cot. Teddy Brown had clambered up the back of the chair and was holding on for dear life as he viewed everything and everyone in front of him.

"Do you want to see my sore leg, Granda?" Doireann asked.

"Yeah. Did you have a bad fall?"

She sat up on Granny's chair in the sitting room and pulled her leggings up.

"Ah, poor you, Doireann. That looks very red and sore," Granda said, and he could smell the ointment on the cut as he viewed it. "When did that happen?"

"Yesterday."

"And where?"

"At home."

"Where at home?" continued Granda.

"In my back," she said, meaning the garden.

"What happened?"

"I fell over the big step."

"You fell over yourself?" Granda said, thinking that's what she'd said.

"No, the big step," she repeated.

"Ah. And who was with you?"

"Mammy."

"And did Mammy give you a big hug, when she heard you crying?"

She nodded, pulled her leggings down, got off Granny's chair, and asked Granda, "Can you put the big telly on?" She meant the one in the sitting room.

"Well, maybe later, Doireann, as we are going out now to play," Granda said.

"That's what I mean—later," she said.

Granny put sun cream on Doireann before they both went out to the back garden to play. Granny soon returned to get the small container for Doireann's soother, as she had just left it on the garden table, and there were a lot of flies around.

Later, Doireann approached Granda, who was sitting on the garden bench. "You know the thing the man on the telly said?" she asked him.

Granda didn't know, but said, "Eh, yes," anyway.

"Well, we are going to do them [that], with the flowers," she informed him.

"Great," he replied.

"Will you come with us, Granda?" she asked.

"Of course, I will," he said.

Then Granny appeared from the shed with some small garden tools to show Doireann how to plant flower bulbs. Granny struggled with the hard ground and knew Doireann would struggle also. Granda loosened up the soil in places and got Doireann to dig the earth to make holes for the bulbs one at a time. Granny did a demonstration and then let Doireann continue, putting one bulb into a hole each time. After about five, Granny said, "Okay, that's enough now, Doireann."

"No. I want to do more," she said.

Granny was firm and said, "No, Doireann. That's plenty."

Granny then showed Doireann how to refill the holes with the soil and explained, "We will have to water them next."

She ran to the back door and said, "Granda, we need water."

"Hold on, Doireann. Where are you going? We can get water from the outside tap," said Granny.

Granny filled the small green metal watering can from the tap. Doireann watered the bulbs and then another one and then another one.

As she went for her umpteenth can of water, Granny said, "Doireann, you can water those flowers over there?" She directed her towards a different area altogether before she drowned the newly planted bulbs. She loved watering and playing with water in general.

The sun went in, and it felt cool. The outdoor temperature gauge read 17.5 degrees. Next, it was Granny's flower boxes that had to be watered, followed by the rocket launcher and everything else she would meet en route. When she used the grey plastic watering can, she managed to avoid spilling any water.

A delighted Doireann, announced, "The flowers will be excellent and grow bigger now." She then said, "I want a flower for my Mammy."

"Wait until she comes to collect you," Granny told her.

Doireann was tired now and sat on the garden bench in between Granny and Granda. Granda took a selfie. As she headed for the kitchen door, Granny asked Doireann, "Are we playing football?"

"No. Yes, just one. The sun is getting in my eyes," she said.

They played football and then touch tag. "You're on, Granda," she said after tapping him.

Granda said to her, "Oh, look over there. What is that?"

She turned to look, and Granda quickly crept up, tapped her, and said, "Ha ha. You're on now," before adding, "I think we need a rest."

Doireann wanted more sun cream, so we went into the house, and Granny put more sun cream on her. The sun was very hot today, but the air was cool whenever it clouded over. Doireann went back out, eating raisins, and Granny brought a bottle of water out for her. Doireann played some footie herself, soloing up and down the garden, and drank some water.

Granny offered to open her water bottle, but Doireann said, "No. I can do it. There, I open it." Then she closed it. She then ate more raisins and started to play with the towels drying on the clothesline. Each time she ran into the large towel, you could hear her laughter from afar.

Next thing, she loudly announced, "I need to go to the toilet!"

Granny took her in.

"*Granda, I'm two, seven now,*" she roared out on her return.

"Well, that's great, Doireann," said Granda. "Well done. You are getting really big now." Then Granda gave her a big hug, and she gave him a big smile back.

"Granny, Doireann is getting really big now," Granda said, and she acknowledged it.

"Granda what's them?" she asked, pointing.

"Oh, they are old tiles from the roof; let me show you." Granda got up from the bench and pointed to the new tiles on his roof.

"How did you do that?" she asked.

"Oh, I didn't do it, pet. I got someone to do it for me—a roofer, he's called," Granda explained. "Come on and I will show you next door's roof." Pointing towards a neighbour's roof, he said, "Now, that is what our tiles used to look like, and they were letting in rain. So, we had to get new ones."

Next on Doireann's instant agenda was to play hide-and-seek with Granny. At one stage, Granny hid, but beforehand, she had sent Doireann up to Granda. He was told to make sure she counted to ten with her head facing away from Granny and wasn't to look. Doireann then set off in the wrong direction. Granda whispered to her and pointed to where Granny was. She crept over and found Granny.

Granny came out of her hiding place and asked, "Doireann, did Granda tell you where I was?"

She looked towards Granda, as he held his hand over his mouth. He then giggled loud enough for her to hear him, and she also grinned.

It was now 12.50 p.m. and near lunchtime. Doireann had just finished eating her raisins.

Granny said, "Okay, Doireann, come in, and I will get lunch ready."

Doireann loved fruit and got plenty of it. She sat and watched some TV, and when her spag-ball was ready, she said, "I'm tired," and went and lay down on the sofa. "Get me a blanket," she ordered.

"Get it yourself," Granda told her.

"It's okay. I have one," she replied.

Granny said, "Okay. You can lie down for a little rest."

A while later, Granda asked, "What is Doireann having?"

"Spaghetti," Granny told him.

Granda hovered around the kitchen table and sized up Doireann's lunch. He then licked his lips noisily and just stared straight at it.

Doireann said, "You have your own," and jumped up immediately and sat at the table. She sucked up the long pieces of noodle into her mouth.

Granda asked Granny to show her how to roll the noodles onto her fork.

"I can't do that," Doireann said and continued to eat her way. Then she said, "I'm tired."

But Granny persisted and encouraged her to finish her spaghetti.

Again, she said, "I'm tired."

But Granny persisted until she had finished all of her lunch.

Granda put the telly on, and Doireann sat back in the TV chair. "I don't want that," Granda was told. Granda checked other channels but couldn't find other children's programmes. He went back to the original channel, which was showing *Go Jetters*. "Your favourite, *Paw Patrol*, will follow this programme shortly," he informed Doireann, and she was happy to wait.

While watching *Paw Patrol*, she leaned over to catch sight of Granny and Granda and proclaimed, "I did a fart," And then she fell off the chair.

She was okay and got back up as Granny joked, "You what? Will you get out of here?"

A little while later, Granny gave her a freezer pop. Granny and Doireann went outside, where Granda was sunning himself. Doireann wanted to play touch tag with Granda, but Granny, while putting her second wash load onto the clothesline, said, "I want you to help me with something, Doireann."

A while later, Granny and Doireann picked blackberries growing in Granny and Granda's back garden. Well, Granny picked them and gave them to Doireann to put into a container. Granny then, washed a load of them for Doireann to eat.

"Why are they called blackberries?" Granda asked Doireann.

She thought for a moment and then, said, "Because they are berries!"

"Very good, Doireann. Well done. That is excellent, and they are black also," he said.

"You had blueberries the other day, and they are berries too and blue," continued Granda. "Why are strawberries not called … Eh, eh, only joking pet. Don't mind Granda."

Doireann pointed to the ladybird garden ornaments and said, "We painted them. I did that one."

"Yes, you did," Granda said, "and you did a great job."

She was delighted, showing them to Granda, who reminded her when she'd painted them. "It was earlier in the summer—when Richard was here. Did you like Richard?"

She nodded approvingly.

"Did you like Gary?" he continued.

Again, she nodded approvingly.

"Richard is in Cambodia now," he told her.

"No. He's on the plane," she said.

"Oh yes, he was on the plane. That's correct. And now he is in Cambodia," Granda informed her. "Do you know where Cambodia is, Doireann?" he asked.

"Is it near Gary['s]?"

Granda marvelled at her response. In Ireland, it is often said that, if you ask an Irish person a question, they will usually answer with another question! Granda then said, "Eh, no. Further than that. Gary is in England."

Mammy called to collect Doireann at about 2.25 p.m., and Granda unlocked the side gate to let her in and then locked it again. "Granny and Doireann are collecting blackberries," he told her.

"Down the end of the garden?" she asked.

"No. Just at the shed, by the water butt."

Next thing, Oisín arrived at the side gate, and Granda let him in as well. "Hiya, Oisín. How was your day?" asked Granda.

"Okay. I just hung around the house today, Granda," he said. Oisín had followed Mammy's car on his bike. He then talked about his fun day in Tayto Park. He had travelled on the largest rollercoaster ride there. It was scary, but he enjoyed it.

Granda took a photo of Mammy, Doireann, and Oisín. Doireann obviously loved the blackberries and couldn't get enough of them. Mammy said, "At last, I think Oisín is looking forward to starting back to school this coming Friday" (31 August).

Granda said to Oisín, "The best days of your life." And he just half-heartedly grinned.

Granny told Mammy about Doireann being very tired today, and Mammy put it down to the antibiotics for her cyst. "They finish today," she said.

Mammy had to hurry away to go to the bank and collected up Doireann's things first. Oisín cycled away first, way ahead of his Mammy.

Daily report from Doireann's crèche (30 August 2018): "Lunch, tomato and bacon rice. Snack, toast and milk. Toilet."

CHAPTER 32

"It's a Cyst"

31 August

Granny and Granda tried to get back to Camolin before 9 a.m. for Oisín's first day back at school after the summer break but got held up with the heavy traffic in Arklow. They were keeping up a tradition since he'd started attending school. The children were lining up in the school playground area as they approached Camolin National School. Granda parked in Camolin Celtic FC car park, in the Community Grounds, at 8.57 a.m.

Granny and Granda jumped out of the car and called after Daddy, as he walked back home, but he didn't hear them. They went up to the school, and as Granny entered the school playground, Oisín ran over to her. Granda waved from the gate. Granny gave Oisín a hug and wished him the best from the both of them.

Granny forgot to bring her phone that morning and saw a missed call from Mammy, at about 8.50 a.m., when they got home. Mammy phoned again at about 9.10 a.m., wondering where Granny and Granda had got to and was happy to hear they had made it in time to see Oisín.

This was the same school Doireann would be attending two years from now. Mammy and Doireann arrived over to Granny and Granda's at about 9.30 a.m. with their new yellow buggy. Granda helped Mammy bring it into the house, and said, "It's a good one. It's heavy and sturdy."

"Granda, can you take a photo of the buggy?" Doireann asked a while later.

Granda handed his phone to her and said, "Here, you take one."

Mammy laughed as Doireann took the photo.

"Look, Granda," she said and showed him her masterpiece.

"Oh, that is a lovely photo," he told her, and Mammy agreed.

She wanted to take another one, and Granda said, "Let's put Snowy into it," meaning the buggy.

She stood back with a silly look on her face, as if to say, *That's weird.* Then she said, "I did a fart," and giggled.

"You what? You did what?" joked Granny.

Granda went and got Snowy, and they took a few photos of him sitting up in the buggy, with the help of Doireann first and then Granny.

Earlier at the hall door, as Granda admired the new buggy, Doireann said nothing, but just stuck out a leg to show him her new pink tights. Granda immediately noticed this and said, "Oh, look at your lovely tights. Look, Granny."

When Granny said, "They are gorgeous," Doireann had a big smile on her face.

Doireann took her smoothie out of the shoulder bag and asked Mammy to fit the straw into it. Granda then held the smoothie in his hands to tease her. Immediately, she loudly said, *"You have yours,"* referring to Granda's unfinished toast.

Next, she held up her new lunch box to show off the contents. She had large blueberries, olives, tomatoes, and nuts. "Granda, I need to do a wee," she said, as Granny and Mammy chatted.

Granda told Mammy, and she took her into the toilet, while Granda congratulated her for telling them that she needed to go to the toilet.

Later, Granda took a photo of Doireann's little elephant hanging from her shoulder bag. It was from Uncle Richard and Aunt Selin in Cambodia.

"Granda, take a photo of my hairband?" she asked because it had a lovely flower on it. "Can I go outside, Granny?"

"Wait until I finish my breakfast," Granny told her.

"We have to drop some books back to the library this morning, and when we come back, we will go outside to play," Granda informed Doireann.

"Granny, can I go to Enniscorthy?"

"We won't be able to fit it in," said Granny.

Granda said, "We will go another day."

"Granny, can I go to Camolin Park?"

"You mean the playground. Yes, all right, Doireann. Why not?" Granny said.

Doireann saw a little spider and drew Granny's attention to it.

"Oh, it's a little one like Doireann," joked Granny.

"*I'm a big girl,*" she screamed.

Granny immediately corrected what she had just said and apologised to the "big girl".

They weren't ready to go to the library just then, and Doireann said, "I want to look at Barney."

Granny set up the DVD for her, while she went to the kitchen press, took out the spare soother, put it into her mouth, and sat in her TV chair "sideways".

"Do you want me to turn your chair around?" asked Granda.

Shaking her head slightly, she quietly said, "No thanks," and sat glued to the telly. "Granny, I need to [do a] wee?" the "big girl" added.

"Again, so soon. Come on then," said Granny and took her into the toilet.

Granny weighed her and she was only two six again. Because she had been two seven the other day, Granny said, "It must have been your shoes."

Doireann was wearing her runners today and said, "That's okay, Granny," and ran into the dining room to continue watching Barney, with his singing and dancing friends.

Doireann finished her smoothie and had some olives, while still glued to the telly. Later on, as she continued watching the telly, she moaned and said, "I'm hungry."

"Hungry?" said Granny, looking surprised, and then asked, "What would you like?"

"Olives."

"There you are," Granny said as she handed her some olives.

Next, Doireann was eating her tomatoes. Granny made Granda a cup of tea. "Would you like a cup of Rosie Lee?" Granda asked Doireann.

She shook her head from side to side as she ate the olives, the tomatoes, and then the blueberries, along with about 60 percent of the nuts, while watching *Pirouette* and then, *Bob the Builder*.

"We will have to put stuff on the floor that's smelly," said Bob the Builder.

Doireann looked up at Granda, displaying a twisted and alarmed-looking face.

"Whatever he is using will give off a strong smell, but it won't be smelly for long," Granda explained to her.

Granny then said, "Okay, Doireann. We are now ready to go." She switched off the telly.

Doireann was putting her runners on in the dining room when Granda appeared and said, "Okay let's go."

Doireann shouted back, "*I am not ready yet.*"

"Okay, Doireann. No need to shout," said Granda.

"I didn't shout," she snapped back.

"Well, there's no need to answer back like that," Granny told her.

When she had put her runners on, Granda asked, "Are we ready now?" She nodded in agreement.

Next thing, the ornamental mandolin that Doireann had been playing with a few minutes earlier made one sound that startled Granda. "You scared, Granda?" Doireann asked.

"Yes," he said, and she giggled.

As they went out the hall door, Granny and Doireann were singing, "We're off to see the wizard, the wonderful Wizard of Oz," and so on as they marched towards the car, now parked on the roadside.

"Look out for cars coming, Doireann," Granda shouted, expecting her to look up and down the road, because a car had just passed.

Granda held Doireann's door open, but she clambered in through Granny's door and slowly crawled her way over to her seat. Because this exercise was taking ages, Granda just closed the door and went and sat in his own seat. Granny said, "Doireann has just said, 'Oh my god, Granda closed the car door.'"

Granny explained to her why Granda had done that as she fastened her car seat belt. Driving along, they sang, "The School Around the Corner's Still the Same," as they passed by Oisín's school.

Then Doireann said, "The doggie one?"

"How much is that doggie in the window, woof, woof," they all sang. Next, they sang, "How much is that sheep in the window, baa baa." Then they sang, "How much is that cat in the window, meow, meow."

"The Wheels on the Bus" was her next song request. Thereafter followed a slight change to the lyrics— "the sheep on the bus"; followed by "the doggie on the bus; and, finally, "the Doireann on the bus". Sometimes, they would sing a particular version many times over.

"I need to do a wee, Granny."

"If you can hold on, we're halfway there?" Granny said.

"No. I have to go now," she said in a hurried state.

"Granda, you'll have to pull off onto a side road. It's my fault for not checking, before we left the house," Granny said.

Granda took a left, onto a side road and pulled over to the side.

He helped Doireann out of the car, and Granny took over from there. When they were back in the car, Granny said, "That's her third one this morning, and the last one was a lot."

Granda turned left and back onto the main road, towards the library. "We are going the wrong way."

"We are not, Doireann," Granny assured her.

As she continued to insist that we were going the wrong way, Granny and Granda just ignored her. Using their own made-up lyrics, they sang to the tune of the theme song from the film *Snapper*. *"Deeee's the best, best; Deeee's the best, best. La la la la. La la la la."* Then, Doireann sang it herself.

"Wheeeeeeeeeeeeeeeeeeeeeeeeeeeeeeeeeeeeeeeeeeeeeeeeeeeeeeeeeeeee," they all shouted after Doireann had requested it, upon entering Gorey Shopping Centre's underground car park. Granda parked in a vacant family bay, helped Doireann put her shoulder bag on, and headed into the basement foyer to see Noddy and Minnie.

"Welcome to Toyland," Noddy said, before Doireann ran to press the lift's up button.

A lady on the lift admired Doireann's clothes, shoes, and hairband. Doireann stood close to Granny, her head slightly held down, as if butter wouldn't melt in her mouth. She darted off the lift and over to the racing car for another car ride.

Granda pretended to sit into the racing car with her. "You can't get in there," she told him.

Granda sat in for the fun of it anyway and got Granny to take a photo.

"Doireann, let me have a look at your eye?" asked Granda.

"It's a cyst," she told him.

"Close your eye, Doireann," he asked again.

"It's a cyst," she said once again.

"Okay. Now, let's have a look at your cyst," pleaded Granda.

She faced Granda with her eyes wide open.

"Close your eye, Doireann," Granda asked.

She closed her good eye.

"Doireann, it's the other eye," Granda explained.

She then had both eyes closed so tightly Granda couldn't see the cyst at all at all and just gave up.

Next, she did her walk-on-the-wall trek and raised her arms up to touch the overhang. She then pointed to the steel capping protruding up from the slabs under her feet that could cause one to trip. Finally, she tried to shove the building wall at the end of the wall walk out of her way. Again, it wouldn't budge, so, down she jumped and darted over to the library doors.

She was now inside the library with Granny, who wanted to return two books and one DVD and pay a €2-penalty charge off her account. Doireann and Granda went to the kiddies' area to read some books until Granny was finished. Granda suggested to Granny that she look for more DVDs for the following weekend. Granny and Granda would be looking after Doireann and Oisín the following Thursday and right through to the Sunday. Granda went to read the newspapers. It wasn't long before Granny and Doireann stood beside Granda to tell him it was time to go.

Doireann did her usual, "*Wheeeeeeeeeeeeeeeeeeeeeeeeeeeeeeeeeeeeeeeeeeeeeeee eeeeeeeeeee,*" and ran, flying down past the courthouse and back up again as soon as they left the library. As she returned, she said, "No catching, Granda." But she ran as fast as she could with Granda in hot pursuit anyway.

As she jumped into Granny's arms, Granda gave her a few tickles. She climbed onto the walk-on-the-wall wall. "Look at the bird," she said, pointing at a crow eating a piece of bread. Then, she advanced on the bird, but it soon took off.

On entering the shopping centre, she said, "It's lovely and warm in here," and removed her cardigan, before dashing over to the racing car, again.

Granda sat on the bench, facing the doctor's surgery to jot down some notes. Doireann joined him and got Granny to help her remove a bottle of water from her shoulder bag for a well-earned drink.

"Ding-a-ling, ding-a-ling. Come on, Granny," she said.

"Where to?" asked Granda.

"To the (pretend) car; we have just got off the train in London," Granny informed him.

She took Granny for a spin, before arriving back at the train station, where the "station master" was still jotting down his notes. "We have to get the plane now," Granny was told.

"Where's the plane?" asked Granny.

Doireann pointed and said, "Over there."

"Oh, the (elevator) lift; that's the place," Granny said.

As both of them ran to catch their flight. Granny called out, "Come on, Granda. You'll miss the plane."

Granda finished his notes and ran to catch his flight, arriving just as Granny and Doireann entered the plane. The plane eventually landed, and when the doors opened, we ran to see Noddy and Minnie again. Doireann sat in with Noddy and covered her ears with both hands and said, "There's something in my ear." She got down off Noddy's car and ran up and down, up and down, and up and down, the foyer, saying, "Get out of my ear. Get out of my ear!"

"Come on, Doireann," Granda said. And they went out to Granda's car.

"*Wheeeeeeeeeeeeeeeeeeeeeeeeeeeeeeeeeeeeeeeeeeeeeeeeeeeeeeeeeeeee*," they all roared as Granda drove up the ramp to the upper car park, before heading out and up the 'Avenue' in Gorey.

"There's the motorbikers," said Granda.

There were dozens of them parked on the footpath chatting.

"Where?" Doireann asked, and Granny showed her.

"Oh, cool," she said.

"Would you like to have a motorbike, Doireann?" asked Granda.

She nodded.

Granda stopped at the traffic lights, and Doireann said, "That's a lovely car. Take a picture, Granda."

Granny said, "You can't just take a photo when you're driving, Doireann."

The car was a large white SUV, a BMW. Granny started to sing, "It's the hard-knock life for you" and so on (from the play *Annie*). Next thing, Doireann started to sing it on her own a few times.

"Where is Spotty the rag?" asked Granda, before Doireann and Granny started to fling it at each other. Doireann couldn't stop laughing, and she then started to fling her cardigan. As she flung one thing at Granny, Granny would return the other thing. Doireann had great fun, with plenty of laughs.

Then, Granny introduced counting into their game. Each time they threw something, they had to count. "Let's do it. I'm ready?" Doireann said.

Throw, one. Return, two. Throw, three. Return, four. Throw, five. Return, six. Throw, seven. And so-on up to sixteen.

Next, Doireann sang, "Baa, baa, black sheep, have you any wool? Yes sir, no sir, three bags full," all by herself.

Granda pulled up on the way home to take a couple of short notes. Next to the car was a flag outside a country lane. "What's that flag, Doireann?" asked Granda.

"Irish flag."

"No, Doireann. It's the Wexford flag," Granda told her, and Granny called out the colours, purple and gold.

Granny then said, "Come on, Granda. It's lunchtime."

Granda started driving again, and Doireann asked for music, "Downtown". Granda switched on the CD and selected number three, knowing it off by heart. Every time the lyrics, "downtown" were about to be sung, Doireann would hold her hands out just before it and ask, "Where?" and Granny and Granda would have to respond, singing, "Downtown," in unison with the singer.

They were just inside the house when Doireann asked, "Granny, can I have a freeze pop?"

"No, Doireann. You have to eat your lunch first," Granny told her. Granny and Doireann were seated at the kitchen table. "Doireann, do you want bread?" she asked.

"No."

"Mammy left this bread for you; will I butter it?" continued Granny.

"Yeah, I want butter, brown butter."

"Brown butter?" Granny said, now totally confused.

Granny then remembered that Mammy had left almond butter for her the other day. When Granda arrived at the kitchen table, Doireann was eating Mammy's brown bread with ordinary butter. Granny said, "Doireann didn't want the brown butter after all."

Doireann, was obviously, not very hungry. This was because of all she ate this morning. And was now looking for her freeze pop.

Granny decided to suss out what food Doireann liked, in readiness for her and Oisín's short stay with them the following week. "Do you like sausages?" she asked.

"Yeah, small sausages."

"Eggs?"

"Yeah, and pepperoni."

Back to the present and Granny said, "Doireann, you will have to eat more. Will I do you a boiled egg—a 'dippy-egg'?"

"No. Eh, yeah, yeah."

"How will I manage to do a dippy-egg?" Granny asked Granda.

"Put the egg into boiling water for three minutes. Or is it six minutes. I can't remember," he said.

"I'll do it for four minutes," she decided.

Granny checked her four-minute boiled egg, and it was a real dippy-egg.

"Okay, Doireann, your egg is ready," Granny called out.

"I don't want it."

"You said you wanted it," complained Granny.

"I don't want it now," Doireann insisted.

Granny gave out to her, and said, "You should never say you want something and then not take it."

Granny dipped some bread into the egg for her, but she stood firm and refused to take it. She then rushed to finish her brown bread, shoving one finger slice into her mouth, while holding another slice.

"Doireann, don't put so much bread into your mouth. It's dangerous. Don't put any more in until you have finished what you are eating," Granda told her.

When she attempted to shove the bread, she was holding, into her full mouth, Granda reminded her what he had just said. "Okay, okay, I heard you," she responded angrily.

"And, Doireann, you are not to talk back like that, okay," said Granda.

When she finished her bread, she sat in front of the telly. It had been switched off earlier so as to get her to sit at the kitchen table.

"Will you eat something else, Doireann?" Granny asked.

"No," she replied, now facing away from Granny and Granda.

"Will you have crackers?" continued Granny.

"No. I want to rest," she moaned.

Granda asked, "Will you have some crackers watching the telly?"

"Eh, yes."

She then wanted to sit in the high chair while eating her crackers and watching *Paw Patrol* on the telly.

Granny ate the dippy-egg with her finger-sized brown bread. After *Paw Patrol*, another animated cartoon, *Honey Bunny*, came on. Doireann really got into it and got very animated. She made loads of different faces—squinting eyes, head held back, a sort of half a laugh, mouth open, mouth open and drawn back, sad look, worried look, chin dropped, aghast look, eyes wide open, surprised smile, and so on. Granda was amused, observing her, and she was literally engrossed in it. Granda asked her when it was over, "Did you enjoy it? Was it good?"

She nodded approvingly, without speaking a word.

Granny let her choose a freeze pop, and she picked a brown (Coca-Cola) one. Granny went to get "changed", and Doireann appeared in front of Granda, with a grin from ear to ear, the size of a Cheshire cat.

"Is Granny changing?" asked Granda.

She just nodded and attacked her freeze pop at the same time.

"What is she changing into?" Granda asked.

"She['s] changing her clothes," Doireann said immediately.

"I thought, she would change into a monster—correction, another monster?" Granda suggested, but he was ignored.

Later on, when Granda changed his clothes, Doireann asked him, "Have you changed?"

"What do you want me to change into, a monster also?" he asked. Silence.

"Okay, let's go outside," said Granda.

Continuing to enjoy her freeze pop, she followed Granda over to the birdbath, which had a low level of very dirty water in it. He emptied out the water and rinsed it under the water butt tap to remove the rest of the dirt. Then he put fresh water in it and left it on the grass for the birds.

"Where does that water come [from], Granda?" she asked.

"Okay, pet, let me show you," he said. He explained to her that the rain fell on the shed roof and flowed into the gutter. "That's the gutter." Granda pointed. "Then the water flows from the gutter down this pipe here into the water butt," explained Granda, identifying the pipe attached to the water-butt.

"We don't have one," she informed Granda.

"Well okay, you tell your Mammy all about it, okay," he told her.

She nodded as she licked her freeze pop.

Granda went to the outdoor tap to wash his hands and explained to her, "Do not touch the birdbath, as that water is dirty and only for the birds. It's okay for them and only them, okay."

Just then, a wasp appeared out of nowhere, and Granda brought Doireann inside with her sweet-smelling freeze pop—just in case the wasp had ideas. Mammy was there, talking to Granny.

"Ah, Mammy," said an excited Doireann.

Granda then washed his hands properly, and as Mammy was gathering up Doireann's things, Granda got the buggy and lifted it outside the hall door for her. Just before they left, Mammy asked Doireann, "Tell Granny and Granda the new word you learnt."

"Devastated," she said.

Mammy stood there with a big proud smile on her face. "What does it mean?" she asked.

"Crying," she answered.

Mammy said, "That's right," and gave her a big hug.

"Doireann picked up a book I had bought for Oisín years ago, and I have been reading it to her. The frog's pal, a rat, leaves or something, and the frog is devastated," Mammy informed them.

Outside, Doireann refused to get into the buggy, and Mammy said, "Okay, you can walk."

Granny and Granda looked out the window as they headed up the road, only to see Mammy running with the buggy and Doireann inside it.

***

Note: Granny and Granda continued to mind Doireann for "one long day" each week up to March 2020, until COVID-19 put a stop to it. Then they were devastated, like so many other grandparents all around the world!

BIBLIOGRAPHY

Shvartz, Anna, and Arthur Bakker, "The Early History of the Scaffolding Metaphor: Bernstein, Luria, Vygotsky, and Before", *Mind, Culture, and Activity* 26/1 (2019), https://www.tandfonline.com/doi/full/10.1080/10749039.2019.1574306, accessed 14 March 2022.